Experiencing Etruscan Pots: Ceramics, Bodies and Images in Etruria

Lucy Shipley

Archaeopress Archaeology

Archaeopress
Gordon House
276 Banbury Road
Oxford OX2 7ED

www.archaeopress.com

ISBN 978 1 78491 056 3
ISBN 978 1 78491 057 0 (e-Pdf)

© Archaeopress and L Shipley 2015

Cover image: view of Murlo. Photo by Grayson Lauffenburger

All rights reserved. No part of this book may be reproduced, stored in retrieval system,
or transmitted, in any form or by any means, electronic, mechanical, photocopying or otherwise,
without the prior written permission of the copyright owners.

Printed and bound in Great Britain by Marston Book Services Ltd, Oxfordshire
This book is available direct from Archaeopress or from our website www.archaeopress.com

Contents

List of Figures iii

List of Tables iv

Acknolwedgements v

Introduction 1
    1.1 Etruscan Places, Etruscan Trade, Etruscan Things 4
    1.2 Agency and Phenomenology in Italian Prehistory 6
    1.3 Seeking Etruscan Experiences 7

Traditions and Trajectories 9
    2.1 Introduction 9
    2.2 Initial Entanglements: 1250-1400 10
    2.3 To Make a Nation: 1723-1800 13
    2.4 Politics of Involvement: 1918-1943 14
    2.5 Division and Development post 1945 16
    2.6 Meanwhile, across la manica.. 18
    2.7 From Romance to Rigour 19
    2.8 Incorporating Ideas 20
    2.9 Conclusions 21

Thinking 'things' through: a phenomenology of objects 23
    3.1 Introduction 23
    3.2 Subject to the Centre: From Hegel to Merleau-Ponty 24
    3.3 Perception to Performance: Judith Butler 25
    3.4 Volatile Bodies 26
    3.5 Throwing Like a Girl 28
    3.6 Phenomenology for Pots 29
    3.7 Objects and Social Discourse 32
    3.8 From Theory to Practice 33

Quantifying Experience – Methodologies 35
    4.1 Introduction 35
    4.2 Making a Corpus, Structuring Data 36
    4.3 Four Sites, Seven Wares 38
    4.4 Experiencing the Etruscan Banquet 41
    4.5 From Table to Tomb 45
    4.6 An Experiential Analysis 48

Touching and Feeling: Vessel Bodies 52
    5.1 Introduction 52
    5.2 Body Proximity Groups: Hand to Mouth, Clay to Skin 55
    5.3 Sizing Pots Up: Height, Rim Diameter, Volume 58
    5.4 Seeking Skill – Secondary Characteristics 63
    5.5 Experience, Performance, Control: Conclusions 67

Seeing and Revealing: Images on Pots 70
    6.1 Introduction 70
    6.2 Angles of Access: Image Placement 72
    6.3 Additional Features, Additional Feelings: Image Stimulation 75
    6.4 Eyes and Fingers: Conclusions 77

Experiencing Bodies: Bodies in Images on Pots 80
    7.1 Introduction 80
    7.2 Human and Other Bodies 81
    7.3 Gendered Bodies 86
    7.4 Bodies on Pots: Conclusions 93

From Being to Doing: Actions of Bodies on Pots **95**
    8.1 Introduction 95
    8.2 Multiple Layers of Experience 96
    8.3 Themes in Activity 98
    8.4 Conclusions 102

Pots, People, and Experience: Conclusions **105**
    9.1 Introduction 105
    9.2 Drink while you think: Ontologies of Pottery and Alcohol 105
    9.3 Changing Pots, Changing Persons 109
    9.4 Back to the Future 111

Pottery Corpus **114**
    Corpus Bibliography 139

Bibliography **139**
    Digital Bibliography 140
    Historical and Literary Sources 140
    Bibliography 141

Index **154**

List of Figures

Figure 1.1: Map of Etruria 3
Figure 2.1: Detail from Giotto's fresco of Hell in the Scrovegni Chapel, Padova. 11
Figure 2.2: Detail from the Tomb of the Blue Demons, Tarquinia. 12
Figure 3.1: Moebius strip..27
Figure 3.2: Young girl throwing a stone into the sea. 29
Figure 4.1: Ceramic groupings by traditional terminologies and user-centric categories. 37
Figure 4.2: Tomb of the Leopards, Tarquinia 42
Figure 4.3: Etruscan pottery in use 2..42
Figure 4.4: Diners from the Tomba dei Vasi Dipinti Adapted from a damaged tomb painting, Tarquinia. 43
Figure 4.5: Crater, Tomb of the Lionesses, Tarquinia 45
Figure 4.6: Funerary Ceramics from Vulci...47
Figure 4.7: Shaping the body through two glass vessels 48
Figure 5.1: Process of 'skill score' calculation...54
Figure 5.2: Pottery by relationship to the body...55
Figure 5.4: Body proximity groups by origin (proportional percentage) 56
Figure 5.3: Pottery by body proximity groups 56
Figure 5.5: Body proximity groups by site. 57
Figure 5.6: A – Vessel height B – Vessel height by production origin. 58
Figure 5.7: A – Indigenous and B – Imported vessel heights and body proximity groups. 59
Figure 5.9: A – Indigenous and B – Imported vessel rim diameters and body proximity groups. 60
Figure 5.8: A – Vessel rim diameter B – Vessel rim diameters and production origin. 60
Figure 5.10: A – Vessel volumes. B – Vessel volumes and production origin. 61
Figure 5.11: Volumes and body proximity groups 62
Figure 5.12: Handle groups and production origin for drinking vessels. 62
Figure 5.13: Rim diameter as a percentage of vessel height 63
Figure 5.14: Diameter as percentage of average hand length (180mm) by body proximity group. 64
Figure 5.15: A – Vessel skill scores B – Proportional percentage of skill scores and production origin. 65
Figure 5.16: Ease of use scores by body proximity group. A – Indigenously produced vesesls and B: Imported vessels.......65
Figure 5.17: Ease of use scores for A – imported and B – indigenous drinking vessels by site. ...66
Figure 5.18: Ease of use scores for A – imported and B – indigenous serving vessels. 67
Figure 6.1: Typology of image placement..70
Figure 6.2: Typology of image stimulation. 71
Figure 6.3: Image placement 72
Figure 6.4: Secondary placement of images on indigenously produced vessels. 73
Figure 6.5: Image placement and body proximity groups. A – All vessels. B – Indigenous vessels. C – Imported vessels. 73
Figure 6.6: Placement of images by site...74
Figure 6.7: Experience of Images by body proximity..75
Figure 6.8: Experiences of images by site. A – All vessels. B – Indigenous vessels. 76
Figure 6.9: Image rendering techniques A – By body proximity group. B – By site. 77
Figure 7.1: Typologies of bodies..80
Figure 7.2: ypologies of gendered body 81
Figure 7.3: Humans and Other bodies All vessels. 82
Figure 7.4: Types of bodies by body proximity group A – Indigenous vessels. B – Imported vessels. 83
Figure 7.5: Types of bodies by site. A – Imported vessels. B – Indigenous vessels. 83
Figure 7.6: Huntsman with dog and rabbits as passive accompaniments......................................84
Figure 7.7: Huntsman being eaten by a large feline (a lion?) PC19690095. 85
Figure 7.8: Male figure with supernatural mount from Vulci. 85
Figure 7.9: Winged female figure. 86
Figure 7.10: Lion-headed male with lions. 87
Figure 7.11: Gendered bodies 87
Figure 7.12: Ages of bodies (all vessels) 88
Figure 7.13: Gendered bodies by body proximity group. 88
Figure 7.14: Gendered bodies by site...89
Figure 7.15: Positions of female bodies...90
Figure 7.16: Positions of female bodies by site. 91
Figure 7.17: Passivity in female bodies in imported pottery: an active woman is pacified and made an object 91
Figure 7.18: The active yet peripheral female body. 92
Figure 7.19: 'Potnia Theron' figure with owls from Poggio Civitate. 92
Figure 7.20: Female with olisbos from Vulci..93
Figure 8.1: Process of activity definition. 95
Figure 8.2: Single and multiple action themes by production origin..97
Figure 8.3: Single and multiple action themes by body proximity group......................................97
Figure 8.4: Action themes on: A – indigenous vessels and B – imported vessels.........................98
Figure 8.5: Action themes by site 99
Figure 8.6: Action themes on imported pottery by date..100
Figure 8.7: Action themes by body proximity group. 101

List of Tables

Table 1.1: Periodization of Etruscan archaeology 4
Table 4.1: Proportions of different ceramic wares included in the corpus 40
Table 4.2: Production origin, deposition context and date range for all pottery by site. 41
Table 4.3: Variables of Experiential Analysis 51
Table 5.1: Categories of vessel height 52
Table 5.2: Categories of vessel rim diameter 53
Table 5.3: Categories of vessel volume 53
Table 5.4: Categories of rim diameter:vessel height ratio 53
Table 5.5: Categories of rim diameter: average human hand length 54

Acknolwedgements

This book owes a great deal to a large number of people: firstly, to the patience and persistence of Yvonne Marshall, who pushed me beyond typology into thought. Secondly, to John Robb and Tim Champion, whose advice and constructive criticism filled in the gaps and reaffirmed its foundations. Eoin O'Donoghue and Theresa Huntsman read the manuscript and their comments were not only helpful but inspiring. Vedia Izzet awakened an intense interest in, and equally intense frustration with, the discourse of Etruscan studies. Anthony Tuck's generosity with his time (and wine), and Ruth Whitehouse, Christopher Smith and Simon Keay's kindness in sharing their experience with me were all integral in its writing. All the errors and issues that slipped through this wonderful net remain my own.

The staff of the Soprintendenza per i Beni Culturali Etruria Meridionale and the British Museum image and copyright teams were deeply helpful with the acquisition of images for the project.

It might seem strange to place an image of a landscape on the cover of a book about pottery, but this is a really a book about sharing experience, and Grayson Lauffenburger's photography does this in exquisite fashion. I am very grateful for permission to use this cover image.

All the students I've been lucky enough to teach from Southampton and Poggio Civitate have made their own contributions (perhaps unknowingly).

This research was funded by the Arts and Humanities Research Council over the course of a Block Grant Partnership funded PhD at the University of Southampton.

And of course, my parents, brothers and Phil.

Chapter 1

Introduction

What is the object most commonly found during almost any archaeological excavation of material from the previous four thousand years? Ask any digger this question and the response will come, often with a groan born of hours of post-excavation analysis, 'pottery.' Ceramic objects are tough and durable, after their fragmentation into multiple pieces which appear with every scrape of a trowel. They are often easy to gloss together, placed in bulk find bags to be counted then forgotten, or sighed over as another piece of an object which can never be reconstituted. While the repetitive discovery of fragments of pottery can be taken for granted, these objects are a reminder of the importance of ceramic products in people's lives. These objects accompanied individuals from the moment they awoke and ate or drank or washed their faces, providing food and refreshment through the day's activities, to a late night of celebration, or simply the containers of a final drink before sleep. In a world without plastics, ceramics, alongside organic containers, were used for almost every substance which required protection or containment: from perfume to porridge. The experience of an Etruscan person, living day to day, would have been filled with interactions with ceramics, making them objects which can recall intimate transactions in the past to the archaeologist in the present.

Characterising that experience of Etruscan pottery is the concern of this book. What was it like to use and live with Etruscan pottery? How was the interaction between an Etruscan pot structured and constituted? How can that experience be related back to bigger questions about the organisation of Etruscan society, its increasingly urban nature and relationship with other Mediterranean cultures? More specifically, I aim to unpick both the physical encounter between vessel and hand, and the emotional interaction between the user of a pot and the images inscribed upon its surface. The decoration of pottery with human images, miniature reflections, distortions and imaginings of the people who once used them prompted a series of potentially deeply meaningful encounters. I will use the analysis of these intensely intimate interactions between people and pots to ask broader questions about Etruscan society during a period of transformation – querying whether four different communities within Etruscan Italy embraced similar or diverse forms of ceramic experience, and the implications of those choices on daily life in each place. These are two inland and two coastal communities, each with a different relationship with the wider Mediterranean world, and each with a ceramic record that bears witness to thousands of pot-person interactions. This book aims to examine social change as exemplified by local Etruscan experiences of familiar and novel forms of decorated ceramics – the daily impact of trade, interaction, belief and self-definition that I argue can be assessed by considering the perspective of the Etruscan *user* of pottery.

To accomplish this bottom-up analysis, I have developed a system of ceramic analysis which suggests that such recreation and re-imagination of user experiences of pottery in the past is possible. By utilising a phenomenological approach, developed from recent engagements between phenomenology and archaeological practice in Italian prehistory, the experience of using any Etruscan vessel is evaluated and made available for analysis and comparison with other pots. Having answered the specific question of individual experiences of singular vessels, this study moves on to answer secondary research questions relating to experience in its wider social context. Were different traditions of ceramic use present in Etruria? Were they associated with particular regional groups or individual cities? How did imported vessels from Greece impact upon Etruscan users? How do the answers to these questions contribute to central arguments in Etruscan studies?

By comparing experiential data from across the region I construct interpretations of Etruscan ceramic use which suggest significant variations in the way pottery was being used in different areas. The data provides an opportunity to examine the impact of imported pottery: not only on the direct experience of Etruscan users, but also on Etruscan communities. The consequences of analysing experience for understanding the complex ways in which Etruscan occasions using pottery were being employed as markers of identity provide a new recognition of ceramics as powerful tools in the construction of individuals and the choreography of society. These are only three of the areas in which experiential analysis has the potential to contribute to wider arguments about Etruscan social practice. However, the analysis of experience is also valuable for its own sake: it considers pottery at a particular point in its biography (Kopytoff 1986; Gosden and Marshall 1999), which has been somewhat marginalised by current approaches to ceramics. Joy (2009) has pointed out the relative difficulty of examining any object in the course of its use-life, as compared to the process of its production (birth) and deposition (death). This is perhaps the longest phase in any object life – performing the function for which it was originally designed until it is discarded. It is this long, sticky interim period, which is ironically when an object is perhaps least visible to the archaeologist, that experiential analysis can interrogate.

Traditional approaches to Etruscan ceramics have focused on the earliest phase of a vessel's biography: its production. This has primarily been through the dual techniques of typological and iconographic analysis (for the former, see Dragendorff 1895; cf Millett 1979; Neff 1993; Orton 1993; Rasmussen 1979, 1985; for the latter, see Arafat and Morgan 1989; Avramidou 2006; Beazley 1962; Del Chiaro 1970; Rausser 2002; Safran 2000; Williams 1982). These traditional methodologies have been focused on three key processes: recording pottery forms, defining their producers, and interpreting images. The former provides a framework for the dating of vessels, and a method for estimating provenance, aided and abetted by petrographic analyses. The value of such an approach, which has created an indispensible tool-kit for ceramic identification, is hard to overstate. The intricate and painstaking work of Sir John Beazley (1947, 1963, 1971, 1978, 1986), tracing the potters and painters of Athens and Etruria, provides a vision of a vibrant industry, and presents a detailed and personal production context for each individual vessel. Analyses of the iconography of painted vases can be used to assess the social context in which each pot was made, the concerns and desires of the audience which consumed it, in addition to the realities of the potter and painter's daily experience. Heavily informed by the relevant historical sources, the stories and allegories, myths and morals which are resplendent on such vases are then used to support a particular argument about an aspect of Greek or Etruscan society (Blundell and Rabinowitz 2008; Bonfante 2004; Jenkins and Williams 1985; Roth 2005; Sandhoff 2011).

More recent archaeological approaches to Etruscan ceramics have moved towards seeing pottery in a different context, rather than cataloguing production processes (Lewis 1997, 2003, 2009; Paolucci 2007a). Paleothodoros (2008:56) has called for the deconstruction of a unitary conception of Etruscan responses to ceramics, and emphasised the agency of families and individuals in their choice of funerary ceramics. However, methodologically, the same systems of categorisation and iconographic analysis have been used to undertake these studies: this time focused on the specific relevance of imagery to individual purchasers, or preferences for particular vessel kinds for burial. The same tried and tested methods developed to analyse the birth of a pot were used to consider vessels at the end of their lives: placed in the tomb, accompanying the Etruscan dead. Between the twin foci of these traditional and more recent approaches, if one assumes that pots in tombs were not simply bought and buried, lies a vast, gaping period of use.

The traditional methods can help to fill in this gap: typologies self-evidently catalogue and record the intricate variations in experience created by pottery forms. Each slight diversion from a stylistic theme would have impacted on an individual using it: each twitch of handle placement and wiggle in profile affecting how a vessel would have felt in the hand. Images of vessels being used on pottery could provide a vision of how they slotted in to physical experience, alongside representations of pottery use in other contexts, such as tomb paintings and funerary furniture. In addition to direct comparison with images of pots in use, iconography can also be used to consider preferences in practice. Osborne (2001, 2003, 2007) has developed an comparative analysis of Greek and Etruscan pottery to argue that the Etruscan consumers of Attic pottery reproduced imported imagery in their own ceramic traditions, suggesting that images were actively considered while the vessel was in use. Giudici and Giudici (2009) performed a similar analysis, comparing the activities shown on vessels from different sites across Etruria and Magna Graecia to establish which were preferred by Etruscan users. Yet none of these methodologies really provide a comprehensive vision of the experience of using pottery in EtruriA – how it felt in the hand, or on the mouth. The use-life of ceramics consisted of series of relationships with individual users and owners, built from thousands of individual interactions with different people. In order to deeply investigate the experience of using Etruscan ceramics, and to develop the results of that analysis into wider conclusions about Etruscan life, new methodologies are essential to augment and build upon traditional approaches.

This chapter is the first step in building and testing such methodologies for examining Etruscan experience, placing the chapters and analysis which follow in context. Firstly, the world of Etruscan users is introduced: the material culture which defines Etruscan assemblages and the traditions of scholarship which shape approaches to them. As discussed in more detail later in this study, the Etruscans occupy a slightly liminal position in terms of archaeological methodologies (Izzet 2007a: 10). A literate cultural group in contact with Greece and Rome, the Etruscans can be approached from a classical perspective, actively engaging with inscriptions and historical sources and developing careful and intricate interpretations from intense analyses of material culture. As the literature of the Etruscans has broadly not survived, however, the application of social theories and anthropological analyses used in prehistoric archaeology is equally appropriate, particularly for the early phases of Etruscan emergence from the Villanovan Iron Age and Late Bronze Age. A key part of this introduction to the Etruscan ceramic sphere is the presentation of one of the most important debates to which the experience of Etruscan pottery can contribute. This discourse surrounds the question of the role of imported ceramics in Etruria. This contentious issue will be considered at length to provide an idea of the potential for experiential analysis to contribute to this debate. Through the development of two anthropological case studies, I demonstrate the relevance of Etruscan experiences of Greek pottery, and suggest that imported ceramics should be conceived of as equally important to their Etruscan users as to their Greek makers. The inclusion of imported Greek material in this study is the result of these principles, while the discussion illustrates the divisions between scholars at work in Etruscology.

Having introduced the Etruscan context of this study in a broad sense, and through a more specific case study of interaction between Etruscan scholarship and the classical world, I turn to the prehistory of Italy and the approaches which have heavily influenced the design of this study. The work of a group of British prehistorians in the context of the Italian Neolithic is summarised in light of their employment of the dual conceptions of agency and phenomenology. The latter is the subject of Chapter 3, which develops the wider concepts of personal agency and phenomenal experience through engagements with feminist thought to form a methodology for investigating their role in Etruscan ceramics. Without agency, this phenomenal engagement could not take place: it is only by acknowledging the subjectivity and power of people in the past to structure their own lives, make their own choices and live in the world on their own terms that their experiences can be isolated and analysed. The majority of these approaches inspired by phenomenology and agency in Italian prehistory are not applied in the specific context of ceramics, yet provide proof that these theoretical approaches can be applied with successful outcomes. The final act of this introductory chapter is to present the structure of the book: how the chapters which follow will put together the material culture and theoretical ideas described here and use them to investigate Etruscan ceramic experience.

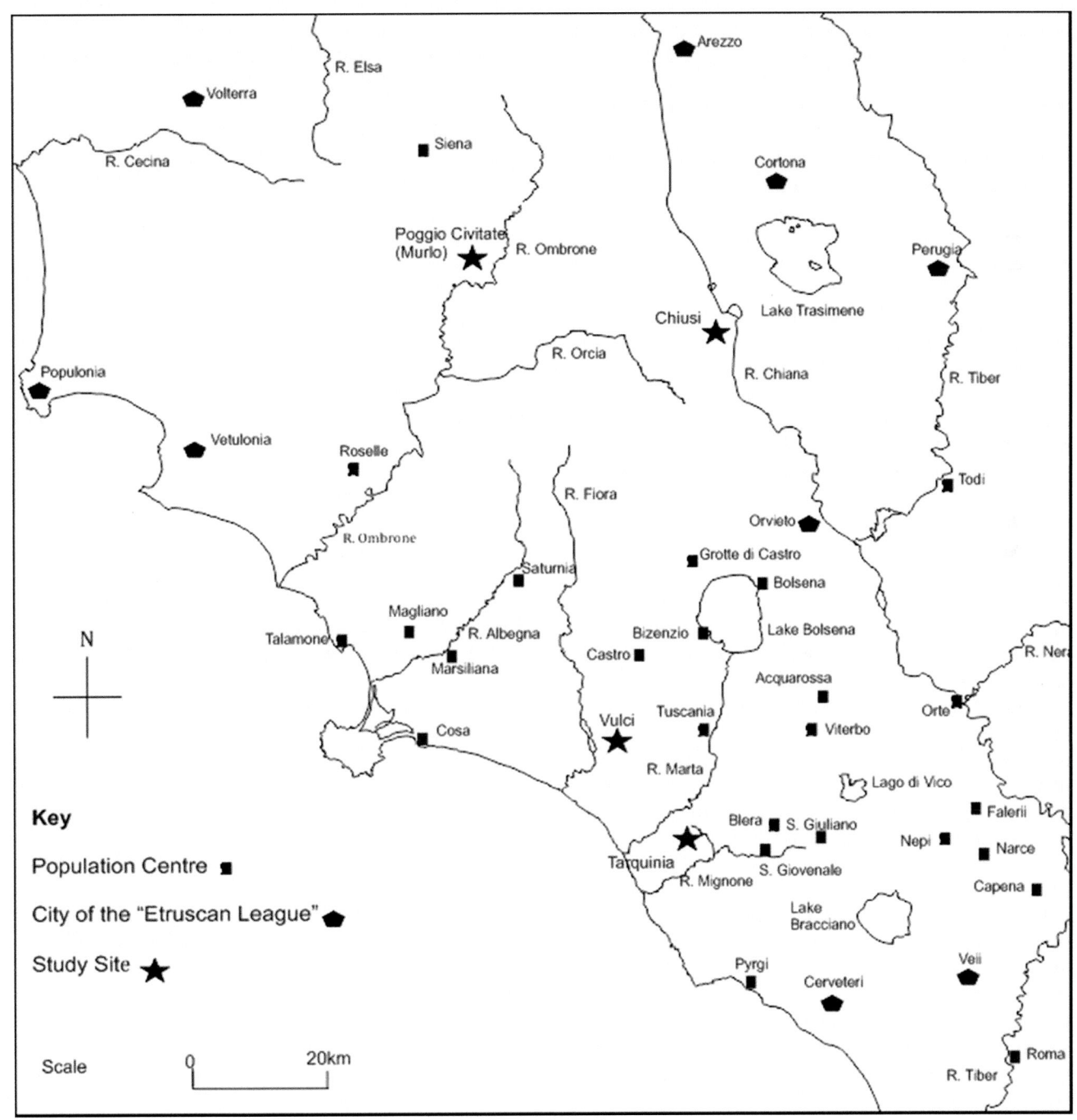

FIGURE 1.1: MAP OF ETRURIA

1.1 Etruscan Places, Etruscan Trade, Etruscan Things

Etruscan communities shared a distinct material culture in central Italy during the first millennium BC. The modern regions of Tuscany, Umbria, southern EmiliA–Romagna and northern Lazio formed the centreof this Etruscan heartland, traditionally defined as bounded by the rivers Tiber and Arno. Although Etruscan influence extended from the Adriatic coast to the Bay of Naples, this central region was occupied by at least twelve settlement centres, and a number of smaller sites, as illustrated in Fig. 1.1. Pallottino (1984b: 124) has argued that these twelve cities formed the largest units of Etruscan society, and were united by shared religious and economic concerns. Banti (1973: 15-16) suggests that the overarching label of 'Etruscans' should be seen as a cultural, rather than a political grouping, and that settlement centres were more important than overarching ethnicity to the construction of identity. The origins of this group of communities remain a sticking point in Etruscan archaeology (Briquel 2001: 43).

Herodotus suggests the origins of Etruscan culture lie in Lydia,[1] a long-standing idea (Briquel 1991) which, with some variations, continues to gain support from modern scholars (Drews 1992; van der Meer 2004). The archaeological record, however, suggests a steady growth in population and a continuity in material culture in the region dating back to at least the ninth century BCE and the preceding Villanovan culture (Camporeale 2004: 170; Torelli 1997:26-43). Recent studies of DNA (Pellecchia et al 2007; Achilli et al 2007) which appear to support the immigration theory have been shown to be methodologically unreliable and deliberately designed to support the immigration hypothesis (Perkins 2009).

Periodization is a slippery and difficult activity, as pointed out by Hodder (1987: 5). However, the time periods shown in Table 1.1 are generally used to demarcate different periods of growth and change in Etruscan culture. The earlier Villanovan and Orientalising phases have names which, in English, are value-laden, with the latter in particular implying intense influence (if not outright immigration) from the Eastern Mediterranean. The Italian terms (in italics) for the earlier periods are less loaded and will be used instead where necessary. This study is focused on the experience of Etruscan ceramic users during the Archaic period, defined here as between 600 and 450 BCE. After a period of economic success in the preceding century, Etruscan urban communities were continuing to grow, with this wealth reflected in increasingly rich burial assemblages. These funerary collections of objects are, in spite of the depredations of centuries of *tombaroli* or grave robbers, the source for the majority of the Etruscan archaeological record: creating a paradoxical situation in which the presentation of the dead is better known than the activities of the living (D'Agostino 1985; Izzet 2007a: 16).

Period	Dates
Villanovan *(Prima età del ferro)*	900-750 BCE
Orientalizing *(Seconda età del ferro)*	750-600 BCE
Archaic	600–450 BCE
Classical	450–300 BCE
Hellenistic	300-100 BCE

TABLE 1.1: PERIODIZATION OF ETRUSCAN ARCHAEOLOGY

The ceramics which are used in this study to examine Etruscan experiences of their use in the main originate from these burial assemblages. The complexity and capriciousness of burial contexts necessitates some caution in the analysis of objects recovered from tombs (Morris 1992; Parker Pearson 2001). The presence of ceramics in tombs has been taken as indicative of their use in life: pottery placed with the dead is assumed to be, even if not itself used directly by the living, materially very close to ceramics which were being used by Etruscans prior to the grave. The different groups of pottery included in the study are discussed in more detail in Chapter 4, but a distinction between two major collections can be drawn at the outset. Some pots in this analysis were made in Italy, but the majority, due to collection biases explored in detail later in Chapter 2, were made in Greece. The inclusion of so many seemingly foreign artefacts in a study of the Etruscans prompts a closer consideration of the relationship between the two groups, and presents an opportunity for the investigation of cultural interactions underlying everyday experience.

The role of Greek ceramics in Etruscan culture, seen as part of the wider relationship between Greeks and Etruscans, has been one of the most hotly debated issues in Etruscan studies (Arafat and Morgan 1994; Boardman 1975; Gill 1991, 1994; Ridgway 1997; Osborne 2001, 2007; Spivey 2006; Izzet 2004, 2007b, 2007c). The central question of this discourse is whether Etruscan consumers were clients of Greek technological mastery in a classic core-periphery model (cf Osborne and Boardman, for core periphery models see Champion 1995, Hall and Chase-Dunn 1993) or actively engaged in consuming and importing Greek produce acquired through trade between equals. The former view was being criticised as long ago as the work of Beazley (1947:xi) while the recent work of Riva (2010a, 2010b), Hodos (2009), Malkin (2002, 2004), Ra'ad (2001), van Dommelen (2001, 2010), Given (1999) and Dietler (1997, 2009) has demonstrated the colonial assumptions which underlie this type of Hellenocentric approach to the Ancient Mediterranean. In order to examine the experiences of Etruscan consumers of Greek ceramics, it is essential to engage with these arguments and develop a coherent hypothesis on the relationship between Greek pots and Etruscan owners. By using two similar historical and anthropological case studies, a clearer idea of the role of imported pottery in Etruria will be developed.

---

[1] Histories 1:94

A relevant historical parallel to the relationship between Greece and Etruria is the work of Felix Chami (1999a, 1999b) on the Iron Age of the Azanian coast of Tanzania. His research provides an example of a supposed peripheral zone, where interpretation has been plagued by colonial assumptions about the nature of trade and exchange within the region. The traditional 'story' of trade in this region was a fable in which Roman traders from the civilised Mediterranean provided the local inhabitants with iron tools in exchange for spices and ivory: a mirror image of later inequalities in trade in Africa. Chami's work with Paul Msemwa at the site of Kisiju demonstrated that not only were local groups in what is now Tanzania making their own iron tools, but that these were relatively common finds, alongside slag and iron making debris (Chami and Msemwa 1997). Additionally, through experimental archaeology work, Chami and Msemwa have shown that the inhabitants of the Rufiji delta and its offshore islands were capable of long sea voyages, and had access to sophisticated sea-faring technology in the form of large dhows. This seemingly peripheral community in fact is re-cast in the role of trans-ocean traders, who may have been actively trading as far away as India. A variety of objects from multiple sources were incorporated into daily life at Kisiju, creating a hybrid mixture of locally produced and imported tools.

Exchanged objects are important in the construction of identity, whether traded as commodities or exchanged as gifts. The networks of relations objects create simultaneously bind communities to each other as partners but also push them apart as separate entities. Anthropologically, there are numerous examples of active and interactive trade which have proved fruitful for discussions of ethnic identity (cf. Barth 1969; Cohen 1978; Horowitz 1985; Comaroff 1987). The model developed by Kipp and Schortmann (1989) suggests that elite exchange in luxury goods resulted in state formation, with exotic imports being used to create social inequality. Theodore-Pena has argued (2011) for an application of the Kipp-Schortmann model to the rise of Etruscan urban elites, suggesting that the formation of Etruscan polities is closely connected to the arrival of goods from the eastern Mediterranean. While I broadly agree with this hypothesis, I would argue that by the Archaic period and the intensification of trade between Greece and Etruria, a more accessible exchange network had developed, involving more, and more knowledgeable, consumers in Etruria.

The assumption that exporting groups are more politically powerful than importers underlies much of the Hellenocentric bias against Etruscan agency. While inequality may have been present in the distribution of goods through exchange systems, this cannot be used to characterise one partner community as lacking in agency or dynamism. One example based on trade between unequal groups which demonstrates the complexity of relationships between importers and exporters is that presented by Levi (1992). He draws together a detailed discussion of the varying levels of trade between Raramuri and Mestizo groups in northern Mexico, and outlines the extent of networks ranging from individual peddlers working from village to village on foot, relying on contacts and friendships, to opportunist large scale traders shipping artworks northwards to the US having obtained them by seemingly exploitative means, with reciprocal gift giving and trading relationships lying in the middle. In the Raramuri case, art objects with relatively little value to the makers are traded for useful objects: Levi describes a coat worth $4 traded for $20 worth of pots (Levi 1992:11). The pots are of little worth to their user, compared to a coat which he could not have made himself nor purchased locally. The apparent exploitation of the Raramuri salesperson in the course of this sale is a fallacy created by the inappropriate ascription of value in this particular situation. This example illustrates the contextual nature of value: the space between one definition of value and another is that in which trade operates.

In a further step, Levi identifies Raramuri as cutting out the Mestizo middleman, and selling objects directly to American dealers themselves, often in large quantities and even through mail order (Levi 1992: 12). As Raramuri traders have noticed the increased value of 'old' pots, they have begun to deliberately break and repair new objects in order to secure a better price (Levi ibid: 19). There are two points relating to Etruscan/Greek relations which this case study helps to make. The first is that even when trading relationships may seem to be founded on unequal terms, things are not always as they first appear. Just as at Kisiju, the Raramuri have taken control of trade in order to obtain what they want and are now active in the maintenance of their identity through the sale of cultural objects. The second point relates to the pots themselves. The Raramuri example shows the production of seemingly culturally specific objects in response to demand from a different group. While Greeks were producing painted pottery for their own use, as the Raramuri still do, they were perfectly capable of incorporating designs more closely allied to indigenous Etruscan preferences. Whether this was happening in the case of Greek and Etruscan commerce will be made visible by comparing indigenous and imported user experiences.

There are several conclusions to draw from the Raramuri and Azanian case studies for the Etruscan situation. Firstly, as at Kisiju, local Etruscan agents actively chose to place imported ceramics in their houses and later in their tombs, and developed their own technologies to create similar objects. The desire to engage with Greek vessel forms and use their images on a regular basis demonstrates their importance to Etruscan lives, just as the seemingly valueless coat was important to the Raramuri trader. Secondly, this desire would not exist were the Etruscan audience not able to relate to and interpret imported images in relation to their own world, and to master and incorporate the skills required to use new vessel shapes. Whether the intricate details of myth were understood (in Greek terms), Etruscan users created their own narratives based on the images they saw before them. It is this combination of relevance and desire which gave Greek ceramics value, rather than an intrinsic artistic worth perceived from the present. Etruscan consumers dictated the value of imported pottery, and their agency controlled the rhythm of trade in these objects. In the same fashion, American consumers of Raramuri pottery develop their own systems of meaning for the pots they buy, while Raramuri potters have changed their practice to suit the purchaser. The shared message from both case studies relates to value: to Etruscan users, Greek ceramics were valuable enough to purchase, and desirable enough to require the development of relationships with new kinds of objects.

This relating to things and styles emphatically does not change the ethnic identity of the person doing the relating and using. Incorporating a certain object into one's lifestyle does not mean a transformation into its producer or designer. Buying Chinese ceramics in the eighteenth century did not make Britons Chinese, although they invented stories to relate to the images on imported ceramic wares (O'Hara 1993). In the modern world, those who buy Raramuri ceramics do not become Raramuri, or even Mexican: they become those who can relate to and explain the presence of these objects in their home and incorporate the objects into their sense of self. The incorporation of the experience of ceramics made in Greece yet used and buried in Etruria into this study is a reflection of their incorporation into the lives of the Etruscans who chose to use and interact with these pots during their lifetime. The opportunity to analyse the experience of using such vessels, and ascertain their role in Etruscan uses which incorporated imported ceramics, provides a chance to consider the development and expression of a distinct form of Etruscan identity.

1.2 Agency and Phenomenology in Italian Prehistory

The debate surrounding relationships between Greeks and Etruscans is just one area of Etruscan archaeology's discourse which an examination of Etruscan experience can contribute to. The inter-connected nature of practice in different Etruscan cities, whether linked to political allegiances or ties of relationships, can also be approached through the ways that individuals were using and experiencing objects. These extensions begin with the action of a single person, and recognising their choices. There are three distinct examples of the investigation of choices, experience and agency in the Italian prehistoric past which are particular influences on the design of this study, in addition to the call for contextualisation in Etruscan ceramic studies. The first of these is focused upon recognising the active nature of choices and actions in the past: the realisation that the individual Etruscan person exercised control over themselves and was the catalyst for change in their own lives.

The work of John Robb has repeatedly demonstrated the potential for applications of archaeological theory in the archaeology of the Italian Neolithic, with a particular focus on the use of agency (1998, 2001, 2005, 2008a, 2008b, 2010). He provides both methodologies for practice, and careful case studies which demonstrate the utility of agency theory in reconceptualising traditional arguments and reframing interpretations to reflect the powerful nature of people and choices in the past. One of Robb's case studies is the analysis of six objects which are used to draw a prehistory of Italy through their entangled social relationships. This narrative uses what he considers the most recent development in agency theory: the specific enaction of agency through relationships with objects, and the recognition that objects themselves are sites of power (Robb 2008a: 507-9). This form of agency is closely linked to individual projects: projects of self-construction, self-definition and the 'production of certainty' (Robb ibid: 502). Each moment that an Etruscan individual picked up a decorated pot, they engaged in one of these agential projects, exercising choice in transforming the body through its connection with a vessel. At the same moment, the pot shapes the exchange, providing the parameters in which the Etruscan subject can refashion themselves and their experiences. The conception that traditions of practice themselves have agency to influence and manipulate past individuals adds another layer of agential relations to the exchange (Robb 2008b), while images and representations also have the potential to impact on the human actor. A flowing stream of different types of powerful social relationships are all wrapped up in the seemingly simple lifting of a vessel, and will continue to mix and move together after the object and actor are separated.

Robb, in his work with Marcia Anne Dobres, suggests that a variety of methodologies can be used to integrate the agency of past actors into archaeological interpretations (Dobres and Robb 2005: 163). One of the methods which they identify is phenomenology, the theoretical heart of this book. The detailed application of phenomenal thought to Etruscan ceramics is the subject of another chapter, but such approaches have been previously tried and found successful in other theatres in Italian prehistory. The work of Ruth Whitehouse (2001, 2007) on the use of caves as ritual places used the physical characteristics of these sites to develop a view of the experience of using them, building this to a re-evaluation of ritual practice in southern Italy and the wider Mediterranean. The same process of using the features of individual sites to draw larger conclusions about experience and society will be employed here. The sites of experience in this case are not dark, cramped spaces in which the body is engulfed: they are rather curving spheres of clay, to be touched and incorporated into the body with the hand and through the mouth.

The same principles of experiential analysis are working in both scenarios: the same features which describe a cave as a liminal space between worlds are perhaps less clear than those which describe a pot as a catalyst for the acquisition and performance of specific identities, but both are extant for the archaeologist. The development of practical methods for the recording and analysis of such experiences, developed at the Tavoliere-Gargano project lead by Sue Hamilton (et al 2006), is considered at length in a later chapter. Suffice to say that this second phenomenological project, also designed in an Italian scenario, this time focused on experiencing settlement sites in Neolithic Puglia, was as successful as the work of Whitehouse and Robb in advancing knowledge about the lives of individuals, and the wider experience of groups in prehistoric Italy.

All these case studies were developed for use in a time far distant from the world inhabited by the Etruscans. The late Iron Age world of Etruria, although perhaps rendered more familiar than the Neolithic through textual and archaeological study, has not previously been approached in such an explicitly phenomenological fashion. The success of such methodologies in earlier periods suggests the potential for such techniques in the Etruscan case. In addition, one scholar of Etruscan archaeology has come very close to considering the experience of her subjects. Vedia Izzet (2007a: 40) presents an analysis of Etruscan material culture from the perspective of the viewer. Her focus is primarily on mirrors, architecture and other objects engaging directly with the individual Etruscan person, and the impacts of objects in the construction of identity. Izzet uses the concepts of boundaries and surfaces as ideas to drive an interpretation of Etruscan society as closely linked to the negotiation of objects and spaces in a ground-breaking and effective archaeological narrative. She makes it clear that 'the object... will be taken as the point at which meaning is generated, interpreted and acted upon' (Izzet ibid: 31). Izzet also clarifies that she does not use ceramics as a case study for her argument as they do not directly manipulate the surface of the body (Izzet ibid: 3). Through the application of phenomenological thought to consider the experience of that Etruscan body, I will demonstrate that pottery has a large role to play in the construction of the Etruscan identity, with far-reaching conclusions for Etruscan social relationships on a local and regional scale.

1.3 Seeking Etruscan Experiences

This chapter has introduced the key research question of this study: what was the experience of using an Etruscan pot like for an Etruscan person? It has also introduced the potential follow-up questions to this primary investigation of a seemingly simple interaction. Through contextualising the desire to ask and answer this question, I have introduced the archaeological background to the Etruscan interaction between pot and person, in addition to the discourse surrounding one of the most fraught debates on which that interaction may shed light. I have introduced the three approaches in Italian prehistory which have inspired the decision to investigate experience in a phenomenological way, and the calls in Etruscan ceramic studies for new methodologies and approaches to consider Etruscan pots in context. To conclude this chapter, I will outline how these arguments are re-formed in more detail, and used to actively answer the question of experiencing Etruscan pottery.

Chapter 2 considers the full disciplinary context of this study. The position of Etruscan studies as betwixt and between classical archaeology and prehistory did not arise by accident, nor is it a coincidence that archaeological theory has been under-applied in Etruscology. To use ideas developed from social theory successfully, it is essential to understand why such approaches have not been tried. By reaching back to the very beginning of Etruscan studies, and tracing the connection between political ideology and archaeological narratives, I argue that the modern situation of theoretical avoidance is the result of centuries of application of political biases to Etruscan archaeology. In the wake of the 20th century cataclysm of World War II and its aftermath, I suggest that Italian Etruscology avoided its connections with fascist political theory by abandoning the explicit use of theory, while continuing to develop interpretations allied to Gramscian marxist thought. In the British case, I suggest that a similar apprehension and nervousness of subjectivity in archaeological practice born from the heritage of Grand Tour literature has restricted the application of social theory to Etruscan archaeology. By undertaking this historiographic analysis, I consider that it becomes possible to make more informed choices about the direct application of theory to the Etruscan world, and to establish that this study is part of a new engagement with interpretive experimentation developing in Etruscology in the last decade.

Chapter 3 outlines the development of a theoretical approach, demonstrating the origin of the phenomenal ideas which are used to develop a direct methodology for the analysis of Etruscan experience. It goes back to Merleau-Ponty's original development of the phenomenology of Hegel, and then argues that feminist re-interpretations of phenomenal thought have the potential to add agency and specificity to his narrower project which pioneered the application of phenomenology to the experience of a single, generic subject. I then examine the application of phenomenology in archaeological practice, demonstrating that rigorous practical methodologies can be formed from phenomenological principles through an in-depth Italian case study. I then develop a specific phenomenology which focuses on objects, and, particularly, on pots, by expanding Gell's object agency beyond art to all physical characteristics of material culture.

The theoretical framework of Chapter 3 sets up a methodology for the investigation of experience, presenting a phenomenology of objects which can be used to develop specific methods. Chapter 4 picks up that methodological thread, detailing how the experience of using ceramics is broken down into four phases, and how pots will be re-categorised according to their relationship with the body of their original user. It then presents the process of gathering together a data set for testing, providing the geographical and technological context of the 1164 pots used to test the specific methodologies used to analyse each phase of experience. Each of these phases is considered in one of the following analytical chapters, and each moves from the specific methods used to extract experiential data from the pottery corpus through comparative analysis of different pottery groups to a growing argument for a clear pattern of Etruscan ceramic use.

Chapter 5 explores the direct relationship between the body of the user and the clay body of a vessel. Chapter 6 moves to the decoration on the surface of a clay pot, and the impact of that decoration's constitution and placement on the experience of the user. Chapter 7 is the first of two chapters focused on the images used to decorate ceramics, and considers the influence of the bodies depicted on clay surfaces. Chapter 8 extends this analysis to what those bodies are doing, and how the actions of static figures immured in clay could impact on the Etruscan person who used them. The final chapter, Chapter 9, pulls together the arguments made in each individual chapter and uses them to build a series of conclusions about Etruscan experience of ceramics, and what those experiences suggest about wider Etruscan society.

Chapter 2

Traditions and Trajectories

2.1 Introduction

Etruscology as a discipline has a deep heritage. That heritage is intensely bound up in the history of the modern state of Italy, which has occupied the lands of the Etruscans since its inception in 1861, and the Tuscan states which ruled the territory in the preceding centuries. The relationship between Italian cultural identities and Etruscan studies has continuously characterised the latter, even when it is practised by those born and brought up outside Italy. Non-Italian scholars, coming from alien lands, are equally caught up in the laden history of Etruscan archaeology. In the early phases of research for this book, my own subjectivities resulted in a sense of frustration: at first I could not understand the rhythm of Etruscan studies, the way the discourse surged and reformed along familiar lines of interpretation. The combative style of Anglo-American archaeological thought was entirely inappropriate, yet the theoretical advances it had resulted in were under-represented. In order for me to be able to develop new ideas about old artefacts, examples of which were first discovered during the fourteenth century, it was absolutely essential to examine the history of Etruscology, both to recognise unspoken influences on my own practice, and place this novel approach within its disciplinary context.

This historiographical research may seem very distant from the experiential analysis promised by the previous chapter, and developed in those which follow. However, there is a key reason why this discussion is an essential part of this study. As hinted at in Chapter 1, Etruscan studies is a discipline which remains to some extent locked in familiar techniques and interpretative tropes, a situation which is particularly apparent in the analysis of ceramics. The majority of these methodologies remain unchanged by decades of archaeological theory, unaffected by recent permutations in anglophone archaeology in other contexts. To understand this stasis, this reluctance to engage with theoretical ideas, it is essential to go deep into the history of Etruscology, to trace the origins of the present situation to their roots. These are the reasons that scholars of the Etruscans have deliberately remained loyal to set methodologies, whether working in English or Italian, and the reasons why an analysis of Etruscan experiences of ceramics has not yet been forthcoming.

In this analysis of the heritage of Etruscology, I argue that such approaches have not been developed for two very good reasons, each specific to the scholarly traditions of Anglo-Americans and Italians. Each group has been caught up and entangled in subjective interpretations based on involvement with political theory and/or personal prejudices. In both cases, this experience was not one which the Etruscological community wished to repeat. By reaching back into the origins of each predicament, facing their effects on the discipline, and being aware of the potential for theoretical engagements to distort archaeological interpretation, my own use of theory to develop a new approach to Etruscan pottery is fully informed. Without the historiographical analysis of this chapter, my own experiential methodology could not have been developed: the history of the discipline was as formative as the writings of social theorists in the construction of this book. As such, it must be included as a precursor to those arguments.

In addition to the contribution this chapter makes to an understanding of the production of modern Etruscan studies, and the delicate balance between new ideas and static repetition, this examination is also the first analysis of Etruscology's past as a grand narrative which takes note of the connections between political events and archaeological practice, although historical summaries (e.g. DeGrummond 1986) and period-specific analyses (e.g. Bartoloni and Bocci Pacini 2004; Cristofani 1983; Pieraccini 2009; Shipley 2013a) have both been produced. Critical historiography has become an accepted methodology for archaeological research (Christenson 1989:1), often allied with studies of nationalism (Champion and Diaz-Andreu 1996:1-7). Guidi (1996: 108-118) has provided a view of the mid 20th century Italian political relationship with archaeology, but his focus is prehistory, not Etruscology in particular. Roman archaeology, too, has had its share of historiographical studies-whether those of Hingley (2002) on the British relationship with Rome in the nineteenth century or the analyses of Munzi (2004) and Nelis (2007) of the use Mussolini's fascist regime made of the ancient past.

It is markedly more difficult to undertake this sort of reflexive research on the influence of political events which are rather closer to the present day, although this is one of the most important aspects of this chapter. The relationship between Italian politics of the later twentieth and early twenty – first century and archaeology has been as important as that which went before, and the same approaches of historiographic analysis can still be applied. Equally difficult is tracing the origins of Etruscan archaeology. The work of Moser (1992, 1997) on the iconography of human origins is helpful in this regard: she has developed a methodology for the analysis of historic images of imagined pasts which I extend into their representation in literature. By considering the development of Etruscan studies during this first, formative period, and by facing up to the more recent involvement of Etruscan archaeology with political movements, this chapter connects the history of Etruscology to its current incarnation, and links up politics and pots.

Before beginning a chronological history of Etruscology, there is a feature of the modern discipline which must be addressed, one which I have used to divide this chapter: the separation between Italian and external approaches to the Etruscans. Some individuals move between and navigate the two streams of study, conferences are organised to bring the two communities together, publications appear in English and in Italian, and occasional articles by Anglophone writers appear in *Studi Etruschi* and Italian scholars in *Etruscan Studies*. Yet these are exceptions rather than regular practice, and such efforts at unification often demonstrate the lack of cohesion between scholars from Italy, Britain and America (to say nothing of the extensive contribution of Swedish, German and French scholars). In order to move forward and provide better research in both key tongues, individual practitioners from both communities must make a more strenuous effort to engage with one another. As an English scholar working on Italian material, it is a personal prerogative to investigate the events which have created the discipline of Etruscology – and those which have divided it into two. This is the other contribution of this chapter, which reaches beyond my arguments about ceramics to the wider development of new ideas in Etruscan studies. It is only by recognising the heritage of the discipline that scholars from both inside and outside Italy can move forward – and it is only by engaging deeply in both traditions of thought that the two groups can be brought together. By recognising the pedigree of Italian Etruscan studies, and the ideals of anglophone Etruscology, the two schools of thought may yet be brought together in self-reflexivity, resulting in shared progression.

To summarise, this chapter has a dual purpose: both to site the present study within the history of Etruscan archaeology, and to demonstrate the importance of historiographic analysis in disciplinary reflection. Beginning from the medieval discovery of Etruscan material culture, I use the story of the discipline to explain the current situation in which theoretical novelty is subservient to familiar patterns of archaeological practice. Having looked at the influence of particularly Italian political events, I move to the experience of the English language tradition, exploring the balance of heritage and romantic tradition with the incorporation of methodological and theoretical developments in the twentieth century. While influences on Italian scholars are perhaps more closely tied to political allegiances and events, those in Britain appear connected to a different sort of politics: the ins and outs of the archaeological establishment in later years, and literary conceptions of colonially inspired attitudes to Italy and Italians in the early history of Etruscan studies in English. Through the historiographic analyses of this chapter, it will be made clear that my research, while explicitly focused on the narrow world of Etruscan pottery, must not only be read in historical context, but is the product of that history.

2.2 Initial Entanglements: 1250-1400

The role of the interest of generations of Tuscan aristocracy, particularly the Medici, in an Etruscan past is widely acknowledged as important to the development of Etruscology (Galdy 2009: 42; Cipriani 1980: 17). It was Cosimo I de Medici (1519-1574) who appropriated Etruscan antiquities to form a personal collection, and who used these objects to create a vision of inherited glory for his family. His ancestor, Pope Leo X (1475-1521), was the first to actively organise excavations searching for Etruscan artefacts. However, this genesis of deliberately organised Etruscan archaeology would have been impossible without a transformation in perceptions of the Etruscans which took place between the late thirteenth and late fourteenth centuries. Over a period of around 150 years, the Etruscans were reconceived for the first time as positive ancestors, rather than reviled pagans, a process which I have detailed elsewhere (Shipley 2013a). My point is that it is no exaggeration to say that the entire history of Etruscan studies is built from the foundations of this medieval role reversal. In this moment of the late medieval period, the stereotypical tropes of Etruscan character were first created, echoes of which can be seen in modern interpretative narratives. The valorisation of the Etruscans, and their connection to Tuscan, and later Italian, national and regional identity, begins amongst the relative security of the later thirteenth century, but is made manifest during the rise of Florence in the wake of plague, famine and war.

The transformation in the image of the Etruscans (and interest in them) is closely linked to the relationship of Florence with the Papacy. In the wake of centuries of insecurity (Randers-Pehrson 1983: 20-29), two key factions had developed in the Italian peninsula: the pro-papacy Guelphs, and the supporters of the Holy Roman Empire, known as Ghibellines. Individual city republics across Tuscany, ruled by citizen bodies (Waley and Dean 2010: 36-38), were characterised by their allegiance to one group or the other: Siena, Arezzo and Pisa were allied to the Ghibellines, while Florence, Perugia and Orvieto were firmly pro-papacy. In spite of the establishment of Ghibelline government in Florence in 1260, Guelph rule was the default political position for Florence at this point, and the city pursued an aggressive policy of intimidation and attack on neighbouring (and rival) Ghibelline cities. It is in this context of tension that the first discovery of Etruscan artefacts was made, ironically in direct response to Florentine aggression. During the construction of a new circle of city walls for Arezzo, a foundation trench was found to contain pottery of a kind never seen before. The chronicler Ristoro d'Arezzo, in his *Composizione del Mondo,* describes the objects in amongst tracts on horoscopes and geology as 'blue and red...light and subtle, without heaviness' (D'Arezzo 1872: 137). The colours and fabric description sound suspiciously like imported Attic black or red figure vases, although Ristoro perceives them as having come from God as a blessing for Arezzo.

It is perhaps unsurprising that d'Arezzo did not make the connection between the Etruscan history of his city and the objects found there. In spite of access to Roman descriptions of the Etruscans in Livy, Virgil and Pliny, the Etruscans as conceived of by the thirteenth century Italian scholastic community were not a group of people to associate with heavenly objects, even in an anti-papal city like Arezzo. In Guelph Florence, the Etruscans were emphatically viewed negatively, as can be seen in both artistic and literary sources. Dante Alighieri, Florentine scholar and later exile, presents a number of Etruscan individuals in his *Divina Commedia* (Schoonhoven 2010). Unlike his Roman guide, condemned to *Purgatorio* as a man born before Christ, Dante's Etruscan characters are firmly placed in *Inferno*. The legendary figure King Porsenna is presented as the torturer of a Roman general found in *Paradiso* (Paradiso IV: 84), while the sorceror Aluns is found in hell (Inferno XX: 46). Other textual sources develop the theme of Porsenna as cruel ruler, with the Etruscans portrayed as violent pagans, in contrast to civilised Romans. The chronicler Giovanni Villani (1280-1348) goes so far in his *Nuova Cronica* as to blame factional violence in Florence on the city's Etruscan heritage: in response to the brutal murder of Roman women and children in 283 BCE, the Etruscan settlement of Fiesole is burned and its inhabitants incorporated into a new Roman city: Florence itself (Cronica Book I 6-11).

This negative conception of the Etruscans, gleaned from Roman sources and perpetuated by contemporary writers, was portrayed in iconography as well as historical chronicles and epic poetry (Jannot 2000: 82). The Florentine artist Giotto, when working on scenes of hell for the Scrovegni family of Padua, must have been influenced by Etruscan representations of demons. There are several similarities between his Satan and the figure of Charun in the Tomb of the Blue Demons at Tarquinia: while not identical, the two images, when seen side by side as in Figures 2.1 and 2.2, recall each other strongly. Both hellish figures share a blue skin-tone, seated pose and outstretched, well-muscled arms. Both grapple with writhing vipers and are shown with a grimacing, open mouth. Giotto's Satan possesses the physical characteristics and reptile accompaniments of Charun, but is provided with a Christian remit for the torture of the damned. In a pro-Roman, pro-papacy regime, there is no room for pagan ancestors except in hell. From the visual association between Etruscans and Satan created by Giotto and the definitive placement of Etruscans in hell by Dante, by the time the later chronicler Leonardo Bruni was writing in 1415 these Florentine archetypes had all but disappeared.

Bruni's chronicle of the History of Florence presents the Etruscans as the founders of Italian civilisation and of classical antiquity, the original incarnation of the ideal form of government that the city republic embodies (Ianziti 2007: 249). This complete reversal was inherently tied to the politics of Florence. After the alienation of the Papacy to Avignon in 1309, and the deployment of menacing mercenary squads across the temporal lands of the Papal States and surrounding cities, allegiance to Rome was crumbling in Florence.

FIGURE 2.1: DETAIL FROM GIOTTO'S FRESCO OF HELL IN THE SCROVEGNI CHAPEL, PADOVA.
IMAGE (C) SOPRINTENDENZA PER I BENI CULTURALI VENETO

FIGURE 2.2: DETAIL FROM THE TOMB OF THE BLUE DEMONS, TARQUINIA.
IMAGE (C) SOPRINTENDENZA PER I BENI CULTURALI ARCEOLOGICI ETRURIA MERIDIONALE.

At the same time, in the wake of the Black Death, the merchant population of the city was recovering more quickly than local rivals, and so was the Florentine economy. The result was a newly confident Florence ready to develop its own iconography and heritage separate from the Roman, papally sanctioned past. The beginnings of this change can be seen in the works of Boccaccio, written in 1336. His *Filocolo* presents the Tuscan landscape as a beautiful garden, in which specifically Etruscan nymphs of love and beauty live (Boccaccio trans. Serafini-Sauli 1985: 5). As the relationship between Florence and the Papacy broke down further after the return of a corrupt and aggressive papal regime to Rome, outright war between the two groups became a feature of the late fourteenth century, providing an opportunity for the Etruscans to take up a more sinister task: that of propaganda. In a letter inciting rebellion against the Pope, the leader of the Florentine government, the humanist philosopher Coluccio Salutati, encouraged the city of Perugia in 1383 to join with their Tuscan brothers to create a new Etruria, independent of Rome (Cipriani 1980: 3). For the first time, but not the last, the Etruscans had become emblems of a nationalist ideal, and the important later trope of liberty and beauty loving Etruscans had been established.

2.3 To Make a Nation: 1723-1800

The medieval reversal in the imagining of the Etruscans, and their first association with the politics of Tuscany would continue in the intervening centuries: Etruscan artefacts were curated extensively by the Medici and incorporated into their collection of curiosities, a key part of the Florentine Renaissance efforts in rebuilding the knowledge of the classical world. However, the role of the Etruscans in these political relationships remained the same as that developed by Boccaccio and Salutati: a mythical brotherhood of ancestors, to be invoked for political advantage or to affirm cultural superiority. Interest in the Etruscan language and culture grew during the sixteenth century, including the first fraudulent rendering of Etruscan texts by Annio da Viterbo and his later exposure (Ligota 1987; Stephens 2004). The first devoted text on the Etruscans, *De Etruria Regali,* was written in 1616 by a Scottish monk, Thomas Dempster.

This text was not a lone example, but part of a wider discourse, itself infiltrated by fraudulent claims eventually dispatched as a result of Papal enquiries (Rowland 1989: 424; 1986; 2004). The next distinct development in the relationship between identity, politics and Etruscan studies came during the following century, and began with the formal publication, for the first time, of Dempster's study for a general audience in 1723. Although this publication was funded and pursued by an English aristocrat, Thomas Coke, in the wake of his Grand Tour in 1713, alongside an Italian scholar, Filippo Buonarroti, suddenly Dempster's ideas on Etruscan society were available for all who could read. The work contains the same images of the Etruscans produced during the Renaissance: a highly cultured society, living in city republics joined together in a League of Twelve, a vision of Etruscan political organisation which continues to this day. Buonarroti also produced a consideration of the origins of the Etruscans, which he connected to ancient Egypt, opening up a question which has been one of the most fractious features of the discipline ever since (Cristofani 1983: 33).

The relative availability of the work opened the Etruscans up to a new audience, separate from the nobles and clergy who had been the primary disseminators of Etruscan information. The lesser gentry and wealthy merchant class, alongside a growing secular intelligentsia, were now able to access the same information. The desire for universal education amongst all classes of Tuscans was exemplified in the creation of a league of self-improvement and education at Cortona, explicitly focused on bringing knowledge of the people's heritage to the general public. The group founded the first public library in Italy and named their organisation 'The Noble Academy of the Etruscans' (Pacini 1992). While individual wealthy patrons still claimed objects from growing numbers of excavations at Chiusi, Montepulciano and Volterra, by the late eighteenth century the first public access museum was opened at Volterra, devoted to displaying to all and sundry the fruits of excavations conducted between 1762 and 1773 (Duggan 2008: 29). In Florence, too, the Uffizi gallery was acquiring more objects and, while still connecting them to the power of Cosimo III, placed them on display to the public. For the first time, one of the most charismatic Etruscan objects, the Chimaera of Arezzo, could now be encountered by visitors – proof of the artistic prowess of their ancestors. These public collections, libraries and study groups were physical expressions of the developing Italian Englightenment, which valued public happiness and scientific investigation highly (Ferrone 1995; Wahnbaek 2004).

While the availability of knowledge of the Etruscans was increasing in Italy, so was a sense of the need for a return to the political values of the Etruscans themselves – or the values that were perceived as Etruscan. Republican rule by the people had resulted in the most prosperous periods of Italian history: the Etruscan period, the glory days of the Roman Republic and the more recent high medieval city states. With the establishment of the French Republic in 1789, the philosophy of equality and brotherhood already visible in the philosophy of the Etruscan study group and public museums found a political expression. Italian political thinkers, scientists and philosophers had been agitating for the introduction of political reforms during the 1760s and 70s, and in the process had developed a conception of Italy as a nation for the first time (Dooley 1987; Venturi 1972). The Piedmontese Carlo Denina portrayed the Etruscans as an unconquered nation in spite of interference from Romans and Gauls – and placed that portrayal in a book whose title left no room for ambiguity as to his political allegiances – *Revolutions in Italy* (Cristofani 1983: 135). These intellectuals were delighted at Napoleon's invasion of Milan in 1796, only 3 years after the first painted tombs at Tarquinia were uncovered to international interest (Duggan 2008: 28). They saw the arrival of the French as the first step in the foundation of an independent Italian republic – something that would not happen for another 65 years.

Dissatisfaction with the French grew quickly as Italians realised they had simply exchanged one form of inequality for another. The political capital of the Etruscans grew under French rule – (incompetent) French excavations at Tarquinia in particular under the orders of the new, French Grand Duke of Tuscany revealed a huge amount of information about what was now coming to be considered the Italian past, before taking that heritage to Paris or selling it for profit. In a reflection of French colonial values, bucchero and other indigenously produced Etruscan (Italian) vessels were smashed, while imported Greek wares swept off to museum glory (Sassatelli 2011). The desire for access to Etruscan archaeology was repressed by the Napoleonic state, but its spectre remained in the new form of committed Italian nationalists. The interest in the origins of the Etruscans established by Buonarroti had also become a question of interest for those working for the foundation of a new Italian nation. This issue would become more important over the following century, but the two sides of the origins argument were already becoming politically entangled. The debate over external immigration or internal development rolls on into the twenty-first century, but was established in the frenzy of Italian resistance to France during the late eighteenth and early nineteenth centuries.

The Etruscans were now being used as a symbol of Italian freedom from foreign invaders – the role given them by Denina had become a rallying cry. Knowledge of the past quickly became a weapon, used to encourage nationalists across Italy – Romans and Etruscans were, for the first time, united in a quest to rouse revolution against French overlords. Although it would take until 1861 for Italy as a nation state to emerge from the confusion of individual kingdoms, abortive national republics and French dominance, the Etruscans would continue to be used to promote the new nation – as representatives of its history and political models for its present. The two key developments of the eighteenth century had changed Etruscan studies from the preserve of the nobility and their paid scribes to a field of study open (and attractive) to the middle classes – a way of expressing nationalistic feelings through scholarly exploration. The foundation of museums and libraries opened the way for these new intellectuals to access the past, and created the sparks of interest which would grow into a discipline during the nineteenth century.

The allegiance to the Etruscan legend of political liberty, unity and freedom of creative expression had by this point transferred from a specifically Tuscan pride to an element of a national consciousness. The nationalist spirit and egalitarian ideals of the Enlightenment had transformed Etruscan studies, but during the early twentieth century the optimism of this period would be darkened during the Fascist years: a time which marked a loss of innocence for Etruscan archaeology and has divided and defined the discipline from the end of World War II.

2.4 Politics of Involvement: 1918-1943

The creation of Italy as a nation state in 1861 provoked an upswelling in national feeling amongst intellectuals (Adamson 1989: 413). In the same moment that archaeology was becoming an acknowledged scientific discipline in northern Europe (Trigger 1990: 74), Italian archaeology formed three distinct sub-groups: classical archaeology focused on Greece and Rome, naturalistica or archaeological science, and paleoetnologia, or the study of prehistory. Guidi points out that the first of these schools was already developed by the time of the Risorgimento, but that the last, paleoetnologia, or prehistory, was a product of this period of searching for united origins (Guidi 2010).

The discovery of shared Bronze Age Appenine and Terramare cultures allowed for a conception of a shared origin for all Italians, in spite of their separation and diversification (Guidi 1996: 108). Indeed, the spread of these Bronze Age cultures from north to south was presented as having mirrored the transformation of Garibaldi's troops spreading across Italy from Piedmont (Guidi ibid: 112). The Etruscans fell squarely between these three disciplines, which is probably the source of the current position of the discipline as uncomfortably stretched between classical studies and prehistory (Izzet 2007a:10; and more obliquely referenced in Bonfante 2011: 233). However, while these nineteenth century traditions remain important, they would have far less impact on the discipline than the period in which the nation of Italy was tested during the early twentieth century.

World War I had been disastrous for Italy, in spite of its position allied to the eventual winners, Britain and France (Burgwyn 1993). The country experienced humiliating defeats in the Alps fighting the Austrians, was devastated in the north-eastern provinces of Veneto and Trentino Alto-Adige, and did not gain the city of Trieste in the Paris Peace Conference as had been hoped. The limitation of state control became apparent with the rise of socialism and the trade unions: greatly alarming the bourgeoisie and threatening the country's economy (Lyttleton 2003: 13-35). The anarchist assassination of King Umberto I in 1900 had left a shadow of mistrust hanging over socialist and anarchist groups, and, rather than allow them control, a rival political party began to form, drumming up support on a promise of the destruction of the socialists and the return of economic and political security: the Fascists (Carsten 1982: 49-62). Through violence and intimidation, the Fascists established control over the weak Liberal government via the democratic process, before removing that process entirely, and establishing a dictatorship under their leader, Benito Mussolini.

Contemporary historians have noted the need for Italy to recognise its Fascist history (Gentile 1986: 179; Sluga 1996). It is also necessary for Etruscology to recognise its involvement in the Fascist past. The Fascist period created a divide which remains visible in the discipline to this day: between students of professors who were accepted by the regime, and those who were outside it. The figures of three particular individuals in the history of Etruscan studies were the founding fathers of this divide: Giulio Quirinio Giglioli, his student Massimo Pallottino, and Ranuccio Bianchi Bandinelli. The latter was the heir of Tuscan aristocrats, and began his investigation into the Etruscans through experimental excavations on his family lands near Chiusi.

Bianchi Bandinelli was a socialist by political inclination from a young age, and this is reflected in his employment record. Although he studied at the prestigious La Sapienza university in Rome, his first academic posts were far from glamorous. After time at Cagliari, he moved to Pisa, before fleeing to Groningen in response to his concerns about the fascist regime. After much cajoling and negotiations of safety, Bianchi Bandinelli returned to a job at Florence – where he was forced to give Hitler and Goering guided tours of the Uffizi, an experience he recounts in his autobiography (Bandinelli 1995). Bianchi Bandinelli's archaeology inescapably reflected his socialism: he was deeply interested in topographic survey, landscape archaeology and the economics of rural Etruria, all methods of ascertaining the realities of life for the ordinary proleteriat during the period (Bandinelli 1927; 1929; 1950; 1961; 1979). Unsurprisingly, perhaps, Bianchi Bandinelli is much more celebrated in modern Italy than his contemporaries, whose politics are harder to accomodate into contemporary values (cf his biographies, Barbanera 2000, 2003; Barbanera (ed.) 2009).

One of Bandinelli's adversaries was the slightly older Giglioli, a veteran of the First World War, whose experience of fighting for his country seems to have resulted in his fervent nationalist beliefs. A scholar at La Sapienza, Università di Roma, his scholarship bears witness to his allegiance to Mussolini's desire for an Italian past unaffected by foreign influences. In addition to undertaking the Corpus Vasorum Antiquorum volumes for the Capitoline Museum and Villa Giulia National Etruscan Museum (Giglioli 1925; 1926), Giglioli wrote *L'arte Etrusca*, a volume which denied any influence from Greece in the development of Etruscan art: an on-message dictum which propogates the myth of Italian cultural supremacy even before Rome (Giglioli 1935). The journal *Archeologia Classica* was founded by Giglioli, providing a secure publishing venue for classical scholars which continues into the present day, forming one of his two key legacies.[2] The other legacy of Giglioli lies in the achievements of his student, the most celebrated Etruscologist of the 20th century, Massimo Pallottino.

Pallottino, who studied under Giglioli at La Sapienza, absorbed the majority of his mentor's archaeological ideas, but managed to avoid embroiling himself in his politics. Emphatically an Etruscan scholar, rather than a classical archaeologist, his first major action in Etruscan studies was his foundation of the journal *Studi Etruschi* in 1927. It is interesting to speculate whether such a journal would have been founded at all without the heavy attention paid to indigenous Italian cultural glories by the Fascist regime, and the early volumes appear somewhat thin, with the same group of scholars publishing articles together: Pallottino and Giglioli, naturally, but also Antonielli and Cultrera, with an article by Bianchi Bandinelli included in the first two volumes from 1927 and 1928. It is interesting to note that Bianchi Bandinelli disappears from *Studi Etruschi* at this point, and has no articles other than short reviews published in the journal until 1959: perhaps an indication of his political alienation, or personal issues –

his obituary in the 1977 edition of Studi Etruschi describes Bianchi Bandinelli as a very difficult man, many years after his original exile. Possibly this exclusion from Studi Etruschi prompted Bianchi Bandinelli to produce his own journal: *Critica d'arte*. First published in 1935, this journal was the first to accept work on any period of art history, and eventually developed into the socialist archaeological journal *Prospettiva* in the 1950s.

Studi Etruschi itself was founded with a distinct structure, reflecting the separation in the discipline of Etruscan studies which remains ongoing. The first part is focused on history, society and religion, while the second is on the interpretation of the Etruscan language and the third on scientific studies including osteology, ceramic analysis and palynology. The split between cultural historical archaeology, science and linguistics remains: and is still present to some extent in the journal. It is unsurprising that these boundaries remain in place, as they are still the three main channels for archaeological research in Italian Etruscan studies. Hence, explorations of personal characteristics such as age and sex in skeletal remains are limited to the science pages, while inscriptions are analysed as texts, not in context. The separation between the three channels discourages direct transfer of ideas between scholars, with a result that there are limited opportunities for collaboration and development. The foundation of *Studi Etruschi* established these tropes of publication which have comprehensively shaped the modern world of Etruscan studies.

The work of Pallottino himself has had an even more significant effect on the development of Etruscology – his publication in *Studi Etruschi* of 1939, on the eve of the outbreak of war, presents the most credible argument for Etruscan origins then published, and remains a seminal text (Pallottino 1939). It is tempting to speculate that Pallottino himself was aware of the dangers to come in an atmosphere of increasing tension, so threw caution to the wind when writing *Sulle facies culturali arcaiche dell'Etruria*, his first major publication. Alongside a convincing reworking of the autochthonous origin arguments, he delivers a stinging critique of the archaeological world in which he worked, stating that:

> 'It could not be said that the study of protohistoric antiquity of central Italy is missing a fundamental methodology, but the major part of scholars do not concern themselves with a critical problem and present conclusions which are accepted without discussion...' (Pallottino 1939:86).

It is striking when reading this article how little the problems of Etruscology have changed – Pallottino lambasts the tendency to impose evolutionary models and cultural labels onto the past, and proposes instead placing objects at the centre of model development, focusing on integration and transition rather than invasion hypotheses. The need to place objects as the centre of archaeological

---

[2] Giglioli was by no means the pet archaeologist of the Fascist regime, although he did organise the Mostra Augustea della Romanità which acted as a showcase for Mussolini's Terza Roma and was visited by Hitler. However, Giglioli's involvement pales in comparison to that of Pericle Ducati. The director of the Museo Civico at Bologna, Ducati was shot by partisans in 1943 as a reaction against his involvement in Fascism – a reflection of just how dangerous and important political allegiances could be for archaeologists at the time.

discussion of society is something I have strongly argued for in Chapter 1 – so it appears that Pallottino's message has been ignored. While he himself went on in 1942 to produce the enormous and successful volume *Etruscologia*, his revolutionary zeal on the edge of war seems to have been forgotten. Rather than endorsing Pallottino's message through the removal of cultural labels, the very act of privileging objects would go on to create ever more complicated labels and distinctions between different groups in prehistoric Italy and create a tangle of arguments of typology and chronology which would mask post-war discomfort with big ideas allied to spurious politics.

2.5 Division and Development post 1945

The intertwined nature of archaeology and politics in Italy have become even more closely knotted together in the wake of the fall of Fascism, and the development of the Third Republic into modern Italy. The end of World War II was a tumultous and violent experience, with Italy itself invaded by foreign forces from both sides. After invasion by the Allies in the south, the government in Rome frantically declared neutrality and expelled Mussolini, only to be taken over by their German allies, effectively dividing the country in two. Partisans prowled the central Appennine mountains, often killing those perceived as connected to the by now hated regime. The damage to the country, economically, culturally and emotionally, was extreme (Zamagni 1993: 321). While the economy of Italy would recover by the 1950s, assisted by both American aid monies and the resurgence of industry, politically and culturally the country had been severely shaken. While the terrors of socialism and anarchy which had prompted some people to turn to Mussolini in the first place had only intensified with the rise of the Soviet Union, there was now a sense that the suffering of socialists under the fascists had earned them at least a voice in parliament, and the power of the trade unions could not be denied (Franzosi 1995: 1-2; Zariski 1956: 255). At the same time, the traditional powers of the Vatican and the nobility had been disgraced by their association with Fascism, and no longer held the same pull over the working and middle-classes, in spite of their eventual allegiance with the American aid-givers against Communism (Filippelli 1989: 5-7).

This fractured state was almost exactly reflected in Etruscan archaeology. The divide between socialists and fascists continued even after the fall of the latter politically, but it is obvious in the pages of *Studi Etruschi*, where Bianchi Bandinelli in particular remained in the wilderness. While politically the Christian Democrats mobilised to fill the centre-right and dominate Italian politics, the group of scholars around Massimo Pallottino, the heirs to Giglioli and the academic establishment of the previous regime, became the focus of Etruscology. It is slightly unfair to connect Pallottino's prevalence to his politics: his archaeological brilliance is at its brightest in his first major post-war work, which is filled with both logical argument and furious frustration. His 1947 *Origin of the Etruscans* is a refinement of his 1939 paper, and the singular 'Origin' of the title is a statement of intent. The article is the first to fully gather together the historiography of the debate over Etruscan origins, from ancient writers to what Pallottino calls 'modern deductions and fantasies' (Pallottino 1947: 14). Perhaps mindful of his own recent experiences with ultra–nationalism, Pallottino identifies the connection between the indigenous origin argument and this set of political beliefs, placing it squarely as part of a long tradition of what is, for him, the wrong way of approaching any argument: to arrive with an a priori conception of the answer, rather than a hypothesis to be tested. The self-knowledge and reflexivity of this volume are matched by the cut and thrust of the writing style, creating a combative and persuasive argument which is perhaps unmatched even today.

In spite of the seeming dominance of the conservatives, certain forms of socialist thought, while excluded from the Etruscology mainstream, would develop into one of the most important features of the discipline in later years, which is still intensely influential at present. It is impossible to consider this period without recognising the importance of the influence of one man's thought, even though that man himself died in prison in 1937. Antonio Gramsci, a Sardinian Marxist, wrote voluminously throughout his imprisonment, and his writings put forward a vision of the maintenance of the bourgeoisie through what he termed 'cultural hegemony' (Davidson 1977). This term was used to describe the claim of the middle classes that they alone represented moral and intellectual superiority, and as such were fit for political power (Gramsci 2010: 20). In order for the workers to overcome the state, they needed to expand from economic aims to incorporate the establishment of their own cultural hegemony of independent thought and virtue. In the creation of such a new order, the role of the intellectual thinker from a working class background would be paramount – an idea guarenteed to appeal to the ranks of individuals enabled to aspire to university after the economic boom of the 1950s (Armstrong 1988). Gramsci's thought provides not only a window into the philosophy of these later Etruscan archaeologists, but also a way of thinking about the developments in the discipline itself. While, in many ways, Pallottino and his advocates had created their own cultural hegemony of Etruscology, this would be challenged in the 1970s and 1980s with the resurgence of the heirs of Bianchi Bandinelli.

The word 'heirs' is particularly appropriate here. Students of the original instigators of the divide between right and left wing Italian Etruscan archaeologists would continue the separation between the two groups into the 21st century. While the political mainstream was dominated by the Christian Democrats until the 1990s, governments would come and go, at an average of 11 months in power each between 1945 and 1996. As a result, perhaps, of this national political deadlock, the personal politics of Etruscology grew more intense, with the heirs of Bianchi Bandinelli and Pallottino continuing to spar in the same manner as their original leaders, in whose image they were made. A triumvirate of past-students of Pallottino have become dominant figures in the traditionalist side of the discipline: Mauro Cristofani, Giovanni Colonna and the late Mario Moretti. They have been prolific excavators, contributing to rescue and research excavations at Cerveteri, Vulci, Veii, Tarquinia, Volterra, Pyrgi and Populonia, and continued the style of Pallottino in their written work, whether as academics in the case of Cristofani and Colonna, or as members of the Soprintendenza, in the case of Moretti. The influence of Pallottino, and the experience of digging are clearly visible in the approach to typology and the use of objects of these three in their many publications, but each has taken up different aspects of their Professor's thought.

Cristofani's wide ranging publications have incorporated Pallottino's interest in the history of the discipline (Cristofani 1983), the cataloguing of funerary objects and iconography (Cristofani 1965, 1970, 1975a) and the development of general works for both new students (1978) and what may be termed an updating of Pallottino's classic *Etruscologia* (Cristofani 1979). Colonna, meanwhile, was more interested in the context of the Etruscan world, its place in a Mediterranean world thronging with different people, whether through contact with Greece (Colonna (ed.) 1996) or with other groups in Italy (Colonna 1970, 2000, 2005). Moretti, meanwhile, worked on the presentation of Etruscan archaeology to both an academic audience and the wider public, through his publications of his work at the Tarquinia museum, Villa Giulia, and Cerveteri(Moretti 1962, 1966, 1970, 1975; Moretti (ed.) 1977). His daughter, Anna Maria Sgubini Moretti, has also worked extensively in public and academic archaeology in Tuscany and Lazio, co-ordinating excavations at Vulci and transforming the Villa Giulia Museo Nazionale Etrusco, in addition to successful mostre and publications which continue the prosaic presentation of the Pallottino school (Sgubini Moretti 1993, 1998; Sgubini Moretti (ed.) 2001a, 2001b, 2002, 2004a, 2004b).

While the successors of Pallottino may have dominated Etruscan archaeology, they have not been alone. Bianchi Bandinelli, too, passed on both his political beliefs and archaeological interests to two particular students, who have gone on themselves to become a source of alternative viewpoints and often combative arguments, as opposed to the studied continuity of the traditional school. Bianchi Bandinelli himself was lionised in the wake of World War II, and seen as an intellectual who had resisted Fascism (D'Agostino 1991: 54). He enthusiastically adopted the ideas of Gramsci, and this is reflected in his *Storicità dell'arte classica* of 1943, which acknowledges the rootedness of art, and indeed archaeology, in society. Perhaps as a result of his new found postwar popularity, or his supposedly difficult personality, Bianchi Bandinelli remained estranged from the Etruscan establishment he had abandoned under Fascism. The first of Bianchi Bandinelli's two students to develop and challenge his thought was Mario Torelli, a scholar who inherited Bianchi Bandinelli's marxism alongside his passion and vision. His comprehensive *History of the Etruscans* (1981) is primarily concerned with economic change and development, and presents the archaeological evidence as a series of dialectical shifts, with each phase accompanied by further distribution of wealth amongst a larger group of individuals, from the Villanovan to Classical phases.

Torelli's 1987 work, *La Società Etrusca* contains a critique of the Pallottino school, while simultaneously praising its original ideas. Torelli writes that while the original idea of pushing for recognition of the importance of archaeology was strong, it has been subsumed beneath the minutiae of object analysis (Torelli 1987: 9-10), a critique which I would echo. His other point for critique is the tendency to blur chronology together by using thematic analysis: Etruscan religion is (he points out) talked of as a singular phenomenon, while in temporal terms it is as separate and could be as different as medieval and nineteenth century Christianity (Torelli ibid). This idea of separation and specificity aligns neatly with the thought of Bianchi Bandinelli's other discipline-changing student, Andrea Carandini.

While perhaps more a scholar of early Rome than an Etruscologist proper, Carandini has nonetheless exercised considerable influence over the discipline. In addition to his early work on lowest social classes in Roman society (Carandini 1979a, 1979b, 1979c) in a Marxist vein, Carandini's more recent use of mythology and iconography in a literal format (Carandini 1997, 2006, 2007) respects folk memory and popular culture in the past, expressing faith in the beliefs of past people as opposed to the preconceptions of the present. While this is a challenging set of ideas, it nonetheless embodies his belief in the Gramscian principles imparted by his mentor, which have been honed and modernised to create a vision of ancient Lazio as an inhabited space. The publication of his own *Diario di uno Scavo* also mirrors Bandinelli's open attitude to archaeological practice (Carandini 2000).

The balance between these two schools of thought has played out over the course of the 20th century and into the first decade of the 21st. Although voices from outside of the traditional divide, such as those of Camporeale (1997, 2004), D'Agostino (1977, 1983, 1985, with Cerchai 1999) and Iaia (1999, 2005, 2006) have periodically moved Italian Etruscan studies in a different direction, the old divisions laid out in this section appear set to continue on into the 21st century. Even as Italian mainstream politics lost its power over the academic world, internal politics replaced it with an equally complicated set of beliefs and allegiances, which have created the modern discipline of Etruscan archaeology as much as any of the previous interactions between the two that created the circumstances in which modern scholars now work. Through an appreciation of the twists and turns of Italian archaeology from the thirteenth century onwards, it is possible for an outsider to approach, although not entirely to understand, the Italian incarnation of Etruscan studies. Without this appreciation for the past of the discipline, there can be no placing of an argument in true context. Without understanding the development of a deadlock in debate, there can be no moving onward from it.

2.6 Meanwhile, across la manica..

The lure of Italian archaeology in England is linked, not to a series of political allegiances and philosophical positions, but rather to a heritage of romanticism and exploration, rooted in the experiences of previous generations in their interactions with the past. Unlike the Italian case, these feelings which have shaped Etruscan archaeology cannot be traced back to particular events or moments: although it is known that English people were travelling and moving around Italy at the time of the first discoveries of the Etruscan past in the late medieval period: Geoffrey Chaucer was clearly influenced by the Etruscan-praising Boccaccio (as discussed from various angles in Boitani (ed.) 1985), while another Englishman, the more martial John Hawkwood, settled near Arezzo, the city in which the first Etruscan ceramics were uncovered a century earlier (Caferro 2006). The image of Italy at this early point seems to have been carried through stories and songs to an audience filled with wonder for a far off land, inspiring travellers to journey to a landscape closely connected with ancient knowledge of Rome, whether conceived of in a religious or quasi-secular (post-Reformation) manifestation. The dangers of travel in Italy, caused by brigands in the space between city-states or disease in the malaria-ridden marshes of the Maremma and the Tiber estuary only served to emphasise the civility of the great cities of Venice, Florence and Milan, presenting a contrast which captured the imagination of English travellers (Brand 2011: 7).

By the sixteenth century a form of travel had developed which would conclusively shape both the discipline of Etruscan archaeology and its practice by non-Italian scholars, as well as the British vision of Italy for centuries to come: the Grand Tour (Black 1992; Naddeo 2005). Guides for English tourists had already been written by the first decades of the sixteenth century, in which archaeological sites and ruins were presented alongside cultural traditions and modern wonders (Bartlett 1980: 48). While the Reformation created distance between the two countries, by the late sixteenth century Italy was re-established as a place of equal danger and romance: a believable location for tragic love stories, comedic routs and slippery courtiers in Elizabethan and Jacobean drama (collectively explored in Marrapodi (ed.) 1997), forming a space in which English society could be safely critiqued at a distance (Hadfield 1998: 200; Höttemann 2011). By the time the Scottish monk Thomas Dempster had left his homeland to work in Italy, a series of connections had been established in English minds about Italy which have been remarkably persistent: firstly, the ancient nature of the land, secondly, the appropriateness of that location for scholarly endeavour, and, finally, the establishment of strong emotional connections with both the Italian past and its study.

It is impossible to reconstruct Dempster's own response to the Etruscans he so diligently studied: he must have been talented to have been chosen to undertake the study by his masters, the Dukes of Tuscany, but it is hard to ascertain whether a personal interest began before or after he began his endeavours. As court historian to James I, he was presented very much as a classical scholar, in stark contrast to his antiquarian and prehistorian predecessor William Camden (Stenhouse 2004: 395). Dempster's idealist vision of Etruscan society may have been a product of the desires of his masters, but could also be a reflection of his own views as a man enamoured with the land and people who had welcomed and employed him after his departure from London. Whatever Dempster's own views, those of the English gentleman who brought his writings to general publication for the first time are well known.

Thomas Coke was an Italophile aristocrat, whose seat, Holkham Hall, in Norfolk, would become a paradise of Italian painting and was designed with Italian architectural principles in mind (Moore 2008: 313). By the time of Coke's rediscovery, a 'Grand Tour' of Europe, including exposure to the classical past in Italy, had become a key part of a young man's education (Chaney 2000). Coke stayed in Italy between 1712 and 1718, in the course of a Grand Tour of extremely long duration, which emphasises his delight in the country he attempted to bring back to England (Moore 1985). Coke's legacy would be the inclusion of Etruscan antiquities on many Grand Tours, bringing young gentlemen into contact with the Etruscans as the most ancient and least known aspect of the Italian tourist experience – and therefore that most susceptible to imagination (Pieraccini 2009: 7). Perhaps the most lasting aspect of Coke's inheritance would be the mania for Etruscan materials produced and presided over by the ceramicist Josiah Wedgwood, whose own fascination with Etruria resulted in the first range of reproduction bucchero wares, which brought Etruscan archaeology into the salons of the British wealthy (Ramage 2011: 189).

The development of the Romantic movement brought into the open the emotional feelings attached to scholarship in Italy, making them respectable. The descriptions of poets of Italian archaeological sites brought them to life through an appeal to the sentiments, rather than through rational description, and the Grand Tour now became an acknowledged feast for the emotions (Chai 2011: 182-3). It was now acceptable to feel stirred to joy or sorrow, laughter or tears by the experience of *Italia*, a country perceived through its past rather than the realities of its present, and held up as a contrast to the burgeoning success of the British Empire (Cavaliero 2007). The young men who would weep at the sight of the ruined Forum would become colonial imperialists, working to replicate the heights and avoid the decline of the Roman empire, and it was primarily Rome, not Etruria, which formed the focus of much of this later

Romantic attention, in contrast to the 18th century interest in the Etruscans (Scott 2003; Hingley 2001; 2002). One eventual colonial officer, however, would prove to be the founder of English Etruscan archaeology, and provide the first popularly read description of Etruscan sites in Italy: inspiring a new generation with tales of adventure and danger. George Dennis' *Cities and Cemeteries of Etruria*, while not explicitly linked to the Romantic movement, contains enough swashbuckling detail of brigands and brambles to form a perfect connection between the dream of Italy of the Romantics and the colonial adventure tale of the later Victorian period: perhaps an explanation for its eventual success (Dennis 1883 [1848]).

Dennis' book did not receive instant acclaim, but grew into one of the most successful publications on the Etruscans of the nineteenth century. He presented the sites of Etruria systematically and sympathetically for the visitor, with warm, personal descriptions laced with a hint of colonial superiority. For the purposes of this discussion of the origins of Etruscan archaeology, however, it is the inspiration that Dennis' work provided which is the most important aspect of his work, provoking the travelogue of Etruria which has been absorbed into the collective psyche of almost all British Etruscologists: the work of D.H. Lawrence. I have previously written about Lawrence's complicated relationship with the establishment of English society, from which he fled into Italy with his new wife Frieda in 1919, and his return to the Romantic traditions of Italian tourism (Shipley 2013b). After a summer spent exploring archaeological sites in Tuscany in 1927, Lawrence wrote his *Sketches of Etruscan Places*, a passionate protest against the political situation of fascist Italy and the constrained nature of English society. George Dennis had been a rebel, excluded from traditional academic circles by his lack of formal education, and Lawrence too styled himself as an exiled hero, akin to the forgotten and denigrated Etruscans that both studied. This act of assimilating the destruction of Etruria by Rome with the defeat of artistic emotions by rationalism, violence and extremism, and the adoption of Etruscan self-identity by the victim of modern tyrany is a striking feature of Lawrence's work (Lawrence 2007 [1932]).

All this romantic imagination is inescapable: it is absorbed into the very fabric of British archaeology. The message is repeated time and again: Italy is a place for escapism and the expression of emotions, a place for the reception of rebels. The vision of the Etruscan past is the ultimate incarnation of this idea of Italy as feeling, liberty and expression. The pattern of archaeological practice mirrors the seasonality and movement of the Grand Tour: whether through summer fieldwork or longer sojourns at the International Schools in Rome. While colonial aspirations have vanished, in this retracing of steps the Etruria of Dennis and Lawrence is conjuured up inescapably. A walk in Tuscany, a vist to an Etruscan site, is coloured by the words written by these previous giants of visitors. If their influence extended only to these moments, to acknowledged reminiscence and the structure of engagement, the phenomenon of English romancised engagement with Etruria would not be problematic. However, the ideals of Etruria as a place of liberty, freedom of expression, art, beauty, and emotion created by the series of interpretations of Italy and Etruria from Chaucer onwards have seeped into the subconsious of the Etruscan scholar. Barker and Rasmussen (1999) acknowledge this influence by commencing each chapter of their general reference work with a quotation from Lawrence. However, to admit to tendencies of subjectivity and individualism has been problematised by a tradition of objective scientific analysis, which rose up, perhaps, to take back Etruscan archaeology from the romantics and bring it to science, while simultaneously creating a cover-up of emotional assumptions and a divide in the discipline.

2.7 From Romance to Rigour

The emotional response to Etruscan archaeology described in the previous section is noticeably concentrated in non-academic sources. From Shakespearean dramas set in an Italy of feelings far from England's green and sensible land to George Dennis and D.H. Lawrence's works of literary travelogues for a general audience, these influential texts were not written by archaeologists, but by interested amateurs. The gentleman archaeologist combined interest with knowledge, but as the twentieth century developed, this type of scholarship was not enough for the developing profession (Daniel 1975: 18). This estrangement from the romantic origins of archaeology was necessary for archaeology to be perceived seriously as a science, and this was true for Italian archaeology as much as for any other sub-discipline. The foundation of the British School at Rome as a centre for archaeological investigation in Italy in 1901 provided a foothold for British archaeologists in Italy (Wiseman 1990). The need for this process is illustrated eloquently in an article by Christopher Hawkes for *Studi Etruschi* emphasising the importance of Transalpine migrations in the development of Etruscan culture: an argument which had already been discarded in Italy twenty years before (Hawkes 1959). The School formed a centre for archaeological studies based on exploration, photography and excavation, although its later relationship with specifically Etruscan archaeology was yet to develop. The archaeological focus of the School was emphatically unromantic – finding out solid facts and developing a coherent strategy of investigation, particularly under the directorship of John Ward-Perkins from the 1950s onwards (Wallace-Hadrill 2001). The South Etruria survey, undertaken under Ward-Perkins, was a systematic exploration of multi-period settlement, begun with the aim of ascertaining the land use pattern of the region, rather than providing a sentimentalised series of images of how a preconceived Etruscan society would have functioned. Growing confidence in survey and excavation methodologies allowed for field archaeology to provide reports of discoveries couched in strictly scientific language, minimising interpretations which could have been undermined by subjective bias.

While excavation provided one way of coping with the dangers of emotionally charged interpretation, the methods used to deal with artefacts themselves were also carefully developed into a strictly scientific format. The development, particularly in America, of art-historical practices based on style and the identification of artists and craftsmen became the dominant methodology for dealing with objects (Davis 1990). Typological analysis, too, was a safe and scientific method of classifying artefacts (particularly ceramics) by matching similarities together, reflecting functionality and connections between different pot-making communities (Arnold 1988: 1). The combination of these two methodologies resulted in the work of John Beazley, perhaps the most influential scholar of ceramics found in Etruscan contexts (Beazley 1947, 1963, 1971, 1978, 1986). Empiricism allowed for the production of meticulous catalogues, presenting objects as isolated extensions of their maker, as opposed to materials collected together in an archaeological context exposed to dangerous interpretations. The symbolism of artistic representation on these objects was another avenue of potential danger, a chance for assumptions about Etruscan society to creep into interpretation. During this mid-century period and later, it has been safer for British and American archaeologists to rely on either interpretations based on 'known' classical sources or other archaeological objects represented in images (Shanks 2004; Snodgrass 1998; Osborne 1997) or focus on transport, production and function (Sparkes 1991, 1996; Boardman 1974, 1979, 1986). In both cases, the textually bounded world of classical Greece is the point of reference, forming an anchor to protect the writer from the internalised inheritance of Lawrence, Dennis and earlier Etruscophiles.

The development of processual archaeology has only served to deepen alienation from potentially subjective theoretical experimentation in Etruscan archaeology. Excavations and surveys produced increasing amounts of data during the later part of the twentieth century, which was catalogued in traditional fashion and used to support familiar arguments. The work of David Ridgway (1973, 1984, 1992, 2002) and Sybille Haynes (1965, 1971, 1985, 2005) dominated the interpretation of this data and its presentation in English in interpretative narratives in two very different styles, although, tellingly, both were classicists by training. Ridgway's scholarship, shaped by post-graduate training in archaeology under Christopher Hawkes, was focused on interaction, exchange and knowledge transfer in the ancient Mediterranean, and his interests lay in the archaeological expression of these through material culture. His excavations at Pithekoussai allowed him to form a view of connectivity based firmly on empirical evidence rather than traditional assumptions (Ridgway 1993).

By contrast, Haynes has always remained loyal to the traditions of classical culture history in which she was trained, relying on single artefact studies of style to interpret movements of people and objects as cultural baggage, rather than as evidence for identities, individuals or innovation. She has continued to use the term 'culture history' in her interpretations of Etruscan material culture, and remained firmly outside theoretical developments in other branches of archaeology, creating and continuing tropes of representation which began with Dempster, but which are continued without criticism, albeit supported by the new wealth of excavation evidence (See Haynes 2005: 2, 47, 52, 133). While Ridgway's work shied away from the romantic history of Etruscan archaeology completely, the approach of Haynes is perhaps more difficult: in adopting the acceptance of Greek descriptions of Etruscan women's independence and the liberal nature of Etruscan society as republican, she accepts unquestioningly a series of stereotypes which have a long history of formation in the non-Etruscan past (as does the American scholar Larissa Bonfante 1975, 1981, 1986, 1989). These two strategies of acceptance or avoidance characterise the work of these two scholars, creating an impasse which could only be bridged by engagement with both the history of Etruscology in English, and the developments occurring in archaeological theory during the 1980s and 1990s.

2.8 Incorporating Ideas

The development of post-processual archaeology encouraged the acknowledgement that the past is the anchor of present practice (Wylie 1992). It is perhaps in this spirit that Barker and Rasmussen's chapter headings from Lawrence are intended (Barker and Rasmussen 1999). They are a visible acknowledgement of the importance of Lawrence's vision for the authors, a gentle warning to the reader of the presence that centuries of romantic visions of Etruria reside inside the mind of the writers, in spite of their objective aims. The increased emphasis on interpretation of material culture in relation to meaning and human experience in the past (Hodder 1982, 1988, 1989, 1991) spread into Etruscan studies in the 1990s, a phenomenon particularly visible in the work of Simon Stoddart (1989, 1990, 1992, 1995, 2007). Nigel Spivey, while focused more on artistic representation, has similarly considered the relationship between material culture and Etruscan society (Spivey 1987, 1988, 1991a, 1991b). Graeme Barker, too, although not a post-processualist himself, developed entirely new conception of Etruscan landscape use and agriculture during this period (Barker 1985, 1988).

A similar approach, influenced by post-processual ideas, is visible in the work of other British scholars of Italian prehistory, working in different contexts, as referenced in the Introduction. To restate their achievements, Mark Pearce has used scientific evidence for the production of metal in earlier Italian prehistory to engage with the experience and practice of miners and smelters in Liguria (Pearce 1998) in addition to exploring depositional practice (Pearce 2008), while John Robb has similarly elevated osteoarchaeological investigations to discussions of identity and social organisation (Robb 1994a, 1994b, 1997) in addition to engaging directly in theoretical debate (Robb 1999, 2001, 2002, 2008, 2009a, 2009b, 2010; Dobres and Robb 2005). Ruth Whitehouse, too, has developed a post-processual approach based on the careful deployment of phenomenological ideas to explore ritual behaviour and the experience of landscape in Neolithic Italy (Whitehouse 1992, 2001a; Hamilton and Whitehouse 2006), in addition to her extensive work on the archaeological expression of gender (Whitehouse 1998, 2001b, 2002, 2007a), while Robin Skeates' work on the same period has focused in detail on interaction between persons, objects and place (Skeates 1994, 1995, 1997, 2000). This collection of work has provided a series of examples for Etruscan archaeology to follow – and, as acknowledged in the introduction, perhaps forms the greatest influence on this study.

Another potential consequence of post-processualism for Etruscan studies has been a new awareness of the importance of textual sources: and a new methodology for dealing with these. It is undeniable that viewpoints on the Etruscans exist from sources outside the Etruscan world, in addition to fragments of writings produced by Etruscans themselves. Livy,[3] Dionysius of Halicarnassus,[4] Herodotus,[5] Pliny[6], Hesiod,[7] Thucydides[8] and Theopompus of Chios[9] are just some of the authors of classical texts which provide brief glimpses into the lives of their western Mediterranean neighbours. The advent of material culture as critical text provides a way of looking at ancient source as critical text (Hodder 2003: 157), opening the door to the incorporation of historiographical awareness into Etruscan archaeology. As opposed to ignoring the texts to focus exclusively on objects, or treating the descriptions of ancient authors as literal fact, a series of post-Derridean historiographical critiques focused on seeing both Greek and Roman texts in context have provided an opportunity for Etruscan archaeology to move forward (Fowler 1997; Habinek 2001; Heath 2002; Miles 1997). The context of literacy (and thus text) in both Greece and Italy has also been an aspect of this type of classics in context (Becker 2010; Becker and Wallace 2010; Bittarello 2009; Cornell 1991; Gillett 2013; Stoddart and Whitley 1988; Whitehouse 2007b). These more aware and contextualised approaches to classical texts have developed in conjunction with a more open recognition of the biases of more recent writings.

Two authors in particular have dominated British Etruscan studies during the first decade of the twenty first century, both of whom have taken on the theoretical ideas provoked by post-processual colleagues working in other periods and the awareness of literary texts described above. Corinna Riva presents a reworking of arguments for the processes of state formation in Etruria, using a post-processual stance to demonstrate the complexity of Etruscan origins. She neatly avoids the pitfalls of nationalist and idealist arguments to examine the changes of the Seconda Età del Ferro through a creative interpretation of material culture and text together (Riva 2010a, see also Riva 2005, 2006). Riva's work, particularly on the social context of drinking (Riva 2010b) and the use of bronze vessels (2010c), is a direct influence on this study.

The work of Vedia Izzet (2001, 2003, 2005, 2007) moves from excavation reports to interpretative innovation effortlessly, carefully constructing narratives which derive from a combination of textual and material culture sources. Her general volume (Izzet 2007a) is particularly remarkable for its opening chapter – the first instance of a reflexive analysis of current Etruscan studies, which forms a critique of traditional discourse (Izzet ibid: 10-41). Izzet is also bold in her use of ethnographic parallels and archaeological theory, showing the extent to which new methodologies can invigorate previously tired discussions. It is no exaggeration to say that without that work in particular, the argument contained in this chapter: that Etruscan archaeology in both England and Italy is the product of political and personal preferences past and present, would not exist. The work of Riva and Izzet is perhaps the most direct influence from Etruscology upon this study, but the shift in the discipline presented in this sub-section has made their work possible – this is a moment in which Etruscan studies can change, acknowledging its past and looking forward to the future.

2.9 Conclusions

This chapter has taken complicated historical issues, current debates and unspoken inclinations and brought them together in a set of two narratives to explore the history of Etruscan studies. Each of the subsections in this chapter could easily have warranted an entire chapter or volume to encompass every argument and machination. The point, however, of this investigation was to fashion a map, a plan, to make it possible to look back into the past and acknowledge the role of history in the modern practice of Etruscan archaeology – to see the routes which have resulted in the position of this re-analysis and the environment in which it was designed and into which it is launched. The current road of Etruscan studies is still divided into two tracks, which, while interweaving with each other on occasion, remain resolutely separate. The Italian school has developed in close conjunction with political struggles, with each engagement forming a twist in the road, creating a winding strada bianca like those that cover the hills of Tuscany. The development of Italy itself as a nation has been allied with the professionalisation of Etruscology as a scientific discipline, while the connection between nationhood and archaeology was tested and re-established during the fascist period. While Italy suffered in the post-war period, Etruscan studies re-emerged as a focus point for the restoration of national pride, although riven by the same divisions which split Italian

---

[3] History of Rome Books 5.1 and 7.2
[4] Roman Antiquities, 1.30
[5] Histories 1: 94
[6] Natural Histories 26.87
[7] Theogony 12: 101
[8] Histories Book IV: 109
[9] Histories 115

society. The story of Italy is interwoven in Etruscan archaeology, and without an awareness of this, the outside scholar will be unable to fully locate their research in the context of this complicated tradition.

The other purpose of making maps is to locate a position, to look for a way onwards. The position of this study sits at the very edge of the pathways I have drawn out in this chapter. Through an analysis of the history of Etruscan studies, I have provided a viewpoint, a place to look back into the past and forward to the future, which, although a point on the English pathway of Etruscology, is, I hope, situated close enough to the Italian track to see its route in equal clarity. The political arguments and theoretical movements which have defined Italian and English Etruscan studies respectively have produced a moment in which new ideas can be developed to move the discipline forward. The process of examining the past of Etruscology demonstrates why theoretical archaeology has been uncommon in the discipline: for Italian authors, engagement with philosophical thought has resulted in interpretations linked to a nationalist past which became intensely problematic after the fall of Mussolini. The replacement of such theories by Gramscian marxism has been made manifest in the establishment and maintenance of a cultural hegemony in archaeological practice, firmly based upon methodologies which are pragmatic, processual and which cannot, seemingly, be manipulated for political ends. In Britain and America, the romantic heritage of the Grand Tour has been resulted in a suppression of subjectivity. In both cases, the result has been the perpetuation of traditional methodologies, in spite of the evident success of theoretical application in other areas of Italian prehistory.

These twin problems of nationalism and romanticism have hampered and hamstrung Etruscan archaeology in both traditions, forming effective roadblocks on each pathway. Their construction was a response to danger: danger of subjectivity, danger of bias, danger of manipulative interpretations. Etruscan pottery studies are as deeply immured in this blockage as any aspect of Etruscology. After a long heritage of engagement with political and social theory, Etruscan archaeology has carefully and deliberately prevented any such engagements and promoted methodologies which imply objective analysis. As the experience of any object or place in the past is intensely subjective, it is entirely excluded by this overarching philosophy. The next chapter embraces that subjectivity through the development of an explicitly theoretical methodology, focused on feminit, phenomenological and materialist perspectives. However, the historiographic analysis of this chapter provides the context to that argument: it demonstrates exactly why such an approach is so important. My initial desire was to move beyond traditional methodologies for ceramic analysis which I saw as hindering the potential for more exciting investigations. By tracing the use of Etruscan objects, including pottery, as political ballast through the centuries, the twentieth century response to political extremism in archaeology of typology and iconography is recast as a justifiable and sensible response. However, by directly engaging with and recognising the events and actions which promoted those biased views, it is surely possible to return to theory in Etruscan ceramic analysis.

Chapter 3

Thinking 'things' through: a phenomenology of objects

3.1 Introduction

The previous chapter outlined the history of Etruscan studies, which, in Italy, has been dominated by two theoretical approaches, closely linked to political affiliations. The hold of cultural historical approaches and Marxist ideology over the discipline in Italy continues to be strong. In Britain, the last twenty years have marked a change in Etruscan studies, which, although still closely connected to the ubiquity of culture-history in the heritage of the discipline, have started to incorporate approaches based on ethnographic analogy, social theory and postprocessual concerns. Anglophone Italian prehistory focused on the Neolithic and Bronze Ages, while not yet fully developed in Etruscology, has experimented more deeply with an approach developed from theoretical engagement. This project is focused on the experience of the users of Etruscan pottery. In a sense this focus is allied to Italian marxist concerns over the 'everyman' of Etruscan society, but the method used to interrogate the nature of experience uses a theoretical tool which has not been applied in Etruscan archaeology previously. Phenomenological thought has, however, been successfully used to design research methodologies in other arenas in Italian prehistory (Betts 2003; Hamilton et al 2006; Whitehouse 2001a). Phenomenology provides a new way of thinking about the lives of the Etruscans, focused on the physical experience of objects. The development of a specific form of phenomenology which can be used practically to analyse things, in addition to places, and which considers the particular experience of objects by individuals, is the task of this chapter.

The decision to use a phenomenological scheme to develop my research methodology was a deliberate action, arrived at from my own personal and theoretical background (cf. Wylie 1992). Just as the intense connections between political or personal preferences and archaeological method have structured Italian and British Etruscology in the past, my decision to use phenomenology to develop a research strategy for Etruscan pots is linked to a growing movement in archaeological theory, perhaps the heir of post-processualism. As post-processualism has disappeared, it has been replaced, not with an overarching school of thought imposed from social theory, but with a plurality of approaches developed by individual practitioners (cf Alberti, Jones and Pollard (eds.) 2013; Preucel and Mrozowski (eds.) 2011) It is possible that in emboldening archaeologists to engage with philosophy, post-processualism destroyed the directionality of archaeological thought, yet created a sense of self-confidence resulting in a vibrant appreciation of theoretical application. It is in this tradition of direct engagement between archaeologists and philosophy that this chapter sits. Within it, I go back to the roots of phenomenological thought, building up through a series of layers a phenomenology which can be practically applied in the context of Etruscan ceramics, and the multiple, variable persons who interacted with them.

The first layer is the development of phenomenal thought by Maurice Merleau-Ponty, which lies at the heart of later, feminist re-interpretations of his ideas. An awareness of the heritage of the concept of phenomenology and the idea of the integrated body/mind subject is essential to understand Merleau-Ponty's personal position. The ideas of Hegel and Heidegger are discussed, before Merleau-Ponty's ideas are considered in detail. This primary analysis examines why phenomenology as a broad series of concepts is appropriate for use in archaeology, and defines the underlying type of phenomenological thought which prompted the application of these ideas to pots. The next aspect is the feminist engagement with Merleau-Ponty's philosophy, the discussion of which is divided by the approaches of three thinkers: Judith Butler, Elizabeth Grosz and Iris Young. From these three different responses to Merleau-Ponty it is possible to move away from a universal phenomenology, and towards a specific theory of embodiment and performance, housed in and particular to an individual body with an individual series of experiences.

From the philosophical roots of phenomenology, the next layer is the way that archaeologists have appropriated aspects of phenomenal thought, and used them to create practical applications which are then applied to the interpretation of the past. Through a detailed analysis of the way phenomenology shaped a particular research project, the aforementioned Tavoliere-Gargano investigation, the utility of the concept for archaeological application which is not only innovative but rigorous is demonstrated. The final piece of theoretical stratigraphy in this chapter uses the thought of Alfred Gell as a bridging mechanism to connect phenomenology to objects. By extending his conception of object agency beyond artistic representation to all physical characteristics of things, it is possible to develop a methodology which records and measures the impacts of such object actors on the experience of humans who used them. The relationship between objects and the body, the recognition of their involvement and inter-dependency on each other, is central to both Gell's thought and this book. For Etruscan pots to be considered in context, they must be analysed in relation to the bodies that lifted, tipped, sipped and swigged from them every day. Characterising those bodies, and seeing them as belonging to subjects rather than faceless automota, is the initial project of phenomenology in archaeology. That process begins for this study with Maurice Merleau-Ponty and his conception of 'being-in-the-world.'

3.2 Subject to the Centre: From Hegel to Merleau-Ponty

The central concept of phenomenological thought is one of rebellion, of a movement away from the thought of Descartes, Kant and originally Aristotle, and their proposal that the mind and body are separate entities. This dualism, which remains reflected in Freudian psychology, enforces a distinction within any human, implying conflict and distance between the two halves of a person. However, the opposition between Cartesian dualism and phenomenological thought was not always present. The term 'phenomenology' first appears in Hegel's *Phenomenology of Spirit* (1807), and Hegel used the terminology to examine the separation of knowledge from the mind. He argues that abstract, structured knowledge does not exist: it can only be present in the context of an individual consciousness. The internalisation of knowledge was the first step to a holistic subject, and the later thought of Husserl (1913) moved phenomenological philosophy forward by considering consciousness further. He proposed that knowledge may be divided into two forms – 'essences' and 'assumptions,' the former of which are universal appreciations, and the latter of which are shaped and created by individual experience. Husserl moved phenomenology onwards from the separation of knowledge to examining the way in which knowledge is created, recognising the role of whole body experience in its construction and application.

Husserl's student, Martin Heidegger (1927), forced the debate onwards through his realisation that before understanding what it is like to be, it is essential to examine what it is to be. This question, 'what is experience?' leads to a recognition that the life of an individual is bounded by time and space, structured by the outside phenomena that act upon and shape both their body and their knowledge. The subject for Heidegger is constantly questioning, seeking to extract from their surroundings answers on the subject of being – how it is to die, to be mortal, to be anxious. He names this subject *Dasein*, a creature which accepts that the process of being itself is a nature of questioning existence. However, to be an applicable methodology in archaeological contexts, Heidegger's question on the nature of experience needs to be extended beyond the construction of knowledge based on a series of questions addressed to a constant external world. The changeable nature of the world outside the self must be addressed, alongside the individuality of the knowledge creating subject. It is here that the work of Merleau-Ponty becomes perhaps more applicable than that of the German school to this particular archaeological phenomenological project.

Merleau-Ponty's journey towards his phenomenological position began with his work *The Structure of Behaviour* (1963). In this, he sets up his philosophical position, attempting to negotiate between objectivism/naturalism and neo-Kantian intellectualism. In his view, both versions of the nature of experience and being are severely flawed. As a response to the development of Gestalt, Merleau-Ponty considers behaviour as a method of understanding existence. However, he develops the idea that experience is holistic, unlike the structured separation insisted on by the supplicants of Gestalt theory. Through his example of the response of a human viewer to a light in the dark, Merleau-Ponty exposes the meaningful nature of responses to stimuli, and demonstrates that this response is whole bodied. An understanding of the structure of this response is impossible: it is unique to the individual who is experiencing the light: response is immured in what he terms milieu. The creation of this milieu cannot be divided by an outsider: it is steadily created by the subject through repeated experience and position in the world. Merleau-Ponty terms this creation of milieu a dialectical experience: thesis, antithesis and synthesis of physical and vital structures in the life of the subject.

The seeds of Merleau-Ponty's phenomenological thought are visible at this point, with many of its key features already in place. The body is important, and the creation of milieu allows for individuality and the recognition of the role of personal experience in the construction of reality. He has already rejected Cartesian duality, alongside all the elaborations on its theme allied with the thought of Kant. The opening pages of *The Phenomenology of Perception* pick up on these themes, and carry them forwards into a devastating critique of Cartesian separation (Merleau-Ponty 1962). Merleau-Ponty goes on to develop his own phenomenology, based on the separation between perception and analysis. He rejects the ideas of the earlier phenomenologist Husserl, suggesting that the reduction of perception to thought removes the inherent vitality of the first perception (ibid: xii). This vitality of perception lies in his theorisation of perception as sensation, as a myriad of feelings, experienced through the living body.

Merleau-Ponty's phenomenology is firmly centred on this living body, with his conception of the *corps propre* or own body as being-in-the-world at its centre. Rather than a creature composed of questions like Heidegger's Dasein, Merleau-Ponty sees the physical body as utterly composed of perception. Husserl's separation of consciousness itself and the object of conscious thought become subsumed in Merleau-Ponty's vision of perception: for him, all consciousness is perceptual consciousness. There is no separation between knowledge of the world inside and outside the body, all are perceived together. This is the ultimate rebuttal of Cartesian ideas – transmuting experience from an abstract question of existence to a jangling chorus of receptive perception. For the archaeologist, the combination of this multiplicity of experience with the idea of milieu or subject position provides a possible way to bridge the gap to the past. Merleau-Ponty's call to the historian (although it is really a call to the archaeologist) demonstrates his persuasiveness on this particular point:

'If one is born into a culture which is structured by historic time... how will he represent a life that is only a flowing present? He will have to reconstitute the lived experience and the actual milieu of this primitive man' (Merleau-Ponty 1962:91.)

While exact reconstitution of the Etruscan subject (or any other past subject) is clearly an impossible task, the excitement of the attempt remains. The shared connections between bodies as sites of inter-location between past and present have been intoxicating for archaeologists, and also for anthropologists, allowing both to dream of overcoming the Self/Other separation. Bourdieu acknowledges the lure of the ideas of Merleau-Ponty, suggesting that he found early on that:

'Merleau-Ponty was something different... a potential way out of the philosophical babble found in academic institutions.' (Bourdieu 1990: 5).

While the clarity of Merleau-Ponty's writing and the seeming simplicity of his ideas of the primacy of perception do seem to provide a 'way out,' what they also provide is a way in to an entire series of other problems. The world is not the same, the body is not the same. It is impossible to reconstitute the lived experience of another person in the present to exact accuracy, let alone the perception of a person who lived in another time, in another country where things are done and perceived differently. While retaining the value in the ideal of finding lived experience through shared being-in-the-world and the possession of our own *corps propre*, the issue of difference must be addressed, for the first, but not the last time in this book. I will do this through an analysis of three different feminist thinkers, whose responses to Merleau-Ponty in particular provide a way to move beyond the issues of the restriction of individual agency visible in his thought. While the three are writers who consider the nature of being through a lens focused by gender, they still provide perhaps the strongest addition to phenomenological philosophy, and give a new freedom to the phenomenological subject.

Feminist concerns with the body have reconstructed its importance in phenomenology from Simone de Beauvoir onwards. They have elaborated critiques of the presumption in the designation of the phenomenological subject as supposedly neutral. The quote from Merleau-Ponty above demonstrates the falseness of that proposal: he is clearly talking about a male subject in the past, a 'man' who is to be interpreted by a male in the present, reconstructing a thoroughly male experience. De Beauvoir's descriptions of female childhood seem to me to be reaching towards performativity, in that the parenting of children actively creates their sexual difference through prescribed actions and speeches, creating self through speaking and doing (de Beauvoir 2012). However, it was not until forty years after the publication of *The Second Sex* that another feminist thinker would bring these ideas to fruition.

3.3 Perception to Performance: Judith Butler

Judith Butler has written of phenomenological thought as reducing the subject to the status of an object (Butler 1988: 519). Her critique, that being-in-the-world reduces the phenomenologically conceived person to a flat receiver, without agency and without action, is a cogent one. While a person may be in the world, a person can also change the world that they perceive and experience. The position of the individual in the phenomenological perception is one of a faceless mass of sensualities, without an informed sense of self. Butler points out the instability of the subject, the personal restructuring of the world in their own image, which she sees as continually taking place through life. Perception is not the only experience of being, there is also action. What that action is, and how it interacts with and through the sensing body, is the subject of Butler's in-depth studies. The development of her solution to the problems of passive phenomenology, the idea of performativity, is at the centre of this work, and provides one way of incorporating the recognition of phenomenology of the importance of the body with a feminist vision of multivocality and action. This term, performativity, refers to the actions of mind and body which make up a performance: the latter term describes the script, the underlying intentions of the performer, which may be of their own making or imposed from outside. It is those performative acts which create the performance as a project. This re-conception of behaviour as performance and performativity, however, is part of Butler's wider engagement with the body as a space for enacting particular identities.

Butler first deals explicitly with the experience of the embodied subject. *Gender Trouble: Feminism and the Subversion of Identity* sees trouble as positive: finding the best way to get into trouble, and how to use it to explore what it is to have a body and be in the world. Butler sees that the distinction of sex and gender is unsatisfactory, and suggests rather that the body has always been wrapped in the cultural conception of self. She asks 'how do we reconceive the body no longer as a passive medium or instrument awaiting the enlivening capacity of a distinctly immaterial will?' (Butler 1999:13). While she allows that phenomenological thought has battled Cartesian duality, she argues that it has instead rendered the combined mind/body as powerless, without an allowance for difference. To solve this problem, Butler introduces the idea of 'regulatory practices' which work to produce the notion that there might be a truth of sex, and which influence the bodily experience of perception. She describes responses to drag artists:

beneath the clothes and the accoutrements of a woman, the viewer perceives that this is 'in reality' a man. But who is the viewer to make that distinction? What vision of the artist's reality can be understood by anyone who is outside their body? The conception that this person is a man is the product of a series of normative deductive processes undertaken to produce binary divisions of sex and gender. In actual reality, the drag artist is neither man nor woman but artist: that is themselves: body, situation and, importantly, performance.

The word performance is key to Butler's conception of reality, whether in the context of the actions undertaken by the drag artist, or (and significantly) in the processes which produce the normative response to him/her. Butler's work in theatre studies, combined with her own situation, formed the background for her development of what she terms performativity. Her interest in iterative acts, moments of speech which bring what they speak to being, applies equally to literature. When Lady Macbeth calls out 'unsex me here, and fill me from the crown to the toe topful of direst cruelty'[10] she is not only speaking words but enacting their outcome: they are performing a function of de-feminisation. These exceptional moments of self-iteration are variables from a far more pervasive system of performance which is undertaken daily:

> '*Performativity is not a singular act, but a repetition and a ritual, which achieves its effects through its naturalization in the context of a body, understood, in part, as a culturally sustained temporal duration.*'
>
> Butler (1999: xv).

In *Bodies that Matter: Notes on the Discursive Limits of Sex* (1993) Butler makes explicit the connection between performativity and the body. From this point, she demonstrates that the body itself is performative: each movement and action is wrapped up within the repetitive acts which make up performance. The misconception that performativity is to be enacted only with the mouth is put right, and the importance of the material body recognised. Importantly, Butler's body is intelligent, specific and owned, unlike the body of the phenomenological subject. Giving the body credit for action is the true overcoming of Cartesian dualism, just as removing binary gender divisions is a way forward for feminists. However, Butler also makes it clear that the agency of the subject is limited to their temporal and cultural context, and that resistance and transgression are relational, defined through the normative performances daily being enacted. The ability of the subject to choose is restricted to only a certain number of culturally defined performative options: hence, the drag artist chooses to rebel through his appropriation of known and accepted performative actions, albeit associated with a different type of body.

It appears to me that the key difference between Merleau-Ponty's phenomenology and Butler's performativity is this attitude to agency. In a phenomenological idea of persons as being-in-the-world, the subject bobs along in a stream of perception, receiving experiences of an outside world through the medium of their body. However, in a performative assessment of being, the subject grabs, shapes and fashions the world through enactment. While the repetitions of performance may be prefigured from the outside, the inner specificities and individual responses to them remain open, and the entire performance is context specific. The drag artist chooses to contravene normative actions on and through his/her body, albeit, as Butler recognises, through the manipulation of familiar acts. Performativity is discursive, rather than representative: the speaking of a word creates it, rather than representing a concept. It transforms both world and subject simultaneously, twisting them into a new material creation. A performative person is a swirling mass of matter and deed, simultaneously changing and being changed by the world rather than simply being in it. As each subject is particular, so is their performance, although it may incorporate and take in shared actions and shared discourse.

3.4 Volatile Bodies

The next scholar whose influence is essential to the design and ideas in this study is also concerned with the body, and unsurprisingly allied to Butler and other writers (including Spivak (2005), Gatens (1996), Irigaray (1993), and Wittig (1994) to name a few) in recognising the importance of difference, particularly sexual difference. However, while Butler uses performativity to express difference and combat binary divisions, Elizabeth Grosz chooses to consider these issues through an elaborate engagement with what she terms phallocentric philosophy (Grosz 1993: xiv). Her aim in her oeuvre *Volatile Bodies: towards a corporeal feminism* is to find a new conception of the body and return it to a central role in the understanding of experience and mind begun by Plato and continued relentlessly via Cartesian ideas. Grosz recognises the complexity and individuality of the body, declaring that 'there is no body as such: there are only bodies – male or female, black, brown, white large or small – and the gradations in between' (ibid: 19). Her insistence on specificity allows for a vision of real bodies – not the visions of phenomenological thought. In this section, I will first examine Grosz's critique of Merleau-Ponty, before moving to discuss her own thoughts on a new shaping of the body, a body more complex than even Butler would envisage.

Before diving into a review of Grosz's critique, it is important to consider the other authors whom she deconstructs, in order to build her own ideas upon them, a tower made up of rubble. She considers Freud and Lacan's psychoanalytical ideas, the concerns of Nietzsche and Foucault with power relations and the thought of Deleuze and Guattari on transformation

---

[10] Shakespeare. 'Macbeth' Act 1 Scene 5 Line 15

and change. It is, however, her work on Merleau-Ponty's phenomenology which is most important to my approach. He forms a central spine to Grosz's work, negotiating the space between psychology and philosophy, a position perhaps inevitable, given his career as a child psychologist. In the initial stages, Grosz focuses on the psychological aspect to Merleau-Ponty's work, reviewing the case of Schneider, a man who can live and act only in the moment due to a cerebral lesion, in order to examine the relationship between the body and space. She notes that for Merleau-Ponty, Schneider's case demonstrates the importance of the self-image of the body as more than object: although the afflicted man can scratch his nose, he cannot point to it – he can respond to sensation within his body knowingly, yet not to experiences of the world outside his skin (ibid: 90). The specificity of Schneider's life is not just an illustration of the intertwined nature of body and mind: it is rather a sympathetic rendering of an individual subject, the very individual who has been seen as missing in phenomenological thought. Grosz also lauds Merleau-Ponty's recognition of the united nature of the senses, although she censures his maintenance that vision is the primary human sense, devoting herself to unravelling the significance of touch. The sexual subject is brought to life through touch, and by denying the importance of both these aspects (and particularly the issue of orgasmic sensation) Merleau-Ponty loses his position as a feminist favourite in the eyes of Grosz.

How can the importance of touch be reconciled with the other senses, and the phenomenological ideas be brought together with the other philosophers into Grosz's new position? The answer lies in her re-conception of the human body as a particular object: the Moebius strip. This object (Fig. 3.1) is a shape with a single side, with a central twist: one can easily be made by twisting and sticking a strip of paper. This object provides Grosz with a metaphor for her conception of both the body and the philosophy surrounding it. Different philosophical discussions apply to different points along the strip, as the shape transmutes between faces that look inwards and outwards. The body, too, sits between these faces, twisting and and changing yet made up of what is undeniably the same substance all the way through. If the mind is the inner face, and the soma the outer, the Moebius strip provides a way to understand their inter-relation and interaction, and come to a clearer knowledge of the subject's negotiation of themselves and the world. However, the Moebius strip can be variable; can be made of any colour or any material: knitted scarves, different papers, graphic representations. In this way, so can the body be coloured differently, constituted differently, experienced differently: yet the substance which makes it up is constant through and through.

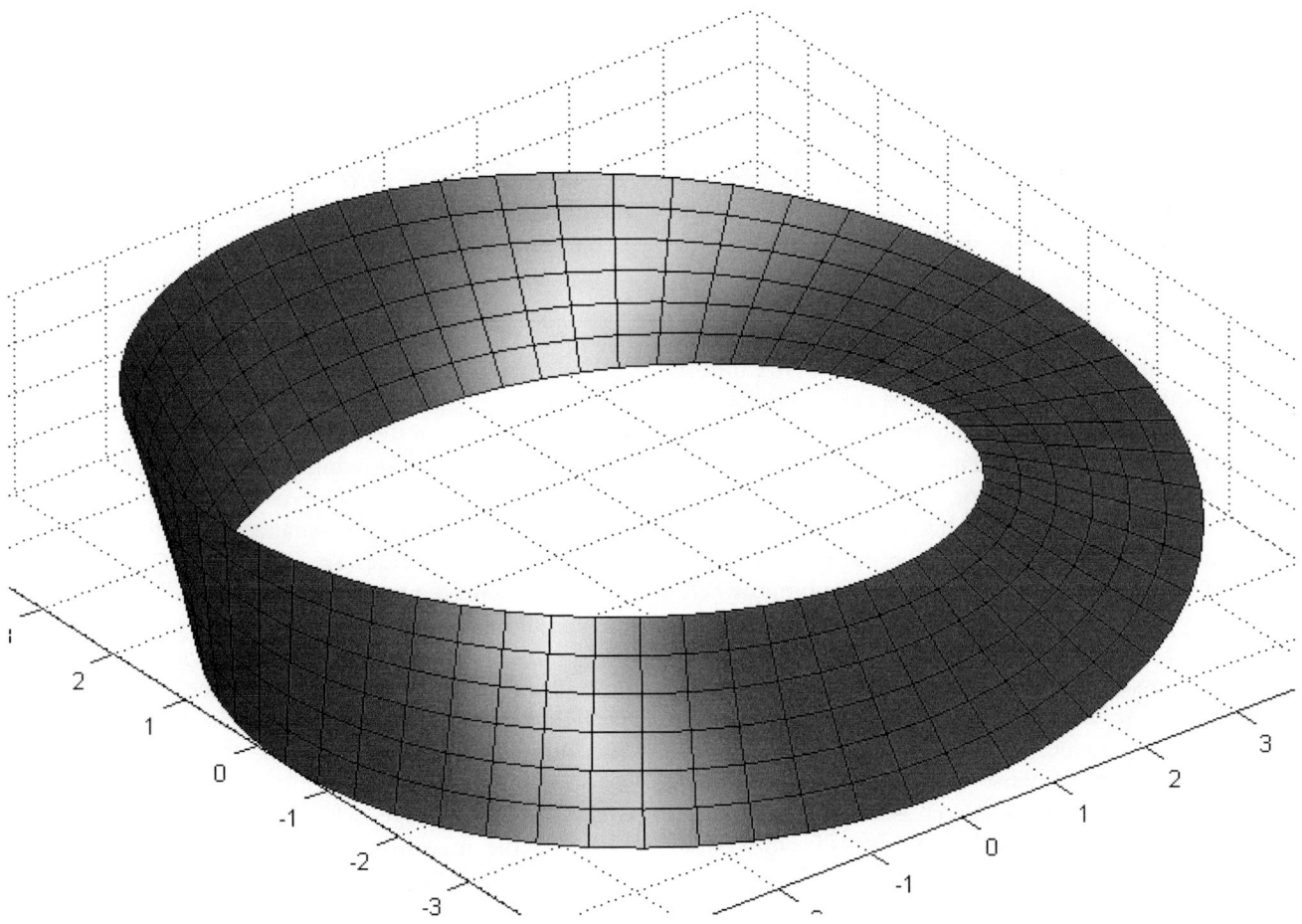

FIGURE 3.1: MOEBIUS STRIP

Grosz's final discussion is one of liquids and flows, a bringing of female specifics to the neutral bodies with which she has previously dealt (Grosz 1993:187). She examines the physical expressions which navigate from the interior to the exterior of the body and back again, flowing from bodily orifices back into bodily perception. The differential responses to bodily fluids develop not only her thoughts on sexual difference in their origination, but also in the responses to them: menstrual blood and seminal fluid, tears and snot. These fluids allow her to return to the flowing shape of the Moebius strip: in the same way that these liquids represent the differences between individual bodies, times, emotions and responses, the Moebius strip represents the spatial expression of her central tenet: that the body is an entire surface to be inscribed and rotated, endlessly changing and pliable. This slippery body expands, contracts and reacts to the world, as do the liquids it produces, intrinsically involved in it yet separate from what is outside it. The only problem I have with this model is that the strip is an object: it cannot move on its own. The strip remains static until twisted by a hand, it is a shape that does not occur without manipulation. Butler's performativity provides the understanding of this action, bringing the inside/outside volatile body to active life, but this conception of action is missing something. The work of the next author on feminist phenomenology seems to me to fill the gap.

3.5 Throwing Like a Girl

Iris Young's work on embodiment and feminist phenomenology is the final piece in this theoretical puzzle (Young 1990). She brings to Grosz's model the action and specificity which is missing in her philosophy, turning the inside/outside body from a piece of paper to living breathing flesh. Young's work also adds to the performative ideas of Butler the humanity and relevance to the everyday they require. It is easy to see how iterative performance can impact on lives at moments of high drama such as 'coming out,' but the idea that we are all constrained by repetitive action seems almost absurd – the assertion in a twenty first century world that I can do what I like with my body unrestrained by gender normative action is a powerful message engrained through self-repetition. The work of Iris Young demonstrates that this idea is a fantasy. Individual bodies are not just blurred sites of action, iteration and inscription, but are specifically constructed in the very image of societal norms, where physicality and performance combine. I will specifically discuss two aspects of Young's thought, both raised through her essay *Throwing like a Girl: a phenomenology of feminine body comportment, mobility and spatiality*. Firstly, I will consider her critique of Merleau-Ponty: the final feminist response to his thought considered here. Then I will outline her chosen case study: the experience of the female body in flight – the action of a little girl throwing a ball, illustrated in Fig. 3.2.

Young, like Grosz, does not so much critique Merleau-Ponty as use him as a stepping off point to her own work. However, unlike Grosz, she does not critique Merleau-Ponty's lack of comment on the body as a sexually aware being, but instead suggests that the initial situation of the body towards things and the environment is more essential than a specifically sexual engagement. Young uses this idea to explore the initial movements of childhood, the body in action in relation to the environment, and not specifically sexualised moments. Although she considers female embodiment in relation to specific circumstances in other essays on the experience of pregnancy (*Pregnant Embodiment: subjectivity and alienation* Young 1990: 160-177) and the possession of breasts, (*Breasted Experience: the look and the feeling* ibid: 189-210), her focus here is on the body's primary orientation to the environment, and its engagement with the outside world, rather than self-examination. Young sees that Merleau-Ponty's ideas apply to 'any human existence in a general way' (ibid: 144) and that they can be used as a base to investigate more specific existences, even without a sexual component. His conception of phenomenal space as created and constituted by the body allows her to examine the phenomenal space created and inhabited by particular types of bodies. By combining his base idea with the account of de Beauvoir of women's experiences of patriarchy, Young creates a feminine phenomenology, examining the ways in which women's bodies are conditioned and created in the image of patriarchal ideology. While not explicitly performative (indeed, the essay was written long before Butler), the ideas of experience and body creation through action loop neatly back to Butler's performativity, providing a connection between subject and society which is specific and active, but firmly constituted through embodiment.

The central example in Young's work is her analysis of the observation of the neurologist and phenomenologist Erwin Straus on the throwing action of a young girl of five years old. He observes that when this girl throws she does not use any part of her body other than her arm, and that the ball she throws is not propelled into the air with 'force, speed or accurate aim' (Straus 1966: 157). In the image above of the girl and the rock, it is possible to see exactly what he describes. The girl lifts and lowers her arm, allowing the stone to leave her hand and splot into the water. The rest of her body is almost still, the feet precariously balanced together, the other arm relaxed at her side. The only part of her which is connected with the throw is the face, she is following the age old advice of 'look where you want the ball to go.' Looking and wanting the stone to move, to go out onto the water as far as the eye can see, is not enough. Without a full body movement, the stone can only end close to its original starting point, disappearing beneath the surface. Straus contrasts this female action to that of a boy of the same age, who would use his entire body to heave the missile outwards, twisting at the waist, using his legs, following through with the other arm. He throws the ball with all his might, aiming it at a point far in the distance, hoping for a strike and a reaction.

FIGURE 3.2: YOUNG GIRL THROWING A STONE INTO THE SEA.
IMAGE © LARS STOKHOLM.

While Straus himself does not comment on the reasons why this difference in the children's throwing techniques should be present, it is the primal point of Young's essay. She goes on to investigate the difference between the boy and the girl, already present in their physical experience of the world at such a young age. She observes that women comport themselves completely differently in the world – from holding books or parcels to the chest to keeping their legs close together or crossed over when seated. Even the length of women's strides compared to their height is, she notices, smaller, taking up less space in the world. What Young takes from this is that the physical expression of patriarchal oppression is created in and on the female body, and come to define female existence. The girl learns that she is a girl through her (lack of) throwing ability. She suggests that female bodies are designed through this learning process to take up as little space and attract as little notice as possible, both as a response to fears of sexual violence and to avoid objectification. The female body has been coerced into action from earliest childhood, in turn creating the phenomenal experience of its inhabitation. While the presence of physical features of sexual difference are the beginning of this differential experience, the way in which the body is created and, I would suggest, performed, demonstrate a physical reflection of the pressures of cultural and temporal context. Through analysis of the body in space, the body in motion, and the body in contact with other bodies and things, it is perhaps possible, if not to 'reconstitute the milieu' of the past man or woman, but to observe their navigation of it, and speculate as to their place within it. Young has developed a phenomenology of action, which incorporates individual agency and external constructs as equal influences, providing a form of thinking through experience which approaches the complexity of real lives in the past or the present.

3.6 Phenomenology for Pots

The primary application of phenomenal thought in archaeology has been to examine experience of places or spaces. This approach was pioneered by, and is continually influential in the work of Chris Tilley (1994, 1996; 2004, 2008, 2012).[11] In his recent study on Scandinavian rock art, Tilley analyses the kinaesthetic manipulations necessary to seek out images in the landscape, and suggests that this bodily contortion

---

[11] Phenomenology has also been used in the context of place by Bradley (1990, 1991, 1997, 2000, 2002, 2003, 2005), Richards (1993, 1996) and Thomas (1990, 1991,1996) but it is the approach of Tilley that I focus on here

forms part of the viewing experience and, as such, part of the image (Tilley 2008: 38-42). He refers back to the work of Bergson (1991:46-47) who presented the body as the seat of negotiation with the outer world and the experience of personality as sited within bodily bounds. The use of phenomenology to examine place and landscape is perhaps tied to its central assumption of the universality of the body. The dimensions of the body in space remain the same, and can be applied to an arena which is relatively unchanged through time, such as Tilley's rock art sites. Rain still makes the body wet, a hill climb presents the same challenges of exertion and balance, exemplified in Tilley's account of his walk along the Dorset Cursus (Tilley 1994: 73-4; 2012). Accusations of subjectivity (Barrett and Ko 2009; Bruck 1998, 2005; Jones 1998; Fleming 2006) have been actively answered by the development of a rigorous research methodology in an analysis of Italian Neolithic landscapes in Puglia by Sue Hamilton and the Tavoliere-Gargano project team (Hamilton et al 2006: 32).

The Tavoliere-Gargano project presents a leap from phenomenology as thought process to phenomenology as archaeological investigation. It is intensely important to my approach: an example of how to integrate phenomenal principles into methodology to produce testable results. Hamilton and her team were interested in the sensual experience of four of these sites through sound, smell and vision. Their first act was to record visual points of interest in the landscape (hills, mountain ranges and areas of obscured vision) in a circular view (Hamilton et al ibid: 41-3), producing a view which represented the visual place of each site in the landscape. Their second methodology explored the impact of different noises, movements and scents to examine communication and shared experience in each ditched enclosure (Hamilton et al ibid: 46-7). This gave a strong idea of communal spaces and shared sounds and scents: the use of different stimuli, such as the crying of a baby and the odour of a flock of sheep on the move, in addition to gendered vocal utterances, allowed for sensory interaction to be mapped across each site, producing repeatable and comparable results. Their final method was the development of a phenomenal site catchment analysis, involving the detailed recording of walked perimeters for each site, which acknowledged the importance of specific walker identities in the production of such landscape experiences and recorded vegetation, aspect, weather and relief to provide intricate reconstructions of routes around each enclosure (Hamilton et al ibid: 55-8).

Tavoliere-Gargano shows that a rigorous methodology can be developed using techniques inspired by phenomenological philosophy. The specificity involved in its parameters also incorporates the variability and physical expression of identity observed by Grosz and Young. It is still focused on landscapes, however, and not on objects. The specificity of knowledge required to use an object is perhaps what lies behind this relative lack of engagement. Feminist forms of phenomenology, particularly performativity, have been used to approach and engage with objects – Joyce (1993, 1998, 2000a, 2000b, 2001, 2003, 2004) has considered a wide range of material culture as active constituents in the iterative performance of identities – for example, the use of clothing and bodily ornaments in the process of transformation from childhood to adult status (Joyce 2000a: 479) although this is closely linked to the analysis of textual sources and images (Joyce ibid: 475). In the Etruscan case, without intricate textual descriptions of the social role and use of pots, how can experience of them be approached in a method which incorporates the principles of feminist phenomenology?

The answer lies in developing an approach which takes note of the relationship between a pot and the body of the person using it. The contents of pots, foodstuffs, liquids and particularly alcoholic beverages, have recently been the subject of analyses based on their effect on the senses (Hamilakis 1998, 1999, 2002, 2008) and on behaviour (Dietler 1990, 2001, 2003, 2006). For both Dietler and Hamilakis, the ceramic vessels which contain such substances are important only as evidence for the presence of their contents: the intermediary things are set aside from the experience of consumption. To reach the role of clay containers themselves, the same process of thinking through effects is key: what did pots themselves actively do to the individuals who used them, and can these actions be recorded and tested? In conceiving of pots as actors, with a definitive effect upon experience and on people, they are conceptualised as agents. Object agency, developed primarily by Alfred Gell, provides a way of recognising the impact of objects on humans, and hence a way of recording those impacts as experience.

Gell was continually interested in the interface between objects and people, which he explored through what he termed art: the production of images (Gell 1998). His work on Trobriand kula canoes (Gell 1992) focused upon the deployment of decorative designs for a purpose: namely, to impress onlookers into trading kula objects on over-favourable terms with the occupants of the canoes. The impact of decoration was purposeful, and this purpose was not aesthetic in a Western conception of the term – the design of the canoes was intended to create an effect upon the viewer as much as upon the surface of the water through which they travelled. The direct integration of the power of markings and decoration with the human body was expressed by Gell in his work on tattooing (Gell 1993), which followed up his observations on the function of decoration through examining the powerful effects of tattoos upon Polynesian subjects. Just as with the kula canoes, the tattoos were designed and implemented to create a series of outcomes: the protection of their bearer and the intimidation of the onlooker.

It is not only ritualised objects and images which Gell argues are designed to have an effect on their viewer or user: he presents the example of a child's bed linen, covered with appealing images to encourage the child to sleep (Gell 1998: 47). This is just as important and meaningful a purpose as the protection of the body through tattooing or the dazzling effect of kula canoes. All three examples are cases of small scale impacts on individual subjects, whose lives are changed by their interaction with an object and its figurative covering. While the design of the images reaches back to societal ideologies, their power is expressed at the scale of the individual interaction. The work of Gell seems very distant from Etruscan ceramics, both geographically and chronologically. Yet there are two key points from his work which are directly applicable to Etruria and Etruscan pottery. The first of these is that images are not simply decorative, but are powerful, with a transformative impact on the body which is specific to the context of their use – during consumption.

The images shown on Etruscan ceramics present a series of bodies which are appropriate to be viewed in the process of using a vessel. These bodies are not blurred blanks, but specific records of particular bodies occupied in specific gestures. As discussed further in Chapters 7 and 8, these are bodies with specifically gendered characteristics, reacting and relating to other bodies and objects in two dimensions. Sociological case studies illustrate the relevance of images to the construction of the identity of a person interacting with them – and the impact of this identification on that person's behaviour. Lavine, Sweeney and Wagner (1999) experimented with television advertisements that portrayed particular images of male and female bodies – some of which presented stereotypically gendered gestures and roles. Showing the (albeit moving) images to a group of men and women, their conclusions were striking: both groups perceived their own bodies differently after viewing the stereotypically gendered adverts – often misjudging their own body size negatively (in the case of the female subjects) or positively (in the case of the male subjects). A similar experiment with young adults demonstrated the same effects on self-image, but this time linked them to actual changes in behaviour (Harrison, Taylor and Marske 2006). The subjects were presented with images of idealised male and female bodies from media sources – and then asked to consume a meal. The amount eaten appeared to co-incide exactly with the images shown – men shown muscular males consumed larger amounts of food than men shown no images at all, while women consumed less after viewing these idealised bodies.

These case studies demonstrate that images can visibly affect behaviour, and their appearance at moments of consumption can impact the specific actions of people engaged in eating or drinking. The images in the examples above were static, solely visual stimuli. Yet a range of case studies of sociological investigation of the power of images demonstrate that when imagery is provided in an interactive, relevant setting, its effect on behaviour can be elevated – with a particular instance, which examined the increased efficacy of online advertisements when a target was inveigled into an interactive engagement with the presented images (Fortin and Dholakia 2005), encountered on a daily basis. These studies demonstrate that when an image stimulates a viewer through multiple senses – accompanied by sound (as in television advertising), or involving the whole body in an interactive engagement, where the user controls the presentation of the image, it is markedly more powerful. The decoration of Etruscan ceramics serves a purpose to influence behaviour, potentially in equally affective and powerful ways. Understanding what that purpose is is central to interpreting experience of these objects.

While these case studies demonstrate the strength and influence of images to transform behaviour, I would extend Gell's idea of the power of things beyond imagery and aesthetics to encompass all objects. To return to his original example, the child's bed linen would not entice and encourage its young owner to sleep if it was not also soft, warm and comfortable – a bed sheet of coarse horse hair would not encourage sleep even if it were decorated with a multitude of dinosaurs or rockets. In the same way, the form of a pot is as carefully designed to impact upon the viewer as the decoration which covers it. While this book is focused on the combination of particular types of images characterised by the representation of the human body with specific pottery forms, the role of every pot's form, regardless of decoration, should not be discounted. Form is as important for shaping the experience of the subject-user as decoration, and both features have an equal power and purpose.

This directly relates to the second lesson to be taken from Gell: the utter absorption of the body into the Polynesian tattoo is reminiscent of the incorporation into the body of the contents of Etruscan ceramics. The function of both these 'art forms' is interlinked: while tattoos take place on the body, these images enter into the body, while the tattoos may mark status through their active creation on the body as lived experience, these scenes mark status through the viewer's access to them, and show how to transport the status of the object into the physical body of the user. By extending Gell's concept of the agency of objects to form as well as decoration, the impact of pot on body is rendered even stronger: the pot physically controls the body of the user, demanding a particular group of skills to balance and use it correctly. Through referring back to the phenomenological observations of Young, the significance of this learned use becomes clear: the integration of the pot onto the body in the hand, and the images of the body on the vessel into the mouth and stomach create a series of powerful effects on the experience of the subject, as designed and planned by the society in which both pot and person inhabit and were created by. In this extension of Gell, and the incorporation of his ideas with feminist phenomenology, it is possible to see a phenomenology of objects, in which powerful things impact upon and create subject experiences which are actively created and constituted both through object effects on the body, and the body's interaction with things.

3.7 Objects and Social Discourse

The feminist phenomenology of Iris Young and the active, engaged role of an individual in Butler's performativity have provided a way for thinking about the human body in space. Gell's thought, and the application of phenomenal ideas by archaeologists, have similarly provided a set of ideas that approach the way in which things influence people. Yet these two channels of thought have not yet come together, as a body and an object do in the living world. The body of Young's girl, her constructed physicality, and Butler's self-affirming actor with his or her deliberate manufacture of identity transmit their messages through the way they use their bodies, often in conjunction with objects. This use of the body as a physical tool to communicate, incorporating or discarding objects to assist in the performance, is central to the coming analysis. Pots may be drafted into the actions of their users, shaping and defining his or her body as they go. The images on this particular group of ceramics provide a secondary point at which user and object encounter and transform one another – reflecting back familiar and unfamiliar bodies and prompting comparison and consideration of the self. These two ways in which pots and people come together provoke a shared series of questions, linked to the relationship between bodies, images and objects. Without words, how do these three different facets of experience come together to communicate, and to contribute to the construction of a particular self?

The use of the body to communicate non-verbally is a phenomenon that is universally recognised and understood. A slump of the shoulders, the flicker of an eyebrow – these often minute movements are picked up on and interpreted by people around us. A pointing finger or a waving arm are the larger cousins of tiny changes in the face and body, responding to emotions, environments and individuals. The relationship between spoken language and the non-verbal communication of the body has been a key issue for scholars of the evolution of linguistics, often using analyses higher primate communication techniques to develop hypotheses of early hominin language (cf. Hewes 1973; Seyfarth 1987). Indeed, the question of whether physical gesture developed over time into speech, or whether the two developed together is still a subject of debate (Arbib, Liebal and Pika 2008) and continues to be examined through neurological investigation (summarised by de Gelder 2006). A key aspect of these arguments is the relationship between particular, specific signals and individual words from a language or cultural meanings (such as a upward thumb, generally assumed to mean 'yes' or 'good' in European and American contexts). Such gestures, while seemingly identical, may have entirely different meanings in another tradition, or in another 'language.' Certainly it would be impossible to connect together this kind of distinct gesture with a specific meaning, linked perhaps to a single Etruscan word, although using the textual record attempts have been made to link together Classical Greek gestures and individual linguistic intentions in the context of theatrical performance (Clarke 2004).

Similarly, some aspects of non-verbally specific gestures can be misleading – the classic example is that used by Clifford Geertz in his development of thick description as a method for anthropological analysis. Geertz (1973: 7) describes a series of boys, all of whom appear to be making the same physical gesture – closing one eye rapidly. However, all the boys have different intentions to one another, different expectations from their use of the eyelid to communicate. The first boy is winking deliberately, with all the conspiratorial implications of that movement of the eyelid. The second boy has a facial twitch, which causes him to blink his eye uncontrollably – he is not attempting to communicate anything with this part of his face. A third boy is mimicking the boy with the twitch, making fun of his disability. Yet, as Geertz points out, a photograph of all three boys would merely show three boys winking – leaving the interpretation of the gesture open. The example strongly illustrates the centrality of context to establishing what an individual intends by the movement of their body. It is at this point that Etruscan ceramics and the images of humans upon them become important – the specificity of knowledge that would enable an archaeologist to triage a wink from a twitch from a spiteful joke may be missing, but the objects themselves provide enough context to investigate less specific gestures, particularly those which incorporate the whole body.

As argued above, the physical features of an object dictate to a human being how to use it, and physically shape the body into specific gestures associated with using a particular thing. The ease or difficulty with which an individual person can perform that interaction with an object is a point of gesture which these physical parameters can help to recreate. The size of an object, its weight, its shape, the material from which it is made, all these dictate how easy or difficult it is to entangle body and thing together in a single action. To return once again to the girl on the beach, heaving her stone into the water – the size of the stone, the type of stone it is made of, the aerodynamics of its shape, all these factors influence the gesture that is created as the stone plops into the sea. Where the features of an object make an action complex and difficult (the stone is heavy, it is sharp and uncomfortable in the hand, it is bumpy and hard for a small child's fingers to wrap around), the melding together of body and thing that creates the gesture is structured primarily by the object. Yet this balance can shift – with practice and application, the girl may learn to control the stone in her hand, to reduce its influence on her action. This control of the object may be translated as skill – the learned ability to perform an activity fluidly, resulting in a successful outcome – the satisfying distance at which the stone eventually finds its mark among the waves.

This definition of skill is a deliberately simplified one. The different arguments over exactly how skill is acquired, grown and curated are as complex as those focused on the evolution of non-verbal language (Ericsson and Lehman 1996; Layton 1974). In archaeology, analyses of skill are primarily centred on the production of artefacts, and their decoration, rather than their usage (e.g. Bamforth and Finlay 2008 in the case of lithic tools, and Costin and Hagstrum 1995 in the case of ceramics. The work of Beazley (1947, 1963, 1978) is thick with references to skill in the production of Attic and Etruscan pots). Yet skill is a central part of the experience of using an object – if a person is familiar with a thing, has extensive knowledge of its shape and feeling, and has schooled the body extensively in its use through practice, even a complex object can be used in a manner that gives an impression of ease. When other people are aware of the problematic nature of the object in question, a reaction is assured – the user has silently communicated their familiarity and experience to those around them. The skilful user lays claim to the connections of the object itself – by demonstrating their easiness with the physical bounds of a pot, an Etruscan user could have implied their familiarity with the world in which the pot was used. As the physical characteristics of the vessel make this demonstration of familiarity more challenging, so that world is rendered more exclusive – and the skill itself more impressive.

This skilful use is a central part of the context of Etruscan ceramic images and their presentation to a user in a moment in which the response of that individual person, the physical form of an object and the content of the images themselves all come together to produce a fully embodied experience. So the experience of using Etruscan pottery is one which incorporates all these different influences together, creating a complex web of intricate interactions between person and object. The strands woven into this holistic experience include the gestures promoted by a pot, the learned control of the body that demonstrates use and experience of similar objects (skill), the influence of images on behaviour, and the heightening of that influence through interaction. All these factors contribute to a contextualisation for the use of Etruscan vessels – one which, while still falling short of Geertz's standard of interpreting an Etruscan wink, has the potential to examine the experience of using Etruscan vessels from the perspective of an Etruscan person. Yet the exact context in which these objects were used was one which itself has a bearing on the encounter between person and pot. As hinted at above in the increased effect of images on eating behaviour when presented alongside a meal, the contents of Etruscan ceramics were equally important in the experience of using them.

An underlying assumption of this book is that the Etruscan ceramics under analysis were used in the consumption of alcohol. The archaeological evidence for this assertion, in addition to the presentation of Etruscan and pan-Mediterranean drinking practice in classical sources is addressed in depth in the following chapter. However, it is important to acknowledge here the deep effects that alcohol can have on the interpretation and presentation of gesture, the acquisition, possession and demonstration of skill, and on the perception of imagery. When alcohol is consumed, vision blurs and distorts, the drinker loses the minute control of their muscles that allows them to undertake intricate tasks, reaction time diminishes. Yet at the same time, social barriers are lowered, tongues loosen and social interaction eases. The balance between these different effects of alcohol on the body is negotiated directly through the objects that contain alcoholic substances – and the images displayed upon them. These contextualising effects impact severely upon the experience of using pots, and the interface between person and object created by such use. While this chapter has delineated phenomenological ideas to define experience from the perspective of the user, and conceptions of object agency to illustrate the perspective of a pot, the space in which the two come together is deeply entwined with the gestures, skills and responses of the user – and the contents of the vessel.

3.8 From Theory to Practice

This chapter has covered a wide range of different theoretical ideas – from the origins of phenomenology through feminist re-interpretations to negotiating phenomenology in archaeology to a theory of object agency based on Gell. However, the central aim of this chapter was to present a theoretical methodology, the framework which literally forms the foundation for the actual analysis, and the smaller questions and answers which build into an interpretation of the experience of Etruscan pottery for Etruscan people. The theory is built into the analysis from this point forwards – every section of this chapter has directly influenced the design of this study, in the following ways.

1. Philosophical phenomenology, particularly that of Merleau-Ponty, demonstrates that experience is the primal activity of existence, and that this experience is constituted through the entire body. In terms of this study, if this is taken to be true, to understand the role of Etruscan pottery it is essential to work towards examining the experiences these pots directly created and contributed to. The Etruscan subject is the central point of the analysis, the person in whom the pottery world is made through bodily interaction and experience.
2. The feminist phenomenology of Butler and Grosz demonstrated the specific nature of that Etruscan experience, and how it is constituted. Butler's work on performativity shows that iteration is central to the construction of experience: the use of a pot is a repetitive action which is deliberately practised in a public performance – using the pot demonstrates and enforces knowledge of how to use a pot. The performativity of pottery also provides the first sign of the potential role of pots in the creation of a body through experience and action. Active subjectivity is another important consideration: the Etruscan user of a pot was making a choice, enacting their own agency and power as an independent individual being.

Further to this agency, the Etruscan subject was a specific bundle of mind, body and experience, inside and outside, as Grosz presents through the metaphor of the Moebius strip. Her work demonstrates the dangers of simplifying the Etruscan person: this is someone made up of a body and a life story as complicated as any other human being, acting in their own individual situation. The relationship between this complex person and a pot can be explored by patterns of use, but each interaction between each pot and each user is absolutely unique.

3. While Butler, Grosz and Merleau-Ponty contribute a phenomenology for the analysis of the experience of being-in-the-world for the Etruscan subject, Iris Young provides a phenomenology for images, a way of analysing the representation of bodies through their manipulation in space. Her observations on the socially constructed body and the physical reiteration of patterns of movement provides a methodology for looking at how bodies are represented and constituted in and on ceramics: the way they move, the way they touch, their component parts. Through an examination of the shapes of objects that interact with the body, in addition to representations of bodily behaviours, it is possible to examine not only constrained choices of representation but constricted physical experience also. The impact of represented patterns of movement can be extended outward, to reconstruct and estimate the physical experiences of Etruscan subjects away from the pottery world.

4. Archaeological uses of phenomenology, in particular the Tavoliere-Gargano project, show that an approach grounded in the idea of embodied subject-centrality can work practically in archaeology. While no exact methodology mirrors that which will be used here, the ways in which experience was constituted in the past are demonstrably approachable and practicable in other archaeological contexts, and, with context-specific adaptation, are appropriate and apt for use in the analysis of Etruscan pottery.

5. The work of Gell on object agency provides a place for objects in a phenomenological world. The decoration on ceramics is acknowledged as having a purpose, a role, making its analysis worthwhile in terms of function – the effect that such images may have on the behaviour of a user. By extending Gell's thought to cover the form of objects, it is possible to explore object function through shape, and the relationship between the force of objects on the phenomenal subject and their experience of the world can be interrogated. By linking the literal structuring of actions by objects with the learned physicality of Young, the Etruscan user of pottery found their body shaped into actions which are prescribed by objects, not only in the interaction between user and image but between hand and handle, mouth and rim. The bodies of pots are actors on the bodies of humans, deliberately causing repetitive physical movements which are a key part of their function.

6. The importance of a specific placement and deployment of the body in social interactions involving objects, as observed by Geertz, connects the physical agency of things with the lived body of a human user, and emphasises the importance of cultural context in the development of relationships between people and pots. The skilled knowledge of how to join together body and vessel, and to incorporate this interaction into a seamless flowing series of other gestures, in a manner which is appropriate, even impressive, to on-lookers, is a result of familiarity and acquiescence to object agency, negotiated through the specificity of the individual body. Therefore, a vessel which demands a heightened level of skill may be used to differentiate between individual users – exposing their level of knowledge through their response to the physical contours of the pot, and potentially facing social consequences as a result.

These six points together form the principles which underlie the design of a research methodology to interrogate the experience of Etruscan ceramics from a user perspective. The example of the Tavoliere-Gargano project demonstrates that it is possible to combine phenomenal approaches with rigorous scientific method. The physicality of Young, specificity of Grosz and object agency of Gell provide a way to transfer the principles of phenomenology to an analysis of pottery, while the sociological case studies demonstrate the relevance of such approaches to an analysis of the Etruscan social world of behaviour, the complexity of which is underlined by Geertz. The next chapter details the exact methods which constitute such an approach, and which use the physical forms and images of Etruscan ceramics to consider their effects on the experience of their users.

Chapter 4

Quantifying Experience – Methodologies

4.1 Introduction

The central question at the heart of this book asks how the experience of using ceramics was constituted for Etruscan users. The interaction between an individual Etruscan person and a vessel is the critical point of engagement. The conclusions from this experiential analysis may be related to wider issues of societal use of ceramics, cultural interaction and shifting attitudes and patterns of behaviour, but they are arrived at through the specific moment at which a person lifts a pot in their hands as an extension of their own body. The previous chapter presented a series of theoretical ideas which specified the nature of experience, and provided a way to approach and examine it through objects. The extension of material agency from artistic images to object forms is the starting point for an analysis of specific user experiences through the physical bodies of pots, reaching back from clay to skin and the bodies of users themselves. This interaction between user and vessel is accessed through a performative phenomenology which emphasises an individual's unique encounter with the vessel, yet allows for the recording of more general features of experience. This balancing of physical effects and specific encounters is played out in the development of a methodology which seeks to quantify experience in a scientifically comparable way, while retaining the particularity of individual interactions between persons and pots in the past.

This chapter lays out the variables which structure this analysis of Etruscan pottery experience. The first of these variables are those which limit the data set – the factors which govern the scope and breadth of the later analysis. The first part of this chapter presents these limiting variables, explaining the decisions which lay behind their implementation, and their implications for the later analysis. This process of explanation, underpinning the choice of a particular group of Etruscan ceramics as subjects for testing, also incorporates three general variables – the geographical origin of ceramics included in the corpus, their original place of production, and their functional relationship to the body of a user. Four sites were chosen to contribute ceramics to the study, and pottery made in Etruria and in Greece was incorporated in the analysis – these decisions are introduced, and then expanded in the second section of this chapter. The detailed excavation history of each site, and the wider social context of the use of pottery in each place are considered, and the distinguishing forms of ceramics that separate imported from indigenous wares are presented. Between these limiting and general variables, the characteristics that defined the data collection process are made clear.

The third part of this chapter opens with a discussion of the role of ceramics in Etruscan society. In it, I firstly examine the use of pottery in formal banqueting events, which is the primary setting for the kinds of experiences which lie at the heart of this investigation: personal interactions between user and pot. Moving from the use of pottery in life to its role in death, the second task of this section is to reconstruct the excavation context of a group of emblematic Etruscan ceramics. The vast majority of the pots included in the data set do not have any information as to their initial discovery – no clue as to their location within a tomb, or within a necropolis, or even within a wider site catchment area. For many, the most detailed information available is that the vessel was found in the region of a particular known Etruscan site, a scrap of information which managed to cling to the vessels as they travelled through antiquarian excavators, dealers and traders to the museums and institutions which still retain them. The earlier discussion of individual sites provides a general background for the ceramics which originate from each place, and an idea of the rough archaeological context of vessels. Through an analysis of more recently excavated pottery from one study site, the second part of this section explores the funerary presentation and use of Etruscan pottery.

These three sub-sections establish the process of data collection, and introduce and expand known information about the ceramics included in that data set. The final sub-section of this chapter puts together the philosophy of the previous chapter with this information, to establish what an experiential analysis is, and how it will be applied to the corpus. The first action is the creation of a new typology of Etruscan ceramics – a typology established by the relationship of a vessel's function to the human body. This typology represents the first direct incorporation of phenomenological thought into the research design, and forms the third general variable alongside site provenance and production origin. Each of these three variables will then be used to structure the analysis of a series of specific and varying pottery characteristics, developed to interrogate and break down the use of any pot into a series of layers. These characteristics fall into groups related to the sensory exploration of a vessel, forming a stratigraphy of ceramic experience. Each group will be generally introduced, with more specific methodologies used to examine each set of individual characteristics presented in each of the chapters that follow. The chapter concludes with a plan of attack, visually presenting the overarching limiting and general variables, and then the specific characteristics considered in each of the four chapters which make up the remainder of this analysis.

4.2 Making a Corpus, Structuring Data

This section presents the central framework of the coming analysis: the limiting variables which I used to establish the data-set, and the general variables that structured the questions I asked of it. The first and most dramatic limiting variable that structures the choice of ceramics included within the dataset is the decision to limit the analysis to vessels only showing human images. This decision arose out of the initial aims of the project – I wanted to explore the relationship between human imagery on ceramics and their living, breathing users. The role of any art as a potentially powerful actor on a human viewer (as discussed in the previous chapter in relation to the thought of Gell) is, I would argue, magnified when the art represents a familiar human figure, with whom the viewer can identify. As observed previously in relation to gestural theory, and the work of Kendon, living humans are continuously using non-verbal communication to assess and inform one another. I would argue that the fixed gestures of humans on ceramics are also undertaking this project of continual information, aimed squarely at influencing any human who interacts with the vessel upon which they are transfixed. In addition to the power of art to intimidate, these images are imbued with an additional strength – they communicate with the viewer using direct methods of gesture which, while they may or may not be familiar, require a response.

The experience and effect of this relationship between the figures of ceramic people, and the reactions of living Etruscan users, was the first aspect of pottery experience that I wanted to investigate. Yet this interaction was presumably not, for the most part, taking place in a gallery space, but in the hurly-burly of use. To be able to examine the experience of encountering human images on pots, I had to interrogate the entirety of the encounter between a user and vessel – Merleau-Ponty's original thought had demonstrated that the different parts of an experience cannot be roped off and separated out from one another – the physical characteristics of a vessel were as important in constructing the effect of the figures as their own placement and rendering. So the central question of the investigation grew and expanded – what was the entire experience of using human-figured pottery like for an Etruscan user? The consequence of this expansion was a realisation of how limiting my initial approach had been – the experience of every Etruscan vessel, decorated with human figures or not, was a complicated series of sensory stimuli. The relationship between a person on a pot and a person using a pot was only one of these layers – yet it was this part of the stratigraphy of ceramic experience in which I was most interested.

To continue the metaphor of excavation, while I would meticulously record each feature and soil layer of a trench regardless of its relevance to my original research question, I would not choose to dig a site which had no relationship to that question at all. The recognition of the importance of those features and objects might overtake the original query – but they would not have arisen were it not for that primary interest. I had originally been interested in the experience of human images on ceramics, quickly recognised that this specific interaction was entangled in the wider context of vessel use, and expanded my research question to incorporate the full spectrum of ceramic experience in Etruria. Yet the focus on human images remained – and had a distinct effect on both the data-set I gathered and the impact of my conclusions.

As demonstrated later in this chapter through a specific case study, the vast majority of Etruscan ceramics do not feature human figures – or any figures at all. Plainwares, geometric or floral decoration dominated the Etruscan experience of pottery – of over 1000 ceramics surveyed from three necropoleis at Vulci, only 26 pots showed human figures. The full analysis, in 4.4, emphasises just how rare these vessels were – and how restricted an analysis focused upon them would be as an investigation of Etruscan ceramic experience as a phenomenon. As such, it is only the experience of a small group of Etruscan people that can be questioned through analysing these specific vessels – a far more comprehensive approach would incorporate all the ceramics from a site or series of sites. Yet doing this would leave the human figured images to one side, ignoring the issue of their impact on the select group of Etruscans who would have encountered and engaged with them. Aware of its effects on my expanded research question, I could not abandon this initial focus – all the vessels analysed would have to feature a human figure.

The second limiting variable was a condition that only ceramics which had been published could be included in the dataset. The decision to use published data made the process of data collection simpler, and removed the time and economic constraints involved in arranging to physically collect data for each vessel from a museum store. The largest single group of vessels were those published under the auspices of the Corpus Vasorum Antiquorum series, incorporating vessels from over twenty different collections. These were followed by those made available online via the British Museum's interactive catalogue. The Poggio Civitate open access excavation archive provided the information for all the ceramics from that site, while the series of publications detailing the collections of Tarquinia's Museo Nazionale (Campus 1981; Ginge 1987; Pianù 1980; Tronchetti 1983) provided a large proportion of the material from Tarquinia. The exact museum provenance and bibliographic reference for each vessel may be found in Appendix I. While the ease of access to published vessels smoothed the process of data collection, its real purpose was to produce a larger dataset than would otherwise have been possible. The testing of experience over a large scale would produce a clearer vision of Etruscan interaction with ceramics, and would allow for more secure conclusions to be drawn relating to the impact of ceramic practice on other aspects of Etruscan life. It is of course possible that unpublished

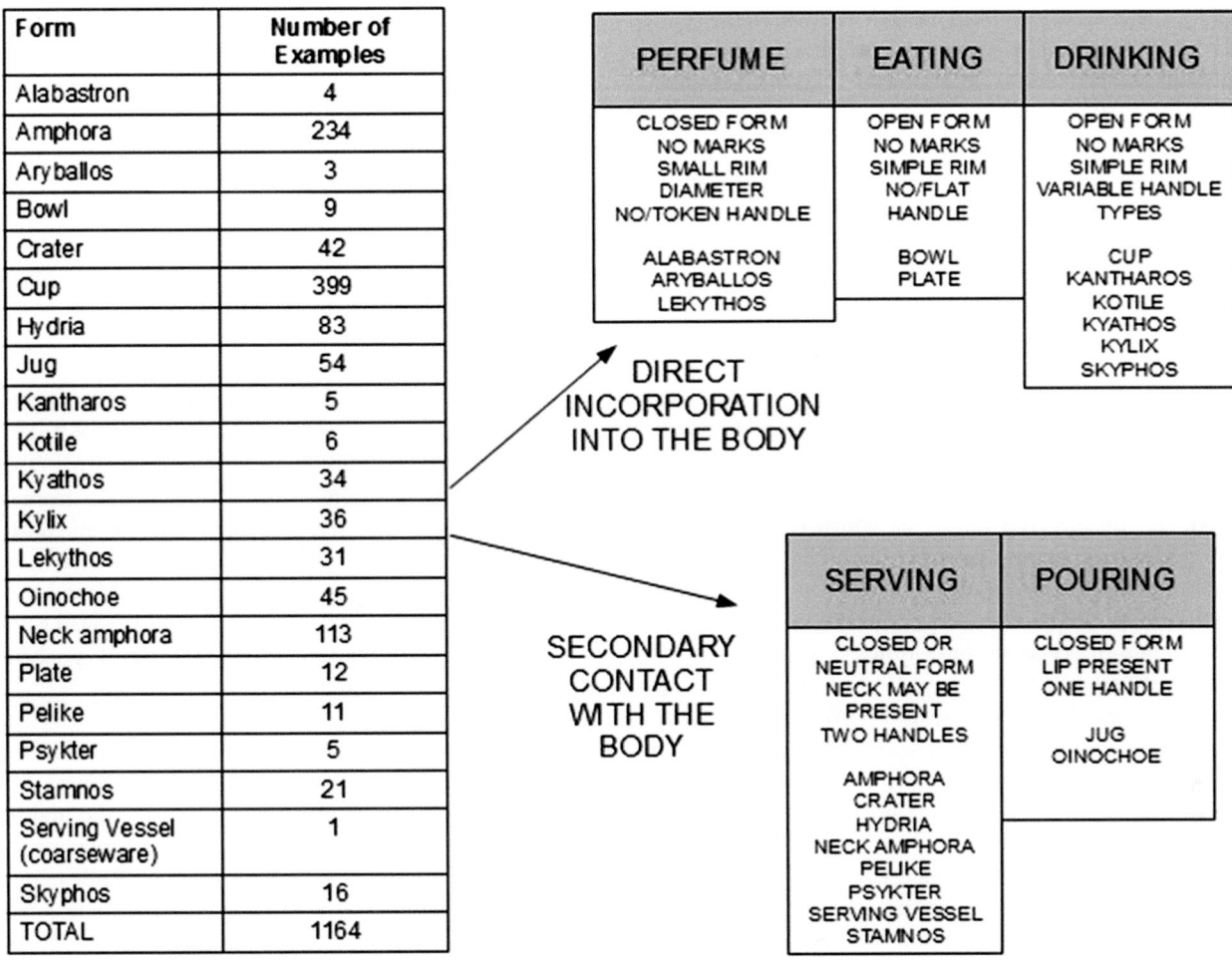

FIGURE 4.1: CERAMIC GROUPINGS BY TRADITIONAL TERMINOLOGIES AND USER-CENTRIC CATEGORIES.

vessels from each of the chosen locations may contradict those conclusions, but in order to acquire a large data set this was a risk worth taking. These two limits restricted the potential data-set significantly, but were underwritten by the types of questions I wanted to use the data to examine, each of which was embedded in a general variable.

The first general variable for the study was geographical provenance – I wanted to assess local variations in ceramic experience across Etruria, and was also concerned about the potential size of the dataset. Ceramics from four sites were chosen in order to present a wide range of ceramic forms, decoration techniques and images, spread across a wide geographical range that would nonetheless remain manageable and easily comparable. The four sites are divided into two pairs by their locations: two to the north of Etruria, and two to the south: they are the southern coastal cities of Vulci and Tarquinia, the northern city of Chiusi, and the non-urban centre of Poggio Civitate (Murlo). The choice of two pairs of neighbouring sites allows for regional, as well as site-specific comparisons. The sites are further differentiated by the nature of the assemblages which represent them: three are predominantly composed of ceramics from tombs, while one is defined by a rare non-funerary assemblage. It would have been preferable to use two of each type of site for the sake of balance, but survival issues made this difficult: ceramics from funerals make up the majority of the Etruscan pottery record. The presence of material from a non-tomb site provides an opportunity to see ceramics in use within a quasi-domestic context, while the tomb sites provided a much better level of preservation and higher number of ceramics available for discussion.

The second general variable was production origin. Pottery produced outside Etruria has been the subject of extensive debate for over a century. The large numbers of imported Greek vessels found in Etruscan funerary assemblages have been continually used as evidence for different models of interaction between the two communities. The conclusions reached through traditional analyses of these ceramics were presented in Chapter One, and focused on typological and iconographic variations. I am concerned with the difference in experience between using the two types of vessel – how was the inherent Otherness of imported ceramics communicated to the user through experience, and what were the physical characteristics which marked such vessels out as different from pottery produced locally? At each phase of the analysis, indigenously produced and imported pottery would be compared to interrogate those differences, and their relationship with the other two general variables. In this way, the conclusions from the experiential analysis are related back to these major arguments, and linked up to traditional interpretations of Etruscan relationships with Greeks and their pots.

The third general variable which forms part of the study framework is a second form of pottery type: vessel body proximity group. This characterisation of pottery function is used at each phase, to differentiate the contexts of use within which an Etruscan person would encounter vessels, decoration and images – a key part of pottery experience. Traditional typological terminologies denote the minutiae of pottery use, and could have been incorporated into the analysis. However, as Figure 4.1 demonstrates, this would have resulted in twenty one different ceramic groupings, as opposed to the five major categories which were developed. These groups were produced by considering the action a ceramic was used for, and the relationship of its contents to the user's body in the course of that action, hence the retained terminology. The features of each vessel demarcate its connection to the body of the user: vessels used for drinking and perfume application bring liquids directly into the body, as do some eating vessels, while pots used for the service of fluids to larger groups or the direct pouring of liquids are more distant. These body-proximity groups retain a functional context, but emphasise the place of vessels in a chain of encounters between an individual and a collection of ceramics, eventually leading to intimate contact and the incorporation of the contents of pots into the body through the mouth or the skin. The development of this ceramic typology allowed for the production of larger groups, making comparison between use contexts simpler. However, the most important role of this system was to re-cast the dataset in the context of use, rather than the context of intricate archaeological analysis.

These three variables examine three different points at which experiences of pottery can be compared: the local level defined by geographical provenance (site of origin), the regional experience defined by place of production and the more personal experience defined by the body proximity group of an individual vessel. Together with the two limiting factors which organised the collection of the datA –set, they form an overarching framework onto which the more specific analysis of different aspects or layers of pottery experience for the individual user detailed later in this chapter. These three general variables, however, each relate to a context of extant archaeological knowledge, which is the focus of the next section. It begins with a discussion of each site, before moving on to the individual imported and indigenous wares included in the data set

4.3 Four Sites, Seven Wares

The site of Poggio Civitate is located 25km south of the modern city of Siena, on a hill above the Ombrone River, which leads down to the Tyrhennian coast. Although stray finds from the nearby necropolis of Poggio Aguzzo were discovered during the early 20th century, systematic excavations on the flat plain of 'Piano del Tesoro' did not begin until 1966, under Kyle Meredith Phillips. As Ridgway and Ridgway point out (1993: xiv), he hoped to uncover a domestic settlement, in order to shift the focus of Etruscan archaeology from the southern necropoleis. Phillips was to be disappointed in this aspiration, but the site proved to be the location of a complex so unusual as to be unique in Etruscan archaeology, and perhaps unique within the Mediterranean Iron Age. The following years of excavation, which remains ongoing, have revealed a huge amount of information about this site and its two phases of development (Phillips 1967, 1968, 1969, 1970, 1971, 1972, 1973; Phillips and Nielson 1974, 1975, 1977). The site has shown signs of occupation from the Villanovan period (Tuck, Rodriguez and Glennie 2012), but developed during the *Seconda Età del Ferro* into a significant central complex accompanied by workshops and smaller buildings. This building was destroyed by fire in around 630 BCE, the time to which a small proportion of the ceramics included in this study are dated.

This complex was rebuilt, only to be deliberately dismantled in the third quarter of the sixth century BCE. This second complex is the origin point for the majority of the material discussed in this study: a group of four buildings dating from the Archaic period. Each wing of the enormous central structure measured 60m in length, making this the largest building in the Mediterranean at this time. While evidence of non-elite settlement on the hill of Poggio Civitate has not been forthcoming, the discovery of a satellite settlement in the neighbouring village of Vescovado di Murlo (Tuck et al 2007) and an Archaic period well (Tuck et al 2010) some distance from the main buildings both attest to other areas of inhabitation in the vicinity of the site.

The majority of the ceramics from Poggio Civitate incorporated in this book have been uncovered over the years of excavation both within the central area of Piano del Tesoro on the site of the buildings, and in the neighbouring Civitate A and B areas, where caches of material from the destruction of the central complex are located. Additionally, the excavated material from the necropolis of Poggio Aguzzo has recently been published, giving a further dimension of analysis (Tuck 2011). The role of Poggio Civitate has been a major subject for debate (Bandinelli 1972; Edlund-Gantz 1972; Cristofani 1975b; Edlund-Berry 1994; Tuck 2000; O'Donoghue 2013), with interpretations ranging from a cult centre to a political meeting place to an elite residence. A tantalising hint of further connections between Poggio Civitate and the Eastern Mediterranean is indicated by a single piece of Attic black figure ware. However, the majority of the materials found here are indigenously (and often locally) produced Etruscan ceramics, a balance of origins which makes Poggio Civitate a site which provides a contrasting parallel to some of the better known sites to the south. The presence of a full online catalogue alongside personal excavation experience and access to material in addition to the geographical and contextual features of the site made Poggio Civitate a clear choice for inclusion in this study.

The city of Chiusi is located around 65km to the south east of Poggio Civitate, and occupies the position of the ancient city. It stands on a hill above the Val di Chiana, and was one of the most significant inland cities of Etruria (Steingräber 1983: 225). The location of the later city was occupied from the late Bronze Age, and the landscape surrounding it is peppered with domestic and mortuary sites from the wider Etruscan period. An important centre of bronze working and bucchero production, Chiusi formed a trading hub in the north of Etruria throughout the archaic period (Camporeale 1994; Romualdi 2009). As the modern city sprawled over the ancient settlement, it was the necropoleis of Colle Casuccini, Poggio Renzo, Fonte Rotella, Poggio Gaiella, della Pania, Dolciano and Vigna Grande which became the focus of archaeological investigation during the nineteenth century. The arrival of the railway line in Chiusi opened up the town to antiquarian exploration, evidenced by the work of Milani (1884) and the discoveries of painted tombs at Poggio Renzo which continued into the early twentieth century (Fabrizi 2001).

The excitement of this period of early exploration unfortunately resulted in a significant amount of archaeological material being separated from knowledge of its initial context: although attempts have been made to re-connect tomb assemblages with contexts and re-catalogue antiquarian collections (Iozzo 2007; Barbagli and Iozzo 2007; Paolucci 2005, 2007b). A significant amount of the ceramics from Chiusi remain associated solely with a necropolis, rather than with a specific tomb or position within a burial assemblage. In spite of this, the amount of ceramic material from funerary contexts at Chiusi is vast, reflecting the variety of pottery used and produced within the town, and deposited with the dead. The assemblage includes a significant amount of indigenously (indeed locally) produced vessels in addition to imported pottery, as a key centre for bucchero production. As a northern inland site with a ceramic assemblage composed from a group of necropoleis similar to those in the south, the Chiusine material acts as a connection between the slight anomaly of Poggio Civitate and the two well-known southern sites of Tarquinia and Vulci.

Tarquinia is perhaps the quintessential Etruscan site. It is located far to the southwest of the two northern sites, only 10km distant from its associated port of Gravisca, and the transport hub of the gleaming Tyrhennian Sea. Occupied from the Neolithic to the Roman period, the settlement area on the 'Civita' hill has been the focus of recent excavations under the direction of Maria Bonghi-Jovino (Bonghi-Jovino 1986a, 1986b, 1989, 1991, 2001, 2010), and found to have origins dating back to the ninth century (Mandolesi 1999; Sgubini Moretti 2001a: 30-2). Aside from these recent excavations and work in the 1940s (Romanelli 1948), however, the focus of archaeological attention at the city has previously been on its burial areas of Monterozzi, Arcatelle, Selciatello, Sopra Selciatello, Impiccato, Poggio Quarto degli Archi and Sorgente. Although records survive of investigations of the tombs during the preceding centuries (Vickers 1985) it was during the early nineteenth century that these necropoleis with their painted tombs and spectacular grave goods formed an irresistible attraction to antiquaries and tomb robbers. This period can be painted equally as a rose-tinted wave of discoveries or as a 'holocaust for Etruscan archaeology' (Leighton 2004: 12). However, a significant number of tombs survived this period intact, to be systematically excavated during the twentieth century and provide information as to the distribution and position of objects within tombs (Cavagnaro-Vanoni 1972, 1977; Sgubini Moretti (ed.) 2001).

Located near to Tarquinia, approximately 20km to the north, the city of Vulci experienced the same boom as its southern neighbour in excavation and exploration during the early nineteenth century, with the discovery of the François tomb a particular moment of excitement. The presence of imported Greek material in so many of the tombs here acted as a magnet to the same individuals working further south at Tarquinia, and objects from the site soon joined those from its neighbour in flooding the European antiquities market. Excavations in the later nineteenth and early twentieth centuries by Bendinelli (Amorelli 1983), Mengarelli (Amorelli 1987) and Gsell (1891) restored a sense of scientific endeavour, providing a clarification on the distribution of imported material throughout the necropolis, and restoring the position of indigenously produced objects which had too often been discarded and vandalised by earlier tomb robbers. Intact tombs excavated by Gsell are now exhibited in the Villa Giulia museum in Rome, where the exact combinations of objects for each tomb may be examined. Excavations at Vulci are still ongoing, under the direction of Anna Maria Sgubini Moretti, who has also worked to restore the connections between objects from Vulci and other sites in southern Etruria and their original contexts (Sgubini Moretti 1993, 2004a).

The site of Vulci itself was occupied from the 9th century BCE, once again on a spur above the river Fiora. The trading networks which would later become so important were already in use at this time, as finds from the early Iron Age demonstrate (Guidi 1985). The city grew throughout the *Seconda Età del Ferro*, until by the sixth century BCE it had become one of the largest cities of Etruria, a hotbed of fashion and exchange. The work of Alain Hus (1971) supports this vision of Vulci as another strong trading city, with a thriving industry in ceramic and bronze production. Elaborate drinking vessels in bronze produced at Vulci have been found as far away as central Germany (Wells 1995: 174), demonstrating the position of the city at the forefront of the luxury goods industry. The production of amphorae suggests trade not only in objects, but also in products: wine and oil in particular, with Volceian wine amphorae excavated in settlements in southern France (Dietler 1997; Riva 2010b). The imported ceramics from

Vulci form the largest single group of objects included in the corpus, while accompanying indigenously made pots demonstrate the use of both object types together in the necropoleis in which they were deposited.

The majority of the ceramics which have been included in the dataset from these four sites were imported from outside Etruria[12]. The combination of excavation bias and restricted availability was largely responsible for this imbalance: Dennis (1883: 450) describes excavators throwing away coarsewares and Etruscan made finewares in their haste to uncover Attic ceramics which could command a higher price. As the two groups were examined separately at every point, this imbalance should not prejudice the results of the analysis. The corpus of imported pots is composed of three different wares: Corinthian, Attic Black-Figure, and Attic Red-figure pottery. The indigenous pots are more variable, and are composed of Bucchero, Etruscan Black-figure, Impasto and Orange wares. The differing proportions of these groups are presented in Table 4.1. The definition of these two groups as 'imported' and 'indigenous' for the purposes of this study is largely based on the ascriptions of previous scholars as published in the individual catalogues. The question of to what extent a vessel made in Italy yet decorated in an Attic style may be considered indigenous, or an Etruscan vessel form decorated in Athens may be considered imported, is left to one side for the present.

Ware	N (%)
Attic Black-figure	628 (54%)
Attic Red-figure	240 (20%)
Bucchero	191 (16.5%)
Corinthian	6 (0.5%)
Etruscan Black-figure	88 (7.6%)
Impasto	8 (0.7%)
Orangeware	3 (0.25%)

TABLE 4.1: PROPORTIONS OF DIFFERENT CERAMIC WARES INCLUDED IN THE CORPUS

The oldest imported ware included in the dataset is Corinthian ware, which uses the same decoration techniques as its successor in popularity, Attic Black-figure. First developed around 700 BCE in Corinth, the creation of images using black paint with incised linear details was 'revolutionary' (Boardman 1974: 9) in allowing the production of detailed figurative representations of humans and animals. When practised on a smooth buff clay extracted from claybeds at Acrocorinth, exquisite finewares could be produced, usually depicting several tiers of animals, humans and mythical beasts marching around the outside of a vessel (Farnsworth 1971: 9). The majority of these images depict animals, although the Corinthian examples included in the dataset are part of a later group which include humans. Etruscan consumers of Corinthian ware developed their own interpretation of this decorative style, producing Etrusco-Corinthian finewares which retained the same decoration techniques and repertoire, continuing to focus upon non-human figures. The popularity of this type of pottery in Italy continued into the sixth century BCE, although a new ceramic style from Greece had begun to challenge the market.

The same technological principles involved in the production of Corinthian black-figure images were adapted and reworked by Athenian painters by around 630 BCE. By abandoning the frieze composition, it was possible to create larger images which occupied the entire decorative space on a ceramic vessel, and hence to develop detailed scenes, often linked to mythological narratives (e.g. Clairmont 1953; Ferrari 2003; Hardwick 1990; Holt 1989; Lowenstam 1993, 1997; Shapiro 1984; Topper 2007; Woodford 1993, 2003) or representations of daily activities (e.g. Berard 1989; Clark 1983; Dover 1989; Poliakoff 1987). Attic Black-figure ware, and its later competitor and eventual successor, Attic Red-figure ware, are the ceramic traditions responsible for some of the most iconic images of the classical Greek world, and the identification and discussion of the potters and painters who created individual vessels and images has been the dominant methodology for their analysis, following the pioneering work of Beazley (1942, 1950, 1956). The works of a wide variety of named individual artists identified by Beazley are included within the survey, but it is the impact of their work on the Etruscans who purchased and used them which is really under scrutiny.

Just as Etrusco-Corinthian ware was developed for an Etruscan market for Greek-style ceramics, Attic pottery was also re-developed in Italy in the form of Etruscan Black-figure ware and later Etruscan Red-figure ware. Utilising the same production techniques, images were produced in Italy with a distinctly Etruscan style of composition and execution (Brendel 1978: 194; Mansuelli 1966: 77). A large database of Etruscan Black-figure ceramics has been gathered by Dimitrios Paleothodoros, which has established the distribution of this ware across Etruria at 58 findspots (Paleothodoros 2011: 37). The lack of examples outside Etruria emphasises the regional relevance of Etruscan Black-figure pottery, and suggests it possessed a specific appeal to Etruscan consumers (Paleothodoros 2010: 2). Vulci was one of the largest centres for the production of Etruscan Black-figure pottery, and the location of one of the most well-known workshops, that of the Micali painter, who was active in Vulci between 530 and 500 BCE (Spivey 1987). By contrast, all Etruscan Black-figure ceramics found at Tarquinia did not originate there, but were imported into the city (Paleothodoros 2010: 3).

The largest group of Etruscan-made ceramics in the study are not inspired by imported wares, but are

---

[12] As the following section will demonstrate, these pots were by no means the majority of ceramics in use at these sites.

exemplary of a manufacturing tradition which dates back to the Villanovan period and the ninth century BCE, the production of bucchero (Camerini 1985). The development of shiny burnished wares which resembled metal began at this early point, but the firing technology required to produce true bucchero pottery was developed much later, around 675 BCE in the area of Cerveteri. The black fabric is produced by high oxidation temperature during firing, alongside the inclusion of carbon in the clay (Leoni and Trabucchi 1962: 275). Intensive burnishing and an organic wash before firing ensures a shiny finish, which is intended to skeuomorphically resemble expensive bronze table wares (Rasmussen 2004: 2). While early bucchero is often undecorated save for small incised geometric designs, later bucchero produced during the Archaic period is decorated both by the addition of moulded figures and the impression of cylinder friezes around the outer sides of the vessel (for a full *chaîne opératoire* analysis, see Perkins 2007: 31). Workshops producing both early bucchero sottile and later bucchero pesante were present at both Chiusi and Vulci, both of which are thought to have supplied Poggio Civitate (Berkin 2004: 128).

The final two groups of Etruscan pottery included in the study are both from the latter site, and are examples of less elaborate finewares. Impasto pottery, commonly of a grey or brown colour, employs similar burnishing techniques to those used on bucchero to produce a shiny, smooth surface. Firing temperatures, however, are lower, and the pottery does not oxidise to the same extent. The last type of pottery, orangeware, is closely associated with Poggio Civitate as a production place. Tobey, Nielson and Rowe (1986) have demonstrated that orangeware from the site was made locally via chemical analysis, and Tuck (2011:25-48) has discussed this fabric as uniquely associated with Poggio Civitate and its accompanying necropolis of Poggio Aguzzo.

The origins, date ranges and excavation contexts for the ceramics used from each site are presented in Table 4.2. It is unfortunate that the sites and ceramic wares are not equally represented in the data set, a reality enforced by the presence or absence of human images at the different sites, and by the available published material. Vulci is dominant, due to the large number of predominantly imported wares available through museum catalogues and the Corpus Vasorum Antiquorum. The relatively small proportion of human figures from Poggio Civitate is a feature of the excavation record, however, and perhaps records the removal of high-value decorated pottery rather than its destruction. While crafting activities record human representation in ivory, in addition to the architectural terracottas, it seems that human figured pots were not placed into the ground in large numbers there, unlike at the three other, predominantly funerary sites. The material is also divided into imported and indigenously produced wares, demonstrating the significant presence of the former at 3 of the 4 study sites. Imported wares are present at Poggio Civitate, and a single shard of Attic black-figure ware from the nearby settlement at Vescovado di Murlo shows a fragment of a human form (Tuck *et al* 2007), but there are no clear examples of human imagery on imported pottery from the site. The dominance of funerary contexts is also relatively unavoidable – a feature of Etruscan archaeology critiqued by Izzet (2007a: 16) and Damgaard-Andersen (1997:345) created by the specific history of excavations in the region. The conspicuous presence of ceramics in burial assemblages has provided much of the inspiration for interpretations of their use, both in life and in death. The next part of this chapter examines those interpretations, before directly considering the specific role of human-figured ceramics in funerary contexts.

4.4 Experiencing the Etruscan Banquet

The assumption that ceramic forms placed in Etruscan tombs reflect their use in life is central to this book. The experiences this study seeks to examine could have taken place in a variety of settings: a cup could have been used to sneak a sip at the end of a long day, at a family meal, or at a formal dining event. This latter instance has been considered the primary occasion at which elaborate pottery was used in Etruria (Small 1994a). Images of banqueting

Site	N Imported Pots (%)	N Indigenous Pots (%)	Total (%)	Deposition Context	Date Range
Chiusi	113 (9.7%)	112 (9.6%)	225 (19.32%)	Funerary	620–450 BCE
Poggio Civitate	0 (0%)	74 (6.35%)	74 (6.35%)	Domestic	650-550 BCE
Tarquini	229 (19.6%)	45 (3.9%)	274 (25.5%)	Funerary	570-440 BCE
Vulci	533 (45.7%)	58 (4.9%)	591 (50.6%)	Funerary	625–440 BCE

TABLE 4.2: PRODUCTION ORIGIN, DEPOSITION CONTEXT AND DATE RANGE FOR ALL POTTERY BY SITE.

FIGURE 4.2: TOMB OF THE LEOPARDS, TARQUINIA
IMAGE (C) SOPRINTENDENZA PER I BENI CULTURALI ARCHEOLOGICI ETRURIA MERIDIONALE.

FIGURE 4.3: ETRUSCAN POTTERY IN USE 2.
ARCHITECTURAL TERRACOTTA PLAQUE FROM POGGIO CIVITATE. IMAGE BY THE AUTHOR.

abound in funerary contexts, and the behavioural etiquette of such events appears to be relatively static. The Greek symposium has been repeatedly used as a comparison for drinking events in Etruria (Cristofani:1987: 126; Sassatelli 1999: 110; Small 1994a). There are certainly similarities between the two kinds of events, particularly in the underlying aims of banquets as an occasion for conspicuous consumption. Both are occasions at which ceramics were used in the communal sharing of drink, and both were hemmed about with specific attitudes and codes for behaviour. Ridgway (1997) interprets the Etruscan banquet as part of a pan-Mediterranean phenomenon in which formal alcohol consumption is a central part of elite identity. In the same fashion, Dietler (1995) and Murray

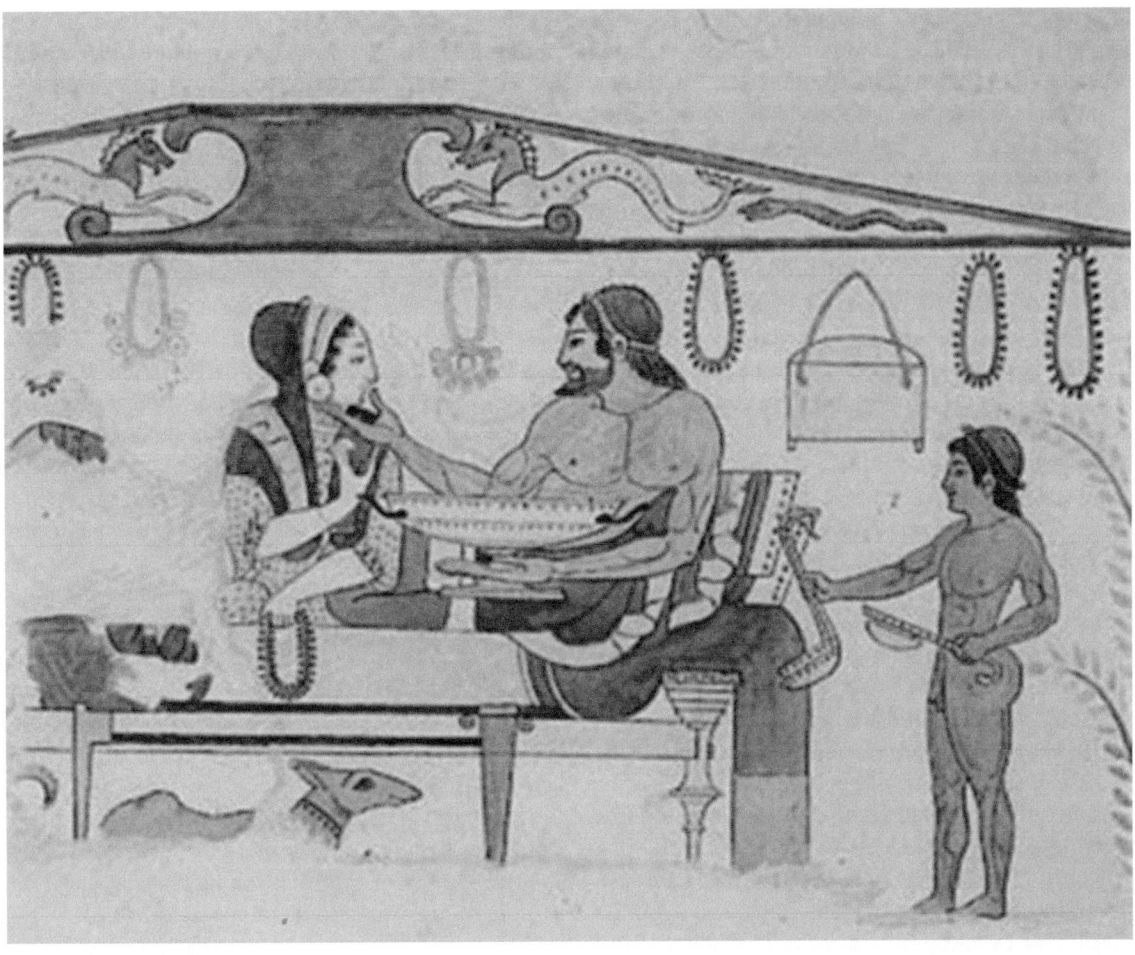

Figure 4.4: Diners from the Tomba dei Vasi Dipinti Adapted from a damaged tomb painting, Tarquinia. Image (c) Soprintendenza per i Beni Culturali Archeologici Etruria Meridionale

(1995) emphasise the importance of feasting and drinking events in central Europe and the south of France, in both cases arguing that hosting and attending such banquets was a central aspect of elite identity. The numerous examples of iconography showing formal consumption events from Etruscan contexts (catalogued as 106 by De Marinis (1961)) provide a corpus of information as to how such events were experienced, or at least, how that experience was represented.

Textual sources, too, provide an idea of how this kind of occasion may have been experienced and organised in Etruria. One particular example, produced from an etic position by a writer from the Eastern Mediterranean, is emblematic of other texts which consider Etruscan society in that it is preoccupied with a desire to construct an image of Etruscan practices which are resolutely and definitively different from the world inhabited by the writer. The goal of such texts, when seen through a post-colonial lens, is not the accurate depiction of the Etruscan banquet, but rather the creation of the Etruscan as Other (Said 1978). In this case, the author, Theopompus of Chios, was writing a century after the end of the Archaic period, in the 4th century BC, when Etruscan communities were once again flourishing after a slump in the late 5th century. He observes one particular difference in Etruscan and Greek drinking practices, based on the gender of the attendants:

'Further, they [Etruscan women] dine, not only with their own husbands, but with any men who happen to be present, and they pledge with wine any whom they wish...they are also terribly bibulous, and are very good looking.' [13]

While the depiction of respectable married women drinking and interacting with strange men may be conveniently alien to a Greek reader, archaeological evidence suggests that some truth may lie beneath the spin. Imagery from both funerary contexts (as shown in Figure 4.2, a scene from the Tomb of the Leopards, Tarquinia) and non-funerary scenes (as shown in Figure 4.3, depicting part of the architectural terracotta frieze from Murlo) certainly confirms the fact that women were present at Etruscan feasting and drinking events. However, Geissler (2012: 268) notes that in no image from Archaic Etruria is there a hint of erotic suggestion, which appears to confirm the hostile

---
[13] Theopompus of Chios, Deipnosopistae. Trans. C. Burton Gulick. 1927. London, LCL

nature of such descriptions. Men and women reclined together on shared couches, although single-sex couches are also displayed. For example, the diners in the Tomb of the Leopards appear to present three couches, occupied by two mixed-sex pairings, and one single-sex masculine pair. These couches are covered with bright cushions, and display carved feet, akin to those represented in funerary stonework in tombs from across the region.

The couples themselves recline in a variety of positions: the famous Sarcophagus of the Married Couple from Cerveteri presents the male diner reclining on his side behind his female companion – resting his hand upon her shoulder. The diners in the Tomb of the Leopards are spaced slightly further apart, but the men remain posterior to the women, while in the Tomb of the Lionesses solely male diners recline leaning on their backs, with bellies up. At Murlo, both male and female diners recline together, although their posture appears slightly more upright than that depicted elsewhere. Regardless of the position of the rest of the body, all are depicted propped up upon one elbow, in what appears to be a standard pose. The impact of this restricted position, and the necessity of sharing a limited couch space with a fellow diner, on the experience of using Etruscan ceramics, must have been extreme. To be able to lift a vessel to the mouth with only one arm requires an additional level of knowledge – particularly when such a vessel is full. The consequences of spillage are also elevated – not only by an individual drinkers' elaborate clothing, but also by the presence of a companion, who will also be affected by a slip or jog. Sharing a couch also provides an opportunity for increased risk – stretching or moving at an inopportune moment may seriously have inconvenienced other diners in the vicinity, while physical closeness and increasing intoxication is a recipe for either intimacy or embarassment or both.

Regardless of the gender of the diner, all those attending Etruscan banquets are depicted in sumptuous clothing, elaborately dressed. Both men and women appear decked out from head to toe: both are regularly represented as crowned with leaf garlands, and women may be shown wearing jewellery: a female diner in the Golini Tomb from Orvieto wears a thick gold necklace, while a woman from the Tomba dei Vasi Dipinti wears what look like uncomfortably large earrings (Figure 4.4). Men and women are shown wearing brightly coloured clothing, with different coloured edgings decorating the hems. Rich reds and greens are shown, with stripes and patterns included in the design of each garment. The process of preparation for attending a banquet must have taken a relatively long amount of time – the readying of clothes, the schooling of hair into particular positions, the donning of jewellery and potentially make up. This elaborate act of self creation prepares an idealised body for display, akin to that observed by Treherne (1995) in the context of warfare.

Such preparations must be considered as an integral part of the banquet, the readying of the body for the onslaught of food and alcohol to come. The richness of apparel also lends a further level of concern to the diner – spillage will not only offend the person with whom one shares a couch, but can also damage both one's own and their clothing, in some cases permanently. The removal of red wine stains from white linen is not an appealing activity.

While the preparation of the body for a banqueting event may be conceived of as relatively similar to that undertaken by a different set of participants in Greece, the substances consumed in Etruria appear to be different. The symposion is an event which is specifically for the consumption of wine – and not for the eating of foods, a fact underlined in the very meaning of the term, developed from the verb sympinein 'to drink together.' Drinking and sociability are at the core of the symposion, while at Etruscan banquets food does appear to have been served alongside wine. The representation of food in funerary art, including the carving of food items in the hands of later funerary represensations of the deceased, suggest that eating and drinking went together in Etruria. Eating vessels and platters in funerary assemblages, then, should be seen as part of a banqueting kit, rather than as objects associated with a different consumption event. The combination of food and drink, in addition to the presence of women and the elaborate preparations before drinking, suggest that the Etruscan banquet would have had perhaps a relaxed, familiar feel, with a variety of activities taking place at once, rather than a sole focus on drinking and being drunk.

There is further archaeological evidence to differentiate the Etruscan banquet from the Greek symposion. Ambrosini's (2013) catalogue of metal dining equipment, focused upon thymiateria (incense burners), candelabra (candlesticks) and kottaboi (stands used during the Greek drinking game of kottabos), found a lesser number of the latter in Etruscan funerary contexts. She also notes that such stands are absent from the Etruscan iconographic record, perhaps suggesting that where such items were being used, they were recent arrivals, and not part of a long-standing tradition represented in imagery. The dating of such finds supports this interpretation – the vast majority are found in tombs which date from the late 6th century BC onwards. The implication of this lack of kottaboi is that drinking games such as kottabos were rarely played at Etruscan banquets. It is tempting to speculate that the kinds of behaviour associated with kottabos in Greece (the flinging of wine dregs) were not considered appropriate in the context of the Etruscan banquet.

While kottabos may not have been a popular form of entertainment at the Etruscan banquet, the playing of music is far more regularly represented. The most famous example of this is the continued scene in the Tomb of the Leopards, in which two musicians caper, playing the double flutes, or aulos, and a lyre respectively. Other examples are known from funerary urns from Chiusi, with a range of instruments played to accompany an event (Tobin 2013). In addition to musicians, young male servants are repeatedly shown as attendants at Etruscan banquets as

FIGURE 4.5: CRATER, TOMB OF THE LIONESSES, TARQUINIA
IMAGE (C) SOPRINTENDENZA PER I BENI CULTURALI ARCHEOLOGICI ETRURIA MERIDIONALE

represented in tomb paintings. In contrast to the elaborately dressed diners, these attendants are shown naked, and are depicted as smaller than their employers. However, they may wear similar head garlands to the diners themselves, made from leaves and perhaps indicating their centrality to the ritual. These servants are often shown carrying jugs or small serving vessels, and seem to be depicted in the act of moving between couches, carrying fluid to the diners. In the Tomba dei Vasi Dipinti one of these attendants carries two ladles, suggesting that he is transporting alcohol from a larger serving vessel which is out of sight.

There are also representations of these large serving vessels, some of which appear as having been feted and decorated. For example, in the Tomb of the Lionesses (Figure 4.5), two musicians approach a huge crater, which itself is decorated with garlands. The question of whether such enormous vessels were being used for mixing wine with water, as they were in Greece, remains confused. It seems likely that had Etruscans not regularly mixed their wine, this would have been pounced upon by classical authors as further evidence of their relationship to the barbarous groups outside Hellas who drank their wine neat. Descriptions of drunken Scythian and Thracian misbehaviour are described by Herodotus [14] and by Plato,[15] and are presented as a direct result of failing to temper wine with water. In addition to serving vessels, drinking cups are also widely represented in funerary images of banqueting. They are presented in a specific fashion, as carried by diners – held balanced atop one hand, with fingers around the stem, balancing the bowl of the vessel on the palm. If this position was the standard method for using particularly wide-bowled drinking vessels such as kylikes, the angles to maintain a reclined pose on one elbow, balance a heavy vessel, avoid jogging a partner and transfer fluid into ones mouth are strikingly difficult. If images represent an idealised vision of vessel handling, the pressures to maintain these visibly uncomfortable poses with an air of studied ease and elegance must have been extreme. The combined impact of the formalised and intimate environment of the Etruscan banquet and the physical discomfort visible in the use of ceramics as shown in imagery on the experience of using such pottery must have resulted in social gatherings replete with opportunities both to demonstrate skill, and shamefully show off its opposite.

4.5 From Table to Tomb

While the focus of the book is the use of Etruscan pottery prior to deposition, 93% of the data-set originates from funerary contexts. The majority of these examples, excavated prior to the establishment of rigorous recording systems, do not possess a provenance more detailed than a notation of the site from which they came. Occasional examples provide a reference to a particular necropolis, but without any suggestion of a link to a single tomb. These pots are without direct context: the other objects which accompanied them into the grave are absent. While

[14] Histories: 6.84
[15] Laws 637

my interest lies in the use and experience of pots in life, the fact of their survival relies on their use in death. The composition of tomb assemblages including ceramics provides an idea of the frequency of human-figure decorated vessels in circulation in Etruria in comparison to other forms of ceramic decoration. Examining complete tomb assemblages also provides a context for the presence of imported vessels in Etruscan hands, as compared to indigenously produced examples. While collection biases, as discussed above, priveleged imported ceramics and destroyed indigenous examples, later excavations can give a sense of the wider composition of grave contents, and the place of imported ceramics in relation to other Etruscan pottery. I will use the specific assemblages, tomb features and ceramic composition of a group of 60 burials from Vulci to provide a comparative context for the largely decontextualised dataset.

The tombs used in this contextualising analysis are from two different necropoleis at Vulci, excavated at different times, but published in full. The first group of 22 tombs, incorporating 35 assemblages, was excavated under the Frenchman Stephane Gsell during the late nineteenth century. These tombs were were located in the Ponte della Badia necropolis, and have been dated somewhat loosely to the Archaic period. Although excavated in the 1890s, all finds from the tombs are recorded, including plainware pottery, and published by Gsell (1894). The second group is from the famous Osteria necropolis, the largest burial ground at Vulci, and are made up of burials from two different publications. The majority of these are those excavated by the Hercle association during the early 1960s, and published comprehensively in 1968 (Hercle 1968), and form a group of 28 tombs, incorporating 33 assemblages. The second collection of tombs from the Osteria necropolis were excavated during the early twentieth century by Mengarelli (Amorelli 1987), and their original contents reassembled by Riccioni (2003), forming a further 10 burials. The total number of tombs analysed is 60, while the number of individual burials, incorporating material from multiple chambers, is 78.

The majority of the burials themselves are inhumations in rock-cut tombs, voids hollowed out from the soft tufaceous rock of the plateaux surrounding the city of Vulci. They are formed primarily of short dromoi entrances, sloping down towards a central square chamber, covered in earth. The physical remains of the deceased from these cemeteries have not been anthropologically analysed, and in some cases are lost or missing. However, as in the majority of Etruscan tombs, the dead would have been laid out on rock carved benches, along the edges and back of the tomb. The bottom of these benches may be carved to resemble a banqueting couch or bed, while pillows and cushions are also carved in stone, organic versions of which may have been placed beneath the body (Steingräber 1995: 56). The presence of two burials in single tombs, alongside burials of more individuals, demonstrates that these graves were places which had to be re-opened and visited, and as such the burial goods would have been visible at each visit before the tomb was sealed. It is highly likely that individuals buried together were related, and DNA analysis has proved this at Tarquinia (Cappellini et al 2004), although not yet at Vulci. Additional chambers are added to certain tombs in this assemblage, such as Gsell's tomb 12, in which four chambers were placed around a single shared dromos entryway, perhaps representing an extended family group over generations. The majority of tombs in the assemblage, however, are single chamber burials for one or two individuals, with a set of ceramics which reflects their size.

The insides of the tombs themselves were undecorated, aside from carvings of roof beams (see Colonna 1986: 395-6), with no sign of the elaborate tomb paintings known at Tarquinia. Into this space were placed groups of pots, some imported from Greece, some made in Etruria, some plain, some geometrically and some figuratively decorated. Disturbances and thefts have made the original placement of pots in the tomb difficult to ascertain, with examples accompanying the corpse on benches and placed on the floor of the tomb, as well as on carved tables (cf. Steingraber 1995: 56). The position of ceramics in tombs, alongside the representation of the deceased as diner, has prompted interpretations of tombs as banqueting chambers for the dead (Pieraccini 2000; Tuck 1994). If such interpretations are accurate, vessels appropriate for use in dining contexts in life could have been placed in funerary contexts in similar proportions to their number in tombs. If this was the case, the visibility and context of human-figured vessels in active use can be reconstructed from in situ excavations of ceramic assemblages such as those of Gsell, Hercle and Riccioni. The total number of pots from all three groups is 1267, of which 390 are from Gsell's excavations, 773 from the work of the Hercle association, and 104 from Riccioni's volume. This is a large sample which demonstrates the position of human figured ceramics in context alongside plain and geometrically decorated pots in tomb contexts.

The 1267 ceramics were divided into groups based on whether a pot was figuratively or non-figuratively decorated. Any representation of any recognisable being was counted as a figurative decoration. Non-figurative designs were composed of geometric shapes. Figure 4.6 A shows the distribution of figuratively decorated pottery across the 78 tombs. Over 50% of the tomb assemblages presented no figuratively decorated pottery at all. The rarity of figurative pottery compared to non-figurative pottery is emphasised further in Figure 4.6 B. Only 83 examples displayed figurative images, of which only 26 showed humans. This demonstrates that human figured pottery is the rarest form of decorated pottery in circulation in this group of tomb assemblages, dwarfed by non-figuratively decorated ceramics. If these conclusions can be extended across Etruria, it can be assumed that the human-decorated pots which makes up the datA –set are examples of an

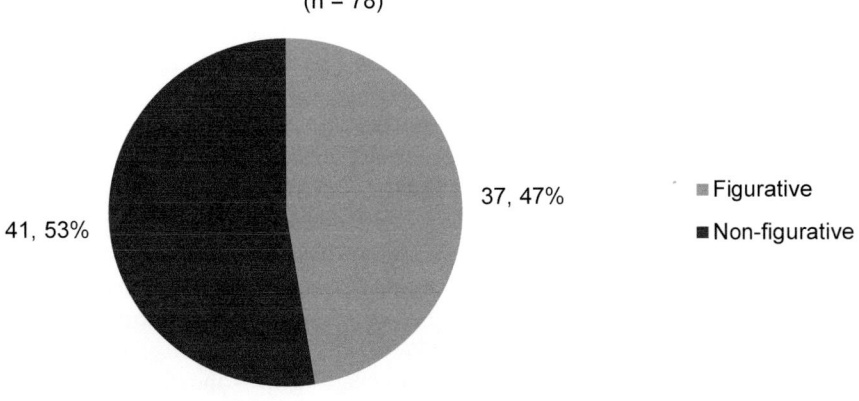
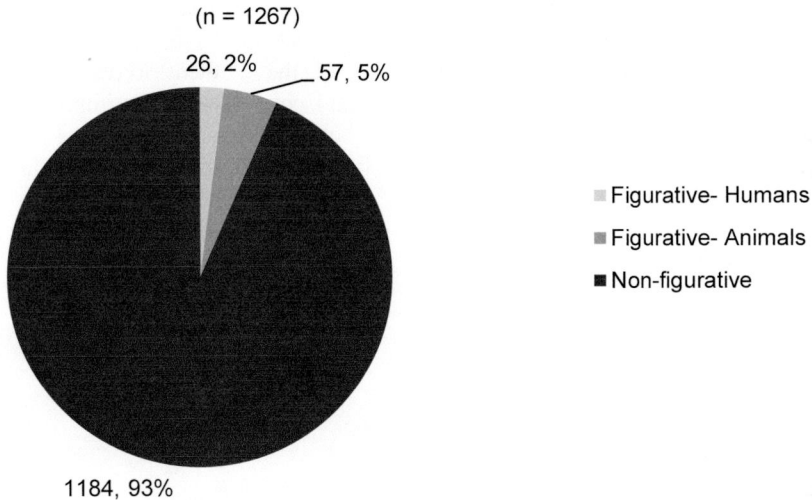
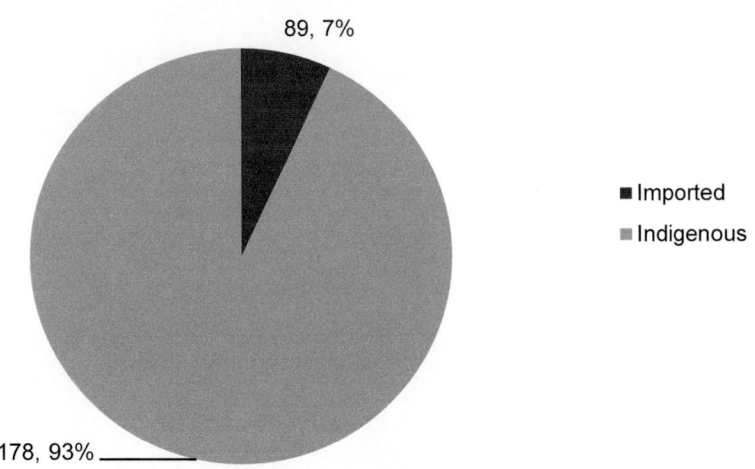

FIGURE 4.6: FUNERARY CERAMICS FROM VULCI
A – PRESENCE OF FIGURATIVE CERAMICS IN VOLCEIAN TOMBS. B – DECORATION TYPES ON VOLCEIAN FUNERARY CERAMICS.
C – PRODUCTION ORIGINS OF FUNERARY CERAMICS FROM VULCI.

uncommon type of vessel, restricted in distribution to particular individuals. In terms of the balance between indigenous and imported ceramics, Figure 4.6 C shows the relative scarcity of imported wares in Volceian tombs. Imported ceramics form only a small proportion of the overall pottery being placed in Etruscan tombs and can be assumed to form a similarly low proportion of ceramics being encountered, used and experienced by Etruscans before death.

4.6 An Experiential Analysis

The first step towards the quantification of experience in measurable parameters is this division of experience into the levels which shape an encounter. Each of these layers forms a chapter of the following analysis, and each provides a slightly different answer to the question of Etruscan ceramic experience. These layers of experience cannot be conceived of as ranked in any way, or as occurring in a series: in practice, they are so entangled that the order in which they happen, and the relative importance of each to the overall experience is almost impossible to tease out. The first aspect of experiencing a vessel which I examine in this book is the direct, physical encounter between hands, mouth and pot. The form of a vessel shapes the initial interaction between user and vessel, demanding the placement of fingers in specific positions, and the development of a relationship between mouth and vessel rim.

Figure 4.7 presents two pairs of images which demonstrate the specificity of physical experience as dictated by modern object forms – on the left, the vessels out of use, and on the right, while in the hands of a human subject (in this case myself). In A, the square-shaped handle of this glass drinking vessel provokes a particular grip – the placement of all four fingers into the handle and the formation of a fist. The rim diameter is small, so the transfer of liquid from glass to mouth is easily accomplished, but there was slight discomfort as the top rim pressed onto the nose. In B, the stem of the vessel provoked an entirely different grip – the fingers were splayed around the body of the vessel, with the fourth and fifth fingers balancing the vessel stem. A wider rim diameter ensured no discomfort while drinking, but was still small enough to control the liquid flow into the mouth.

The experience of using both these vessels was created by their shapes, but it was not essential to actually use them to estimate how the experience would be. The physical impression of vessel form can be measured with the eye as well as with the mouth and hands, but the instinctive calculations made to produce a prediction of how one's body will interact with an object are opaque.

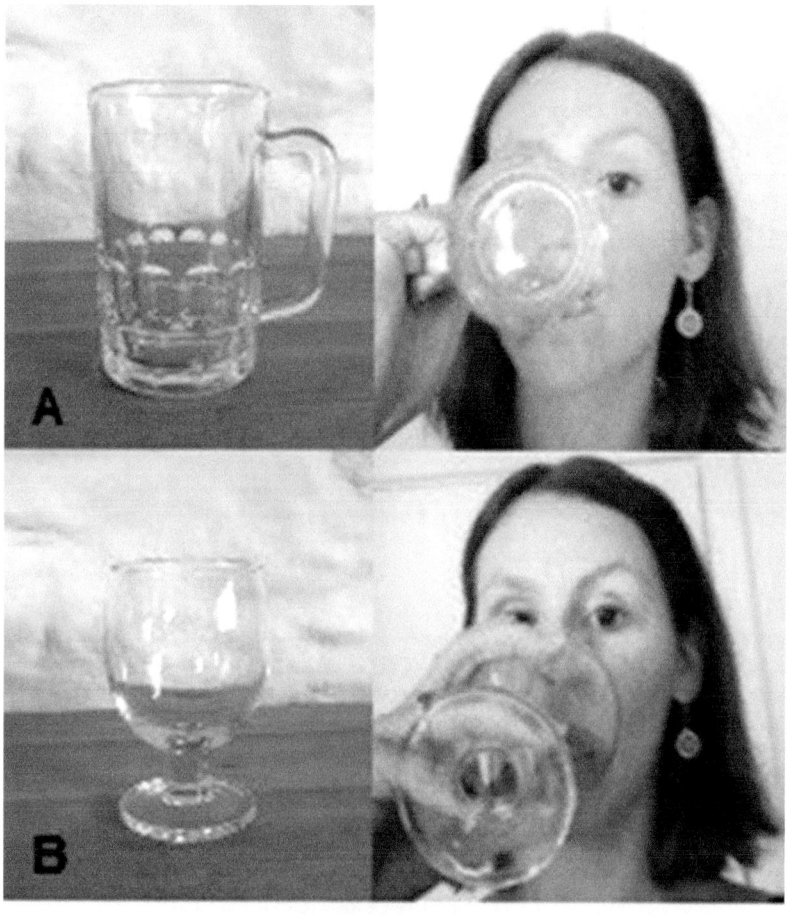

FIGURE 4.7: SHAPING THE BODY THROUGH TWO GLASS VESSELS
IMAGE BY THE AUTHOR.

Through experimenting with a range of modern vessels, as shown in Figure 4.7, and manipulating a combination of replica and original Etruscan vessels during fieldwork at the site of Poggio Civitate, I developed a series of vessel characteristics which appeared to be colouring my experience of using a vessel. These fell into two groups:

> Primary characteristics: Vessel height, rim diameter, volume, handle form.

> Secondary characteristics: Rim diameter: height ratio, rim diameter: average human hand length ratio.

These characteristics were directly measurable, could be compared across the data-set and could be estimated from the most basic recorded details of any vessel: rim diameter and height. They were also the characteristics that I perceived as most strongly influencing my physical interaction with the vessel. Each one had a distinct impact on my own ceramic use experience, which is best recorded through thick description (Geertz 1973).

Height – The height of a vessel instantly transformed how I approached the container. A tall vessel demands that the drinker work out the right angle from which to access its contents – and this angle changes all the time as the fluid diminishes. When I commenced drinking, only the slightest tip of a vessel was necessary with my hands, and the glass or pot could be held around the rim, controlling the discharge of liquid into the mouth. As I continued to drink, my hand or hands slid down the vessel, increasing the angle between my mouth and the container, moving from the initial perpendicular angle between mouth and vessel to one that is obtuse, well over 180 degrees. To access the final dregs, a tall vessel needed to be tipped almost upside down on top of my mouth – a completely distinct experience never necessitated by a short glass or cup. When pouring, I needed to hold the vessel at both ends, balancing with both hands – one on the top of the vessel and one at the bottom.

Rim diameter – While height primarily changed the angle at which I held a vessel in relation to my mouth, rim diameter had more of an effect on the position of my hands. The wider a vessel, the more likely it was that I used two hands to hold it, and to balance it to avoid spilling any of the contents. Even when I continued to use one hand, my fingers were splayed out, stretched to keep hold of the vessel. A narrow vessel, by contrast, could be held almost between finger and thumb, or by all five digits wrapped around its outside. When the rim diameter was much larger than my mouth, I also had to be extremely careful when drinking – it was safer to move my mouth and to sip, sucking up the liquid without moving the vessel to avoid spilling any. Tipping the vessel was a risky business – the contents could seep out at the corners of my mouth and ooze across my chin if I tipped the vessel too quickly or at an extreme angle so that the fluid rushed out. In addition, a specific size rim diameter would prevent my tipping the vessel at all – squashing my nose uncomfortably and forcing me to try and position the vessel at a greater distance to my face – a distinct and unpleasant user experience. A vessel with a very small rim diameter allowed me to place the rim inside my lips – creating a new series of issues as air locks developed inside the container, causing me to cough and splutter and put the drink down if I attempted longer, sustained draughts. When pouring, similar problems arose – I needed to hold the vessel a greater distance from its intended target, to allow the liquid to develop a narrow flow – and the initial tipping of the vessel was filled with trepidation. The presence of a lip substantially solved this problem, creating a false impression of a reduced rim diameter, restricting the flow of fluid.

Volume – The volume of a vessel was a deeply influential factor in my experience of using it. If the vessel was very full, I was forced to be careful in how I balanced it in the hand – a slightest wobble and the contents would spill over the sides. It was also far heavier – a full vessel weighed a great deal more than one that was almost empty, and while in the case of the smaller vessels this did not matter, holding a large, full vessel (such as a 3l bottle) became uncomfortable fairly rapidly, resulting in shaking in the arms and aching wrists. The volume of a vessel also, crucially, dictates how long it takes to empty – a very small container could be drained in seconds, while a larger vessel, even with sustained consumption, took far longer to consume. This had a distinct effect on pouring as well as drinking – I had to hold such uncomfortable vessels for far longer to pour out their contents into smaller vessels, moving the pouring vessel around in my hands, shifting their position constantly to distribute the load.

Handle form – The presence, absence and form of handles was a highly influential factor in my use of a vessel. While the presence of handles does not dictate that one uses them, I usually attempted to – when I did not it was often difficult to use the vessel without encountering and interacting with the handles in some form. Vessels without handles were the easiest to use – I could put my hands wherever I chose without the handle getting in the way. Where handles were present, their size and shape deeply impacted on my experience – small handles squashed my fingers together uncomfortably, while awkward angles also created pressure points on the hand. Vertical handles allowed me to thread my hand through the hole, taking the weight of the vessel on my fist, while horizontal handles made me grasp the handle itself, using it to lever and steer the vessel in a more precarious manner. A single handle made for easier pouring, while double handles were distinctly difficult – I had to hold the vessel on each side and pour it away from me – there was no flexibility in usage.

Rim diameter: height ratio – The relationship between rim diameter and height exacerbated or reduced the issues created by each of these individual features. If both were extreme, the experience of using the vessel became significantly different – a vessel that was both tall and wide was almost impossible for me to use for either drinking or pouring without spilling the contents everywhere. By contrast, a short narrow vessel was very easy to use, almost thoughtlessly, but was restricted in the amount of fluid that it could contain, meaning irritating and continual refills to consume the same amount of liquid.

Rim diameter: average human hand length ratio – I suspected that this relationship lay at the heart of my problems with extreme rim diameters. In addition to demanding a particular level of attention, and dictating whether I held a vessel with one hand or two, the relationship between rim diameter and the size of my hands largely structured how much control I had over the vessel itself. When my hands were spread out and working hard to keep control of the vessel, a large area of it would not be controlled by me to a confidence-inducing level. The larger the disparity between the diameter of the vessel and the length of my hands, the more uncomfortable I felt using it, both in terms of physical discomfort and in terms of my apprehension about spilling its contents and making a mess.

To be able to access these different variables which I had identified through my own experience and experimentation, I needed to gain this information from the published sources of vessels from which I had gathered together the corpus of ceramics. Relying on published material only forced me into a situation in which I was reliant on the measurements of others for my own analysis. The two primary measurements which I required were rim diameter and vessel height – information that was regularly provided in the published information about each vessel. The authors of the majority of the catalogues from which I extracted my dataset had performed these measurements themselves, or supervised their production by others. Many of the earlier publications used imperial measurements, which I converted back to metric myself. The online databases, those of the British Museum and the Poggio Civitate Excavation Archive, were more problematic. There was no record of the individual curator or staff member who had done the measuring – and, indeed, many of the British Museum records were inconsistent in the information they provided, with some vessels providing metric and others imperial measurements, and still others missing one or both of these crucial pieces of information. This variation in authors, while unavoidable, may have resulted in variation in the recording of vessel heights and rim diameters affecting the accuracy of the data collected. Similarly, while the definition of different vessel shapes is largely dictated by the categories established during the early 20th century and catalogued by Richter and Milne (1935), this is not always explicit and could also be subject to variation between authors.

A further issue arose regarding the estimation of volume. While I had planned to use the formula for calculating the volume of a cylinder (Volume= $\pi r2 h$), it was clear that many of these vessels, particularly drinking vessels, were absolutely not straightforward cylinders. To partially resolve this, the result produced by the basic formula would have to be scaled down based on the proportions of the actual vessel bowl. Using photographs and drawings where available, and reliant on the proportions of similar vessel classes where they were not, I scaled down the volume produced by the formula using this method. While entirely imperfect, this method allowed me to access at least an estimated idea of volume. As all vessels were subjected to the same process, they could still be compared against one another, with each group of measurements affected by the flaws of this process to the same degree. By retaining the broad groups of different vessel forms based on their relationship to the body, the imperfect estimation of volume would be minimised as much as possible. The creation of scatter graphs of the exact figures would have been impacted more severely by the problems caused by this inaccurate method of volume estimation, potentially resulting in mismatches between different vessel types that were wildly different from one another in terms of form but misrepresented by inaccurate calculations.

While this primary layer of experience was perhaps the most complex to unpick, and the most reliant on recorded information over which I had little control, the next layer of experience, analysed in Chapter 6, was a clearer and simpler phenomenon to explore. This part of the analysis bridges the gap between the form and decoration of vessels, and is the first chapter to relate to the images on vessel surfaces, being focused on the impact of image production techniques on the user of a pot. While the physical form of a pot may have a more obvious impact on the user, pottery decoration similarly structures the exchange between the two. The first part of this experience is dictated by the placement of decoration, which controls the concealment or revelation of images to the user. The second is the way in which decoration interacts with the human body. An picture which can be felt, in the form of a tactile decoration involving moulding or stamping is a different experience to a painted image which can only be seen. For both these aspects of the experience of vessel images, typologies are developed which differentiate between different encounters for the user, allowing for the categorisation of ceramic decoration by impact.

The third layer of experience is also focused on the images used to decorate ceramic vessels, but is focused on the subject of the image. The two previous phases of experiential analysis could be undertaken on any decorated vessel, but this third layer of experience is focused on the representation of human figures in ceramic decoration. The user experiences the human subjects of images on the surface in a visual way, but also may make direct contact with them using the hand or mouth. The contents of a vessel may also come to be associated with the images which contain and contextualise them. In both cases, there is a mental response to the images, involving identification of and potentially with the individuals and scenarios shown. It is along these lines of response that this form of experience is divided for analysis: between the bodies displayed on pottery, and the activities they are undertaking. The former analysis, developing a typology for bodies based on their physical characteristics including species, gender and age, is presented in Chapter 7. A second typology of activities is considered in Chapter 8. Together, these chapters provide a methodology which considers the contribution of imagery to experience through two levels of representational analysis. The relationship of these specific variables to the overarching limiting variables is presented in Table 4.3, which forms a guide to the structure of the analysis as it moves through the different layers of experiencing Etruscan pottery. In the next chapter, the analysis begins with the first layer of experience, that created between the body of a pot and the body of a user.

Variable Type	Application	Variable
Limiting	All Analyses	Presence of human images
Limiting	All Analyses	Publication availability
General	All Analyses	Provenance (site of origin)
General	All Analyses	Production Origin (site of manufacture)
General	All Analyses	Body Proximity Group (experiential function)
Specific	Chapter 5 (Vessel bodies)	Vessel height, rim diameter, volume, handle type, rim: height ratio, rim: hand ratio
Specific	Chapter 6 (Images on vessel bodies)	Position of images, composition of images
Specific	Chapter 7 (Bodies in images on vessels)	Type of body, gender of body, position of body
Specific	Chapter 8 (Actions of bodies in images on vessels)	Actions of bodies, number of actions of bodies.

TABLE 4.3: VARIABLES OF EXPERIENTIAL ANALYSIS

Chapter 5

Touching and Feeling: Vessel Bodies

5.1 Introduction

This chapter unpicks the first layer of the experience of using an Etruscan pot, and examines the relationship between the body of the user and its clay extension. The sliding scale of incorporation developed to categorise different pottery activities is used as the primary method to interrogate the accompanying characteristics and attributes of ceramics which influence the experience of using them. These attributes fall into two separate groups:

1. Simple characteristics which are formed from a single measurement relating to the vessel. These include vessel height, diameter and volume, in addition to the shape and form of handles. All these primary characteristics have a direct impact on the experience of the user, but are assessed separately.
2. Composite characteristics are devolved from a combination of primary characteristics, or the relating of these to an additional parameter, or external measurement. These include rim:vessel height ratio and rim:hand length ratio.

There is also a final, composite assessment of what the combination of primary and secondary attributes meant for the whole-body experience of the user.

Each of these specific vessel characteristics is then related to the three general variables (provenance, production origin, and body proximity group), as described in the previous chapter. Having completed the analysis, it is clear that the physical experience embodied and encoded in these vessel characteristics was strategically and deliberately formed, and may be directly related to the production origin of individual pots. The ceramic record provides evidence for a significant change in the experience of the Etruscan user of pottery associated with the arrival of imported pottery – a change which is enacted on and through every part of both bodies involved: that of the person, and that of the pot. Before presenting the data which supports this claim, the process through which it was produced is presented.

The first action was to divide the pottery by the categories established in Chapter 4, based on the sliding scale of incorporation into the body. This was done by utilising traditional terminology to establish the action accompanying the use of a vessel, and then placing it within a particular class. This resulted in two distinct groups of pots: those used to present their contents directly onto the surface of the body, and those used to transport substances to other pots, which nonetheless will be later applied into or onto the body of a user, or group of users. These vessel categories were then divided further, with the titles of their primary actions forming their nomenclature.

The closest group of vessels to the body are those used primarily for drinking, bringing fluid directly into the mouth. The next group of vessels are those used for perfume, which, while it was rubbed into the skin through the intervention of the hands, are still closely bound up with direct application. Similarly, vessels used for eating, while foodstuffs are mediated through a utensil (which could be food itself, for example the use of flatbreads to scoop up soft foods) or the user's hand, before entering into the body. The second category of vessels is divided in two, once more based on the methods used to bring their contents to the body. Vessels used for pouring spill their contents directly into pots which will then be used to carry liquids into the body, while those used for serving will either be dipped into with direct consumption vessels, or plumbed using utensils such as ladles or spoons. Direct pouring is also possible from serving vessels, but the lack of a distinct lip would have made this process more problematic.

Having established these categories for analysis, the next method of analysis was the acquisition of primary data about the six characteristics of each vessel, each of which directly impact on the experience of the user. The first of these was height. The height of a vessel determines interaction – the position of the hands, the movement of the vessel in space. Tall vessels must be lifted and manipulated in a very specific way, with both the upper and lower parts of a vessel supported to be sure of secure handling. Height was divided into five categories, from very small to very large, as presented in Table 5.1. This height measurement was taken as the distance between base and rim, with large extending handles, as seen in the case of kyathoi and kantharoi, noted separately in the handle-specific analysis.

Category	Height (mm)
Very Small	<100mm
Small	>100mm <150mm
Medium	>150mm <250mm
Large	>250mm <350mm
Very Large	>350mm

TABLE 5.1: CATEGORIES OF VESSEL HEIGHT

The second primary characteristic was vessel diameter. The experience of removing the contents of a pot is intensely linked to diameter. A large rim diameter will make the process of pouring more difficult for the user, demanding close attention to avoid spillage of a wave of contents, while a small diameter will produce a more concentrated flow. In direct contact with the body, a small diameter forces a pursing of the lips, in contrast to the wide open mouth necessitated by a large diameter. Both may result in fluid being poured into the mouth, rather than sipped with direct contact between the lips and the rim. As with height, vessel diameters were divided into five categories ranging from very small to very large, as presented in Table 5.2. To put these measurements into their geometrical context, the circumference of any vessel over 300mm is at least 942mm, far larger than any vessel regularly used in modern contexts.

Category	Rim Diameter (mm)
Very Small	<50mm
Small	>50mm <100mm
Medium	>100mm <200mm
Large	>200mm <300mm
Very Large	>300mm

TABLE 5.2: CATEGORIES OF VESSEL RIM DIAMETER

Having established vessel height and diameter, the next primary pot attribute to investigate is volume. It is all too easy to forget that pottery was used for transporting liquids, substances which formed the focus of their existence. The amount of fluid a vessel could carry was an integral part of the experience of the user: dictating the weight of the pot[16] and mediating the amount that a user could consume. The ceramics were divided by approximate volume, calculated from the radius and height of the bowl of each vessel, taking each vessel as roughly cylindrical and using published measurements.[17] Bowl-specific measurements for height were used, where available, for vessels with long stems. Bowl volumes for vessels with long stems without bowl height information were estimated from photographs or proportions of standard forms. These were then divided into five categories, presented in Table 5.3. This table also presents the modern equivalent size vessels which were used to define these categories. These sizes are deliberately generous, as they provide an idea of the scale of individual and group consumption in the modern world, and their size allows for flexibility in the calculation of vessel volumes, a necessity given the lack of information and difficulty calculating volume of specific vessel forms.

The final primary attribute assessed was the presence or absence of handles, and their form. While a pot can always be lifted by its body alone, different handle shapes promote different methods of interaction between the body of the user and the vessel. This analysis was only undertaken for the vessels which would be lifted directly to the mouth of the user, as these vessels had a particularly prominent role for handles, if present. The handles were grouped by their impact on the hand of the user, as determined by their shape, number and position. The first handle category was formed of pots with no handles at all, which had to be grasped around the body or stem (Group 1). The second group (Group 2A) was formed of vessels with a single handle in a vertical position, while the third (Group 2B) was made up of vessels with a pair of vertically placed handles. The final group (Group 3) were those with horizontal handles of any form. Handles would have had a significant effect on the user: the difference between wrapping the entirety of fingers and palm around a handle-less vessel is entirely different to the balancing motion required to lift a vessel with flat handles.

Category	Volume (ml)	Modern Equivalent Vessel
Very Small	<300ml	Beer bottle (330ml)
Small	>300ml <750ml	Wine bottle (750ml)
Medium	>750ml <3000ml	Large cider bottle (2500ml)
Large	>3000ml <5000ml	Double magnum of wine (3000ml)
Very Large	>5000ml	Commercial water dispenser (5000ml)

TABLE 5.3: CATEGORIES OF VESSEL VOLUME

The first composite characteristic was devised to interrogate the relationship between vessel height and rim diameter. The ratio of diameter:height was calculated, and expressed in percentage terms (i.e. rim diameter as a percentage of height). This was done to investigate the balance required to move each vessel around – where rim diameter is significantly larger than height, controlling the pot to avoid spillage becomes more challenging. By contrast, it is much more difficult to spill the contents of a very tall pot with a small rim diameter – even if tipped over, the liquid will ooze, rather than gush, out of its container. A comfortable ratio makes for easy, even thoughtless use of the vessel, while an extreme ratio will necessitate a very specific series of movements for successful use. As with the primary characteristics, the categories of rim diameter as a proportion of height were divided into five groups presented in Table 5.4.

Category	Rim Diameter as % of Height
Very Small	<50%
Small	>50% <100%
Medium	>100% <200%
Large	>200% <300%
Very Large	>300%

TABLE 5.4: CATEGORIES OF RIM DIAMETER:VESSEL HEIGHT RATIO

The second composite measurement also used rim diameter, but related it to a human parameter: that of the length of the average human hand. This was established

---

[16] Although vessel thickness will impact upon the overall weight of a pot, volume provides a close estimation of this figure.

[17] There are a range of computer programmes which can be used to calculate vessel capacity, but the majority required detailed inputs (i.e. vessel profile drawings) which were impractical for use with a large data set.

at 180mm, calculated from the mean of male (189mm) and female (172mm) average hand sizes, as recorded by Agnihotri et al (2008). In terms of the experience of the user, the hand is the primary measuring tool, and the central means of interaction with the body of the vessel – it is the hand that incorporates the pot into the body, sticking it to the skin through grip. Pottery with a rim diameter significantly larger than the length of a single hand could not be lifted with one hand, but required the employment of both to manage its associated larger circumference. Pots significantly larger than two hands would have necessitated an intricate balancing act, with very specific hand positioning. As with the analysis of rim diameter:height relationships, the ratio between rim diameter and human hand length (180mm) was expressed as a percentage. The results of individual pots were then divided into groups, once more ranging from very small to very large and presented in Table 5.5.

Category	Rim Diameter as % of Average Hand Length
Very Small	<50%
Small	>50% <100%
Medium	>100% <150%
Large	>150% <200%
Very Large	>200%

TABLE 5.5: CATEGORIES OF RIM DIAMETER: AVERAGE HUMAN HAND LENGTH

The final assessment of user experience in this chapter is entirely composite. A combination of three attributes assessed through the primary and secondary analyses are put together to produce an overall vision of the experience of using a vessel, through the lens of ease of use. At each phase of analysis, the ceramics were divided into groups based on their differences. At each point, the difference would have impacted on the user, making their experience more or less difficult. So, each phase was given a score, which would count towards an overall total number which represents an assessment of how difficult each vessel was to use. The first attribute to contribute to this final score was volume. As volume takes into account both height and weight, the use of a single figure avoided over-complicating the score-calculation process. The other two attributes were the secondary data describing vessel diameter/height and vessel diameter/human hand relationships. In the case of vessels which had been subjected to a handle analysis, this was also included. The calculation process is illustrated in Figure 5.1.

At each point in the analysis, the data from each of the pottery characteristics is presented first without any other accompanying information. Then, the data is divided by the groups which establish distance from the body, to explore links between pottery forms and attributes. The body-distance group data for the entire corpus is then split between those made in Etruria, and those made elsewhere, to examine whether production origin has a connection with the specific attribute's

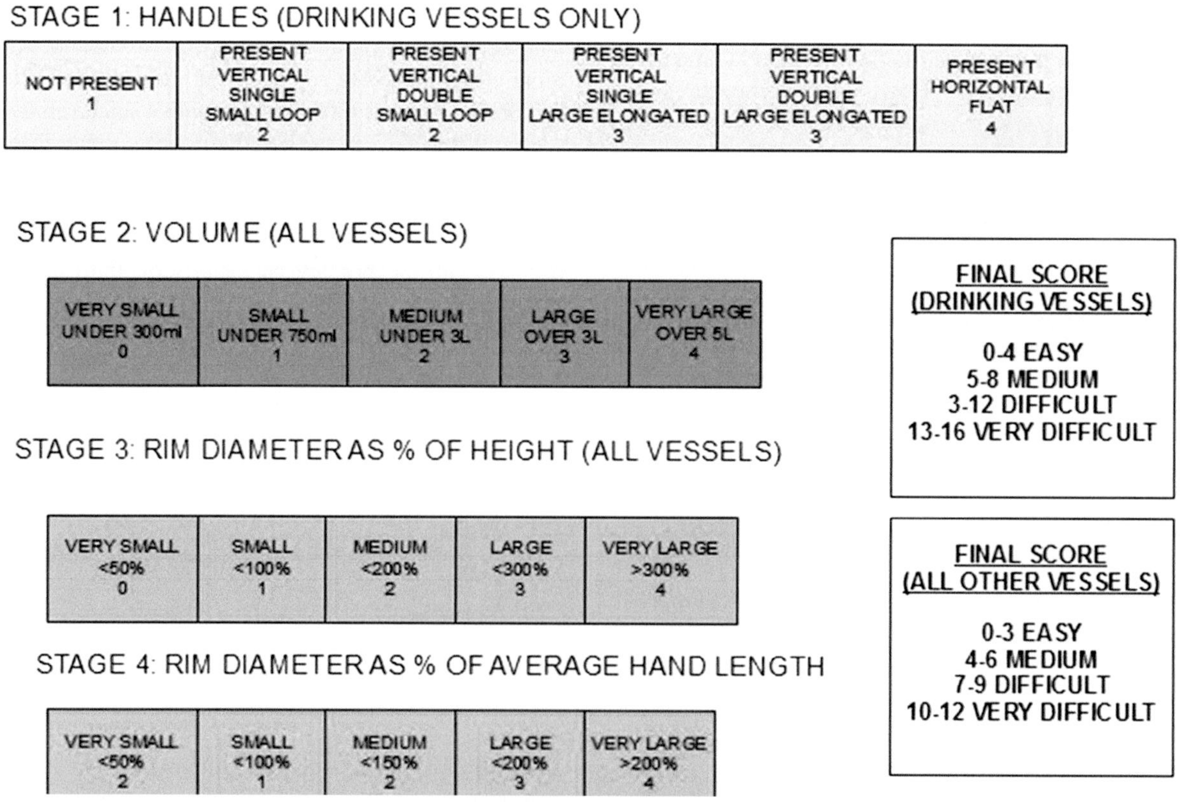

STAGE 1: HANDLES (DRINKING VESSELS ONLY)

| NOT PRESENT 1 | PRESENT VERTICAL SINGLE SMALL LOOP 2 | PRESENT VERTICAL DOUBLE SMALL LOOP 2 | PRESENT VERTICAL SINGLE LARGE ELONGATED 3 | PRESENT VERTICAL DOUBLE LARGE ELONGATED 3 | PRESENT HORIZONTAL FLAT 4 |

STAGE 2: VOLUME (ALL VESSELS)

| VERY SMALL UNDER 300ml 0 | SMALL UNDER 750ml 1 | MEDIUM UNDER 3L 2 | LARGE OVER 3L 3 | VERY LARGE OVER 5L 4 |

STAGE 3: RIM DIAMETER AS % OF HEIGHT (ALL VESSELS)

| VERY SMALL <50% 0 | SMALL <100% 1 | MEDIUM <200% 2 | LARGE <300% 3 | VERY LARGE >300% 4 |

STAGE 4: RIM DIAMETER AS % OF AVERAGE HAND LENGTH

| VERY SMALL <50% 2 | SMALL <100% 1 | MEDIUM <150% 2 | LARGE <200% 3 | VERY LARGE >200% 4 |

FINAL SCORE (DRINKING VESSELS)

0-4 EASY
5-8 MEDIUM
3-12 DIFFICULT
13-16 VERY DIFFICULT

FINAL SCORE (ALL OTHER VESSELS)

0-3 EASY
4-6 MEDIUM
7-9 DIFFICULT
10-12 VERY DIFFICULT

FIGURE 5.1: PROCESS OF 'SKILL SCORE' CALCULATION

presence or absence. Finally, the material is divided by site, to search for any local preferences for particular attributes or experiences which may relate to the relationship between users and pots in specific places. By dividing through these three avenues, it is possible to probe for connections between different pressures external from the pots themselves which impacted upon their user, and which perhaps prompted specific types of engagements which resulted in the pots' very existence.

Through these processes, the physical experience of engagement with Etruscan pots has been analysed in a quantifiable way. Ranging from the most accessible and simple height and diameter measurements to the final composite skill score, the way that vessels and users interacted with one another can be assessed through repeatable examinations. Unfortunately, some parts of the datA –set were excluded from this analysis due to gaps in their publication records. As the study relied entirely on published data, this was unavoidable. An extension for the project could be to expand and check the methods developed here, and their results, by directly measuring ceramics from a wider range of sites in person, to produce a larger set of results for comparison with those achieved here. As discussed in the previous chapter, due to the scope of the project, published data was the only way to reach a large and diverse data set within the limits of time and funding. However, the results from this analysis demonstrate the potential for these techniques both in Etruscan ceramic contexts, and elsewhere.

5.2 Body Proximity Groups: Hand to Mouth, Clay to Skin

The pottery corpus was divided into two broad forms of interaction between pot and body. Direct relationships were formed by direct contact between the contents of a vessel and the surface of the body while the vessel itself was in use. Secondary relationships are those where a vessel is used to carry liquids which will later be incorporated into the body. The two groups of pottery were relatively evenly distributed in the dataset, as illustrated in Figure 5.2. Ceramics with a direct relationship to the body formed 48% of the total dataset, at 555 examples, while vessels tied to secondary relationships formed 52% of the total, or 609 examples. The difference between the two groups is not statistically significant, while the even split was not created by deliberate data manipulation or collection strategies. It is apparent that pottery with both a direct and secondary relationship to the body was essential to ceramic experience in Etruria. Both types were evidently appropriate sites for the placement of human-figured decoration. The expression of the Etruscan experience of pottery in two halves emphasises the importance of both groups to ceramic lives: both direct and secondary pots contributed to Etruscan ceramic worlds.

Direct contact vessels can be divided by their role into three groups: pots for drinking, eating and perfume application. Secondary contact vessels can be divided in half: pouring vessels for direct transport and serving vessels for transport via an additional implement. Figure 5.3 presents the dataset when divided amongst these five groups. The assemblage is dominated by two vessel types: those used for drinking, and those used for serving. The largest of these groups is that of ceramics used for serving, with 510 examples, or 43.7%, and this is closely followed by pots used for drinking, at 496 examples or 42% of the total. While pouring vessels (99 examples, 8.44%) do form a sizable chunk of the total, it is pots used for drinking and serving which are the primary types of ceramic being used in Etruscan Italy, according to this assemblage. These are the vessels which are central to the Etruscan experience of pottery, the main forms in which that experience is constituted and constructed. While other forms are present and contributing to different forms of experience, the primary interaction between people and pots takes place between users, drinking and serving vessels.

Why are the most common types of pottery, drinking and serving vessels, identified in Figure 5.3, so apparently popular? When the dataset is divided between indigenously produced and imported wares, expressed proportionately to avoid the collection biases of the dataset, the reason for their high visibility in the dataset becomes apparent. Figure 5.4 displays the body proximity groups divided by their places of origin: where they were made. Drinking and serving vessels are the groups most evenly divided between these two categories. Although the balance is slightly skewed in both cases, both indigenous and imported workshops were making human-decorated serving and drinking vessels, which were in turn being purchased and used in relatively equal measure. The split between production places is different for both groups: drinking vessels were made in Etruria in just over 55% of cases, while serving vessels were imported in 52% of examples. These were the only two groups of pottery which were not dominated by one production place or the other: perfume and pouring vessels were predominantly formed of imported wares, while eating vessels were mainly made in Etruria. It is only drinking

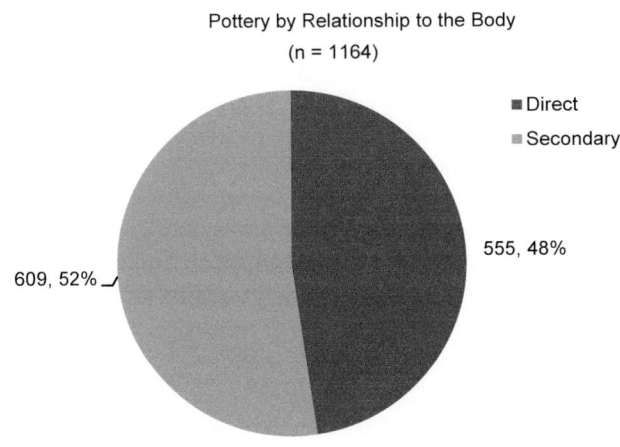

FIGURE 5.2: POTTERY BY RELATIONSHIP TO THE BODY

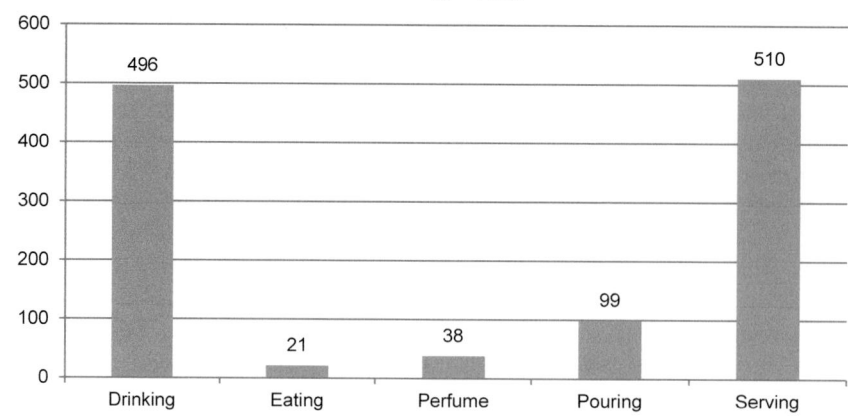

FIGURE 5.3: POTTERY BY BODY PROXIMITY GROUPS

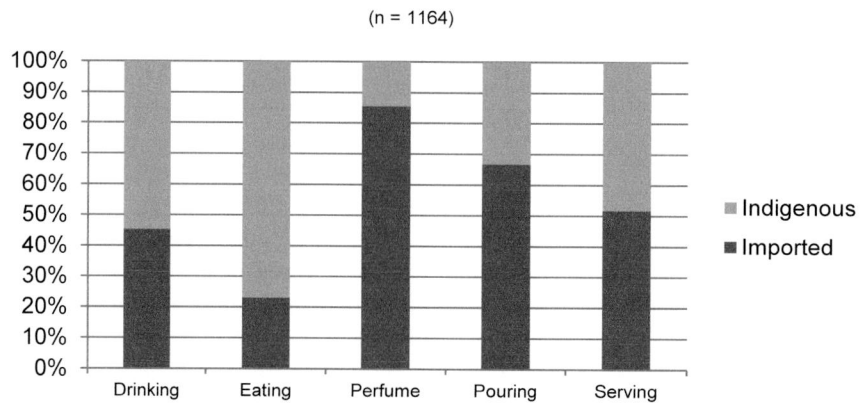

FIGURE 5.4: BODY PROXIMITY GROUPS BY ORIGIN (PROPORTIONAL PERCENTAGE) PROPORTIONAL PERCENTAGE USES THE PERCENTAGE OF EACH GROUP, RATHER THAN THE RAW DATA, TO PRODUCE A CHART WHICH REFLECTS THE RELATIONSHIP BETWEEN IMPORTED AND INDIGENOUSLY PRODUCED POTTERY WHICH NEGATES THE EFFECTS OF COLLECTION BIAS.

and serving vessels which are produced in equally large numbers in both places. It is impossible to distinguish whether this is a symptom or cause of the popularity of drinking and serving vessels, but underlines their central role in Etruscan experiences of pottery.

Drinking and serving vessels may be the most popular pots in the assemblage, but is this a universal preference at all four study sites? Figure 5.5 presents the body proximity groups by site, firstly for the entire corpus (as a proportional percentage), then for imported and indigenously produced pottery separately. There are clear differences between the sites at each phase of analysis. In graph 5.5.A, that presenting the entire corpus, Poggio Civitate stands out as unique. The site's assemblage is dominated by drinking vessels, with very few pots used for serving. The experience of using pottery here is entirely different from that anywhere else: expressed mainly through drinking vessels alone. The material from Chiusi is also dominated by drinking vessels, albeit to a smaller extent, implying that the Poggio Civitate preference for many drinking vessels

and fewer serving vessels is not caused by collection bias. While Chiusine pottery contains far more serving vessels than Poggio Civitate, it is nonetheless similar, the first indication of a northern type of pottery experience which is manifestly different to that created by the southern assemblages from Tarquinia and Vulci.

The difference between Poggio Civitate and Chiusi and Tarquinia and Vulci becomes even more obvious when the indigenously produced pottery is considered alone, as shown in Figure 5.5-C. The two southern sites have an entirely different pattern of indigenous vessel use: while the Volceian material contains slightly more drinking vessels than that from Tarquinia, both groups are heavily dominated by serving vessels, forming over 60% of indigenously made Volceian pottery, and over 80% of pots made in Etruria and found at Tarquinia. Chiusi and Poggio Civitate present the opposite pattern: at both sites over 50% of vessels were used for drinking. The material from Poggio Civitate could have been suggested to only represent the remnants of interaction between users and ceramics in indigenous pottery at a moment in time prior to the site's destruction but the connection with Chiusi and divergence from Tarquinia and Vulci demonstrates that this is false: there is an entirely different culture of ceramic experience taking place in these northern sites to that preferred in the south.

This pattern of a divide in practice between north and south is also hinted at in the imported material. Once again, Tarquinia and Vulci are almost identical in the high presence of serving vessels, although there are slightly more drinking vessels at Tarquinia. At Chiusi, however, the imported material is very similar to the indigenous assemblage: drinking vessels form over 60% of the total pots. This not only confirms the presence of a different type of experience of pottery use at Chiusi and Poggio Civitate from that at Tarquinia and Vulci, but also suggests that Chiusine consumers of imported pottery were deliberately choosing pots to fit into their established use-patterns, rather than absorbing pottery types previously unpopular. The Chiusine material is also from funerary assemblages, similar to those at Tarquinia and Vulci, so specific context does not lie behind this difference. The visible divergence in pottery use patterns is not confined to ceramics used in conjunction with dining: perfume vessels, popular in the south, do not form the same proportion of the Chiusine assemblage. Etruscan

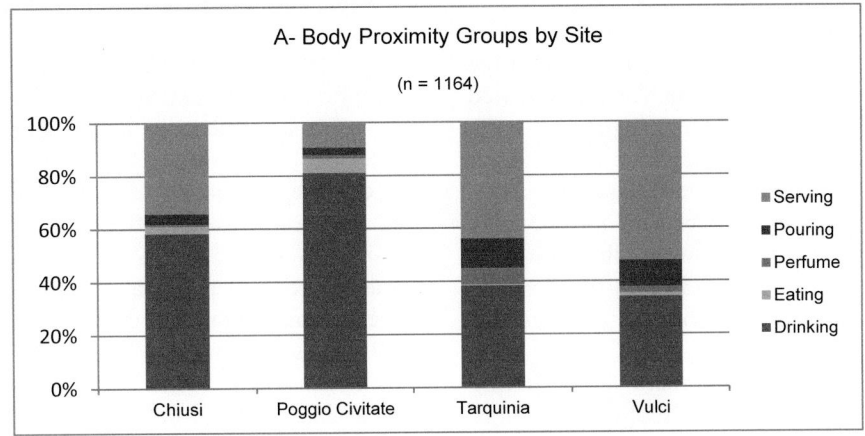

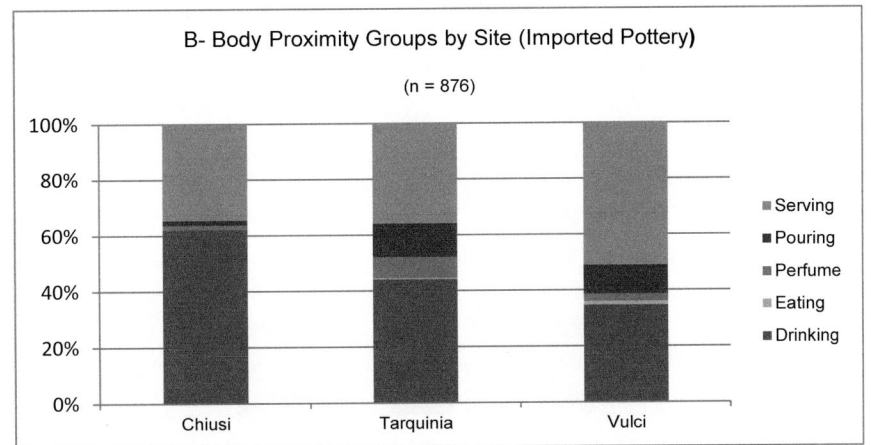

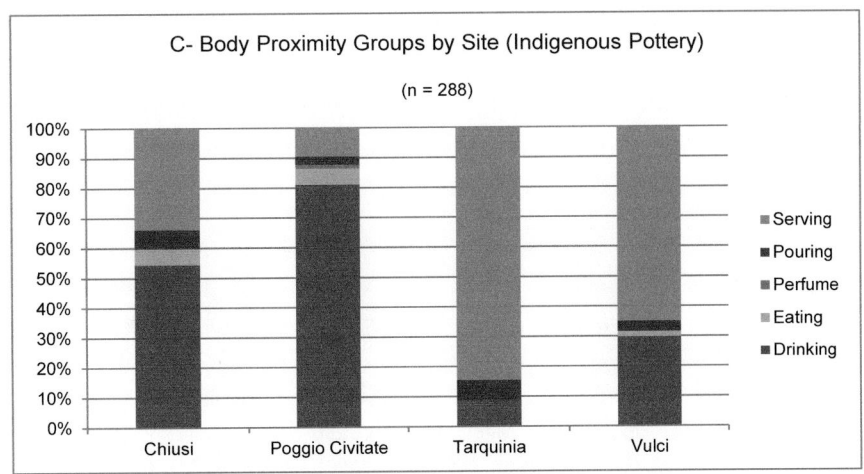

FIGURE 5.5: BODY PROXIMITY GROUPS BY SITE.
A – ALL POTTERY. B – IMPORTED POTTERY. C – INDIGENOUS POTTERY.

users were making deliberate decisions about the adoption of pottery forms, and those decisions were structured by two different traditions of ceramic practice.

This initial division of the data set by phenomenological methods has exposed the presence of different types of experience present in Etruria. There are four key conclusions to take forward:

1. The primary vessels through which Etruscans experienced human-figured pottery are those used for drinking and serving fluids. While vessels for direct and secondary contact are equally present in the corpus, these categories are dominated by drinking and serving pots respectively.
2. Human figured decoration is also found on three other vessel types, all of which are associated with a single production place, as opposed to the equal division of provenance seen in drinking and serving vessels. Eating vessels are primarily made in Etruria, while perfume and pouring vessels are primarily made outside the region.
3. There are two different traditions for ceramic use visible in the assemblage, dictated by geographical location. Poggio Civitate and Chiusi present larger numbers of drinking vessels, while Tarquinia and Vulci possess more serving vessels.
4. Etruscan individuals were deliberately incorporating imported vessels into their own local ceramic useways.

The next phase of analysis is to break down these categories further, to examine the exact constitution of these two emerging traditions of experience. Drinking and serving vessels appear to lie at the heart of Etruscan ceramic practice, but how are these vessels actually experienced by their user, and can differences in experience produced by new ceramic attributes suggest change in the nature of interaction between pots and users?

5.3 Sizing Pots Up: Height, Rim Diameter, Volume

The primary characteristics of pots are obvious things – the typologies and associated terms carry an expectation in terms of basic attributes – a neck amphora is not going to be small in height, while an alabastron will not have a large rim diameter. Reviewing these seemingly simple aspects can, however, reveal differences in experience which terminology obfuscates. The different aspects of ceramic use associated with provenance and body proximity are only to be approached through the material attributes of pottery itself. Going right back to height and rim diameter, before moving forward to volume and handle type is essential to ground experience in primary features before moving on to their combined effect on the user. From the division of

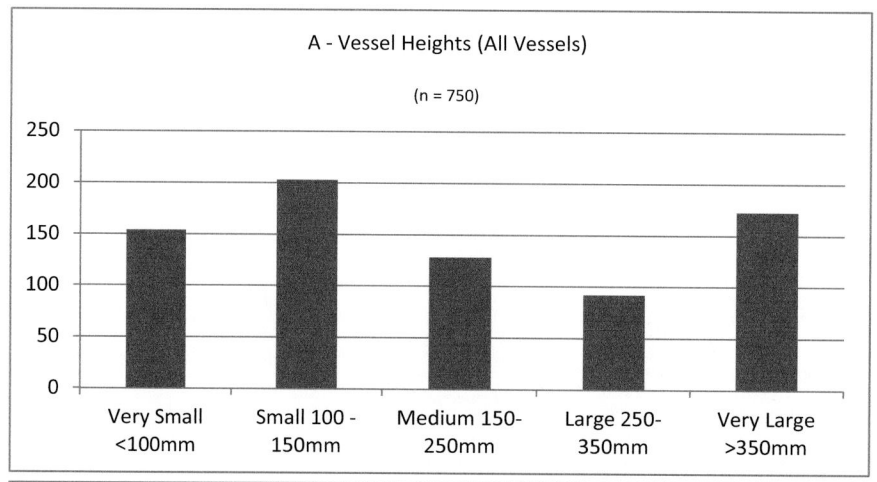

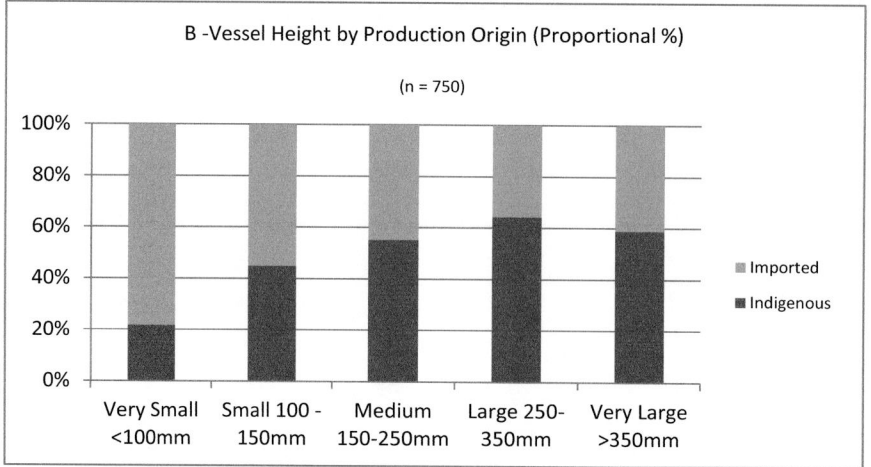

FIGURE 5.6: A – VESSEL HEIGHT B – VESSEL HEIGHT BY PRODUCTION ORIGIN.

pottery by body proximity in the previous subsection, certain experiences tied to particular vessel roles have been linked to geographical location and production origin. However, within these groups pottery forms and shapes varied: the body proximity groups are too blunt to alone examine the difference in experiences of Etruscan ceramics. By assessing the physical characteristics of each pot which makes up the dataset, it is possible to see a strong difference associated not with site of discovery, but with production origin. The changing balance of pottery interactions at each site, and the transformation in practice associated with particular shapes and experiences within these interactions are intertwined.

Figure 5.6.A presents the vessel heights for all pots where height measurements were available. The two largest groups were Small vessels, and Very Large vessels. These corresponded almost exactly to drinking and serving vessels, which, as observed above, dominate the dataset. So, it could be assumed from this that vessel sizes were relatively standardised across the corpus. Figure 5.6.B demonstrates that this is untrue. It shows the proportional percentage of indigenously produced and imported vessels which form each size group. It is clear that imported vessels were smaller in height than indigenously made pots, albeit with a slight increase in imported vessels over 350mm. When the body proximity groups are used to divide the dataset, however, this becomes less clear-cut.

Figure 5.7 shows the indigenous and imported vessel heights divided by body proximity groups. It shows that while, as a group, imported vessels are smaller in height than indigenously made pots, in some individual groups they are actually taller. Drinking, eating and pouring vessels made in Etruria are all taller than imported counterparts, while imported serving vessels were taller. The difference in experience is obvious: a long drinking vessel with a high stem requires a completely different mode of operation to a short cup. However, this is only half the picture: rim diameter is the other central facet of pottery characterisation.

Figure 5.8 provides the other half of the initial vessel encouter experience. Rim diameter is presented for all vessels in A, which shows a completely different pattern to that for height. Vessel rim diameters are very rarely under 100mm, with the modal group being medium sized diameters between 100 and 200mm. The supposedly clear groups of drinking and serving vessels associated with small and very large heights can be linked to the medium and large/very large rim diameters, illustrating that the modal ratio between height and rim diameter is unbalanced in favour of the latter. Etruscan ceramics, in contrast to modern vessels, were wider than they were tall. When the data is divided between imported and indigenously produced wares, this pattern becomes more

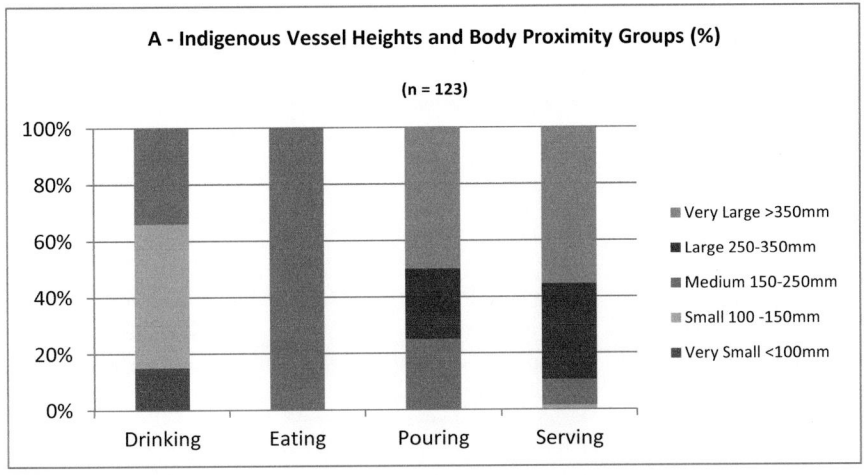

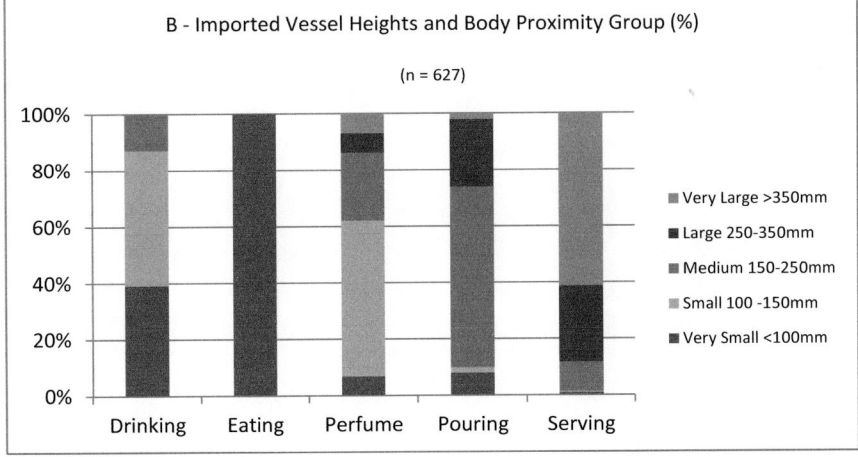

FIGURE 5.7: A – INDIGENOUS AND B – IMPORTED VESSEL HEIGHTS AND BODY PROXIMITY GROUPS.

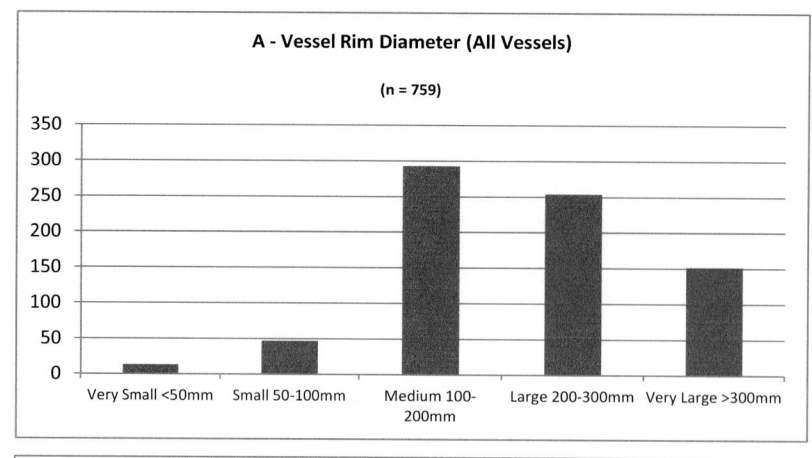
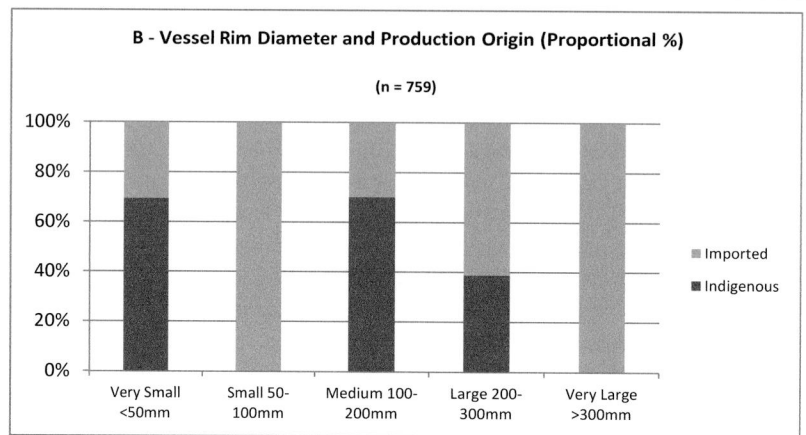

Figure 5.8: A – Vessel rim diameter B – Vessel rim diameters and production origin.

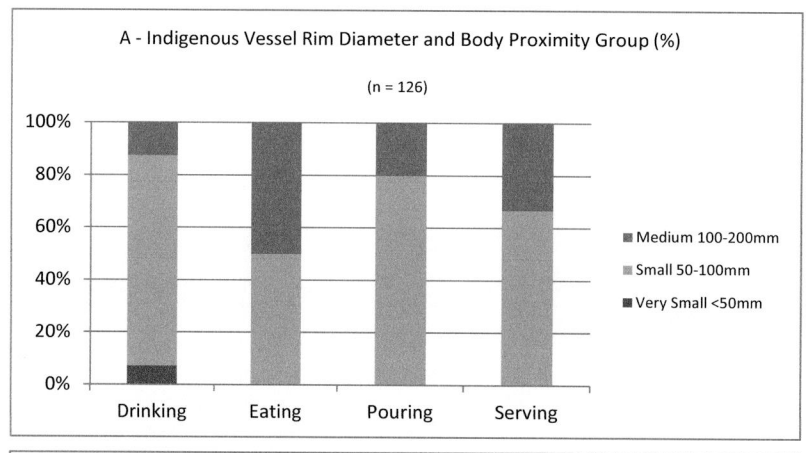
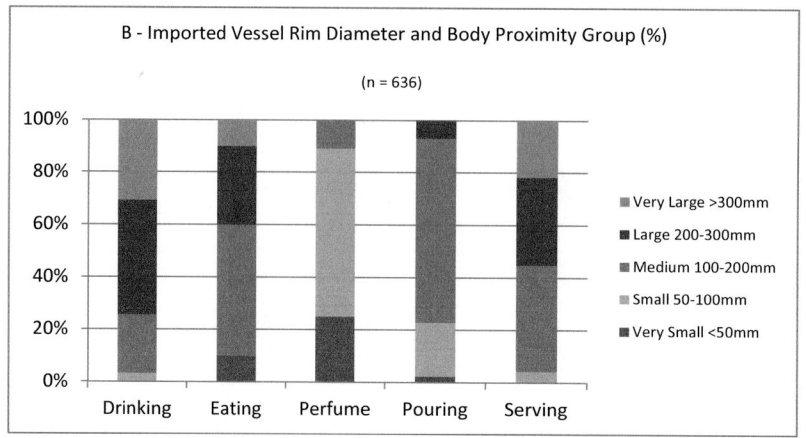

Figure 5.9: A – Indigenous and B – Imported vessel rim diameters and body proximity groups.

clearly associated with imported pots, which are much wider, as demonstrated in Figure 5.8B. Imported rim diameters are not only more variable, but are wider, while indigenously made Etruscan pots are more standardised, focused on very small and medium rim diameters.

When distributed across the body proximity groups, the standardisation of indigenous Etruscan vessels becomes more obvious. Drinking, pouring and serving vessels are all of similar rim diameter, which is far narrower than that of an imported vessel. Eating vessels come in two clear sizes, perhaps related to sharing plates and individual plates. By contrast, imported vessels are far more variable: eating and drinking vessel rim diameters range from under 50mm to over 300mm! In addition to this variety, imported vessels are far wider than imported pots being related to the body in the same fashion. From this basic initial comparison between height and rim diameter, it is possible to already see differences in the type of interaction between user and pot created by the adoption of imported ceramics. They are far wider, making for difficult pouring and manipulation, with the unbalanced height:width ratio creating an experience fraught with spillage. By contrast, Etruscan vessels are taller and narrower, with a large surface area which can be grasped directly: in terms of simplified shape, these pots are more akin to a tall cylinder than a low sphere.

Putting together vessel height and rim diameter results in volume. Figure 5.10.A presents the volumes for all measured vessels, then divides these by production origin. The most common vessel volume is between 750ml and 3l. Larger vessels as a whole dominate the data set, a phenomeon explained in 5.10.B, in which it is visible that imported vessels have larger volumes. In every size category above 750ml, imported vessels were more frequently represented. While indigenous vessels did reach sizes of over 5l, these were in the minority – vessels between 300 and 750ml were the modal group for indigenously produced pots. Before moving on to the specific body proximity groups, there is a key point to be made: imported vessels as a whole carried more liquids than indigenously produced Etruscan ones. This increase in size would have had a strong effect on user experience, reducing the necessity of refills and decreasing vessel malleability.

The divide between indigenous and imported ceramic experiences becomes more apparent when the body proximity groups are divided by volume, as shown in Figure 5.11. In all groups except eating vessels,

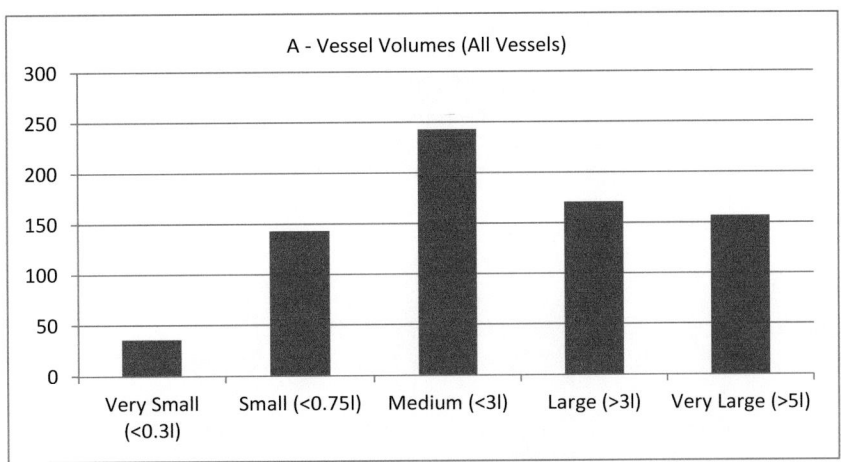

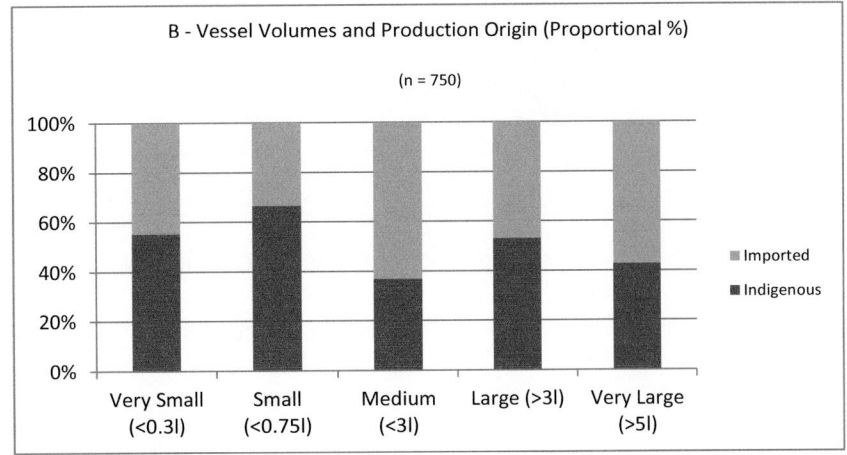

Figure 5.10: A – Vessel volumes. B – Vessel volumes and production origin.

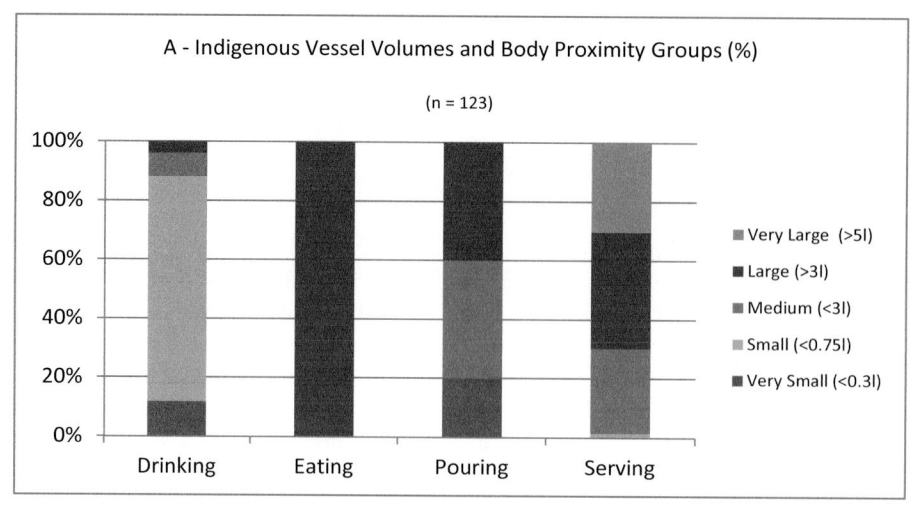

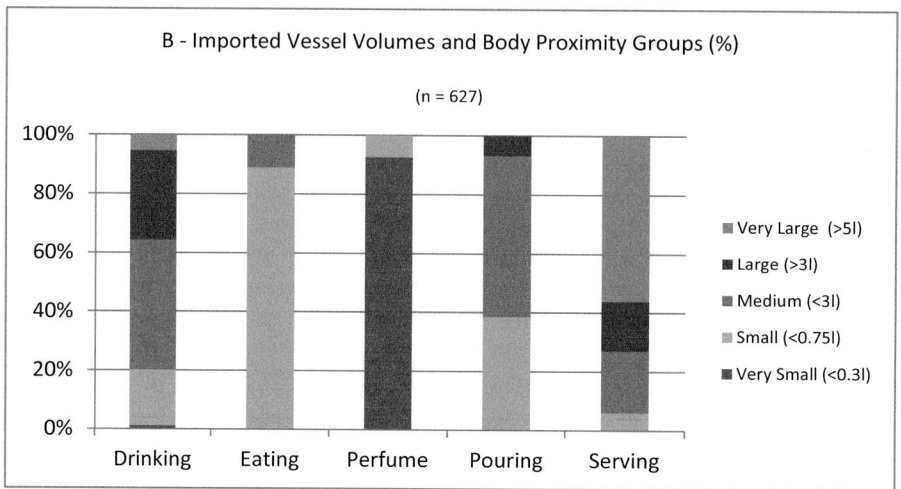

FIGURE 5.11: VOLUMES AND BODY PROXIMITY GROUPS OF A – INDIGENOUS VESSELS. B – IMPORTED VESSELS.

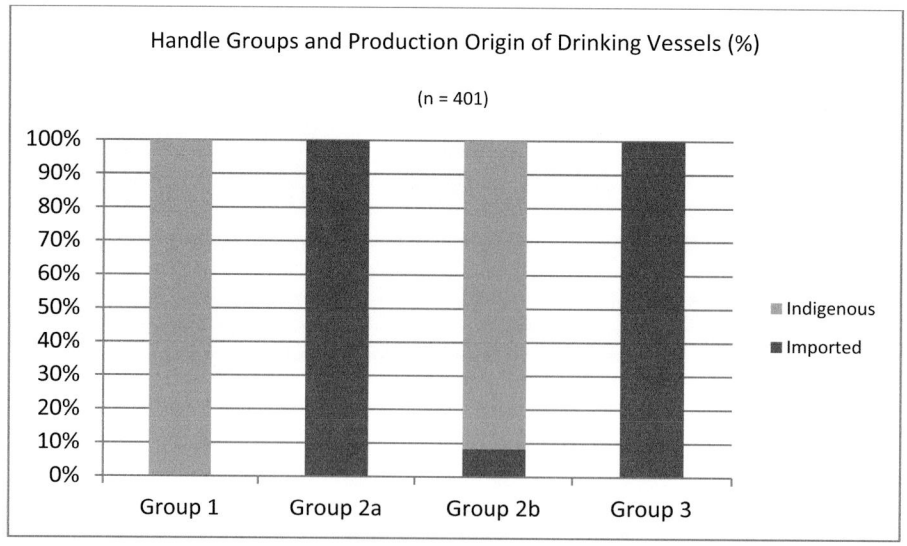

FIGURE 5.12: HANDLE GROUPS AND PRODUCTION ORIGIN FOR DRINKING VESSELS.

imported pots had a higher capacity. The difference is particularly dramatic in drinking and serving pots: the two most commonly represented groups in the dataset. Imported forms of both are significantly larger: over 50% of serving vessels produced outside Etruria are over 5l in capacity, while all drinking vessels of this capacity were imported, rather than indigenously produced. Imported ceramics as a whole have high volumes: the average imported serving vessel volume is 7.89l, while the average imported drinking vessel volume is 2.44l, as opposed to indigenously made average volumes of 600ml for drinking vessels and 5.14l for serving vessels. The impact of this increase in vessel volume on interaction is hard to overstate: indigenous vessels would have produced an entirely different experience to the new imported pots.

The final primary characteristic is handle type. Figure 5.12 presents the handle types for the drinking vessels divided by production origin. This is the most problematic aspect of the dataset – a single example of a kantharos skews the dataset, giving the (false) impression that vertical double handles are incontrovertibly associated with imported wares. Leaving this aside, there are two strong features which can be observed: all imported drinking vessels possessed handles of some kind. Pots without handles were exclusively indigenously produced, while pots from this assemblage with flat handles requiring complex balancing were all made outside Etruria. In addition to the wider-reaching impacts of height, rim diameter and volume, imported vessels were also transforming experience through handling practice.

To sum up the results of the primary characteristic analysis:

1. Etruscan made vessels are taller, but narrower than imported vessels, which are generally smaller but wider.
2. This does not have an effect on volume, as imported vessels are so much wider that their volumes are significantly larger. Indigenously made pots had a smaller capacity, and could have carried far less liquid.
3. Flat handles are exclusively associated with imported pots, while indigenously vessels commonly had no handles at all but were directly lifted via stem or tondo.

This initial analysis has exposed some serious impacts caused by pottery form on Etruscan experience, and demonstrated these to be connected to imported ceramic wares mixing with indigenously produced pots, potentially creating a hybrid culture of practice. The intricacies of that practice, and the implications of vessel characteristics on user experience beyond initial encounter is the subject of the next part of the analysis. The difficulty or ease of using a vessel has already been alluded to, and the quantification of this skill factor through secondary characteristics and a calculative process fleshes out the bare facts provided by the primary attributes of Etruscan ceramics.

5.4 Seeking Skill – Secondary Characteristics

The primary characteristics of Etruscan pottery, which formed the initial contact between user and object, provide a similarly primal insight for archaeological study. The difference between imported and indigenously produced pottery is already visible, but what was its impact on the Etruscan user? Through using composite analyses designed to interrogate the user experience, it is possible to illustrate the practical difference between using an indigenously produced pot and one made in Greece and imported to Etruria. At each phase of the analysis

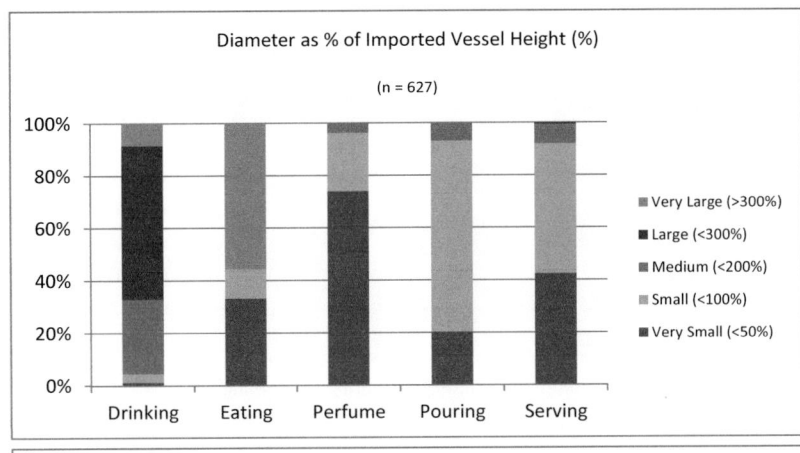

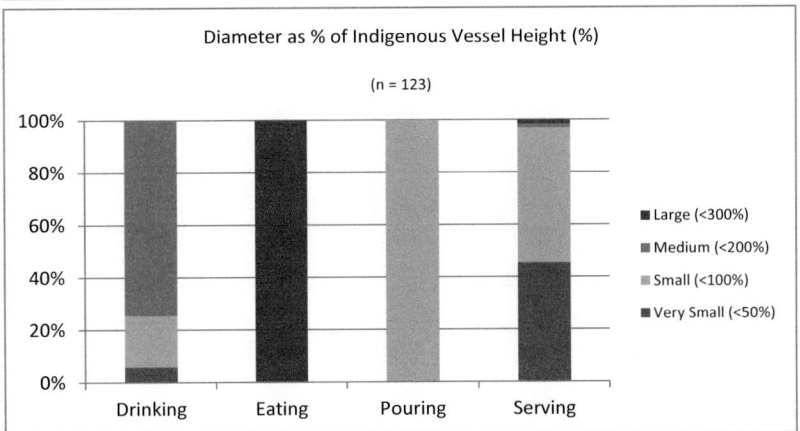

FIGURE 5.13: RIM DIAMETER AS A PERCENTAGE OF VESSEL HEIGHT FOR A – IMPORTED VESSELS AND B – INDIGENOUS VESSELS BY BODY PROXIMITY GROUP.

the data for indigenous and imported pottery will be presented divided by body proximity groups, to enable direct comparison between the two sets of results across the different roles of pottery. The first of these composite measures relates diameter to vessel height, the second rim diameter and average hand length. These two figures both provide an idea of balance and ease of use – how difficult was a vessel to lift and use, to pour or drink from? How easy was it to avoid spilling the potentially valuable contents?

Diameter/height and diameter/average hand length ratios are then built into a difficulty score alongside handle type and volume. The differences in these ease-of-use scores between imported and indigenously made wares represent sharp impacts on Etruscan users, learning to negotiate new and increasingly difficult pottery forms. These scores give some indication of the level of skill required to use a vessel without spilling its contents or dropping it: the amount of practice necessary to master successful use, the scale of potential damage caused by inattention. The skill scores are then related back to the data from 5.1, in which it was observed that drinking and serving vessels were the most common types of pottery being used at all sites, but in different proportions. The skill scores for these two groups are re-formed by site provenance, fleshing out the difference in practice observed between northern and southern Etruria. The balance between drinking and serving vessels is only one phase of a complicated system of pottery use which emphasises the active experience of the user in its navigation.

Figure 5.13 shows the relationships between rim diameter and vessel height across body proximity groups for both imported (A) and indigenous (B) vessels. The two groups are completely different from each other. As with the primary characteristics, indigenous vessels are less variable across all four groups: two are composed entirely of a single size. The suggestion of longer, thinner vessels is also maintained, with very few vessels outside those used for eating having a rim diameter over 200% of height. In contrast, imported vessels are very variable, particularly in eating and drinking vessels. Serving, perfume and pouring vessels, in addition to being more standardised, are much more similar to indigenously made vessel proportions. It is imported drinking vessels which exemplify both the widest range and highest level of divergence for indigenously made forms. Over 60% of imported drinking vessels had diameters of 200% of height or more.

Figure 5.14, showing the relationship between average hand length and rim diameter, presents an opposing pattern of difference. Indigenous pouring and serving vessels are both more variable and more extreme in the relationships of hand size to diameter, while the opposite is true for drinking and eating vessels. There is a strong difference between indigenous and imported pots which is

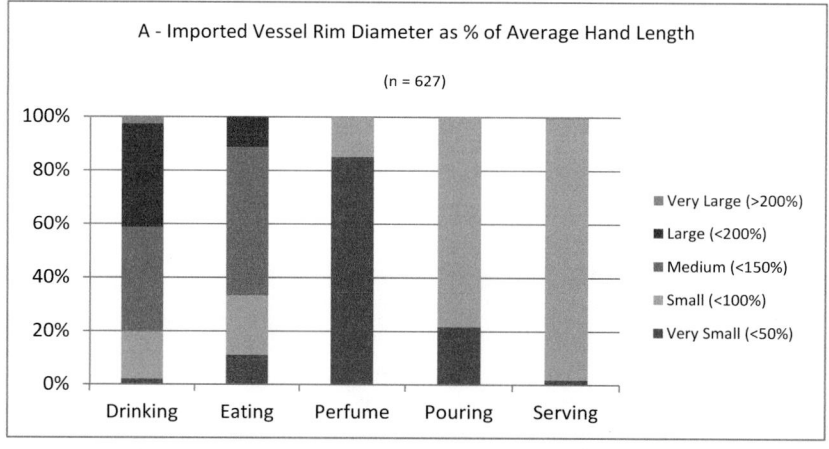

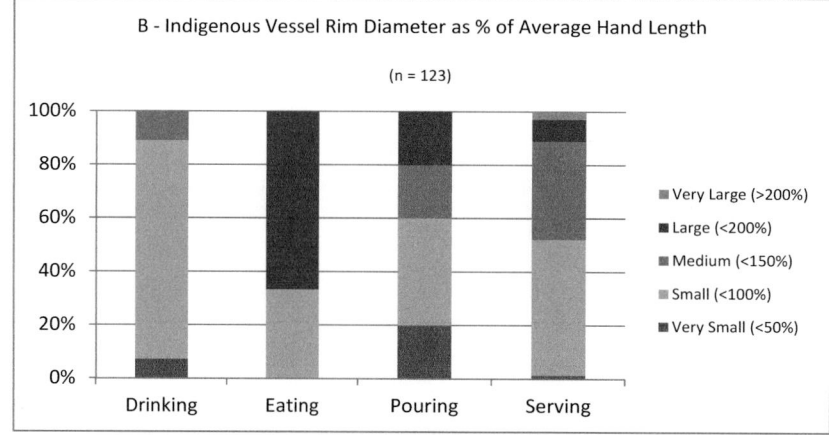

FIGURE 5.14: DIAMETER AS PERCENTAGE OF AVERAGE HAND LENGTH (180MM) BY BODY PROXIMITY GROUP. A – IMPORTED VESSELS AND B – INDIGENOUS VESSELS.

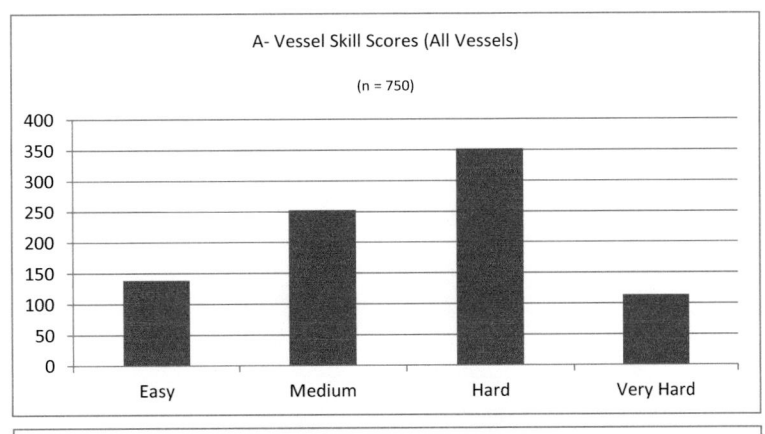
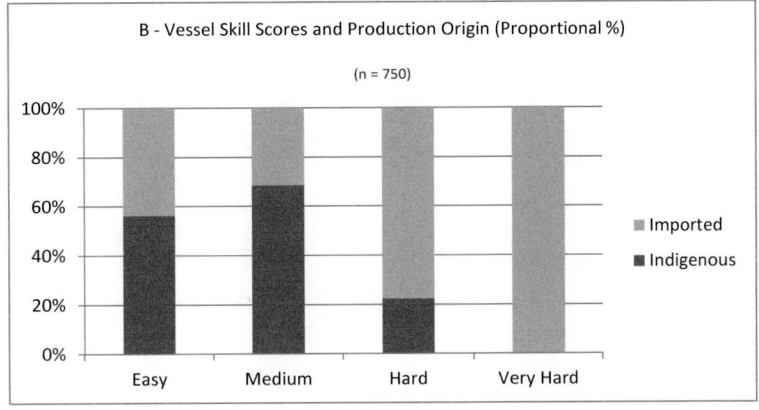

FIGURE 5.15: A – VESSEL SKILL SCORES B – PROPORTIONAL PERCENTAGE OF SKILL SCORES AND PRODUCTION ORIGIN.

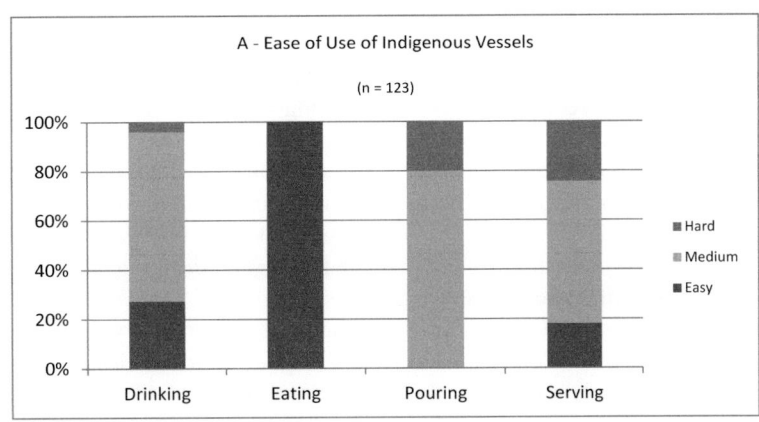
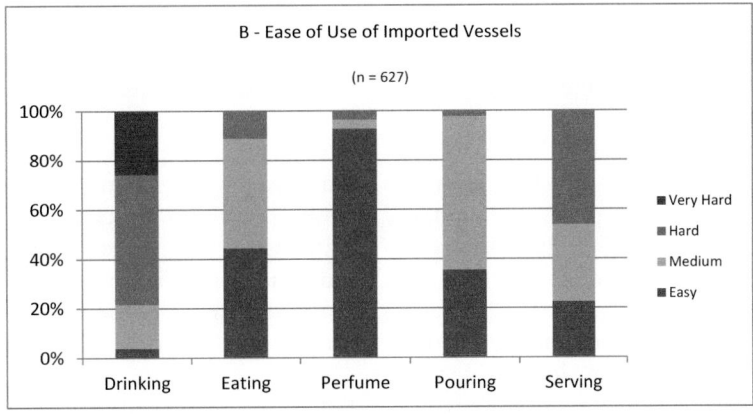

FIGURE 5.16: EASE OF USE SCORES BY BODY PROXIMITY GROUP. A – INDIGENOUSLY PRODUCED VESESLS AND B: IMPORTED VESSELS.

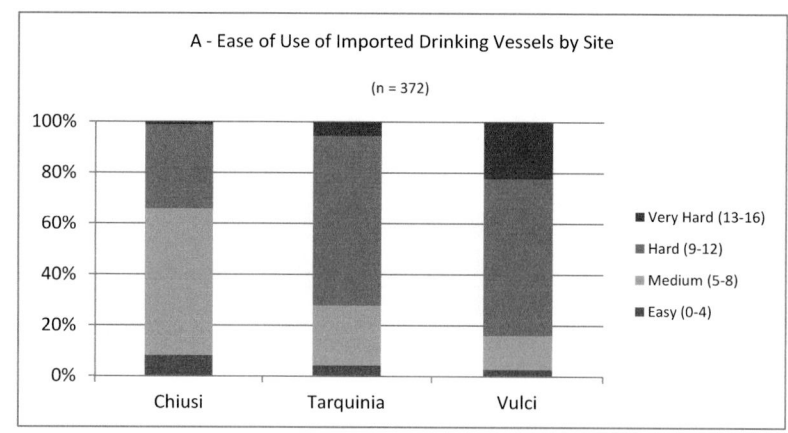

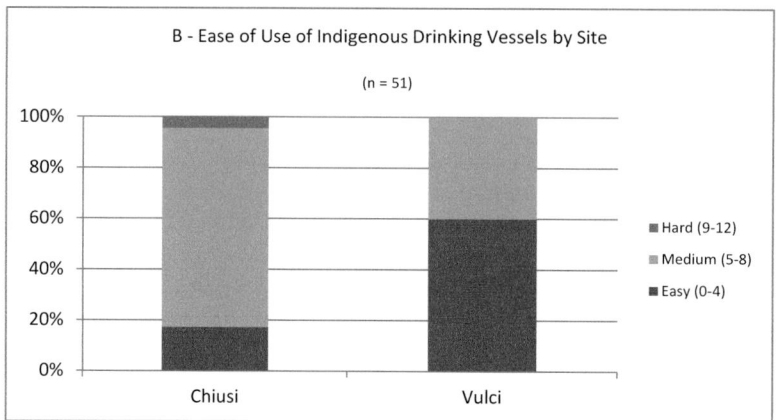

FIGURE 5.17: EASE OF USE SCORES FOR A – IMPORTED AND B – INDIGENOUS DRINKING VESSELS BY SITE.

focused on their body proximity group: imported vessels used in direct contact with the body are more variable and have a higher ratio of hand-length to rim diameter, while the reverse is true for indigenous vessels. The two groups demonstrate a different location for attention on the relationship between hand and pot: for indigenous pots, secondary contact vessels, for imported, direct body contact pots.

Figure 5.15 presents the composite skill scores for vessel use. A shows the total number of pots falling in each category, but is skewed by the proportion of imported vessels included in the assemblage. B demonstrates the contrast in skill level for vessels produced in and outside Etruria. 5.15 B shows clearly that indigenous vessels were significantly easier to use than those made in Greece: not a single indigenously made pot scored in the 'very hard' region. This is borne out by the mean skill scores: indigenous vessels scored an average of 5.31, while imported vessels scored an average of 7.57. Pots brought in from outside Etruria were, as a group, demanding new and more difficult forms of interaction from Etruscan users, changing their daily experiences of pottery.

Figure 5.16 shows that in all body proximity groups except perfume and pouring vessels, imported pots were more difficult to use. Perfume vessels were the only imported pots with a majority of vessels classed as 'easy' to use. Serving vessels show a relatively similar pattern, but drinking vessels, the direct carriers of liquid into the body, are the most divergent in terms of difficulty. Indigenous vessels were much easier to use, with no pot scoring above a 'Hard' in terms of difficulty. Imported drinking vessels were the most difficult body proximity group, with over 20% scoring as 'Very Hard' to use. The increase in user skill requirement associated with imported vessels observed in Figure 5.15 can now be recognised to be focused on drinking vessels in particular.

The first pattern of vessel use practice observed was the higher ratio of drinking to serving vessels at the northern sites of Chiusi and Poggio Civitate. Figure 5.17 demonstrates a difference in the difficulty level of those drinking vessels between northern and southern sites. Imported drinking vessels at Chiusi are significantly easier, while indigenous versions are harder than those from Vulci. It is Vulci which has the hardest to use imported vessels and easiest indigenously made pots while Tarquinia sits in the middle. The north/south divide in practice is more complicated than drinking/serving vessels, but related to skill scores too: indigenous drinking pots are more difficult to use in the north and easier in the south, while the reverse is true for imported vessels.

Figure 5.18 shows the imported (A) and indigenous (B) serving vessel use level scores divided between sites. As with drinking vessels, there is a difference in terms of

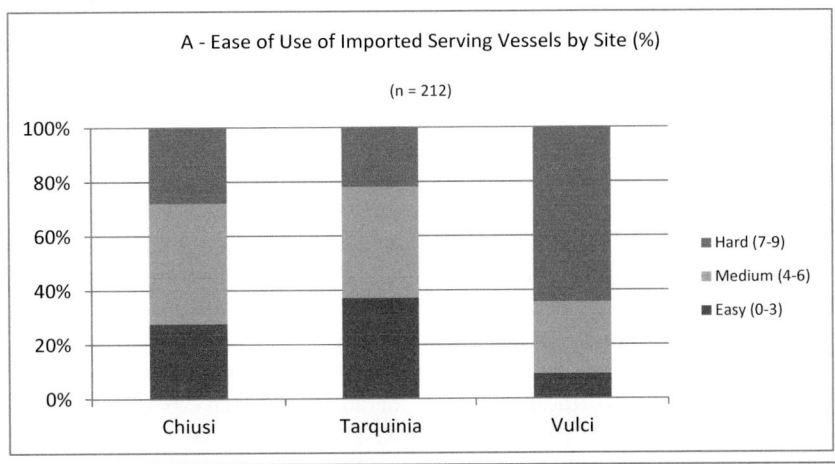

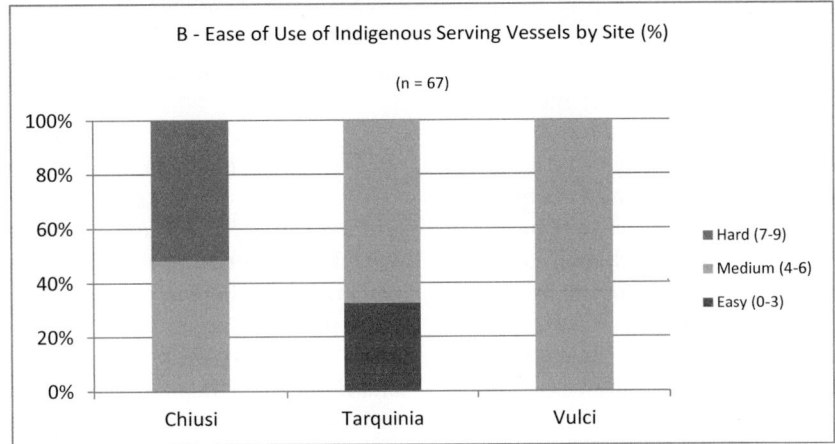

FIGURE 5.18: EASE OF USE SCORES FOR A – IMPORTED AND B – INDIGENOUS SERVING VESSELS.

ease of use. Exactly as with drinking vessels, indigenous serving vessels were more difficult to use at Chiusi than at Tarquinia or Vulci. The easiest to use serving vessels produced in Etruria were found at Tarquinia. In the imported wares, Chiusi and Tarquinia presented a relatively similar pattern of incorporation of imported serving vessels with an increased difficulty level, while Vulci had a higher number of 'Hard' imported serving pots, forming over 60% of the total serving wares.

There are three key conclusions to take forward from the analysis of composite vessel characteristics and skill levels:

1. Imported vessels were more difficult to use than pots produced in Etruria.
2. Drinking vessels were the most difficult body proximity group to use for imported vessels, while pouring and serving vessels were the most difficult to use for indigenous vessels. In other words, direct body-contact pots used by an individual were more complicated in imported examples, while secondary body-contact, shared vessels were more difficult to use in the indigenous assemblage.
3. Chiusi has a larger number of more difficult to use indigenously made drinking and serving vessels than the two southern sites, but a lower number of difficult to use imported pots in all categories.

These three conclusions all have a direct bearing on the experience of the Etruscan user of pottery in different locales, but also contribute to an understanding of the traditions of ceramic usage developed at the different sites and expressed through different specific pots. The final section puts together these conclusions with those from the primary vessel attribute analysis and the body proximity groupings to argue for two different forms of ceramic experience in Etruria, and their potential hybridisation.

5.5 Experience, Performance, Control: Conclusions

The data at all three phases of investigation strongly suggests two different co-existing types of ceramic experience, each associated with imported and indigenously made pottery forms. The spread of the former across south Etruria, visible at the sites of Tarquinia and Vulci, indicates a level of creolisation in practice, with pots from Greece accepted into Etruscan ways of using them. At the same time, the physical characteristics of those pots would have transformed the experience for the user, without allowing for hybridity. It is hard to establish from this data whether a separate southern Etruscan culture of ceramic usage existed prior to the introduction of imported wares, which were already being refashioned and adapted by indigenous craftspeople by the Archaic period. This southern tradition may or may not have been similar to that which is still visible in the northern sites of Chiusi and Poggio Civitate. At Poggio Civitate, while small fragments of imported wares have been uncovered, one of which, found at the neighbouring settlement of Vescovado di Murlo, featured a human figure, these were not large enough to recreate pottery forms. Although imported pottery had reached Poggio Civitate, and certainly was being used at Chiusi, it is possible to discern continuity in pottery use at both sites and the maintenance of an indigenous culture of pottery interaction. These two traditions of pottery use each configured an entirely different user experience, as revealed by the conclusions from the analysis of primary and composite attributes.

The northern Etruscan experience of human-figured ceramics, as seen at Chiusi and Poggio Civitate, is one focused on the use of many drinking vessels with a smaller number of serving vessels. The very small number of perfume vessels compared to pots used in the context of the service and consumption of food and drink suggests that the primary forum for pottery experience is communal eating and drinking events, whether on a small, familial scale or extensive public gatherings. While there are many more secondary-contact serving and pouring vessels in the assemblages for both sites, they are not decorated with human figures as regularly as ceramics used for drinking. The focus for the image is on the individual experience of a personal vessel, which happens in the interaction between a person and their own pot, in the moment of use. Shared vessels are not as appropriate for the placement of these images, and the relative lack of human figured imported serving wares at Chiusi emphasises this. This focus on individual drinking vessels as vehicles for image placement is important, and will be returned to in the following chapters.

In terms of the specific experience, indigenous drinking vessels were relatively straightforward to use. The majority could be gripped either directly by their body or stem, and lifted to the mouth without undue concern for spillage or balance. Handles, where present, were vertical, and the hand could be inserted into the loop rather than used to support the vessel from underneath. Even if a vessel was overturned or unbalanced, only a small amount of liquid would be wasted due to their small volume. The smaller volume of indigenously produced drinking vessels also created a key aspect of the user experience: they would have had to be refilled regularly, and, due to their ease of use, could have been emptied quickly! Anecdotally, a thirsty person, particularly in the heat of the summer, could easily drink 600ml of fluid over the course of 20 or 30 minutes. This ease of use of drinking vessels created a need for regular refilling from serving and pouring vessels: and this refilling process was more difficult than simple drinking, as is visible in the data from Chiusi in Figure 5.18. The display of skills related to the use of pottery, and the need for their creation, was focused in the indigenous, northern tradition of ceramic use on the transfer of liquids, rather than their consumption. The person who performed this role needed to be able to manipulate difficult vessels filled with large volumes of liquid capably and without wasting their contents: a specialist skill set. While individual drinking was easy and relatively relaxed in terms of skill requirement, the regular refilling demanded by small vessel forms created an opportunity for the display of manipulative skills grown through practice. It is hard to speculate as to who undertook the distribution of liquid: it could possibly be connected with the role of host or hostess, or have been undertaken by servants. In any case, the experience of Etruscan-made pottery, at its most visible at Chiusi and Poggio Civitate, would have been one of easy drinking and complex serving, breaking up events through possibly formalised refilling.

The experience of using imported pottery, and, to some extent, indigenous pottery made in southern cities influenced by outside ceramic useways was an entirely different affair. The balance between serving and drinking vessels is different: both groups are almost equally used as carriers for human images: serving vessels are clearly appropriate places for this type of decoration: their images have an impact which is important for all those who see and use them. The process of drinking, too, is completely different. Imported drinking vessels were difficult to use – in many cases extremely so. They required an intense concentration to avoid spillage, balancing the vessel on the flat of the hand, negotiating the enormous difference between rim diameter and height without tipping the vessel. The discomfort caused by the contortion of the hand to support such a vessel, particularly when filled with a large amount of liquid, regularly over 2l and weighing 2kg, must have been extreme. Once the vessel had been lifted to the mouth, the balance required to tip fluid into the mouth from such a wide rim without spilling any down the chin needed to be perfect. These large drinking vessels also would have lasted a lot longer without needing refilling: 2l is a huge amount of fluid, particularly if that fluid is alcoholic! Even in the midst of an event requiring high liquid consumption, these large volume drinking cups could not have been emptied quickly, creating instead an extended, slow interaction between user and vessel as the cup was drained over a longer period of time. In Tarquinia and Vulci, while very easy to use indigenous wares continued to be made, it is conceivable that these were used specifically for less formal occasions, while intricate imported wares took over at communal consumption events. It may be that such a sharp increase in volume is connected to differences in drinking practice – potentially providing evidence for the dilution of wine with water in Greece, and the consumption of neat wine in Etruria. Whether or not Greek practices, including the mixing of wnie and water, accompanied the imported vessels across the Mediterranean is intensely difficult to estimate.

The size of drinking pots also impacted on serving vessel usage: imported serving wares are simultaneously larger and easier to use than indigenous forms. Their increased size was a necessity to provide for the higher volume cups they were required to fill, while their ease-of-use is evidence for a complete shift in focus for the demonstration of ceramic use skills. The complex system of refilling, with its associated demanding serving vessels, was replaced by a user experience intensely concentrated on the role of the individual. The manipulation of such difficult vessels, potentially in the context of increasing intoxication, necessitated the acquisition of a set of practical motor skills which were intensely visible. These skills were required of every person participating in a consumption event, not only a specific server. These skills demonstrated familiarity with a group of imported ceramic wares which were purchased, rather than produced: a marker of access to potentially expensive ceramic forms. The successful use of imported drinking vessels relied upon extensive experience – the lack of which would have been all too visible in a mess of smashed shards or a stained garment.

While these two different user experiences are vastly different in practice, there are two key principles which underline both of them, and which perhaps form the underlying common ground which eventually resulted in a hybrid experience of pottery, incorporating ceramics from both traditions in Etruria by the end of the Archaic period. The first of these is the opportunity provided, albeit at different points in the two traditions, for the performance of skills associated with access to high value ceramics and their contents. While related to individual drinkers in the case of imported pottery, and to a specific server in the indigenous experience, both provided a moment for the display and recognition of a specific type of knowledge, an opportunity for the recognition of shared values through practice. The increased importance of this for every person present through the introduction of complex individual drinking vessels demonstrates the visiblity of such skills, and their importance in the construction of elite identities. Allied to this performative use of ceramics is the use of perfume vessels: in both indigenous and imported contexts these vessels appear to be primarily pragmatically designed – easy to use, long in length with small rim diameters to dissuade spillage. The small volume of these vessels implies the value of their contents, and the need for this group of pottery to be personal and portable. While not connected directly to consumption events, perfume application would have been a central part of preparation – and also linked to the performative use of ceramics, in this case to produce scent, demonstrating access to expensive fragrances.

The second shared theme in both types of ceramic practice is that of social control. It is not an unreasonable assumption to assume that the vessels associated with liquid consumption would have been used for alcoholic substances, and specifically that of wine. While the strength and potency of Etruscan wine is unknown, it is probable that excessive consumption would have resulted in the usual effects of alcohol, which, when taken to extremes include aggression, stupor, vomiting and unconsciousness.

To avoid these negative effects of extreme alcohol consumption, both the physical characteristics of vessels for the provision of such liquids themselves, and the performative context in which they were consumed, can be seen as acting as forms of social control. While Etruscan made drinking vessels slowed the intoxication process by requiring refilling and breaks in consumption, imported wares did the same by problematizing the process of drinking itself, requiring a slow rate of consumption and a careful approach to alcohol. In communal drinking events with large numbers of people, such controls would have been essential for maintaining both the safety and dignity of participants, simultaneously avoiding violence and embarassment through the built-in controls present in the clay under their hands.

This chapter has focused on the physical form of clay, and the impact of pottery bodies on the persons using it. It has identified two different forms of experience existing together in Archaic period Etruria, both of which possessed shared underlying drivers of performativity and social control. The physical form of pottery, however, is only one part of the experience of using it. The next chapter considers the physical constitution of clay decoration, asking how the augmentation of pottery with images changes the experience of using it. What was specific about the experience of using a decorated vessel, as opposed to a plain one? How were these decorations linked to the two different traditions of ceramic use identified in this chapter? The answers to these questions flesh out the experience of using an Etruscan vessel, beyond aching wrists and wine-stained lips, to the impact of images, and their role in the whole-body experience of pottery use in Etruria.

Chapter 6

Seeing and Revealing: Images on Pots

6.1 Introduction

The previous chapter developed a method for quantifying the user experience of Etruscan pottery in relation to the physical shape of a vessel. The presentation of those clay surfaces is the focus of this chapter. The smooth contours which squash or spread the fingers or enforce a carefully balanced tipping motion are also distinguished by their markings, the images which are concealed or revealed through movement and manipulation, and which may be encountered in a range of different ways. All the pots within this dataset use images on their surfaces to colour the experience of the user – how these images are constituted, and what their contribution is to the all-round experience of pottery, are the twin foci of this part of the investigation. Using the same parameters of body proximity group and geographical origin as drivers for analysis, how does the constitution of ceramic decoration impact upon the experience of the Etruscan user, and the patterns of practice observed in the previous chapter?

This analysis of surface decoration is focused on the form of images, and their constitution, rather than their subject. The constitution of images is influenced by two key factors, the first of which is the location of decoration on the surface of the vessel. Image position strongly structures the experience of the user: the images are concealed and revealed to different viewers at different moments, and felt by different parts of the body. An image on the bottom of a cup will only be revealed after its contents are drunk, and encountered solely with the eyes. An image on a handle is half-hidden beneath the hand and fingers which trace its contours. An image on the outside of a pot is invisible to the drinker when it is lifted to the mouth, but can be seen by every other person present in the room. The experience of a pot goes beyond the user: images can reach out to every person who sees them. To interrogate this, a typology of image placement was developed, illustrated in Figure 6.1.

The typology divides images primarily by their accessibility. Images on the inside of vessels are visible only to the user, unless deliberately displayed to others once the vessel's

Figure 6.1: Typology of image placement.

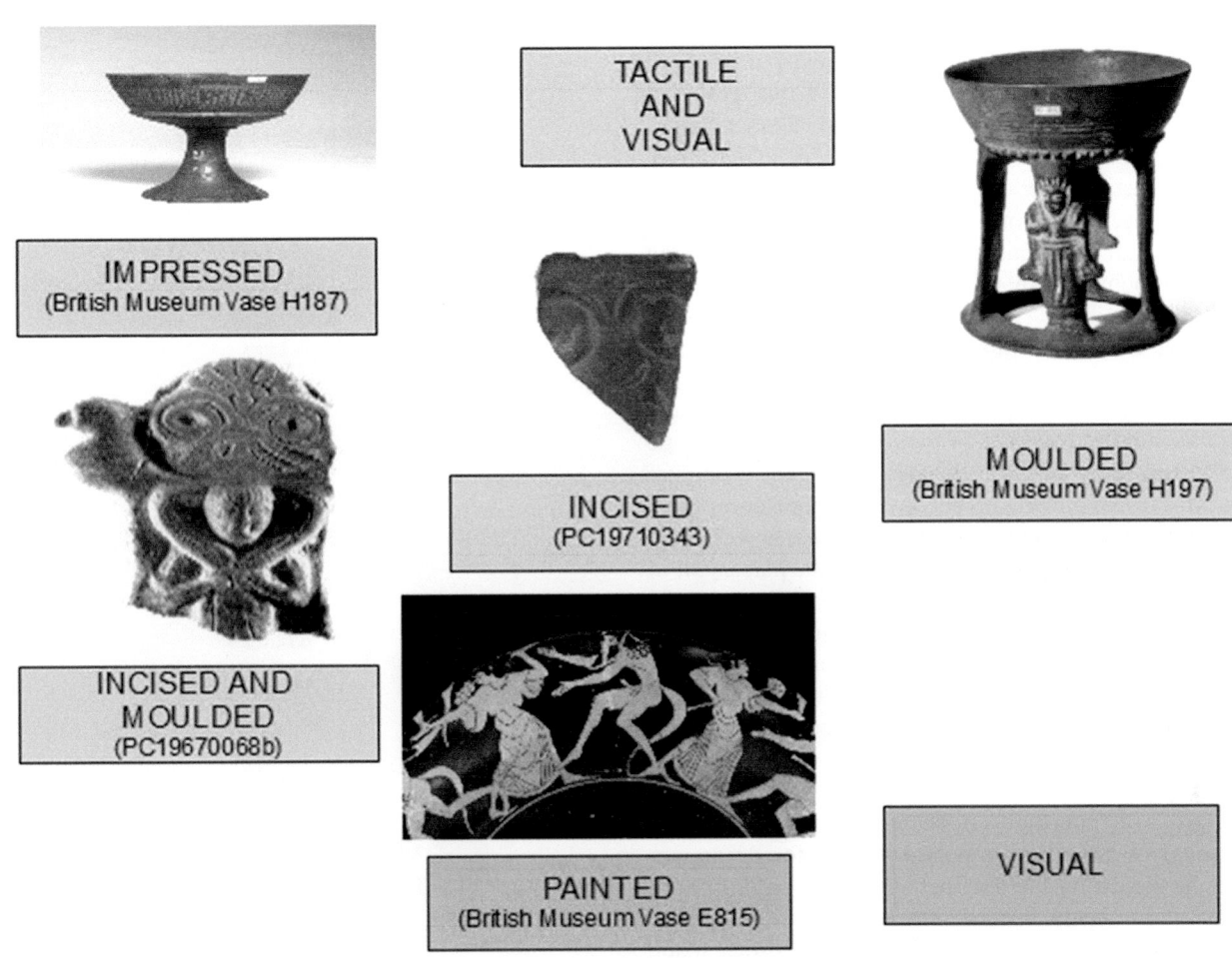

FIGURE 6.2: TYPOLOGY OF IMAGE STIMULATION.

contents have been drunk. This group of images could be revealed slowly by continued consumption, or quickly in a shot-like swallow. The other major group of images is those on the outside of vessels, which can be seen by all those who care to look – except by the drinker in the moment of consumption. When the vessel is lifted to the mouth this type of decoration disappears, and all that can be seen is the yawning mouth of the pot, and the liquid inside. There is also a third group of pots which combine both types of image: those with decoration on both the inside and outside of a vessel surface. The decoration of these pots can be seen by both drinker and their companions, and as the outside images are concealed, the inner image comes more clearly into focus as the vessel is slowly emptied. These three groups are categorised as inside, outside and combined image vessels.

These three primary categories can be divided further, depending on the specific placement of decoration. The majority of images in all three groups are found on the body of the pot, placed so as to make contact seemingly with the vessel contents and the hand. Others are found on handling surfaces, both on the exterior legs of the vessel and the handle space. The former is reminiscent of exterior body decorations, but the handle space is characterised as both interior and exterior decoration: it can be seen by others when the vessel is turned towards them, or can alternatively be concealed by the drinker's hand. It is hidden by the side of the face when the lip of the vessel is in contact with the mouth, but remains under the fingers. These primary and secondary characteristics of image placement are then incorporated with three other factors: body proximity group, production origin and geographical provenance. In this way, the experience of users of different vessel types, from different places and used at different sites can be probed, to examine whether traditions of image experience in practice can be seen in addition to differences in form.

The second key aspect of image experience, after placement, is the sensory stimulation of the image. Every form of vessel decoration included in the corpus is visually stimulating, appealing to the eyes, and the subject matter of that stimulus will be examined in the next chapter. However, a group of vessels within the corpus also appeal to the fingers, transforming the user experience through tactile means, rather than the solely visual. What other characteristics are shared between this group of vessels, and how are they related to the solely visual pots? The experience of using tactile pottery would have been entirely different for an Etruscan person – where would these touch pots be encountered, and how did they relate to the body? Having identified this group of ceramics through a second typology of pottery sense stimulation, illustrated in Figure 6.2, the body proximity groups, production origins and geographical provenances of this group of objects are queried to examine whether this type of pottery had a similar role in ceramic practice as its solely visual relations. Tactile experience was manufactured in Etruria in different techniques of decoration, yet what do all these groups have in common, and why are these pots required to impact upon the body of the user?

6.2 Angles of Access: Image Placement

The first aspect of the relationship between user and image is constructed through the placement of an image on a vessel. Each position dictates a different encounter between eye and picture. Images are concealed or revealed by their place in relation to the liquid contained within the vessel, and by their location as related to the placement of the hand of the user. All vessels in the dataset are visually stimulating, but this stimulation is constituted in different ways. The three primary positions for image placement are presented in Figure 6.3, firstly presented as an entire corpus, and then divided into indigenously made and imported pottery.

Figure 6.3 demonstrates a shared preference beween indigenously made and imported vessels for decoration which is placed on the external surface of pots. In both groups, the 'outside' decoration was the most frequently represented form. However, indigenous Etruscan made pottery is also characterised by a large group of vessels which were decorated in a composite fashion, with both external and internal faces used. By contrast, the second most popular image placement site for imported vessels is the internal surface, although this is only slightly more usual than composite image placement. The exact constitution of indigenous composite images can be explored further by dividing the indigenous datA –set into secondary image locations. As the imported pottery images are all concentrated on the body, they are not represented visually.

Figure 6.4 shows that, while the most common place for images on indigenous vessels to be located is, like imported vessels, on the pot's body, a sizable number are located elsewhere. The body of the pot is used in 61% of instances, as opposed to 100% of the imported dataset. All the composite images on imported wares are located on the body, while all save one of those from the indigenous assemblage are located on the handle, or on both the handle and body. There is also a single example of decoration on the legs of a vessel. In both these cases, there is a different experience for the user – the image is placed at the point at which direct contact with the hand is encouraged. While the body of the pot can also be used to lift a vessel, the handle scenes emphasise the agency of the drinker in the revelation of the image in their possession. It is in the power of the drinker to show others the handle of their vessel, perhaps creating a parallel with the interior images preferred in the imported ceramics.

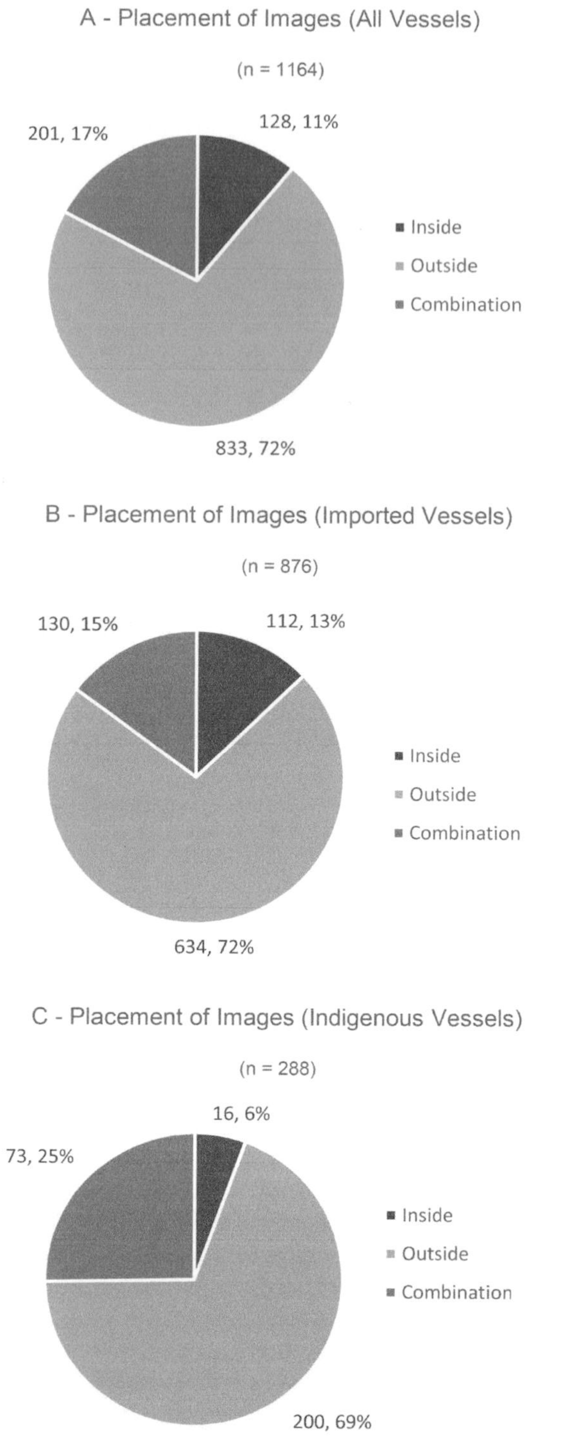

FIGURE 6.3: IMAGE PLACEMENT
A – ALL VESSELS. B – IMPORTED VESSELS. C – INDIGENOUS VESSELS.

Figure 6.5 relates image placement to body proximity groups, and divides this by production origin. It shows that, for all vessels, body proximity and use are the factors which primarily dictate image placement. All perfume, pouring and serving vessels are composed of external images in both imported and indigenous cases. This is caused both by form – perfume vessels are so closed in form that they cannot possess internal images that can be seen – and by audience – serving and pouring vessels are shared, hence the images they carry must also be able to

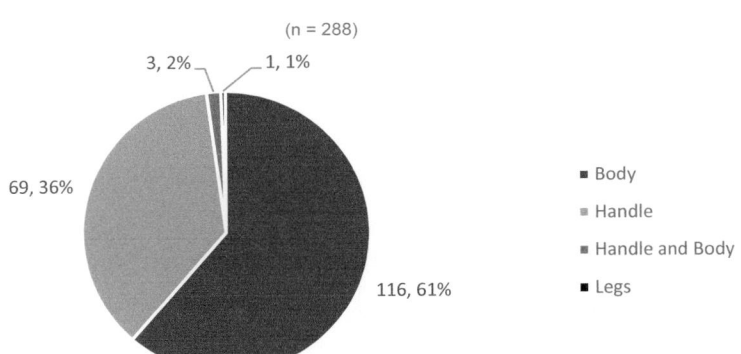

FIGURE 6.4: SECONDARY PLACEMENT OF IMAGES ON INDIGENOUSLY PRODUCED VESSELS.

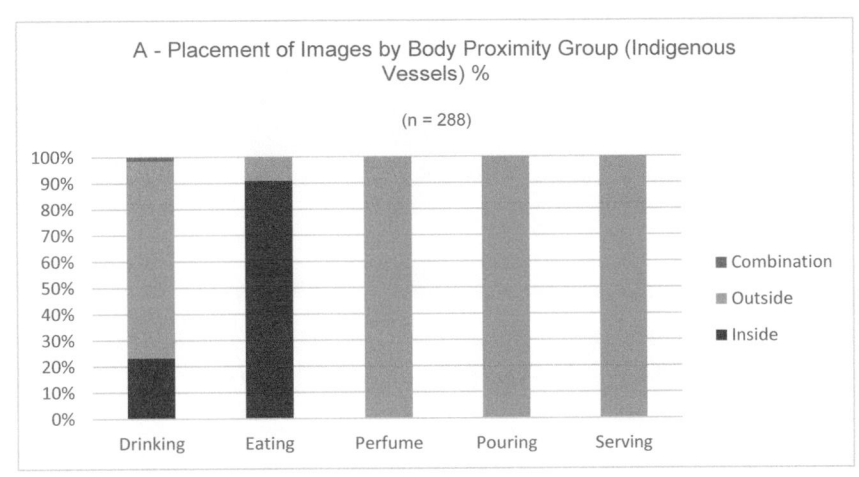

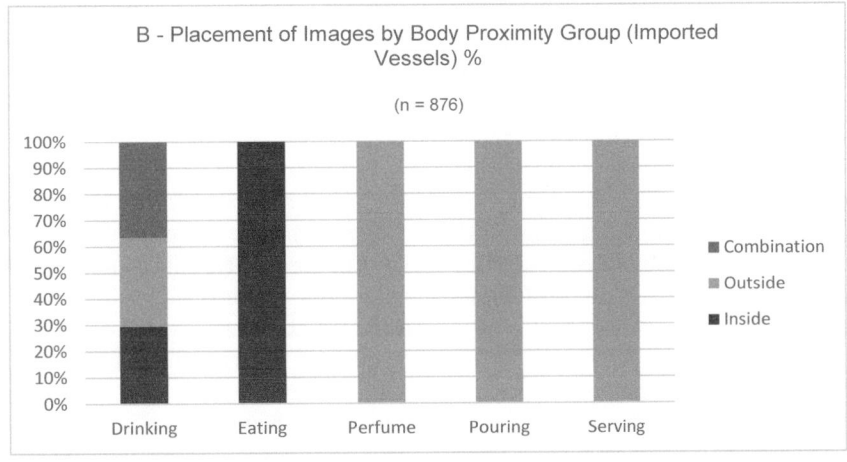

FIGURE 6.5: IMAGE PLACEMENT AND BODY PROXIMITY GROUPS. A – ALL VESSELS. B – INDIGENOUS VESSELS. C – IMPORTED VESSELS.

be shared. The flat plate or platter like forms of eating vessels, while resulting in their images being categorised as located internally, are similarly controlled by accessible surfaces. It is drinking vessels, in both groups, which are the site of variation, and also of difference. Indigenous and imported drinking vessels are decorated differently, with exterior placement preferred for the former, and a more or less equal split between all three forms of image placement present in the latter.

Figure 6.6 shows the relationship between image placement and site. While somewhat dictated by the vessel types present at each site, there remains a strong trend visible in this data: the unique position of the ceramics from Poggio Civitate. The pattern of imported image placement is almost identical at all three sites, albeit with slightly more use of composite decoration at Chiusi. However, in the indigenous material, Poggio Civitate is revealed as completely different in terms of image placement: the vast

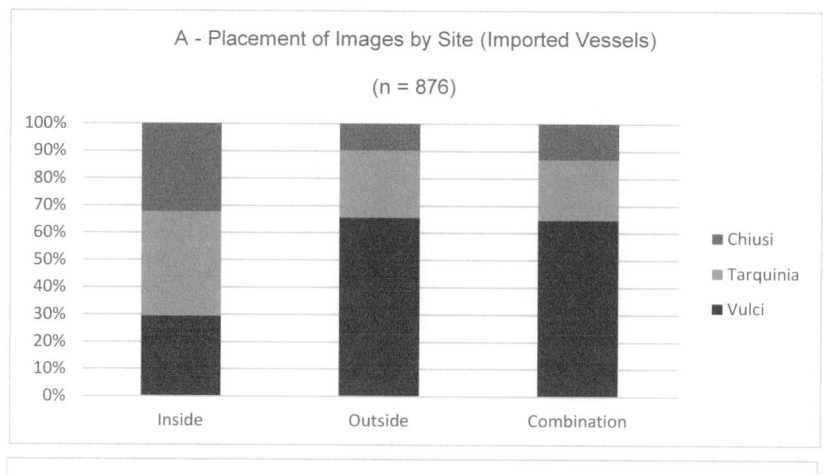

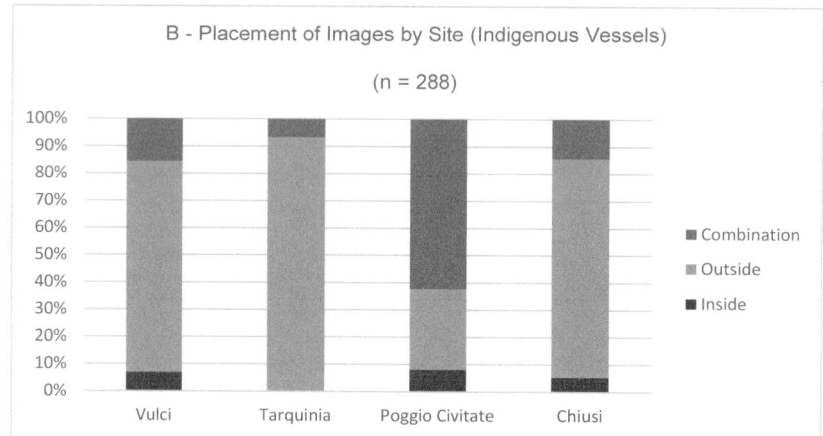

FIGURE 6.6: PLACEMENT OF IMAGES BY SITE.

majority of pots from the site are decorated in a composite way – and these are all examples of handle placement. While this is linked to the large number of drinking vessels at the site, it seems fairly conclusive that decoration on these particular ceramics from Poggio Civitate was being placed in a specific position, and used in a way which is divergent from the three other sites. The proportion of drinking vessels at the site only makes visible a tradition of vessel decoration which is largely absent from the other three sites, and perhaps is only preserved due to Poggio Civitate's destruction.

The most striking pattern from this analysis of image location has been the recognition that the majority of both imported and indigenous ceramics display images on their outer side. In terms of user experience, these images are invisible when the vessel is in direct use – they can only be observed between servings, when the pot is placed down on a surface, or held in the hand. While inner images, both alone and in conjunction with external scenes are present in the data set, the emphasis is firmly on decoration on the outside of a vessel. This external placement of images demonstrates that the decoration on a pot is not only present for its user: every other person present can see the pictures which an individual is drinking in with their liquid contents. This is important: images on pottery are not only designed to impact upon the person using the vessel on which they sit, but also on everyone else in the room. These external images, both Etruscan-made and imported, are designed to be seen, and to be displayed openly, creating an association between the user who experiences them directly and the observer who experiences them indirectly.

In terms of associations between image placement and the location of pottery in relation to the body, the clearest connection is between drinking vessels and an increased level of variability. This could suggest a playful, individual placement of images, with each vessel providing a different experience which could be tailored to the desires of the user. Interior and handle images which can only be accessed by the individual drinker provide an additional interaction between the two, while exterior images can only be viewed by the user when the vessel is placed downwards. The lack of variation in other function groups appears to be largely dictated by their form and use: these vessels are designed for more than one person to look at, so utilise exterior space for images to achieve the widest possible audience. The privacy of revelation of interior images is a particular feature shared between drinking and eating vessels, as food and drink are removed to reveal an image, but in the context of the closed form of drinking vessels this effect creates a specific, intimate experience.

To return to the two different traditions of pottery use identified in the previous chapter, there is far less evidence for a similarly divergent pattern of image placement between imported and indigenous ceramics. While handle-decorated vessels are exclusively associated with indigenously made vessels, and there are more examples of interior decoration on imported pots, there appears to be no clear spread of new image sites from the coast inland. Rather, new methods of representation are incorporated into indigenous traditions alongside imported vessels, replicated in Etruscan-made pottery. The unique pattern of image placement at Poggio Civitate may represent a 'before' snapshot of indigenous traditions prior to contact with imported image placement preferences, or may be indicative of site-specific practice. In any case, it is clear that the relatively standardised location of images across sites cannot be assimilated with the traditions of practice previously identified as associated with imported/indigenous pottery experiences. If image location is not specific enough to either group, what can image constitution contribute to the different experiences created by form?

6.3 Additional Features, Additional Feelings: Image Stimulation

Early on in this chapter, I identified the presence of a group of ceramics which are not only visually stimulating, but also tactile. These vesssels use not only the eyes, but also the fingertips, to communicate with the person using them. Where do these vessels come from, and what characteristics do they share? What was the difference in experience for an Etruscan person using pottery that did not just affect the eyes, but could also be felt directly beneath the hand in the action of drinking?

Figure 6.7 shows the major shared characteristic of these tactile vessels. They are all pots made in Etruria, with three of the indigenously produced body proximity groups being entirely dominated by touch-sensitive vessels. The dominance of tactile/visual methods is evident in all groups except for serving and perfume vessels. The association of tactile/visual techniques of pottery decoration with Etruscan-made ceramics becomes clearer: in the indigenous decorative tradition, the physical experience of pottery was not solely focused on the eye. Drinking and pouring vessels, perhaps linked to specifically Etruscan practices of drinking, prior to the advent of large volume serving vessels, are almost entirely decorated using indigenously developed methods. By contrast, a large proportion of serving vessels are painted, perhaps implying the continued association between an imported form of ceramic and an imported decorative technique, themselves allied to an imported employment of pottery. Perfume vessels, with their associated scent, may also represent a third form of sensory stimulation in pottery, with particular scents being released in conjunction with images. To return to the specifically tactile pots, these are clearly linked to indigenous Etruscan ceramic useways, but where are they located?

Figure 6.8 shows the proportion of visually stimulating and combination (visual/tactile) vessels from each site. In 6.8 A, it is possible to view a clear difference between the southern and northern sites, as might have been predicted based on the different patterns of ceramic use established in each region in the previous chapter. The two southern sites are hugely dominated by visual modes of image experience alone, with Tarquinia exhibiting a slightly larger imbalance between visual and visual/tactile decorative forms. In contrast, Poggio Civitate is entirely composed of visual/tactile decorated human figure pottery, while Chiusi illustrates an almost equal split between the two decorative techniques. If Poggio Civitate is excluded, the data strongly reflects the relative distance of each site from Tyrhennian trading ports, and, it could be inferred, from Greek influenced methods of pottery decoration. The demise of Poggio Civitate before large-scale changes from outside Etruria could percolate up the Ombrone River probably accounts for its exceptional nature – had the site

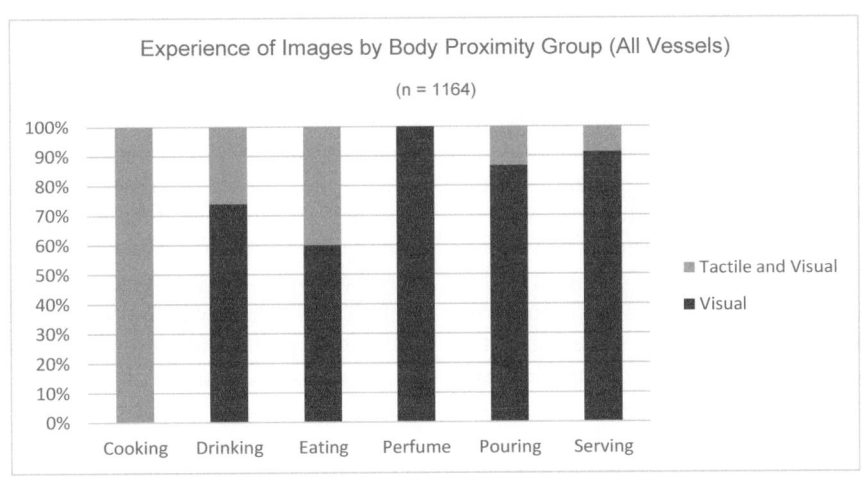

FIGURE 6.7: EXPERIENCE OF IMAGES BY BODY PROXIMITY

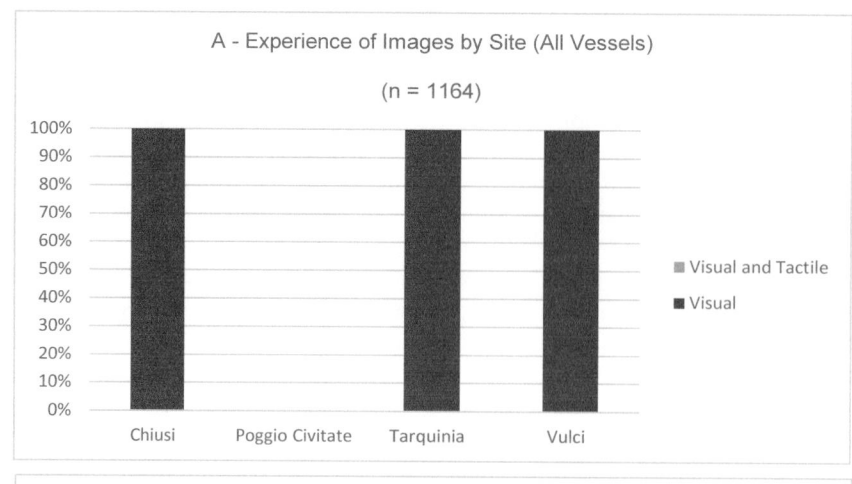

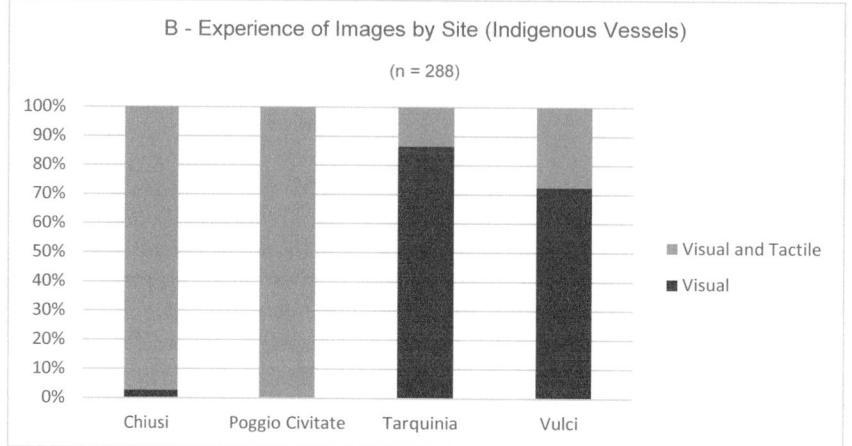

FIGURE 6.8: EXPERIENCES OF IMAGES BY SITE. A – ALL VESSELS. B – INDIGENOUS VESSELS.

continued to be occupied, a pattern similar to that at Chiusi might be expected.

In 6.8 B, in which the imported painted wares are removed from the data set, the continued influence of imported decorative styles in the southern cities of Tarquinia and Vulci is clear in the large number of vessels which deploy visual stimuli alone. The strong traditions of using pottery using a combination of tactile and visual techniques remain present in small numbers in these southern centres, but it is at Chiusi, a centre for bucchero production, that the continuity of tactile vessels is really evident. Human images were produced in a variety of forms, yet the association of visual and combined visual and tactile experiences with imported and indigenously produced pottery delineated a difference in the methods considered appropriate for this rendering. The continued use of geometrically decorated pottery employing tactile methods in southern Etruria demonstrates that these techniques continued to be used, but usually not for representation of the human form.

The existence of a northern tradition of tactile vessels is very visible in Figure 6.8, particularly in figure B. However, how were these tactile images constructed at each site, and which techniques were being employed to produce a specific tactile experience? Figure 6.9 presents the decorative techniques used on the tactile vessels divided by body proximity group and site.

The most commonly used decorative techniques employed to produce a tactile sensation associated with human images are moulding and impressing. The combination of moulding with incised decoration is also found, but only in two types of vessel: those used for drinking, and those used for pouring. The difference between body proximity groups is small, but in terms of distribution of these techniques across sites there is further evidence for a difference in ceramic experience in the northern and southern sites, and even between individual sites. Chiusi, already identified as a centre for bucchero production, is dominated by impressed images, while at Poggio Civitate moulded figures are more commonly found. This is also the case at Tarquinia and Vulci, which are the origins for the majority of images which use a combination of sensation techniques, perhaps reflecting the use of incised decoration for geometric decoration in this region. The experience of touch is constructed differently across Etruria: at Chiusi, it is primarily formed through the subtle encounter between cylinder frieze and fingertips, in which the cartoon-strip of frieze must be carefully examined by both eye and hand. At Poggio Civitate, Vulci and to a slightly lesser extent Tarquinia, moulded figures are being used to create a more

FIGURE 6.9: IMAGE RENDERING TECHNIQUES A – BY BODY PROXIMITY GROUP.
B – BY SITE.

intense interactive experience, involving the user of a vessel in the physical form of the miniature human under their hands.

6.4 Eyes and Fingers: Conclusions

The placement and form of images on Etruscan pottery is central to their effect on the viewer and user, and their experience of ceramics. As the form of a vessel demands a mode of drinking which displays technical knowledge, so the images on a vessel demand a mode of looking and feeling which, while not demanding skill, insists upon engagement. The way in which images are formed and displayed structures this specific interaction, demonstrating the correct way to construct relationships with images on pottery, and incorporate them into vessel use. The placement of an image forms the first part of this construction process, controlling who sees and has access to human figures on pottery. The dichotomy between concealment and revelation evident in the placement of images on the inside and outside of vessels, in addition to the physical contact with images required by handle-placement, presents a series of different forms of human-ceramic interaction, which may be largely divided into two traditions allied to those associated with the use of indigenous and imported ceramics in the previous chapter.

The process of defining the effect of a vessel on those who see it begins with the decision to use an image as decoration in the first place. While I have argued in Chapter 3 (page 96) that Gell's object agency should be conceived of as beginning with form, in the moment that an image is placed on a pot, a further series of intentions come together and are absorbed into the clay. The placement of a picture confirms or queries an object's functional role – who it is designed for, how it will impact upon that person, or persons. The choice of public or private imagery, exposes the power of a vessel to the world or creates an intimate possession between user and pot. In Gell's conception of objects as sources of power and meaning that transform the lives of humans, this placement of an image is a central factor (Gell 1998: 24).

Indeed, that images are designed to be 'seen' is central to Gell's definition of what is and is not art. The specific choices in the placement of decoration dictate to whom the power inherent in the image is directed – whether the vessel will work its magic upon an individual or a group. The technique used in the construction of an image is of equal importance – how will the powerful picture appear to its future users, how will they experience and respond to its demands? Different senses are moulded and impacted upon by the power of the image – shunted and shoved into sensations and emotions by a supposedly innocent etching. As Gell observes, the more an object enthralls the senses with its complexity, the more power it gains (Gell 1998: 23). These twin features of decoration – who has access to imagery, and how they encounter them – dictate how an object is absorbed into the body of its user – and how it can transform that body through its own personal pressures.

In the case of the Etruscan material in this study, the predominant form of image location across the whole corpus, as demonstrated above, is the positioning of representations of humans on the exterior of a vessel. While enforced by closed vessel forms as the only visible location for imagery, this prevalence also exists in open form pots, particularly indigenously produced examples. There is only a small group of vessels, primarily drinking cups and open form eating vessels, which employ interior decoration. Images on the outer side of vessels are clear for all to see: they are shared by all who look upon a particular vessel. The sole employment of exterior decoration for serving and pouring vessels, used communally, emphasises the shared nature of both the contents of the vessels and the images which adorn them. Every person who consumes a part of the contents of these ceramics is enabled to see the images which lie on the outer skin of the vessel. Just as the fluid inside will be shared, so the vessel decoration is held in common – and so are its effects.

The placement of decoration on the exterior of drinking vessels has similar connotations. It is impossible to see the outside of a vessel while drinking from it. The exterior decoration can only be viewed by the drinker when the vessel is set down between sips. However, for those surrounding the drinker, the exterior of a vessel is visible at all times, whether it is being drunk from or placed upon the table. The inter-visibility of individual drinking vessels provides an opportunity for personalisation and the association of particular images with individual owners or users: a person may repeatedly have used the same drinking vessel with the same set of images, marking out their preference for particular scenes, or allegiance to particular figures. Alternatively, the choice of a vessel with exterior decoration may have been used in formal drinking contexts to differentiate between attendees, with the function of making visible a clear demarcation of status and position through the visual display of specific images to the entire drinking group.

Interior images have an opposite series of connotations, particularly in the context of neutral formed vessels. If the open form, flat eating vessels, for which interior decoration is as visible as exterior decoration on a closed-form serving vessel, are excluded, the only vessels which use interior decoration are those for drinking. The major part of this group of interior decorated drinking vessels originate from Greece, with a very small proportion produced in Italy. These Etruscan-made interior decorated drinking vessels appear inspired by the imported versions, suggesting that interior decoration is a form of image placement imported from outside the region. This form of image placement is completely different from exterior imagery – even when combined with decoration on the outer face. An interior image is visible only to the user, and remains visible as the cup is brought to the mouth and drunk from. It is only when the liquid is fully drained that the image becomes fully visible, resulting in a teasing process of revelation as the vessel is tilted into the mouth, and concealment when returned to a flat level in the hand or on a table.

In terms of audience, an interior image is only visible to other drinkers if the user of the vessel chooses to show them, or when the vessel is re-filled. The interior image is directed at the drinker alone: its impact is designed to fully focus its power on a single individual. The connotations of playfulness and surprise associated with interior images revealed through drinking are a light-hearted aside to a serious intimacy, deliberately created to connect together the image and the sensation of drinking. This is an entirely different interaction to the shared observation of exterior images, and its connection with imported wares emphasises their impact on Etruscan drinking practice. The advent of this change must have transformed the individual experience of drinking, particularly on the first occasion: the sudden revelation of an image to an unsuspecting user forging a new and intimate connection between the two.

If interior image placement can be associated with imported imagery, and a form of image interaction connected to drinking practices influenced from abroad, a firmly indigenous tradition of image placement is the location of human figures on the interior face of vessel handles. No imported vessel used this form of image placement, which was most popularly used at Poggio Civitate. The location of an image on a vessel handle intentionally creates an entirely different form of interaction between user and vessel. The image has to be felt with the hand – while the body of the pot dictated the exposure and covering of exterior and interior images, it is the fingers and thumb of the user which control the revelation of a handle image. A handle placed image is not directly visible while drinking, facing the drinker as the interior images do. However, it can be seen out of the corner of the eye, with a larger or smaller area revealed depending on the method used to hold the vessel. What is lost in terms of a visual connection is gained through the tactile nature of handle placed images – the drinker feels the image, strokes it with the fingers, and builds a connection not only with the eyes but with the hand. This link begins from the moment the hand clasps the handle, and is not completed until it releases the vessel again: image and hand are in contact all the way through the drinking process.

A focus on touch, rather than on vision, as a method for images to communicate their intentions, appears to be connected to indigenous Etruscan ceramic experience more widely. The placement of images on handles is only one aspect of what appears to be a far larger tradition. The proportion of indigenously-made pottery which combines both visual and tactile stimulatory techniques, 70% of the indigenously made assemblage, emphasises the importance of touch in the Etruscan drinking experience. Different types of tactile experience can also be distinguished, with each method of image production creating a different interaction between finger and picture. Impressed scenes rolling around the outside of a vessel provide a continuous stimulation for the fingers around the vessel, but demand a high level of sensory perception to distinguish scenes from touch alone. Incised images are similarly difficult to feel with the hand alone, requiring a combination of vision and touch to fully appreciate. Plastic moulded images allow for the most obvious image interpretation through touch – the direct movement of the hand over a represented figurine, albeit attached to a vessel. This method of image rendering, the simplest of the tactile modes to access, is by far the most common decorative technique. Its wide-scale deployment perhaps reflects the level of detail it is possible to render and to feel when using a moulded vessel. The bumps and curves of a moulded figure sculpt the fingers of the user into set patterns, allowing the user to experience an exploration of the ceramic human body as intimate as touching their own flesh. The intimacy of touch is an entirely personal experience: no other person can create the same experience of interaction with a moulded figure. In the context of communal drinking, no other drinkers can have the same relationship with a moulded figure as the person touching it.

The contrast between tactile Etruscan-made pottery and visually stimulating imported wares could not be clearer in the way that they impact upon their audience, and enforce their power over the user.

The bright colours and complicated imagery so often used in Attic black figure pottery are very different to the monochrome moulded contours of bucchero wares. The image needs to be interpreted with the eye – a touch of the hand proves the flat surface cannot create the same stimulation as a moulded decoration. It is tempting to connect this simplicity in tactile decoration with the increased complexity of vessel form design noted in the previous chapter. As vessels required more skill, the tactile senses were fully occupied in negotiating new pottery shapes. The imagery can be absorbed and observed without the hands being distracted from their task of avoiding spillage. The personal and intimate connection between touch and vessel created by tactile pottery decorations is transformed in imported pottery. As observed, interior images, visible only to the viewer, are closely associated with imported wares. With the spread of imported vessels with interior-images, privacy of vision replaced privacy of touch.

While the personal nature of drinking vessel images remained a continued theme in Etruscan drinking practice, the shift from touch to vision transformed the experience of the individual user. What these images showed, and the impact of their subject matter upon that experience, is the subject of the next chapter.

Chapter 7

Experiencing Bodies: Bodies in Images on Pots

7.1 Introduction

The previous two chapters have considered the experience of using Etruscan pottery by focusing primarily on the bodies of pots themselves. They have explored the nubs and swirls which form images to touch or look at, and the curves and lips of clay which shape the pot's motion in the hand and incorporation into the body. Those investigations have exposed clear differences between Etruscan indigenous pottery and imported Greek wares from the perspective of experience: although easier to interact with, Etruscan vessels employ a more variable form of decoration, while Greek vessels are diverse in shape, yet conformative in the decorative experience they offer. This chapter explores the experience of those images themselves: their subjects. The individuals painted, moulded or stamped on the surface of clay are not placed there idly. They are an interactive vision, intended for the eyes of the user of a pot. Whether placed internally or externally, on a vessel which can be lifted and used easily or which demands thought, practice and skill, the bodies on Etruscan ceramics coloured and shaped the experience of the bodies using them. The differences between imported and indigenous representations add continuing shades of divergence between the two groups, suggesting two very different interactions for an Etruscan user.

The analysis of experiencing bodily images is perhaps more problematic in terms of methodological design than that of the shape and complexity of pottery forms, or decorative techniques. In the previous chapters, a phenomenological view was employed which made active use of parameters of the human body which have changed only a little: the length of the hands, the decision to use touch or vision to investigate an image. The exact meanings and nuances of images on Etruscan pottery are almost entirely unknowable: they cannot be exactly reconstructed. However, by re-imagining typologies and types of image, the persons for whom they were designed, and who knew them intimately, can perhaps be approached. This calls for a more specific conception of Etruscan users: the individual gender, age and, perhaps, social class of the person picking up such a pot and making it a part of themselves. Assuming that similar categories of personhood are being employed in the world of users as well as pots creates an opportunity: the types of being engraved on vessels are relevant to particular kinds of user, and give an additional insight into who might be using different pottery forms, or, at least, who their painter intended them to be used by. The meaning of a vessel is different to anyone who uses it, but what patterns of meaning are being created, and are they universally present in imported and indigenous wares, and spread across Etruria?

This process of re-assessing the imagery of Etruscan pottery from the perspective of a user and their relationship and identification with the bodies on a vessel is two-fold. It involves the division of body types on pottery in two stages through a new typology of the kinds of bodies which are found on ceramics. The first set of divisions, illustrated in Fig. 7.1, divides clay bodies into those which are human, and those which are Other. These non-human bodies are a mixture of animals and supernatural figures which combine human and animal features, or use the characteristics of a mixture of species to produce a composite beast. Human bodies are clearly visible in Etruscan ceramic decoration, with features which are recognisable.

These bodies are then taken and divided in a typology based upon gender. A binary system of gender seems to be being employed in ceramic representations: males are

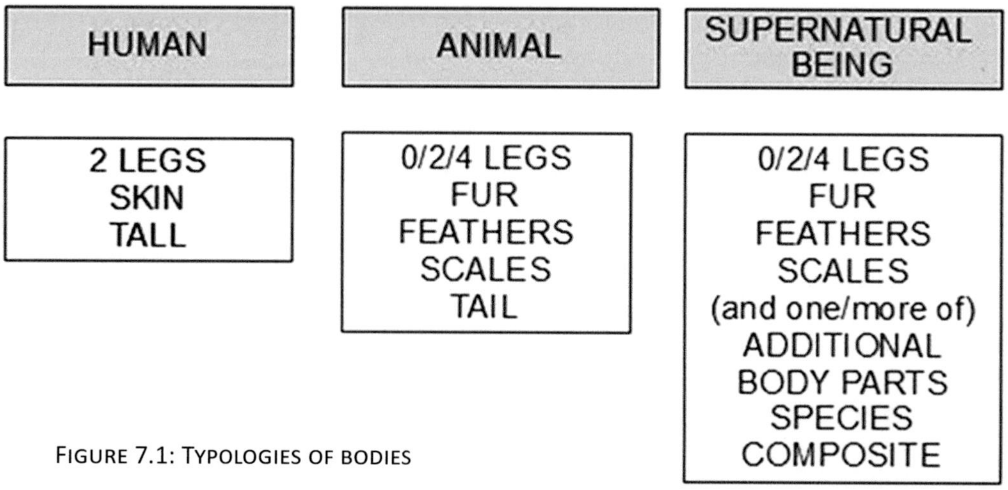

FIGURE 7.1: TYPOLOGIES OF BODIES

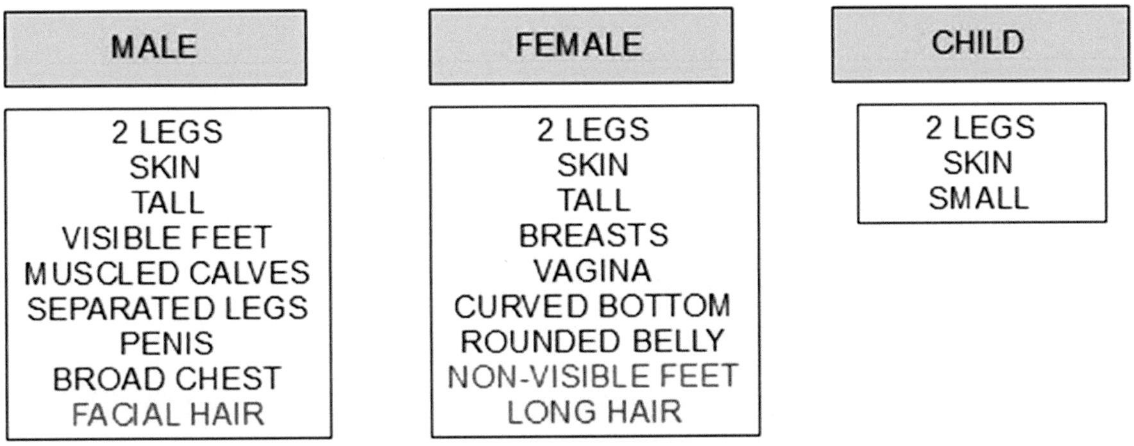

MALE	FEMALE	CHILD
2 LEGS SKIN TALL VISIBLE FEET MUSCLED CALVES SEPARATED LEGS PENIS BROAD CHEST FACIAL HAIR	2 LEGS SKIN TALL BREASTS VAGINA CURVED BOTTOM ROUNDED BELLY NON-VISIBLE FEET LONG HAIR	2 LEGS SKIN SMALL

FIGURE 7.2: YPOLOGIES OF GENDERED BODY

clearly demarcated from females through the form of their body, in addition to clothing, jewellery and cultural features. These characteristics are illustrated in Fig. 7.2. Age was also considered in this process of division, but, as will be examined in more detail later, proved rather irrelevant to the results of the wider analysis. For both types of division of the dataset, a vessel was considered to be placed in a single category (e.g. 'human' or 'female') if a single type of body was shown on its central display surface. Vessels which displayed more than one kind of body, or more than one gendered body type, were classed as composite vessels.

These two phases of dividing bodies and defining persons are considered separately, with each type suggesting a different series of relationships between image and user. In each segment of the analysis, I begin by contrasting imported and indigenous ways of dividing bodies and persons in pottery images: which types of body or person are shown in each case? This initial difference is then broken down by the body proximity groups used to divide pottery forms, exposing where differences lie in relation to the use of vessels. Then, the Etruscan provenance of site of origin is used to divide each phase by geographical connections, examining whether similar patterns of image experience are being employed at each site. In the course of each of these secondary analyses, the different origins of pots are used to produce a continual comparison, and to explore whether imported images are universally similar across the three Etruscan communities where they were being encountered.

In addition to the analysis of the dataset as a whole, in this chapter, and the chapter which follows, individual case studies which exemplify particular patterns of imagery will be discussed as case studies. Their relevance as singular objects to a specific experience is drawn out to illustrate the contrasts between different types of body representations, and the different groups of pots which bear those images and their impacts upon a user. This form of examination of singular case studies is more subjective than statistical exploration of a wider data-set. It is based upon a compositional analysis of each individual image, considering the placement and position of the different bodies grouped together and their relationships with each other. This analysis uses the space of images to unpick the way in which such powerful decorations are structured to impact upon different users, and provoke specific reactions. The relationship between the body of an Etruscan user and the body imprisoned in the clay would have changed with each mood, but by considering the construction of the bodies which have survived in the archaeological record, it is possible to approach the bodies of the dead.

7.2 Human and Other Bodies

The different kinds of bodies to be found on Etruscan pottery are presented in Fig. 7.3, which shows the use of bodies in imagery across first the whole corpus, then the imported and indigenous vessels separately.

In both cases, humans alone were the most common types of body. However, in terms of accompanying bodies, a clear difference is visible between the indigenous and imported assemblages. Animals are the accompanying bodies of choice for the former group, while supernatural and hybrid beings are preferred for the latter. When the two sets of ceramics are divided into body proximity groups, as shown in Fig. 7.4, the distribution of these bodies across pottery uses demonstrates further differences between the two.

The distribution of different bodies across indigenous pottery types is far more variable: large numbers of animal bodies are shown on pouring and eating vessels, while serving vessels are more usually decorated with supernatural beings. The imported assemblage is more uniform, with humans the dominant body type in every class of pottery. Supernatural beings are always thinly represented, usually included in less than 25% of scenes. The only shared point of reference between the variable indigenous vessels and standardised imported pottery is the surge in animal imagery on eating vessels, perhaps linked to the serving of meat.

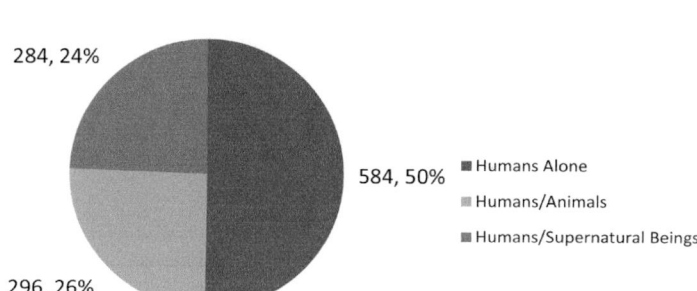
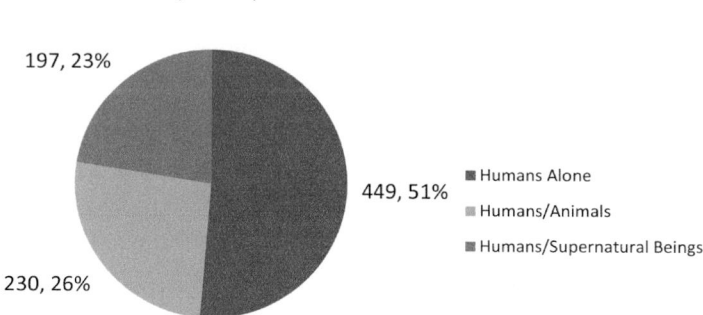
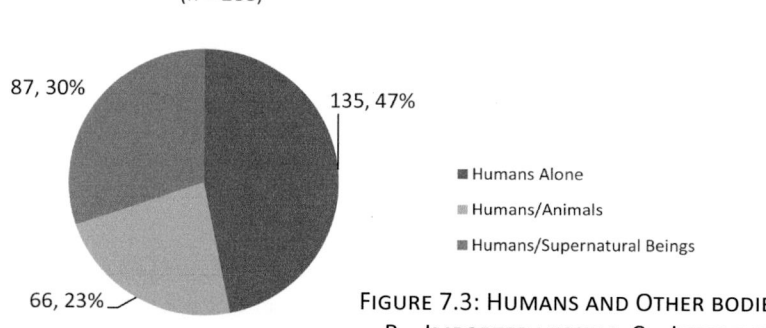

FIGURE 7.3: HUMANS AND OTHER BODIES ALL VESSELS.
B – IMPORTED VESSELS. C – INDIGENOUS VESSELS.

The difference between the two groups is even more obvious when geographical provenance within Etruria is used to divide the dataset, as shown in Fig. 7.5. At the southern sites of Tarquinia and Vulci, imported wares are almost identical in the kinds of bodies they employ as decoration. Indigenous pottery is different at every site. Chiusi and Poggio Civitate are similar in the distribution of bodies, continuing the link between them which was observed in both pottery forms and decorative methods. Tarquinia and Vulci are completely different, with Tarquinian examples displaying a far smaller interest in images of animals. The same patterns of standardised imported representative patterns and variable indigenous imagery observed at the outset are repeated and confirmed: while indigenous pottery is being produced and decorated in site-specific fashions to regional preferences, imported ceramics are being imported with standardised subjects. An exception is visible in the case of Chiusi: the very small number of animal bodies suggests deliberate choice on the part of northern Etruscan users: a continued preference for supernatural beings over earthly animals at Chiusi suggests that a proportion of imported wares were not purchased or used depending on the desires of buyers.

The dominance of scenes of humans alone in both indigenous and imported pottery hides a further difference between the two groups: the role of humans in scenes with other types of body. Each type of

Experiencing Bodies: Bodies in Images on Pots

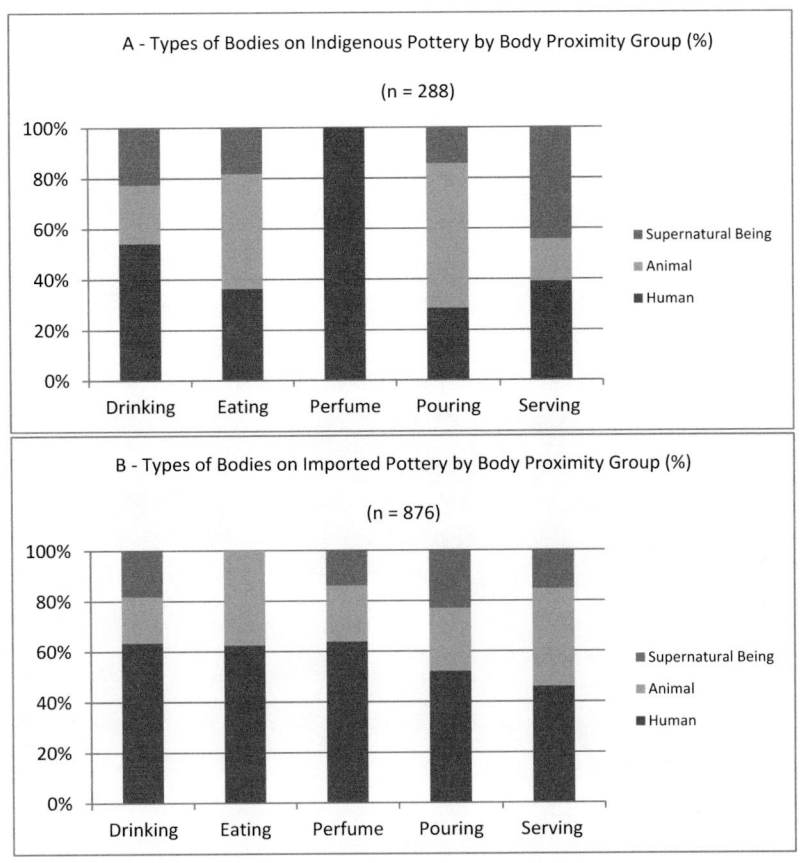

Figure 7.4: Types of bodies by body proximity group A – Indigenous vessels. B – Imported vessels.

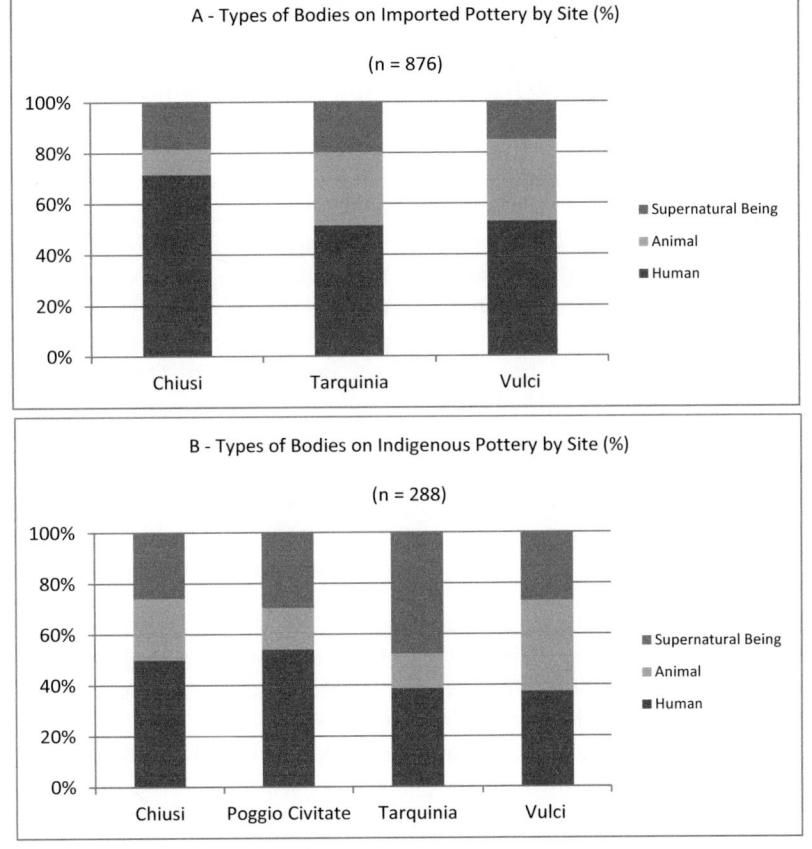

Figure 7.5: Types of bodies by site. A – Imported vessels. B – Indigenous vessels.

FIGURE 7.6: HUNTSMAN WITH DOG AND RABBITS AS PASSIVE ACCOMPANIMENTS. BRITISH MUSEUM VASE B421. IMAGE (C) TRUSTEES OF THE BRITISH MUSEUM.

interaction with other bodies presents further diversity between the two collections of images. Animals are popular subjects in both indigenous and imported pottery: familiar additions that can be used in images to instantly provide attributes or agency to a human subject. A warrior riding in a chariot uses the horses as tools to demonstrate wealth and the fruits of prowess, as well as to provide him with transport. However, clear differences in the configuration of relationships between humans and animals in Etruria and Greece are being illustrated in pottery, as two contrasting case studies demonstrate.

The first example, shown in Fig. 7.6, is characteristic of the role of humans in imported imagery: human bodies are marked out as the most important type of beings. They are the focus of action in scenes, actors who can be related to the life of the person using the vessel. In the composition of Fig. 7.6, the two species of animal body shown in the image are cast to the sides of the scene – the dog is sycophantically placed at the feet of its master, with paws and head turning towards him. This pose gives an idea of the animal half-leaping in pleasure towards the running male figure, an action

which is simultaneously realistic and servile. If the white dog occupies a passive role in the composition of the image, the dead prey are utterly arbitrary. They are hares, their long ears and strong hind legs drooping as they dangle from the staff of the hunter. Their boxing paws are clasped to secure them in death, as their heads loll, necks broken. They are behind the running hunter, unworthy of his attention now that they are dispatched, placed on the very edge of the image. The male body is at the centre, catching the gaze. Both types of animal, in their liminal spaces around him, serve as passive objects which define the male figure as hunter. His control over both the dog and hares emphasises his power over them both.

The indigenous image shown in Fig. 7.7 could not be more different. It shows another male figure, once more sharing the vessel with an animal. The animal is a large feline, probably a lion, which grasps the leg of the man in its jaws. The consequences of such a wound for the lion's victim will be fatal – even if escape from the feline were possible, infection caused by bacteria from its saliva would end the life of the man. He is powerless in the situation, as devoid of agency as the flopping hares of the previous image. The composition of the image is also different: it is a moulded decoration placed on the handle of a drinking cup. The curves of the man's thigh, the thick lines of the lion's jaws, could be felt by the user. The implication for the viewer of this image is entirely different: humans are not beings with control over their surroundings or lives, but can be chewed up and destroyed by more powerful beings. If imagery on pottery is being used as a source of self-identification, unless a complex myth of rebirth lies behind this image, the viewer is perhaps being encouraged to take on the characteristics of the beast, not least its continued survival.

This is not just a difference in the representation and characterisation of wild and domestic animals, or predatorory and prey species. A large group of imported vessels (134 examples) show a man and a large, dangerous feline in combat. The man may be identifiable as the hero Hercle, but is nonetheless determinedly human. There is no suggestion that the lion may be the dominant force in the image. It will lose, it will die, and it will become the skin that will go on to define the heroic representation of its killer. There is no possibility that Hercle will be eaten by the lion, as the man in PC19690095 is being. The motif of humans being the victims of animals recurs at Poggio Civitate in other contexts, notably architectural terracottas (Rathje 2007; Winter 1997, 2009). The myth of Actaeon, eaten by his own dogs, is one of the very few Greek narratives which involve a human being overpowered by beasts, and his demise is the result of the wrath of a supernatural

FIGURE 7.7: HUNTSMAN BEING EATEN BY A LARGE FELINE (A LION?) PC19690095. IMAGE: POGGIO CIVITATE ARCHAEOLOGICAL PROJECT.

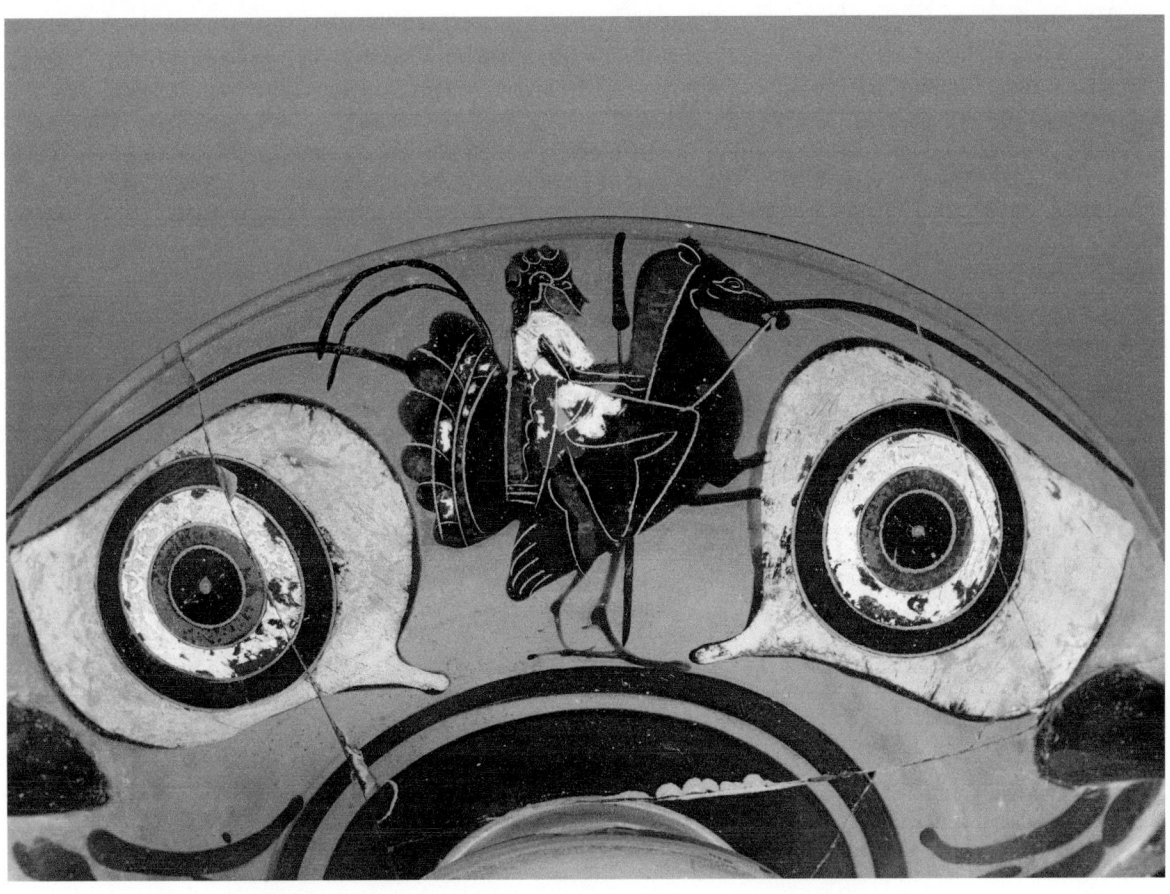

FIGURE 7.8: MALE FIGURE WITH SUPERNATURAL MOUNT FROM VULCI. BRITISH MUSEUM VASE B433. IMAGE (C) TRUSTEES OF THE BRITISH MUSEUM.

being, and while no imported vessel in the corpus shows this situation, it does appear in a very late indigenously produced vessel from Tarquinia (British Museum Vase F480) and has been examined by Tuck (2010). While not all Etruscan images display such violence directed from animal bodies onto those of humans, and there are many scenes of peripheral beasts (such as dogs under tables, or horses being ridden), the existence of such images hints at a different intent in the representation of animals. It is possible that the role of big cats, which would not have been wild in Etruria and may have been entirely unfamiliar to the viewer, is closer to supernatural beings than actual animals. In contrast, a drinking cup from Vulci made in Athens, British Museum Vase E57, presents a male figure leading a cheetah – a particularly rare feline which is clearly subservient to the will of a human body.

The representation of supernatural beings with humans is also different in the indigenous and imported traditions of imagery. In both cases, however, supernatural beings lend a divine sense to proceedings, which may perhaps point to the interpretation of these scenes as imagined, and the activities performed by the bodies present being irrelevant to those which humans might have undertaken in a 'real-life' scenario. The primacy of human bodies in imported representation continues even in scenes incoporating the supernatural: gods and goddesses are depicted as humans, with composite characteristics reserved for lesser figures or monsters. Fig.7.8 shows an image of a male figure riding a composite animal, made up of a horse and a cockerel. In spite of its otherworldliness, this being is still subject to the will of a human rider. British Museum Vase B403, which features a male figure (Theseus) and a composite minotaur, repeats the message of human dominance. The supernatural features of these hybrid beings do not differentiate them from domestic beasts, which can be controlled or killed at will by humans. That all these humans possess specifically male bodies is a point which will be examined in more detail later.

By contrast, superhuman beings in Etruscan indigenous representation are presented in a very different fashion. The vast majority of examples in the dataset show winged female figures, as in the example shown in Fig. 7.9 from Poggio Civitate. These supernatural humans are often presented alone, placed on a vessel without other beings to distract from their central position. In cases where other bodies are present, in all but one example these are animals which flank the central female figure, occasionally with their paws entwined in her hands. The connection with animals is underlined in the example shown in Fig. 7.10, in which a lion-headed man masturbates between two lions. It is unclear whether they have been produced through this interaction, but, as with the winged female figures, the animals act as peripheral guardians to the central composite human. These superhumans are clearly distinct from usual human bodies, and are accorded a more iconic position: their impact on the viewer is instant and striking, presented singly without a running narrative which requires imagination or remembrance.

The variation between imported and indigenous pottery in terms of the presence or absence of different bodies overlies strong differences in the ways in which those bodies are used in imagery. The different preferences of individual sites are clear in the local variation in body types present in indigenous ceramics, pointing to differences in the user experience of pottery at each different location. The imported wares are far more concise in their repertoire, and, with the exception of Chiusi caused by indigenous

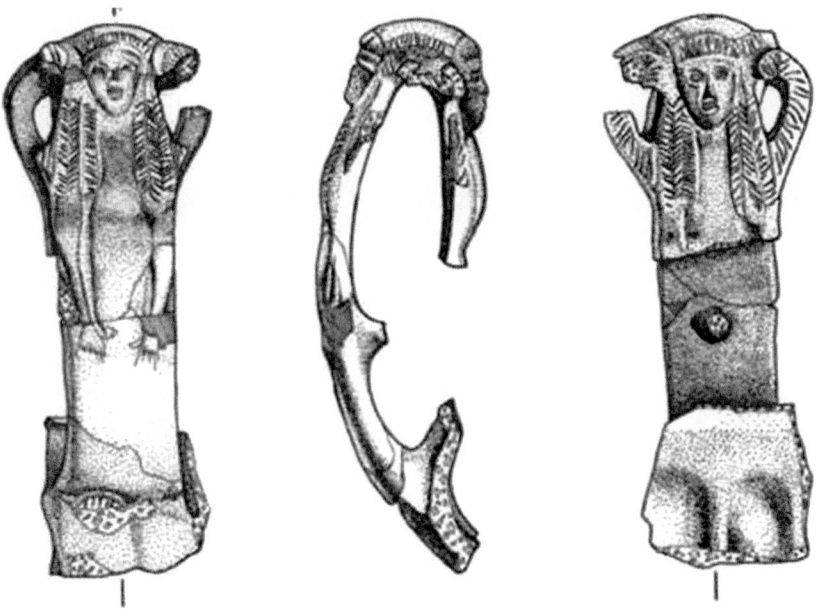

FIGURE 7.9: WINGED FEMALE FIGURE.
PC 19710563. IMAGE (C) POGGIO CIVITATE ARCHAEOLOGICAL PROJECT.

FIGURE 7.10: LION-HEADED MALE WITH LIONS. TARQUINIA MUSEO NAZIONALE RC1979. IMAGE (C) SOPRINTENDENZA PER I BENI CULTURALI ETRURIA MERIDIONALE.

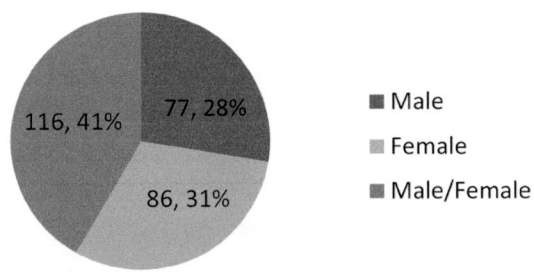

FIGURE 7.11: GENDERED BODIES
A – INDIGENOUS VESSELS. B – IMPORTED VESSELS.

purchasing power, are fairly standardised in the types of humans, animals and supernatural beings they represent. That imported tradition places humans as dominant figures in images, with animals and supernatural figures relegated to human agency: even divinities are represented as largely human. By contrast, indigenous images depict a more complicated relationship between humans and other beings: humans, while dominant in some situations, are nonetheless vulnerable to attack, and are not the primary attendants of the divine. There are already suggestions of further differences in the types of human bodies which are being displayed in indigenous and imported contexts, and these specific variations form the next component of this bodily analysis.

7.3 Gendered Bodies

The different types of human bodies displayed on Etruscan pottery are a central part of the experience of ceramics. Seeing a body which is familiar or different to one's own relates the vessel to the user, alienating or reassuring the user that this object is relevant to them. Pots themselves may be gendered by the bodies marked on their surfaces, rendered male or female by association. The stark variation between representations of different kinds of human bodies in indigenously produced Etruscan ceramics and those imported from Greece is another facet of the divide between the two. The implications of these differences for the user are hard to quantify. Yet through an experiential perspective, the gendered bodies on ceramics can be used to analyse not the gender relationships which existed between their users, but the changing role of ceramics in the construction of individual identities. The first division is by the gendered typologies presented earlier in this chapter, the results of which are presented in Fig. 7.11. In this stage of the analysis, a small group of nine human figures were removed from the indigenous assemblage as they possessed no clear characteristics which could be used to diagnose their gender.

The two groups present two entirely different systems of gender representation. Only 6% of imported vessels do not show a male body and are focused on females alone, compared to 42% of indigenous pots. The indigenous assemblage is divided relatively evenly between all three types of image, with images of females alone being the most popular. The imported assemblage is almost equally divided between male bodies and male and female bodies, with exclusively female pots very rare. These vessels are deeply divided in their presentation of persons and, if this is taken as an act of specifying the gender of the pot, their own gendered personae. Stark differences in preference for the representation of males and females are visible. To examine whether other personal qualities were equally divisive, I repeated the division of the dataset, this time using age to divide the figures. The results are presented in Fig. 7.12, and are conclusive – juvenile bodies are very rarely represented, with the vast majority of individuals displayed as adults. The opportunity provided by the

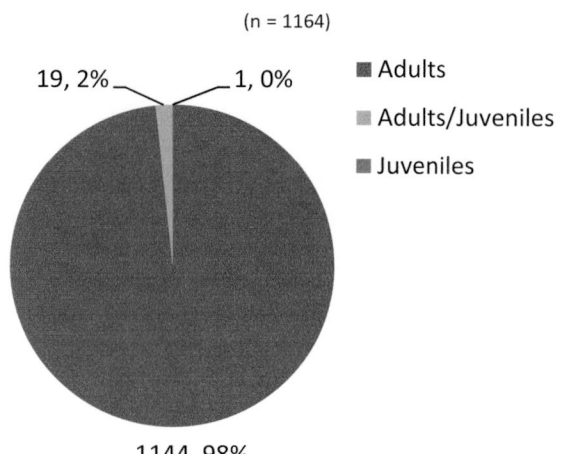

FIGURE 7.12: AGES OF BODIES (ALL VESSELS)

The overarching patterns of gender representation identified from the two assemblages as a whole continue in the individual body proximity groups. The results of this analysis are presented in Fig. 7.13. Imported vessels present a similar picture of representative practice across all five pottery types: the only exceptions are a slight inflation in the number of composite male and female images on serving vessels and a slight increase in female bodies on eating and pouring vessels. These types of pot are the two groups which are closest to indigenous representative preferences, although both retain a higher proportion of males than any indigenous pottery form except for the two perfume vessels, which cannot be taken as significant. The two vessel forms which involve direct contact with the human body are both dominated by female bodies, while the two more remote serving vessels are more mixed. While in the imported assemblage, gendered bodies are being used to decorate pottery with relatively little variation between ceramic types, indigenous pots are divided between those used for direct incorporation into the body and those which facilitate and provide the fluids which will be incorporated. If this is related back to audience, female images are most relevant at the point of consumption, while male bodies and male/female combinations are appropriate for earlier phases in pottery use.

adult form to categorise those mature bodies by gender, and to clarify their position as different types of person, in addition to the relevance of vessels to a primarily adult audience, may be a motivating factor in the alienation of children from ceramic imagery.

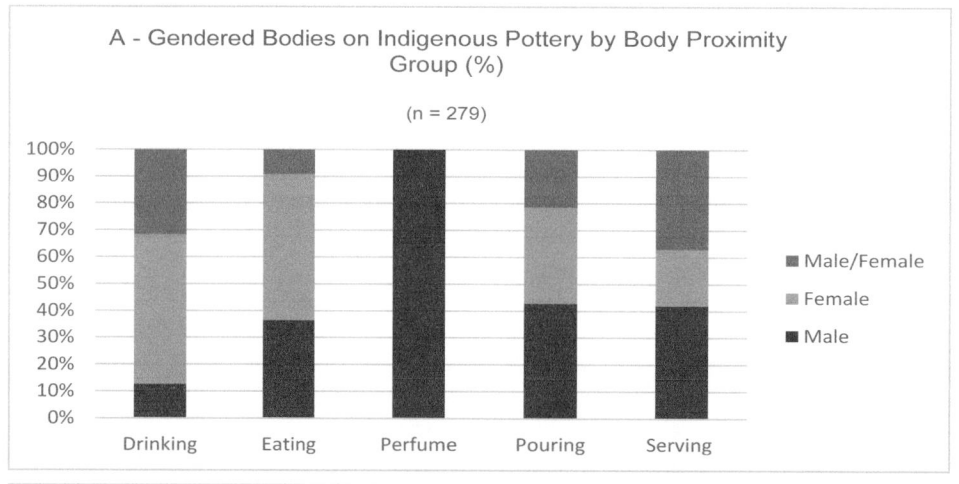

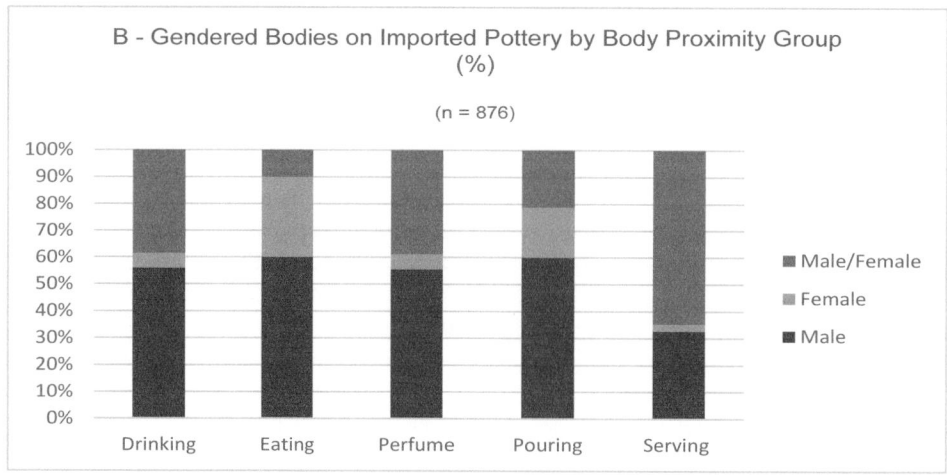

FIGURE 7.13: GENDERED BODIES BY BODY PROXIMITY GROUP.
A – INDIGENOUS VESSELS. B – IMPORTED VESSELS.

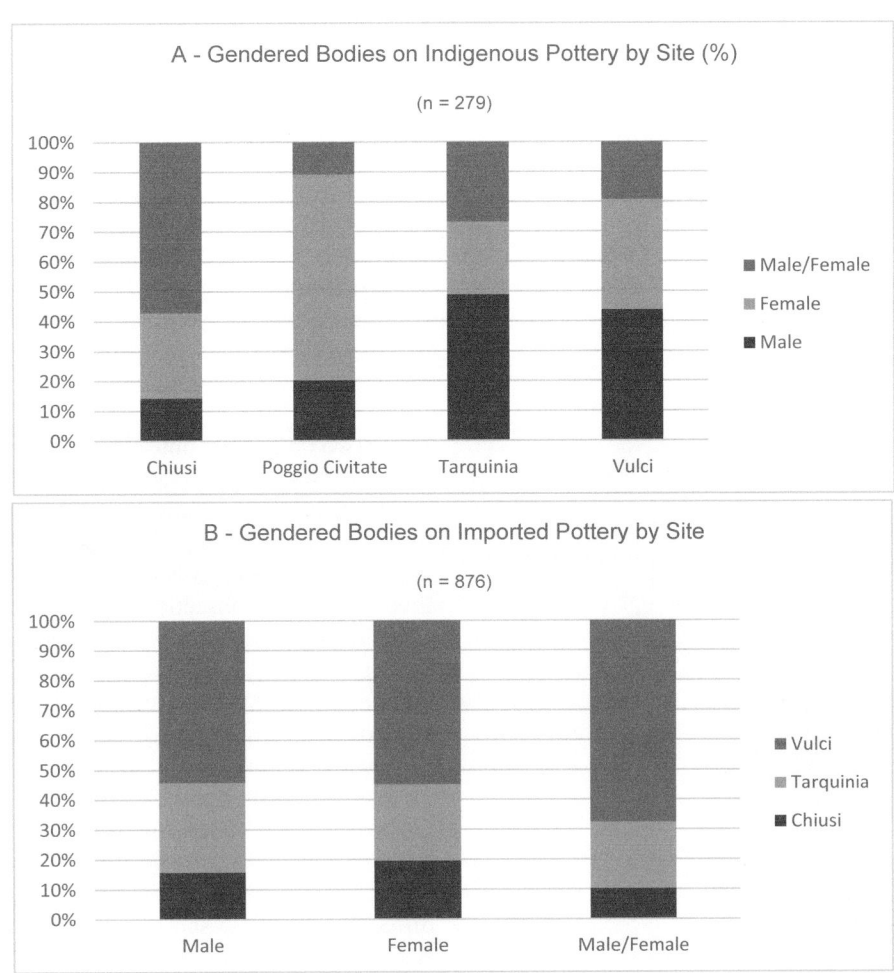

FIGURE 7.14: GENDERED BODIES BY SITE
A – INDIGENOUS VESSELS. B – IMPORTED VESSELS.

When the data is divided by site, as in Fig. 7.14, a now familiar pattern emerges. Exactly as for the types of bodies and decorative techniques, the indigenous pottery represents a variable pattern which is suggestive of local traditions of pottery decoration and different preferences in the viewing of gendered persons. The two pairs of northern and southern sites are retained, suggesting that the regional traditions of ceramic use and experience were also influential in the placement of gendered bodies onto the clay. Just as unsurprisingly, the imported material is almost identical at all three sites. There are slight differences (more female bodies at Chiusi) suggestive of local choices made by discerning Etruscan customers, but the repeated pattern of gendered representation confirms the suggestion that imported wares reflect a selected corpus directly transferred from outside Etruscan representative traditions. It is unlikely that the variations in indigenous representation indicate variation in relationships and the treatment of persons based on gender: the position of specific bodies in indigenous and imported images point to a more complicated role for gendered pots, caught up in changes in the meaningful use of ceramics.

The compositional analysis in the previous suB – section indicated differences in the representation of human bodies between indigenous and imported pottery in terms of their agency. For the user, a human body engaged in a project which actively changes or dictates the imagery of a vessel is a different prospect to a human body as marginalised as a dead animal. The use of a particular group of bodies, those of women, forms a case study in different styles of representing persons. The imported vessels, while featuring males in 94% of images, do also include females in 54% of cases. The position of those female bodies, both alone and in relation to the male bodies around them, defines their contribution to the images in which they feature. While females are more regularly represented in the indigenous vessels, appearing in 73% of examples, the same question of their role in image composition applies. Images depicting female bodies were divided into those showing active females, fully involved in a project central to the image, passive females excluded or objectified from the activities of other bodies, and iconic females who form the singular focus of an image. The results, presented in Fig. 7.15, underline the striking difference in the representation of women in imported and indigenous pottery.

Indigenous representations of female figures are largely iconic, while imported images display women as passive figures. The clear focus of imported images is the male

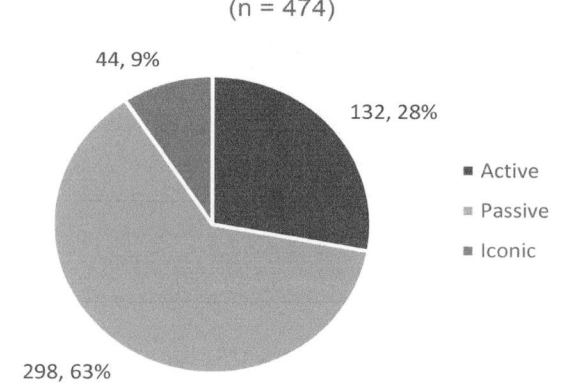

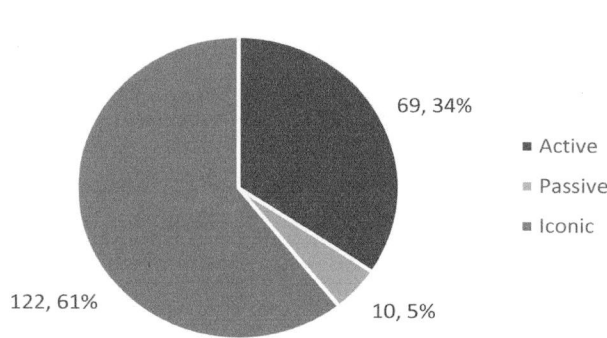

Figure 7.15: Positions of female bodies. A – Imported vessels. B – Indigenous vessels.

body, which is almost always the centre of any composition. Indigenous female bodies are rarely represented as passive: they are either the iconic single focus of an image, or heavily involved in an activity which defines it. When the positions of female bodies are divided by site, as in Fig. 7.16, female passivity in imported pottery is shown to be ubiquitous at all three sites using imported ceramics. Indigenous treatment of women's bodies is different at each site: the two northern sites use more iconic images of females, while the two southern sites, and particularly Tarquinia, employ women's bodies in active positions.

The specific representation of gendered bodies is clarified in individual examples from both traditions. Fig. 7.17 depicts two vessels imported from Greece, both of which engage with the idea of the female body as active and then firmly discard it. On the left, in a famous composition, a male and female warrior are fighting one another. On the right, the female warrior has been killed and is slung over the male's shoulder in a fashion disconcertingly similar to the position of the slaughtered hares in Fig. 7.6. The woman's body is used in the first image as a foil, similar to the employment of composite beasts for male figures to dispatch. While the bodies of the fighters occupy a symmetrical position, the woman is carefully placed below the man. If an Etruscan audience knew a variant of the Achilles and Penthesilea myth, they could have contextualised the vessels through the narrative, giving the female bodies in both pots a specific role as active yet doomed. If they did not, the two images are entirely different: the first depicts an active female figure vigorously involved in the scene. The second shows the female body flopping and objectified in death. The contrast between the two, once the mythological context is removed, presents an entirely different experience for the users of the two vessels.

These two images are unusual in the imported assemblage. More commonly, women's active bodies are depicted peripherally: accompanying male bodies which form the centre of the image. In one group of scenes, women hands a male child to a superhuman figure: while she is involved in the transaction as the child's mother, it is the child himself who is the focus of the image. A male infant pushes both a divine and mortal woman to the liminal areas at the edge of the scene. In one of the most common compositions within the corpus, shown in Figure 7.18, a male warrior bids farewell to another male figure. Though his feet are pointed towards the woman on the far right, his head is turned away. She is isolated in the corner of the composition, further away from the male body than the dog at his feet. These active yet excluded women are very different from those shown in indigenous representations. A series of images from cylinder impressed vessels (detailed in Scalia 1968) show female bodies involved in a ceremonial presentation or courtly event: women are both enthroned and represented as providing gifts alongside males. In indigenous images of men and women together, both are involved in similar kinds of activities.

Images of females alone are equally divergent. The indigenous tradition of iconic females presents a repetitive vision of the lone, divine female. Defined by her long hair, plaited or loose over her breasts, this woman stands alone on vessels, or is accompanied by two wild animals or birds, as in Figure 7.19. This type of image, often referred to as the 'Mistress of Animals' or 'Potnia Theron,'[18] presents the female body as a source of control and has origins in Near Eastern goddess motifs (Andersen 1992; Valentini 1969). The woman controls the animals in her grasp, without violence. Even without her animal accomplices or divine wings, this type of female body is repeated over and over again on Etruscan indigenous pottery. The few images of imported females alone are very different. These women are active, often engaged in activities which emphasise their bodies and their difference from the familiar male

---

[18] Although the worship of a female deity associated with animal control at Tarquinia, who appears to have been particularly closely linked to deer, has been identified through inscription evidence as the Etruscan goddess Uni(Bonghi-Jovino 2001: 21-29). The presence of a sanctuary to a goddess associated with animal control at Tarquinia is perplexing in light of the representation of female bodies at the site and relative lack of ceramic imagery associated with such a figure. It could be that in certain regions this deity was appropriate for placement on pottery, while in others she was not.

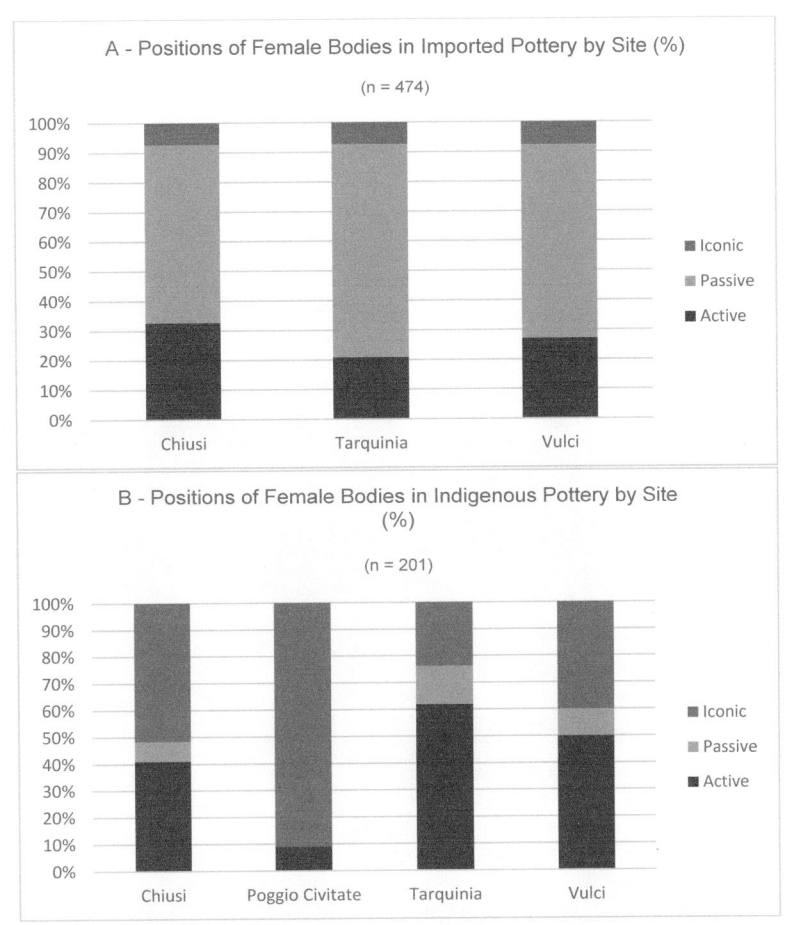

FIGURE 7.16: POSITIONS OF FEMALE BODIES BY SITE.
A – IMPORTED VESSELS. B – INDIGENOUS VESSELS.

FIGURE 7.17: PASSIVITY IN FEMALE BODIES IN IMPORTED POTTERY: AN ACTIVE WOMAN IS PACIFIED AND MADE AN OBJECT
LEFT: BRITISH MUSEUM VASE B21. RIGHT: BRITISH MUSEUM VASE B323.
IMAGES (C) TRUSTEES OF THE BRITISH MUSEUM.

FIGURE 7.18: THE ACTIVE YET PERIPHERAL FEMALE BODY.
BRITISH MUSEUM VASE E448, FROM VULCI. IMAGES (C) TRUSTEES OF THE BRITISH MUSEUM.

FIGURE 7.19: 'POTNIA THERON' FIGURE WITH OWLS FROM POGGIO CIVITATE.
PC19710560. IMAGE (C) POGGIO CIVITATE ARCHAEOLOGICAL PROJECT.

form. In Figure 7.20, a woman points at her vagina, while simultaneously waggling an enormous olisbos towards her mouth. Her body is twisted uncomfortably to display her to the viewer frontally, while her eyes are averted, focused only on her phallic accessory. This image is intensely different from the abstract gaze of the female faces shown in indigenous representations of women, and further differentiated from the Potnia Theron style icons.

To summarise, the gendered representation of bodies in indigenous and imported Etruscan pottery presents a continuing series of contradictions. Indigenous vessels employ different types of bodies, preferring female bodies to males, while the opposite is true of the imported wares. The way that each type makes use of those bodies is also different: female bodies are passive and objectified in imported imagery, but iconic and engaged in activities in indigenous scenes. The exact choice of gendered images in indigenous vessels varies at each study site, while imported vessels present a restricted series of bodies which is almost identical across Etruria. Taking these observations, and those on the relationship between human and animal bodies, what is the effect of such images on their user, and what is the implication for the role and purpose of pottery decoration in Etruria?

Figure 7.20: Female with olisbos from Vulci.
British Museum Vase E815. Image (C) Trustees of the British Museum.

7.4 Bodies on Pots: Conclusions

The overarching patterns of body type distribution across Etruria match up very closely with those observed in the previous chapter. The imported wares provide a stock collection of body types, for the most part focused upon human males. The steady repetition of similar motifs at each study site strongly suggests the presence of a set repertoire of imported bodies available to Etruscan users, in spite of small variances suggestive of the preferences of those users. The indigenous assemblage is far more variable, both in terms of the types of bodies shown and the gender of those bodies. Each site has its own distinct distribution of indigenous pottery bodies: all four are different. The regional similarities between Chiusi and Poggio Civitate continue, while those between Tarquinia and Vulci are slightly more disparate. These patterns of the distribution of bodies between indigenous and imported wares provide an important additional impact of imported pottery on Etruscan users and their experience of pottery. The role of persons on pots, the point of bodily decoration in ceramic vessels, was changing.

In terms of types of bodies, the primary change was in the position and representation of human bodies. The indigenous interest in supernatural bodies, primarily supernatural female bodies, contrasts with imported preferences for human, male bodies. The relationship between those male figures and the creatures and beings with whom they share a vessel is strictly hierarchical. The human male is in command, central to the image, even when he shares it with divine beings. There are already implications for changes in the representation of gender in this conclusion. The imported assemblage seems to conform to a vision of Greek women as peripheral to male bodies, occupying the edges of images, bound in passive positions or, when active, forming entertainment or doomed opponents for male protagonists. The contrast between indigenous imagery of females and males joining in processional scenes together, and the iconic representation of female faces on drinking vessels is stark. The experience of using an imported vessel which shows a male figure dominating a dangerous animal, or which excludes a female user from identifying with a powerful personage, would have been vastly different for an Etruscan individual.

This change in representation, and the associated change in experience for specific Etruscan users, suggests a different function for imagery in the two types of pottery. They are so different, almost incompatible, that the desired effect of each type of visual tradition must also be different. The agency and power of each type of image suggests a transformation in images linked to the revolution in vessel forms suggested in chapter 5. The placement of specific images on particular pottery types is further confirmation of different purposes for imagery in particular contexts, yet there is a broad sweep of practice uniting these different forms. Indigenous Etruscan imagery is ambiguous about the role of human beings. Hybrid animals and supernatural figures create a ceramic world in which humans are by far the least powerful figure, and occasionally are represented as the victims of these stronger beings. The image of the winged female, to be physically felt as a moulded image in the midst of an intense experience between an individual drinker and their cup is a particular icon of this form of ceramic agency. In the dangerous world represented in the Etruscan tradition, this figure suggests personal protection.

To pursue this idea further, the presence of a source of supernatural power is both a control for the behaviour of the drinker and a source of protection – the presence of the goddess is absorbed into the food or liquid, preventing actions which might denigrate her figure. That power also acts as an apotropaic force, preventing poisoning from food and drink, safeguarding the physical health as well as the behaviour of the consumer. In addition to these protective powers, iconic supernatural female images can be linked to one of the effects of moderate alcohol consumption: an increase in libido and attractiveness of the opposite sex, experienced by both male and female drinkers. The presence of exhortative inscriptions to Aphrodite on early drinking ceramics made in Greece, particularly that on the 'Nestor's Cup' from Pithecussae (Faraone 1996; Hansen 1976; Murray 1994; Ridgway 1992: 55-57, 1997), indicates a recognition of the connection between alcohol consumption and desire. Shorter inscriptions on ceramics from Etruria, such as the 'Mi Uni' cup from Tarquinia, in addition to single figure sigla, have also been linked to deities and the everyday rituals involving the use of ceramics (DeGrummond 2009: 159). The combination of control, protection and the promise of fertility is a potent cocktail. This most popular form of representation in the indigenous dataset connects up with the other images in its function: Etruscan indigenous imagery is designed to influence the user through references to divine figures who provide security and the promise of fertility.

The function of imported ceramic images could not be more different. The dominance of male bodies over females, animals and divine figures discounts the power of the latter almost entirely. The images are confident depictions of idealised bodies: the males are perfectly positioned in relation to the beings around them, displaying their superiority through their central position and continual activity. These images do not require the benevolent intercession of a divine figure: their power lies in the perfect figures on their surface. The overarching purpose of these images is self-affirmation. The user is encouraged to identify with the bodies in the image, to recognise their own physical characteristics reflected in the perfect power of the male actor. In the case of perfume vessels, the oozing oil changes the scent of the body into that of the ideal male on the bottle. In the case of vessels associated with alcohol, the effects of the drug create a feedback loop: the drinker self-identifies with the idealised figures on the vessel, while the contents of the vessel, having absorbed the power of those figures, make the user feel that they have taken on those idealised attributes.

This change in image function must have had an extreme effect on Etruscan drinkers, with that effect to some extent dictated by gender. The intoxicating feeling of confidence associated with the imported vessels' portrayal of male bodies must have transformed the experience of drinking for men. Imbibing the passive alienation of women's bodies in imported wares must have felt very different for Etruscan women to the consumption of divine femininity. In spite of a hint of buying practices that tried to diminish this effect, and the continued use of indigenous ceramics, the representation of bodies shows another clear experiential difference between the two forms of pottery, this time with specific and potentially gendered implications.

The impact of such a stark change in the experience of seeing a deeply familiar kind of body placed in an entirely unfamiliar situation is hard to ascertain. For an Etruscan woman to find herself surrounded by images that depict bodies like hers forced to the fringes by those of males – for the trusted image of a divine female body embued with control to be replaced with scenes of women's bodies entirely dominated by those of males – must have been a jarring and jolting experience. In Butler's terminology, the script of a gendered performance is being rewritten, providing a new series of norms from which to reconstruct an entirely different performative self. The act of using such vessels might become iterative – an act of tacit approval, a decision to equate one's body with those on the pot. For a male user, splashing on perfumed oil or drinking from an imported cup, the action creates a new self – the rubbing in of the perfume is the ultimate performative gesture, bringing into being a new character, with new lines and a new way of being.

Continued exposure to such images must have a continued effect which is enacted on the body. Just as the female child in Young's case study knows that people with bodies like her own cannot throw stones well, an unconscious awareness of the changing role of female bodies shown on such vessels must have grown in women and girls coming into contact with the new passive female body. The small gestures, body positions and relationships visible in the vessel imagery forms a microcosm of potential reactions – the man who barges to the centre of the gathering, the woman who physically alienates herself from male company, folding in on herself with arms and legs at the side of the room. The consequences of a shift in gendered imagery on pottery, and their myriad tiny effects on individual lives, are easy to imagine. The next chapter goes beyond the first impressions gained of bodies on pottery, the first layer of a performance. It examines the specific tasks and actions that define the active or passive body – the way in which divine protection and idealised self affirmation are constructed and confirmed through the behaviour of people on pots – and their continued effects on the lives of people who use pots.

Chapter 8

From Being to Doing: Actions of Bodies on Pots

8.1 Introduction

The bodies represented on Etruscan pottery are figures caught in a moment. They are frozen in position, deliberately placed in certain poses or in the midst of specific activities by the craftsperson that placed them there. The types of bodies which are used to illustrate these objects, and the positions those bodies occupy in relation to each other, have been demonstrably linked to the places in which those craftspeople worked, and suggested two very different traditions of representation. By extension, these two styles of imagery also suggest a relationship with pottery, and the images on that pottery, which is equally divergent in the two groups. Imported ceramics were being used for the promotion, production and confirmation of idealised identities, with a focus on the male body as the central subject of representation and desirability. Indigenous ceramics appear more concerned with volatility, change and the creation and continuation of connections between humans and the supernatural. Bodies themselves, however, are only one part of the construction of images. The particular actions which those bodies are undertaking provide a clearer idea of the the differences between imported and indigenous wares. The analysis of actions also provides a vision of the different activities which were used to characterise idealised bodies, and to forge links between humans and divinities. Regional and local differences in those activities allow for a more specific vision of variety across Etruria, one a little obscured in the observation of bodies alone. The Etruscan person using a vessel would have put its form and decoration, the bodies and actions displayed on its surface together into a single, fluid interpretation: by the end of this chapter, all four of these parameters will have been examined. An interpretation of the full experience of using different Etruscan pots, in four different Etruscan places, will be possible.

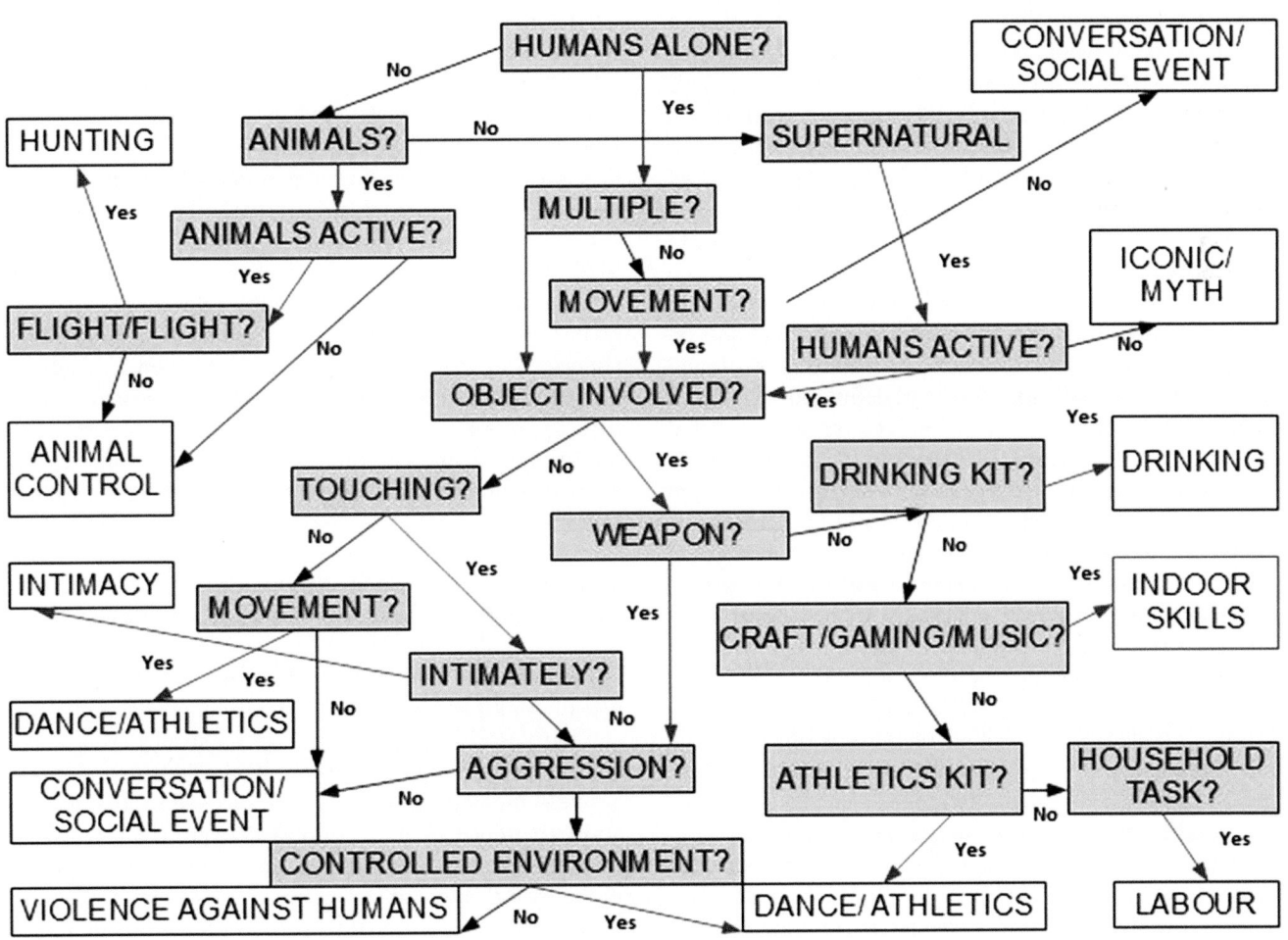

Figure 8.1: Process of activity definition.

In order to add this final piece to the experiential analysis, a method for the analysis of actions being undertaken in pottery images was put together. The work of Giudici and Giudici (2009) considered the activities shown in all pottery imported from Greece to Italy. The resulting categories, while comprehensive, were as unwieldy as traditional pottery forms for a statistical analysis: the sheer variety of imagery made their dataset very complicated. Before becoming ensnared in specific activities, the first question for this study was to investigate the combination of activities on vessels: what proportion of ceramics at each level of analysis (production origin, body proximity group and site) showed multiple types of image? The experience for a user of interacting with a vessel with multiple activities shown is potentially more nuanced and complicated than that of using a pot which contains either a single image or multiple images presenting the same action. The vessel can be twisted and turned, to ensure that one of the two images is presented, or a contrasting interior image can be revealed in the process of use. The presence of these multiple activity pots, their origins, forms and locations, forms the first part of the activity analysis.

The second part of that analysis returns to the difficult task of recording and contrasting the specific activities shown on Etruscan pottery. The first decision was to assign each image an overarching theme. The specific actions of each individual body would have made for a very complicated analysis, so the broader theme to which those bodies were contributing was made the central unit of comparison. To categorise those themes, I developed a series of questions which were employed like a flow chart for the division of the dataset into comparable categories. Starting from the compositional analysis of bodies, the questions moved to the actions of those bodies and their interactions with each other and objects in order to arrive at categories of action which were broad enough to incorporate all the variants on an overarching theme. This map of questions is illustrated in Fig. 8.1, and details the process of definition which lead to each of the twelve categories. This process avoided the problem of becoming immured in the detail of each individual composition, allowing for comparison between groups of pots on a defined level. While this process of question and answer provided a satisfactory categorisation for the majority of vessels, some very specific images demanded a more subjective analysis. In the case of those images, I placed each in the overarching category which seemed most appropriate.

Having divided the activities on vessels through this method, the same comparisons between indigenous and imported pots, body proximity groups and sites are made. The results of these comparisons are then followed, as in the previous chapter, by a more subjective compositional analysis of activities. Through more detailed case studies, the illustration of particular features of ceramic experience as produced through different vessel types and in different spaces is possible. This use of case studies serves as a reminder of the complexity and individuality of experiencing each type of image: the full impact of pottery on a user. Through these three phases of analysis, the representation of activities and their relationship to the design and purpose of Etruscan pottery in influencing experience and action in the living world is put forward. The action of these ceramic bodies, caught in a perpetual state of motion, involved forever in a carefully chosen activity, would have created a response from the Etruscan user who encountered them. That response might include the repetition of activities seen in pottery, the recreation of idealised actions which defined persons and bodies. By categorising the particular actions being used at each point of pottery use, and each location in Etruria, it is possible to assess whether this process of transferring action from image to reality was taking place. The motivations for decorating Etruscan pottery with human figures, and the power of those images, are both made clearer through the frozen activities in which those figures are eternally occupied.

8.2 Multiple Layers of Experience

The presence of multiple forms of action on a vessel presents a different experience to the viewer from the use of a single continuous theme. This type of ceramic forms a minority of the dataset as a whole, so this type of complex experience involving the manipulation of vessels to display different images must have been relatively uncommon. As shown in Figure 8.2, multiple action pots are primarily imported into Etruria, although a small group of indigenous vessels also use multiple images. More imported pots display this kind of multiple action, with contrasting scenes provoking different responses in the viewer depending on the way they are approached or encountered. This phenomenon could not have been a common one in indigenous pottery experience, suggesting that indigenous vessels were either not required to bear images of multiple relevance to viewers, or that the power and purpose of indigenous pottery was connected to images which needed to be viewed singly in order to be taken seriously. By contrast, imported vessels were appropriate spaces for the provocation of suprise, or the display of images which were entwined together for a singular purpose, and which could depict very different scenarios.

Having identified that it is primarily imported vessels which employ images of multiple activities in their decoration, the relationship of those vessels to the body is presented in Fig. 8.3. The few examples of indigenous use of multiple activities are focused on drinking and serving vessels while multiple action scenes are present within each body proximity group. All interactions between the body and a pot could be used for the display and experience of these imported examples: the small number of cases in perfume and pouring vessels are probably indicative of lack of space caused by the slender, closed or neutral form of these two groups, while larger open form serving, drinking and eating vessels provided more opportunity for the display of multiple images. The

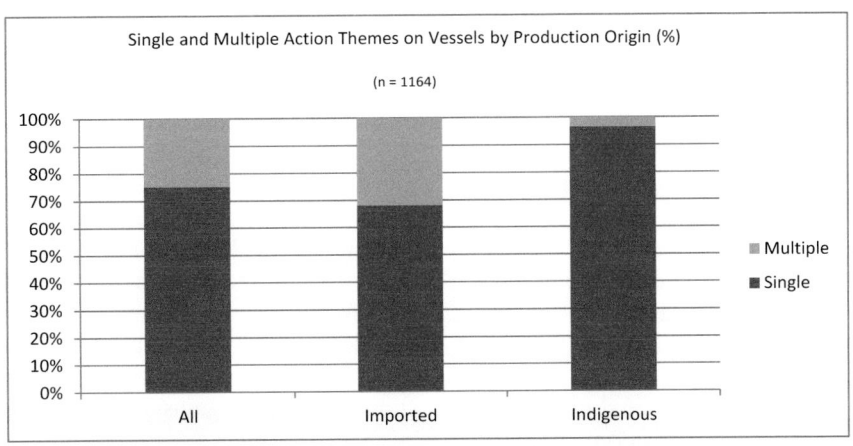

FIGURE 8.2: SINGLE AND MULTIPLE ACTION THEMES BY PRODUCTION ORIGIN.

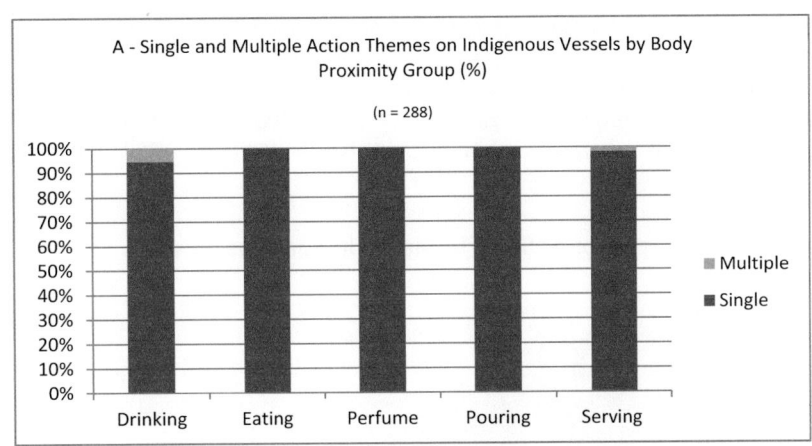

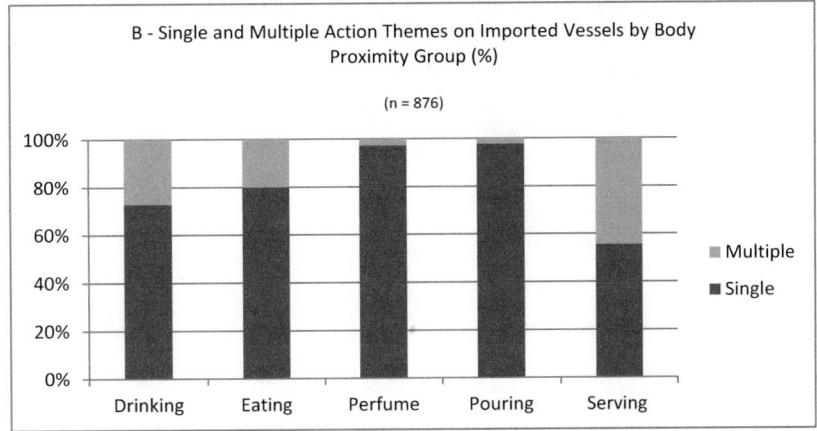

FIGURE 8.3: SINGLE AND MULTIPLE ACTION THEMES BY BODY PROXIMITY GROUP.
A – INDIGENOUS VESSELS. B – IMPORTED VESSELS.

relationship with the body is not a significant motivation in the design of this group of vessels.

While body proximity groups do not appear to be closely connected to the presence of multiple activity images, their distribution across the four sites does clarify the association of this group of pots with importation. The two northern sites have only one example of a multiple action themed indigenous vessel, while these are more common at Tarquinia and Vulci. The influence of imported wares on the design of indigenous vessels in these coastal cities is probably the main factor in the presence of multiple activity pots in these sites. The presence of imported versions of these multi-layered vessels is spread relatively evenly across the three sites: further evidence for a standardised set of pottery which was being peddled across Etruria having been imported in bulk. The hints of variety in uptake of these standardised groups of ceramics visible in the previous chapter are stronger here, with each site having a slightly different proportion of multiple action vessels.

The use of multiple images on a singular vessel appears to be closely connected to imported styles in pottery decoration, and hence in ceramic use. Singular images are all that is required in the vast majority of indigenous pottery, with multiple scenes only employed in areas with high contact with the new influx of vessels. These two patterns ally neatly to the two different traditions of ceramic practice and experience which have been continually observed in previous chapters. They also connect with the ideas about the purpose of ceramic decoration put forward in the previous chapter. Indigenous Etruscan vessels, with their focus on acting as conduits for divine power facilitating change in the body through alcohol consumption, do not require multiple images which contrast with each other. The relationship with deities or supernatural forces can be established quickly, and is presented in a consistent fashion, through a single image. If imported wares can be associated with the promotion and creation of idealised identities primarily linked to masculinity, the presence of seemingly contrasting types of action makes sense. There are multiple actions which can be used to assert and grow this type of identity: images ranging across the gamut of masculine experience can be employed to decorate ceramics filled with substances which physically change the bodies of those who use them. What those activities were, and how they acted on Etruscan experience of pottery, is the next phase of this analysis.

8.3 Themes in Activity

Figure 8.4 presents the different action themes used in the indigenous and imported assemblages. The two are vastly different. It is clear that in addition to a different focus on body type, the actions that those bodies are undertaking are completely diverse in the two groups. Indigenous vessels are dominated by iconic images of single figures, while the most popular type of activity represented on the imported pots is violence against other humans.

From the most popular to the least popular, the two groups of action themes are ordered very differently. The only shared interest between the two is the representation of dance and athletics – apart from this the types of activity which are being imported into Etruria are, while representing the same kinds of action, ordered in a very different way. Imported pottery is dominated by violent

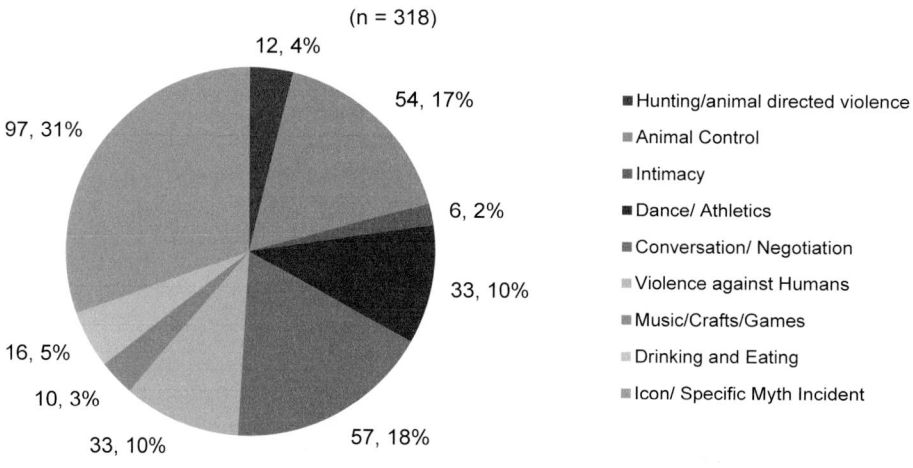

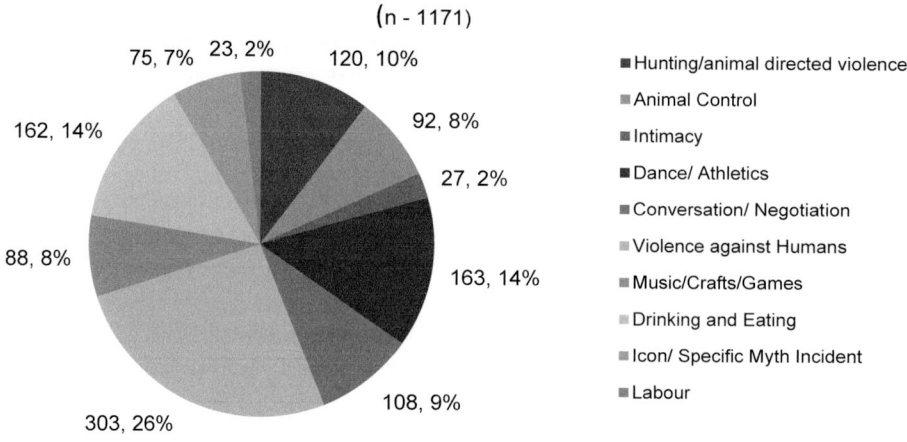

FIGURE 8.4: ACTION THEMES ON: A – INDIGENOUS VESSELS AND B – IMPORTED VESSELS

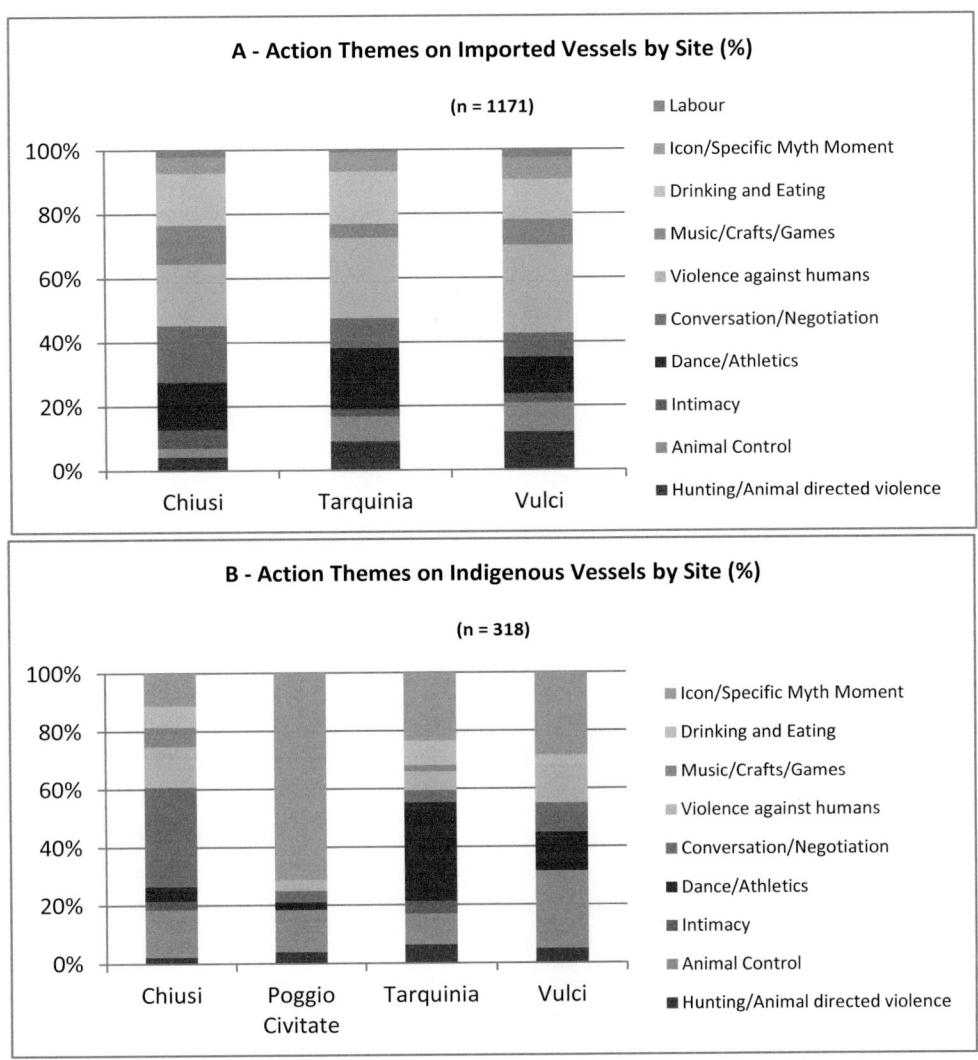

FIGURE 8.5: ACTION THEMES BY SITE

imagery – whether directed at animals or humans, while indigenous actions are more static – incorporating iconic scenes and structured social events. The idea of standardised imported wares being brought into Etruria, alongside activities which were valuable to a non-Etruscan audience holds firm. The indigenous assemblage presents less variety in terms of the types of activities displayed: a contrast to the types of bodies and decorative methods used, which were far more variable.

When the data is divided by site, the indigenous assemblage is exposed as far more variable between sites. While the repertoire of action themes is limited, different types of image are preferred at each site: regional differences in action theme are strongly visible. The link between the two northern sites is gone: Poggio Civitate and Chiusi exhibit very different types of activity, and Vulci and Tarquinia, while not as strongly divergent, also vary from each other. The strongest difference remains between the northern and southern sites. If preferences for body types are shared across sites, the action theme analysis is the strongest evidence for local traditions of representation in pottery decoration: different activities are important at different places. This is closely linked to a wider regional difference between northern, inland Etruria and the southern cities of the Tyrhennian coast. To relate these variations back to the idea of Etruscan ceramics as focused upon bodily transformation through relationships with divine entities, the widespread preference for iconic figures fits this narrative neatly. However, other activities are also being used in decoration which have less obvious connections to external forces. At Chiusi, the focus is on images of structured social intercourse, conversation and negotiation. At Tarquinia, it is on dance and athletics, while at Vulci the most popular scenes are those of animal control.

These secondary scenes are not connected as obviously to the relationship between alcohol, bodily change and divine powers. However, in the individual images the connection between human and divine is clear. In a large group of social intercourse scenes from Chiusi, males and females approach enthroned figures with gifts, while winged female figures are also shown behind these seated individuals. The procession and dedication of gifts are closely linked to intercession with figures of power: whether human or immortal. Scenes of animal control, too, recall the divine – images of untethered wild animals with humans, or marine creatures. The scenes of dance and athletics also feature

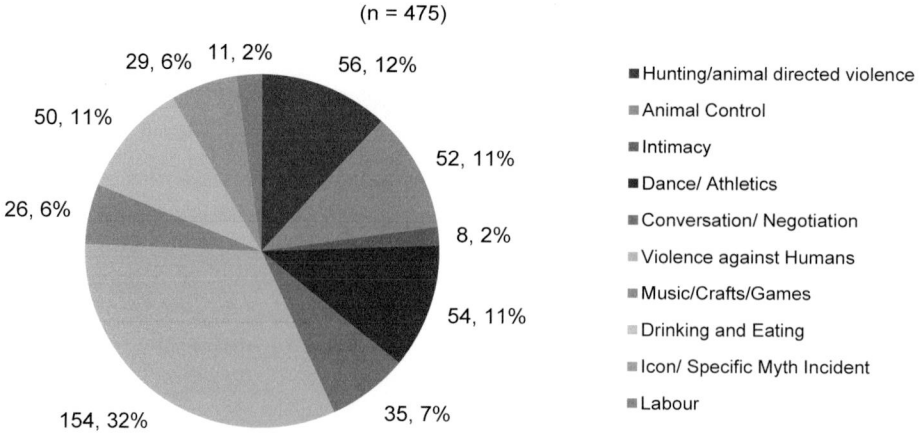

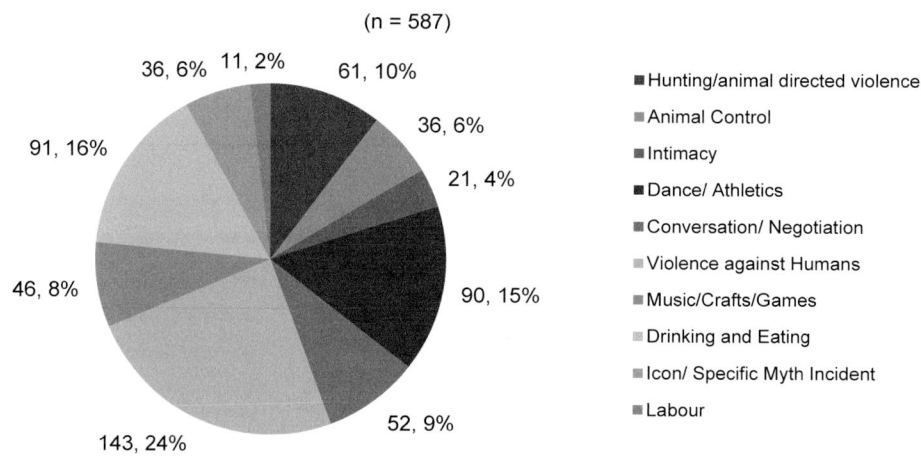

Figure 8.6: Action themes on imported pottery by date. A – 600-500 BCE. B – 500-450 BCE

unusual beings: winged youths using strigils to remove oil from their skin, or women and composite humans dancing together. The relationship between the consumption and experience of alcohol and the divine clearly does not always need to be represented in solely iconic fashion: active experiences of transformative substances, or other activities which incorporate the world of deities into everyday practice, reference the same philosophy that the body is changed through contact with a vessel which carries a reminder of the power of the divine to influence the living world.

The imported action themes, unlike the indigenous assemblage, follow the same pattern as observed for bodies and decorative techniques. All three sites present a very similar set of action themes, with the same preferences for particular types of activities. There is a slight variation between the pottery from Chiusi and the two southern sites – a variation that might have been expected based on the earlier results. Chiusine consumers do appear to have been more particular in the activities they chose to incorporate into their lives, in addition to the bodies they wanted to interact with through pottery. There is a continued interest in images of formalised social intercourse visible in the imported wares, providing strong evidence for the agency of Etruscan consumers. The slightly larger number of images showing dancing and athletics at Tarquinia is further evidence for the choices of Etruscan users being important to their purchases, even if their acquisitions were restricted to a set imported stock. Indigenous preferences are subtly continued in imported pottery, in spite of divergent roles for pottery: the same familiar images are being recycled and reused to support new ideas about the impact of pottery on its user.

The agency of Etruscan consumers becomes even more visible when the imported wares are divided by date of production, as shown in Figure 8.6.[19] In the later assemblage, from 500 to 450 BCE, activities which are more popular

---

[19] A group of nine pots were excluded from this analysis as they were not conclusively dated.

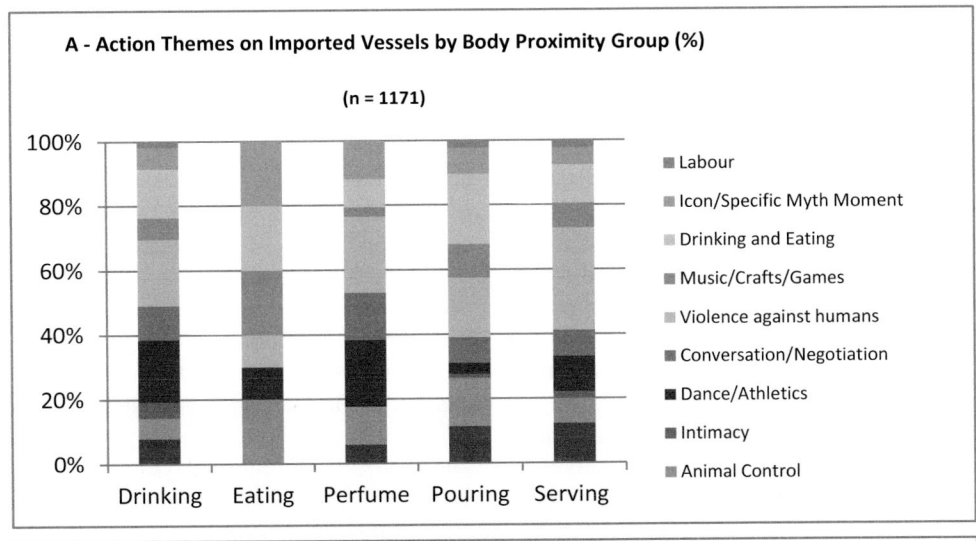

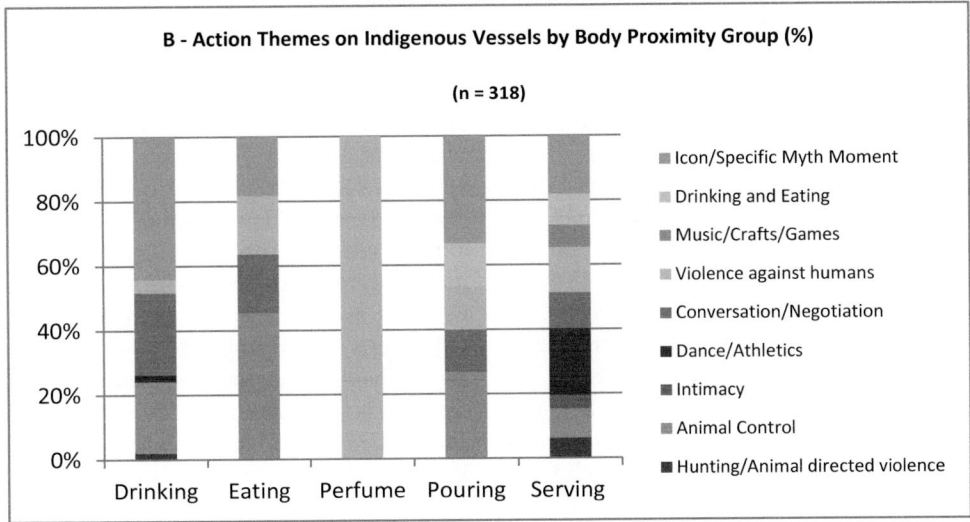

FIGURE 8.7: ACTION THEMES BY BODY PROXIMITY GROUP.
A – IMPORTED VESSELS. B – INDIGENOUS VESSELS.

in the indigenous assemblage, such as conversation, dance and athletics, and drinking and eating have all increased in number, while scenes of violence against humans and hunting have decreased. Importers of Greek ceramics had, by this later period, realised the preferences of an Etruscan market which, while happily accepting images of some imported activities, also wanted a number of vessels which reached back to earlier traditions of ceramic decoration.

The difference between imported and indigenous wares is also visible across the different body proximity groups. Aside from eating vessels, the imported wares display the same uniformity in action themes that has been observed in every phase of their development. There are slight differences between groups, but overall the distribution of action themes is remarkably similar across the board: the same activities are repeated again and again across contexts of use and through different relationships to the body. This group of actions is clearly important: they need to be brought into the body at every stage of using a vessel. Whether rubbing perfumed oil into the skin, moving liquid from a large communal serving vessel or sipping it from a personal cup, the same actions are used to characterise that liquid, and its effects on the body. To return to the idea of imported vessels as vehicles for physical change, and for the taking on of new social identities, this group of activities are used to define what those identities are at each stage of pottery use. The most important images in this process of self-definition and transformation through alcohol are those relating to violence, but other activities are being used to promote similar idealised actions. Dance, athletics, hunting, animal control and drinking itself are all being used to simultaneously inspire change and re-shape the body of pottery users. These actions are all linked to activities which require both knowledge (incorporating physical skill and hours of training or practice) and economic assets (hunting parties riding expensive horses, youths wearing costly armour). Absorbing those idealised bodies, and the actions they are undertaking, provided a way of changing the body of ceramic users into similarly perfect forms – at least until the scent or alcohol wore off.[20]

---

[20] The perfume vessels stand out in this assemblage – but as there are only two examples, it is essential not to overinterpret this data. It is tempting to suggest that perfume vessels with violent images were being used to promote the scent of a 'beautiful warrior' (cf. Treherne 1995) through physically changing body odour.

The indigenous vessels present a far more variable picture. Drinking and eating vessels present a more restricted range of activity types, while serving vessels are close to the imported pattern. The types of activity on those drinking and eating vessels are those which are closest to divine imagery: iconic single figures, intricate social events and images of seemingly impossible animal control. This clarifies the use of Etruscan ceramics for communication with exterior forces, and links up to the use of moulded and tactile decoration in these groups. Vessels with close proximity to the body are being designed to promote intimate contact between the body of the user and the divine forces of superhuman figures. The experience is intimate, and the change in the body of the user is evidence of a personalised interaction between the two. The specific effects of food and alchol are focused on an individual user, while their experience of using a vessel is dictated by their relationship with either the individual deity or ritual activities shown on the sides of the pot. The change in the body is acknowledged as temporary, and its cause is not directly attributed to the vessel and its contents: rather, it is the interaction with the divine which causes the physical and mental changes in the constitution of the body.

8.4 Conclusions

This chapter has clarified the two different types of ceramic experience being accessed by Etruscan users through an analysis of the activities being presented to them on pottery. These two groups of activities link up to the differences in body type and method of decoration observed in the previous chapter, but provide a conclusive piece in the full experience of the Etruscan user. The role of activities of bodies on pottery is a central part of the power of ceramic imagery, and hence of the agency of the pot as an object interacting with and influencing its user. The distinction between indigenous and imported activities on pottery is strong: while both groups utilise similar types of activity, the proportions of those actions are entirely different. The experience of using an imported vessel would have entailed contact with and exposure to a set of images presenting activities which, while perhaps not unfamiliar to an Etruscan audience, provided a very different set of demands and expectations to those associated with indigenous pottery.

Indigenous Etruscan pottery images usually put forward a single type of human activity, aside from some small examples influenced by imported design. This ensures that the experience of the user is intensely focused on the singular action, concentrating all their attention onto the type of activity being represented. The prevalence of single figures represented in an iconic fashion suggests a direct interaction structured between user and icon. These images of individual persons present a one-on-one experience for the user, with a particularly intense experience involved in using vessels close to the body for direct incorporation of fluids. In other contexts, particularly more communal vessels, while the focus on intensity and single activities continues, the range of activities is extended. Popular actions, however, retain connections to the supernatural: images of processions and offerings, or of supernatural beings interacting with humans. The experience of using an indigenously produced vesssel was carefully structured to promote intense interactions with forces outside the human body. The transformation of the body which comes through the consumption of alcoholic substances or the application of perfume appears to be attributed to supernatural deities whose power is channelled into the body through the pot. The images on Etruscan pottery, whether iconic or active, are designed to remind the viewer of their position in relation to these powers, emphasise that the changes in their body are outside their control.

The majority of imported vessels also use images of a single activity. However, there are a group of examples of multiple action themes on vessels. The experience of using pottery with multiple activities is entirely different: when the liquid is consumed to reveal an inner image, or twisted and turned to show a favoured side, the agency of the user and power of the object are united in putting together a personalised experience of particular actions. The repertoire of activities used to decorate imported vessels is restricted to a set range, which are almost uniformly present at each site of use. The direct importation of preferences from outside Etruria brings a range of activities which are relatively unpopular in the indigenous assemblage. Scenes focused on violence or aggressive interactions with other humans or animals are the most popular group, which grows even larger if athletic events are included as incidents of controlled aggression. Within these broad action themes, individual images are very variable, presenting a wide range of different forms of violence, dance or hunting activity. The experience of using such a vessel appears more personalised, with a user or buyer deciding on the images which appeal most strongly to them. The purpose of these images, too, is personal. The ceramics themselves are important in the transformation of the body through liquid substances – the images provide an ideal vision for that change, a flawless model for the user to aspire to. The chance to transform the body with the help of perfume or alcohol is firmly with the user of these imported vessels – they are exhorted to channel that change into these particular idealised figures. The prevalence of violence suggests the glamour and admiration for aggressive behaviour, closely linked to masculine identities. While the exact replication of violent acts is not required of users by these vessels, the ultrA – macho bodies presented to the Etruscan drinker provided a vision of their own increased confidence, created and confirmed by the transformation in their bodily odour or increasingly drunken ebullience.

Further evidence for a connection between the consumption of alcohol and the construction and maintenance of relationships with the divine may be pursued in a number of different avenues, both inside and outside Etruria. While the giving of libations, pouring out wine upon the ground, is a phenomenon attested to and known across Greece and into Etruria, the vessels used in this activity are highly specific in their design, and in the resulting experience of their use. Flat and broad-brimmed, this type of pot is ideal for the slow drip of fluid upon the earth – it is not well designed for human consumption. Yet in Etruria other forms of alcohol containers were being used for dedications at sanctuaries – an Attic kylix from Tarquinia declares that 'Venel Atelina dedicated this vase for the sons of Tinia' (Becker 2009: 88), while a bucchero vessel from Veii similarly claims that it was dedicated by one Apile Vipenna (Bonfante and Bonfante 2002: 140). That both imported and indigenously produced vessels were appropriate for dedication is an indication that the connection between divinity and drunkenness was not restricted to libation practice alone, but could be extended to any vessel used for drinking – a pot could become sanctified at a moment's notice.

In both Greece and Etruria there was a specific deity associated with the consumption of alcohol. Although their roles and accoutrements differ in Greece and Italy (Bonfante 1993), Fufluns/Dionysus is intrinsically linked with the production, consumption and enjoyment of wine. Paleothodoros (2004) has explored the iconographic tradition of representing Fufluns on Etruscan Black and Red Figure vessels from across Etruria, observing that outside the sphere of ceramics, the figure of the god is much less commonly used in decorative imagery. In the pottery corpus, the figure of Fufluns is notably popular (appearing in 137 scenes), and he is regularly attended by his female consort, the Greek Ariadne or Etruscan Areatha. She is also shown in an additional 15 images by herself. The figure of Ariadne is intriguing – her popularity in Etruria is not commesurate in Greece. The female figures on indigenously produced Etruscan vessels, with their hybrid animal features, may have been equated with a female deity associated with alcohol. Merging with the mythology of a mortal woman who became a goddess through her association with alcohol and a divine male, the figure of Ariadne as an exhortative and inspirational model for behaviour matches with that of Dionysus as a divinity devoted to the positivity of alcohol.

However, in the Greek context at least, even Dionysus himself has rules for how wine should be consumed appropriately. Lynch (2011: 77-78) presents the process of preparations which is essential to the organisation of a drinking event, and observes the importance of mixing wine with water to avoid excessive consumption. While the smaller volumes of indigenously made Etruscan vessels observed in Chapter 5 could indicate that this mixing process was originally not taking place, the importation of specific mixing vessels such as craters implies that Etruscan consumers were taking on board the norms and etiquette associated with Greek drinking practice, including the dilution of wine. A part of this process may have been a full or partial abandonment of the intense relationship with the divine implied by imagery on the indigenous vessels. By 375 BC the poet Eubulus, in a play devoted to the relationship between Dionysus and his mother Semele, places the following telling statement in the mouth of the wine god himself:

> 'Three bowls do I mix for the temperate – one to health, which they empty first; the second to love and pleasure, the third to sleep...the fourth bowl is ours no longer, but belongs to violence'.[21]

Dionysus not only explicitly mixes and prepares the wine and water to be consumed himself, demonstrating the centrality of this process in the production of the banquet, but also outlines the affective qualities of his brew. The effects of the fifth to tenth bowls become increasingly unpleasant and indicative of the loss of control over the body – the tenth bowl induces the greatest terror of all – madness.

However, Dionysus the deity in this text is explicitly distanced from the behaviour of the drinker to excess – he provides a clear warning as to what will happen, but disowns the alcohol after the fourth bowl. The emphasis is on the individual drinker to maintain an appropriate level of intoxication, and to avoid shame and loss of control through over-consumption. The power of the god only holds so far – it is the drinker who is responsible for his or her own fate. The alienation of a deity from drunkenness in Greece by this point is a confirmation of the increasing self-reliance visible in the iconography of alcohol consumption vessels from the Eastern Mediterranean, and the message they brought with them to Etruria. While the continued popularity of both Fufluns and Areatha is a testament to the continued links between Etruscan drinking and the divine, the position of the deities has changed irrevocably, excluded from the direct consequences of consumption.

The relationship between these two different types of ceramic experience is difficult to establish. Etruscan users were clearly involving both imported and indigenous vessels in their lives, and were using and interacting with both groups. Whether the indigenous use of pottery as conduit for the divine was being applied to new imported wares, or the self-affirming experience of imported vessels was embraced fully remains unclear. It is evident, however, that Etruscan users at different sites were producing their own local traditions of ceramic use. The stark differences in action themes on indigenous pottery between the four sites points to strong local conceptions of the activities which constituted relationships with supernatural powers. It is possible that this overarching conclusion about the role of indigenous pottery may have been more strongly adhered to in certain sites: particularly those in the inland north of Etruria. This may also be related to the reproduction and adoption of an imported philosophy of ceramic use in the coastal trading centres. All over Etruria, however, the activities shown on imported vessels changed as traders in imported ceramics grew familiar with the desires and values of an Etruscan market. While

---

[21] Eubulus, *Dionysus and Semele* 2.37c

at specific sites indigenous preferences can be discerned in the imported wares, at all sites indigenous motifs and activities are present in later imported vessels. While the exact formula for hybridisation of imported and indigenous representations of activities on pottery remains unknown, it is evident that Etruscan users were deliberately choosing particular images to incorporate into their lives. The agency of the Etruscan user to structure their own experience of pottery is at its most visible in the types of activities they chose to interact with, whether or not that relationship was linked to divine forces or a transformation of the self.

Chapter 9

Pots, People, and Experience: Conclusions

9.1 Introduction

This study started with a straightforward aim: to investigate the experience of using Etruscan pottery. I wanted to explore ceramics from the point of view of a user, putting pottery into the context of hands and mouths, skin and eyes. In the preceding chapters, I have moved from the direct encounter between an Etruscan vessel and the hand and mouth to the tangled relationships evoked by images of static humans imprisoned on vessel surfaces. These explorations have led me to two distinct traditions of ceramic use in Archaic period Etruria, each of which is closely allied to a particular kind of pottery. This overarching pair of divergent experiences, associated with imported Greek ceramics and indigenously produced Etruscan wares, present two very different approaches to the use of pottery, particularly in the context of alcohol consumption. The first part of this concluding chapter defines and clarifies these two types of practice, pulling together the conclusions from the individual analyses to present a characterisation of the entire experience of using each type of Etruscan vessel – the new forms and images from Greece, and the familiar indigenous shapes and icons. These patterns of practice made visible from the experiential analysis are suggestive not only of different experiences for users of Etruscan vessels, but also different conceptualisations of that usage. The two types of vessel are closely linked to the ontologies of the individuals who used them – pots and their alcoholic contents were literally reshaping the world of Etruscan users. The meaning of that transformation, I argue, is as different as the imagery, forms and figures on the two groups of vessels, although I suggest that at the heart of each approach lies the same social purpose.

These two divergent types of experience and accompanying cosmology are only one aspect of the conclusions from the experiential analysis. The pattern of adoption and scale of transformation in Etruscan approaches to pottery use and alcohol consumption is subtle – each of the four sites included in the survey presented a different set of experiences being incorporated or excluded from the regular use of ceramics there. These relationships are suggestive of deeper currents of change running through each individual place: the pace and rhythm of change in ceramic experiences hints at different values, ideas and beliefs which served to create and maintain regional identities. These more local variations in pottery experience are the subject of the second part of this chapter, in which I argue that the northern, inland sites of Poggio Civitate and Chiusi were places in which pottery experience was related to local preferences and referred to a heritage of ceramic usage, while the southern coastal cities of Tarquinia and Vulci chose to value and experiment extensively with new ceramics with new values attached to them. These observations of variability in ceramic experience across Etruria relate to wider questions about change in the region – particularly changes related to increasingly urban living and changes inspired by the adoption of objects acquired from outside Etruria. I suggest that the experiential analysis of ceramics provides a view of one potential motivation which lay behind these transformations – a change in the conception of personhood itself.

The final part of this chapter looks to the future. Having presented the specific conclusions of each phase of the analysis in their own dedicated chapters, and built those conclusions together into wider arguments for the role of pottery in Etruscan society and the relationship between ceramics and social change, I appraise the study methodology and its potential for expansion. The arguments made within this chapter are sweeping – to support and refine the conclusions of this study further experiential analysis is necessary. The different routes for that additional study, the different options to explore, are presented and reviewed in relation both to the specific and more general conclusions. Finally, I argue for the potential of the ideas which lay behind that methodology – the desire to actively consider Etruscan agency, the will to apply theoretical ideas in an Etruscan setting – and suggest that further engagement with these principles could form an exciting new avenue for Etruscan archaeology in the future.

9.2 Drink while you think: Ontologies of Pottery and Alcohol

The initial parameters of this study restricted the ceramics involved to those bearing human images. As discussed in Chapter Four, almost all these vessels are finewares – ceramics which, while potentially used in a wide variety of situations to carry a range of substances, were presumably used in the main at formal or familial consumption events. Of those, the vast majority were used in connection with drinking liquids – some of which (milk or water) have relatively little effect on the body of the user and the experience of a vessel, providing sustenance in a similar way to food. Other liquids had a stronger impact on their Etruscan consumer – brewed ales made from grain, or wine (Barker 1988, Pieraccini 2011). An underlying assumption of this book has been that many of the vessels included in the analysis were used in the context of drinking such beverages – both at communal dining occasions and potentially at smaller family events. The experience of using such vessels is closely tied to the effects of alcohol on the body – and those effects are extreme and transformative. The drinker's sense of the world changes – their senses are simultaneously heightened and dulled by the effects of what is a powerful drug. The consequences of this consumption on behaviour are potentially extreme – vomiting, violence, unconsciousness – and even lesser levels of consumption can have strong influences over behaviour – increased libido and confidence, a higher level of fluency in spoken language, the garrulous gaiety of the cheerful drunk. All these actions and transformations, these variations in the self created by alcoholic liquids, are controlled and mediated through the experience of pottery.

In examining the experience of pottery itself, I have also traced the management of these different reactions to potent and transformative alcoholic liquids. The shapes and images considered in the previous four chapters catalogue a series of systems created in ceramic bodies to control and structure particular responses to alcohol. The experience of using an Etruscan vessel is one of building and securing such responses, and required the user to relate the changes in their own body and mind to the liquid consumed – and the container it was consumed from. This system of control is linked to a cosmology of intoxication – an understanding of the way in which alcohol impacts upon persons. The variation between the two overarching types of pottery experience documented in this study suggest that that system, and hence that cosmology, is very different in indigenously made Etruscan and imported Greek vessels. The full experience of each type of alcohol consumption, recreated from each phase of the analysis and woven together into a single narrative, presents two methodologies for Etruscan people thinking about and conceptualising their response to alcohol through the pottery used to bring it into their bodies.

The indigenous experience of pots is characterised by a deceptively simple series of vessel forms for human consumption. At every stage of relationship with the body, indigenous vessels contained less fluid, and were relatively straightforward to use. The initial access to a vessel, the first contact between hand and pot, was a simple affair. Without a heavy weight of liquid sloshing around inside, the indigenous vessels were easy to balance, requiring minimal concentration on their manipulation. From large serving vessels to personal drinking vessels, this theme of simplicity in design continues, contributing to an overarching experience of easy access to ceramics. The small volume of indigenously produced Etruscan vessels has a continued effect on the experience of using them.

Regular refilling must have been required, particularly of small, personal drinking vessels. The truncated, stop-start effect of emptying a vessel and waiting for it to be refilled before recommencing use created a series of gaps. These voids in experience, moments in which the pot cannot be used, but can only be looked at, must have been an important aspect of indigenous Etruscan vessel use. The larger the vessel, the longer the gap – the refilling of a large serving vessel, if required, must have required careful staging and organisation. These pointed moments, caused by pottery forms, suggest a deliberate structuring of vessel use, perhaps designed to ensure a formal refilling of vessels.

The physical form of indigenous ceramics: easy to use, but requiring regular refills, was perfectly designed to co-ordinate with the imagery used to decorate it, and the intended effect of that imagery on a user. The production of decoration on indigenous Etruscan pottery resulted in increasingly complex techniques for accessing imagery. This representative tradition required the use of touch as well as vision, particularly in order to examine the results of decorative methods developed in Etruria and not influenced by imported vessels. Tactile decoration, whether constituted through moulding or impressing, creates a deep engagement with an image – the physical contours of a human body can be accessed through the fingers. The Etruscan user of a vessel needed to combine eyes and hands in order to skim the surface of an impressed cylinder design, feeling the individual, exaggerated bodies pressed into the clay. Larger moulded figures are regularly placed on handles and almost always on exterior surfaces which come into direct contact with the hand. While tactile images can be continually stroked and examined while the pot is in use, a break in vessel use provides a moment for deeper exploration of these images. An Etruscan person could have taken a moment to rotate a cylinder-impressed image in their hands, rubbing the palms on the image, or traced the wings and body of a moulded figure on a handle with the fingers, rather than feeling them as potentially uncomfortable bumps squashed into the hand.

The types of images shown in these tactile scenes, and in later visual imagery, provide further emphasis on the need to actively commune with a vessel. The predominant theme in experiencing images on Etruscan vessels is the relationship between humans and supernatural powers. This relationship is clearly not one between equals. The primary experience of seeing these images, while in the process of consuming substances that change the body, was designed to promote a specific type of relationship between human and divinity, and to define that relationship. The process of transformation in the body caused by alcohol consumption is firmly attributed to deities, and the individual user of pottery is disenfranchised from the changes taking place in their own body.

Both the positive and negative effects of alcohol are absorbed in the power of the miniature figures embossed on indigenous pottery, who are particularly visible on individual vessels. The opportunity to stop and consider those figures while waiting for a refill provided a moment to understand the supernatural power of the divine wrapped up in a vessel. To return to the initial point of experience, the shape of pots, there is no requirement for complexity in ceramic form if the vessel is laden with the relationship between a deity and a user. The entire experience is bound up in the power of a supernatural figure, who can be seen and touched. As the body floods with fluid, so the user experiences an external force, flowing through the body from the vessel into mouth, throat and brain.

The connection between the use of pottery in Etruria and the power of divine figures has been made before, particularly in the context of sanctuaries and libation pouring (Pieraccini 2011; Warden 2009: 112-12). However, these case studies have referred to specifically ritualised contexts, places in which the power of the divine could be accessed easily by mortals. The ritual consumption of alcohol and the use of accompanying ceramics, however, does not have to necessarily require a serious and stratified type of activity. The realisation that the divine and everyday were closely entwined for people in the past has been one of the strongest threads in recent advances in British Iron Age archaeology. Hill (1995) conceived of deposits containing a mixture of seemingly unusual objects placed in specific positions as simultanously ritualised and trivialised: equal parts ritual and refuse. He considers that such deposits are the result of both ritualised and quotidianal, and that the individuals who put them together were comfortable with mixing the two. The disposal of a day's rubbish may be as meaningful as the deliberate slaughter and careful manipulation of a large animal.

Chadwick (2012) expands on this idea, suggesting a continuum of practices which result in such deposits, all of which are simultaneously related to ritual invocations of supernatural forces, and yet required in the daily round. The idea of purely utilitarian, or purely ritual, activities presents a false dichotomy: the lives and acts of past people are more complicated and fluid. Hill and Chadwick are focused upon specific archaeological contexts. Hamilton (2002) has applied similar ideas to the distribution of pottery in Iron Age Britain, suggesting that ritual activity heavily influenced the use of ceramics. Transferred to the Etruscan context, this idea of the supernatural entwined with the everyday in pottery use provides an intriguing role for indigenous vessels. The idea of 'ritualised' drinking suggests a litany of libations, speeches and po-faced formality, with divine figures staunchly in charge of the proceedings. This is not at all what I am suggesting. The creeping presence of supernatural powers into the ceramics of Etruscan consumption rather presents an acknowledgement of ever-present powers, a positive acclamation of the involvement of the divine with the everyday round. As Hill, Chadwick and Hamilton's work points out, ritual and routine can become so entangled it is impossible to separate them.

Kay Read has arrived at similar conclusions about the nature of sacred and profane in pre-Hispanic Mexico, arguing that 'multitudinous powers continually course through everything' (1998: 193). Mitchell (2004: 17) uses Read's arguments in the context of modern Mexican alcohol consumption, forming a helpful ethnographic parallel for the Etruscan case. He observes that for drinkers of both weaker corn beers and stronger liquors distilled from the agave plant, the experience of drunkenness is conceived of as a state of being allied to transformations in time – the drunken individual becomes a time traveller, with hours passing by in a state separated from the harsh realities of labour and poverty. He also points out that the drunk is conceived of by his community as a speaker of truth, a figure akin to a holy fool, who may insult and sabotage social structures with a relatively free remit (Mitchell 2004: 89). Both situations are constructed through the role of alcohol in making contact with the other world, a world of spirits and deities and to recently departed ancestors and/or favoured saints. In the Mexican context, particularly during fiestas associated with the *Dia de los Muertos* or Day of the Dead celebrations, alcohol brings back the dead to speak with and comfort the living, while simultaneously promoting the production of new generations. The spiritual use of alcohol in Mexico as a tool to change time, contact the dead and secure fertility is, I suggest, very close to the role of alcohol in Etruscan society – a transformative substance of everyday ritual, the effects of which are carefully controlled through ceramic bodies.

While the Mexican parallel provides tantalising hints as to the potential contexts and concerns created by spiritual drinking, the experiential data suggests a particular expression of the entwined relationship of drinker and deity in an Etruscan context. The organisation of consumption is suggested through the sizes and types of vessels, while the divine figures on drinking vessels emphasise the lack of agency of Etruscan drinkers – the drinking individual is a tool to be used by the deities who control the response of the individual to alcohol. The deities on indigenous vessels can be touched and explored at length, while their effects on the body can be felt more and more strongly as the user of a vessel succumbs to the alcohol they consume. This experience can be repeated again and again – at both formal occasions and at each instance that the wine-jug and cup are brought out. The relationship between user and divinity can be reformed and reconstituted, reassuring the user of the continued presence of the divine in their life. This acceptance of the divine interaction and interference in everyday life is reflective of an entirely different configuration of ritual and religion: a matter-of-fact engagement with the supernatural. It is tempting to relate this to the continual and everyday interference of deities portrayed in classical literature, notably the works of Homer. A strong relationship with the divine is perhaps not only a concern for heroes.

The experience of using imported vessels is an entirely different proposition from the outset. Picking up and moving an imported pot, whether for individual or communal use, is an act which required either prior knowledge or forethought. The experience begins with a visual appraisal of the form of a pot, perhaps a desperate scraping of past encounters to find a method for interacting with complex vessel forms. The need to demonstrate familiarity with such vessels, the potential social pressure of making the wrong decisions, resulting in embarassing and visual spillage and stains, must have coloured the Etruscan experience of imported vessels almost entirely. The concentration required by the form of these vessels, awkward to hold and difficult to use, is the primary relationship established between user and pot. When a form is familiar, while this intense attention is lessened, risk will always remain: the user may have practised lifting and moving a vessel multiple times, but a slip of the fingers, a wobble of the wrist, and the pot is dropped and its contents spilled. The lifting of individual or communal vessels, filled with a far larger volume of liquid, would not only have been fraught but also painful. The pressure of a vessel on the hands and wrists could have prompted aches and shaking as muscle exhaustion set in. The ordeal of negotiating such vessels tests the commitment of the individual to the project of using the pot in the first place.

It is not just the individual sensory experience which was changed by the use of imported vessels. The indigenous phenomenon of continual refilling is no longer required of such large volume pots – the individual drinking vessel can hold enough fluid to sustain its user for far longer, while refilling a large serving vessel is an intimidating prospect, requiring large amounts of fluid on standby. The role of jugs and other pouring vessels is reduced, as the volume difference between serving and drinking vessels is far less. The experience of individual vessel use changes from a regularly interrupted series of actions to a continual flow of experience, stretched out over a long period of time. The difficulty of using imported vessels, and the amount of liquid they contained, must have slowed down the drinking process, forcing the user to maintain a steady relationship with the vessel. The tactile decoration of indigenous vessels is not required: the strong stimulation of the vessel form on the hand takes its place. In the process of negotiating imported pots, there is no room for tactile imagery – the body is fully occupied with the form of the vessel. Decoration has to be primarily visually stimulating – the hands and fingers are just too busy to fully engage with tactile imagery. The move away from tactile decoration to purely visual stimulation appears to be linked to an increasing variety in image placement: a user can visually access images on the inside of a vessel, slowly revealed over the course of a drawn out interaction between pot and person. There is no need to touch the inner surface, resulting in sticky fingers. It is only the eye that links image and user, changing the balance of touch and vision in pottery experience.

The visual images themselves contribute to this diverse experience of using imported vessels. While the initial encounter with the image can take place in different positions, the type of encounter on offer can also vary. Different types of decoration put together on the same vessel provide a series of options for the viewer, allowing the user of a vessel to structure and shape their own experience of interacting with the pot and its decoration. The type of images used in imported vessels have a specific effect on the user – just as the shape of imported pottery requires the user to dredge up former experiences of such objects in order to negotiate them safely, imported imagery demands that the user relate their own experience to that of the human figures painted on the clay. The user is expected to find relevance in the image: whether concocted from real life or half-remembered, half-invented from a mythological narrative. There is a message beyond the power of the divine – a specific intention and purpose behind each image of the human body. These messages are being infused steadily into the contents of such vessels – as the body of the user changes, that individual can feel those images take effect. The idealised figures on vessels come to life as the scent from a perfume bottle transforms the sweat of a user, or as a drinker is filled with confidence and desire. Knowledge of the exact narrative on display is not important in the construction of experience: the transformation comes with the identification of the self with the positive models available on the vessel.

The imagery on imported vessels emphasises that these transformations of the individual self are carefully targeted at a specific, gendered audience. The overwhelming focus of imported ceramics is on the promotion of a particular kind of body and its deeds. That body is male, dominant and overwhelmingly powerful. The power of this male body is emphasised in a wide sweep of activities – from hunting to athletics, drinking to warfare, each action is designed to emphasise the agency of the male figure at the centre of almost every image. In the few examples of female bodies, they too are configured in an ideal fashion: passively undertaking tasks of adornment, or domestic labour. The establishment of gender norms apart, these vessels are undertaking a very different task to the indigenous vessels. The figure of the supernatural divinity is marginalised. The images on vessels reflect back an idealised image of the user – a user who is, in the world of the producers of such objects, characterised as male. Unlike the powerful figures of indigenous vessels, who can be applied to either a male or female user's life and circumstances, imported wares are firmly directed at this specific audience. While females are able to access and relate to the images which reflect their own bodies, the woman user is restricted to a set position of passivity and exclusion. With the power of the divinity removed, the images on vessels themselves become dictators of behaviour, pushing hard for a recognition of the self in the ideal.

The ability of alcohol to result in self-confidence so strong as to allow for self-identification with such clearly ideal figures provides the latter with their power. Even before the alcohol takes effect, the promise of the imagery is bound up with the transformation of body and mind which will come. The same principles are used in modern contexts to sell particular brands of alcoholic substance, and similarity with advertising also connects up with the use of gendered poses and activities to promote particular ways of being. Goffman (1979) observes the use of specifically gendered characteristics to sell specific products, while Belknap and

Leonard (1991) demonstrated the continued application of female subordination and submission in advertising material targeted at women. The creation of an ideal self, alongside the means to attain that persona, is a powerful force. Just as advertisements present an object which can provide the means to becoming an idealised vision of perfection, so too did imported vessels present a gendered image of exemplary being, and the alcoholic substance which allowed the user (particularly the male user) to feel themseves becoming this inflated self. The process began with recognition of potential similarity between user and image, and concluded with the vessel and its contents working together to produce a user reconfigured in the idealised light of the image.

Ethnographic case studies underline the relevance of this sociological work on the role of alcohol in the construction and maintenance of idealised alternative selves. Alasuutari (1982:44) describes the use of alcohol by men in Finland as a form of escape from their everyday lives and selves, a methodology for the creation for ideal masculinities which are free from both self doubt and self-discipline in equal measure. He goes on to argue that drunkenness allows Finnish men to 'gain a measure of self-respect through the symbolic ordering of their environment' (Alasuutari 1982:50). Drinking alcohol, and, indeed, being drunk, allow these men to restructure their old selves or construct new identities. Imported Greek vessels provide an opportunity to channel that self-construction towards socially idealised models – their images providing a template for behaviour and their shapes acting as a simultaneous test and expression of belonging. Even when the images on such vessels appear violent, degrading or inappropriate to modern eyes, this does not remove their potential for the provision of self-respect to an Etruscan user. The difficult forms and large volumes demand a particular level of skill, providing an experience of self-construction through touch to attach to this imagined idealism. Together, the intoxicating substance within the vessel, and pleasure of imagining an idealised self created by the vessel itself, formed an irresistible experience for Etruscan pottery users.

9.3 Changing Pots, Changing Persons

The two kinds of ceramic experience described above appear resolutely separate from one another. Indigenous Etruscan vessels, relatively easy to use, containing smaller volumes, and focused on a relationship with divinities which assures and smoothes the experience of alcohol, appear to present an entirely different set of concerns and values to imported vessels, difficult to use, providing access to large quantities of alcohol and actively stimulating and encouraging the inflation of an idealised and personal ego. Ethnographic parallels from the modern world emphasise these differences – the conception of alcohol in Finland and Mexico supports the existence of these two models for thinking through drinking. However, in Archaic Etruria, these two ceramic worlds, linked to diverse ways of managing the transformations evoked by alcohol consumption, were colliding. Etruscan people were obtaining access to imported vessels, and to their associated messages – the emphasis on the idealised figure of the individual, particularly the powerful male individual, and the refiguring of alcohol consumption from a divine to a personal activity. Yet indigenous vessels were not abandoned entirely – the forms and images of Etruscan made pottery continued to be used and experienced throughout the Archaic period, influencing the types of vessels imported into the region in later years. Both indigenous and imported ceramic experiences were available to Etruscan individuals, and both were voraciously purchased, used and deposited, often together. The impression, particularly when undecorated and non-human figured ceramics are taken into account, is of an increasingly hybrid ceramic experience. Each phase of this analysis has demonstrated, however, that the extent of that hybridity varied from site to site and, presumably, household to household.

The geographical distribution of the two different kinds of ceramic experience, and the implied changing makeup and balance of Etruscan hybrid ceramic experience across space, relate to two related arguments. The first of these is the swirling mass of discourse surrounding different models of change in Etruria, and the balance between extraneous influence and indigenous ingenuity – a phenomenon discussed at the very beginning of this book. Each site presents a different case study for ceramic change – the ways in which experiences of individuals were being shaped by pottery at a local level. The levels of hybridity in each place build into arguments over the rate and form of change in other aspects of material culture or social organisation – transformations in burial practice, political organisation or the expression, maintenance and definition of values. These relationships are at the centre of the first part of this section, in which I explore how the different sites express and reproduce their own composite ceramic worlds. Lying behind this series of interpretations is a question succinctly asked by Robin Osborne in 2001 – 'Why did Athenian pots appeal to the Etruscans?' In the introduction, I argued that novelty and externally ascribed aesthetic value were unsatisfying answers to this question. The results of the experiential analysis, their geographical expression, relationship with ontologies of alcohol consumption and connections with other forms of change provide a new response, focused not on economics or aesthetics but on personhood.

The data from all four phases of the experiential analysis strongly suggested particular patterns of adopting new ceramics and retaining traditional forms for each site. The data from Poggio Civitate suggested that the imported form of experiencing ceramics decorated with human imagery was not incorporated into daily use at the site. While imported vessels are present from the Archaic complex, these do not challenge the iconographic dominance of indigenously produced vessels with their strong adherence to the indigenous representation of alcohol consumption as a form of every-day ritual controlled by deities. Indeed, the combination of imported vessel styles such as kyathoi with indigenous iconography featuring iconic females suggests that while particular shapes may have been incorporated into use, imported imagery was excluded. The deliberate destruction of Poggio Civitate in the late sixth century provides a chronological context to this relative stability in ceramic iconography – unless all imported forms of ceramic experience that incorporate human images were removed prior to the destruction of the complex, such vessels were not a part of consumption practices at the site. The Etruscan community that inhabited the complex appear firmly bound up in the model of alcohol consumption focused upon divine interventions, with the continued use of vessels which control and maintain transformative drinking through a relationship with the divine female emblazoned on their surfaces. Other forms of material culture from the site – architectural terracottas and frieze plaques in particular – support a conclusion that prior to the abandonment of the complex, the community at Poggio Civitate were deeply concerned with the reproduction of a familial identity through a strong relationship with the divine. In this context, the continuity of ceramic experience forms another link forged between the inhabitants of Poggio Civitate and their deities through everyday rituals. The stability in ceramic experience observed at Poggio Civitate is also echoed in the experiential data from Chiusi. Of the three urban sites surveyed, the material from Chiusi suggests continuity in ceramic preferences most strongly. Images of conversation and negotiation in particular are popular in both imported and indigenous ceramics from the site, while the imported imagery from Chiusi is clearly differentiated from that of Tarquinia and Vulci. In terms of physical experience, too, the imported Chiusine material retains echoes of indigenous practice – the intensely difficult to use imported vessels of the south are largely absent, yet complex, hard to use indigenous vessels are popular. There appears to have been an emphasis on the maintenance and continuity of local ceramic useways, with new pots being deliberately chosen to slot into this scheme of vessel experience.

Poggio Civitate and Chiusi both present models of relative conservatism and a strong allegiance to traditions of ceramic experience with a long heritage of expression in Etruria, the experiential data from the coastal cities of Tarquinia and Vulci suggests both an entirely different relationship with ceramics, and with change. Both Tarquinia and Vulci present a pattern of ceramic experience which almost fuses together the new imported shapes and iconography with their indigenous counterparts. By the late Archaic period, the development and extensive distribution of Etruscan versions of imported forms and images in this region emphasises the increasing dominance of imported images as the appropriate model for ceramic representations of human beings. While the preferences of both sites for particular kinds of activities and bodies seem to refer back to indigenous practices, the contrast with the northern sites is striking – at Tarquinia and Vulci, the imported ceramic experience is a central part of alcohol consumption, and the traditional relationship between drinkers and the divine is distorted and transformed into a new encounter – between the extant self and the desired self of the drinker as an individual. These conclusions support the assumption that the coastal cities of Etruria experienced change in patterns of ceramic consumption at a faster and more intense rate than sites located inland and to the north. This assertion, however, begs the question as to why any site in Etruria would change their ceramic experiences at all? Why incorporate new shapes and images, new skills and stories, into daily use? Why did Attic pots appeal to the Etruscans?

My response to this question is developed from the twin cosmologies of alcohol consumption identified through the experiential analysis, and experience itself lies at the heart of this answer. Conceptions of value focused upon aesthetics and economics are demonstrably unsatisfying drivers for ceramic change in Etruria. Thinking of value through the lens of experience, however, provides a clearer and, I suggest, stronger, solution to the problem of ceramic transformations, which can then be related more effectively to wider patterns of change and stability across Etruria. The two models of alcohol consumption associated with imported and indigenous pottery present two very different experiences for the user, and place that user in an equally different position. In the indigenous model, she or he is an agent for the divine – the identity and actions of the drinker are entirely bound up in the connection between their body and that of a deity. The agency and power of that drinker is removed from their body, which acts only as a conduit for another force. The imported ceramic experience is completely different. The imagery and shape of the vessel emphasise the skill and power of the user as themself – it is their actions, not those of a divinity, which allow them to manipulate the complex new forms without losing face. The alcoholic transformation of the body is an extension of the agency of the individual drinker – it is their choice to interact with and consume the idealised bodies of a particular vessel. In the indigenous experience, the consumption of alcohol is pressurised and intense, a recognition that the drinker will lose control over their body and is reliant on an outside source to avoid unpleasant consequences and achieve desired outcomes. In the imported ceramic experience, the drinker is in control. The alcohol allows him or her (and the iconography is particularly directed at a male drinker) to deliberately channel and produce a drunken self which is idealised to a high degree – a self which is simultaneously pleasing and self-produced. In the difference between these two experiences lies the appeal of imported pottery to an Etruscan audience. Imported pots enabled their Etruscan users to take control of and credit for their intoxicated personalities. The redistribution of agency from deity to drinker is what made these vessels so appealing, and resulted in the scale of their adoption in Italy, far from the social context of their production in Athens.

If the difference in individual agency provided by the experience of using imported pots resulted in increased enjoyment of using such vessels, then why, at Poggio Civitate and Chiusi, were Etruscan communities holding fast to less pleasurable ceramic experiences? The coastal cities of Tarquinia and Vulci may, by virtue of their location, have been more open to new technologies, ideas and experiences, but this environmentally deterministic argument is not enough to explain the complex hybrid ceramic culture developed at Chiusi in particular. It is certainly not sufficient to explain other instances of northern conservatism, such as the continued use of cremation as a method for the disposal of the corpse at Chiusi, long after inhumation was adopted in the southern coastal cities in a variety of formats. Even into the Classical and Hellenistic periods, Chiusine burial ritual demanded the consumption of the corpse by fire. The continuity in burial practice at Chiusi and the unwillingness of that community to adopt imported vessels and their associated promotion of individual agency is, I suggest, linked to a model for social change which is focused on the definition and ascription of personhood – the attributes and ideas which allow a community to clarify and ascertain who is or is not a 'person-' a full member of society (Gillespie 2001; Fowler 2001, 2004; Brück 2001, 2006; Jones 2002, 2005). I have argued elsewhere that biconical urn focused burial rites of the earlier *Prima Età del Ferro* deliberately represent the deceased in a manner which defines them as a partible person, ascribing the dead a form of personhood which is communal (Shipley 2015). That form of communal personhood, developed from the work of Strathern (1988), in which a person is conceived of as the sum and site of their relationships with others, rather than as a distinct individual with their own identity and agency, is closely connected to the indigenous model of ceramic usage. In the indigenous experience of alcohol and pottery, the identity of the individual is subsumed entirely in their connection to a deity, potentially with an aim of maintaining a family. In cremation burials, such as those at Chiusi, the singular body is made generic by the flames, and reconstructed as a sum of their relationships with others – represented solely as a communal, rather than an individual person.

Indigenous ceramic experience, cremation burial and communal personhood, then, are bound up together. There is no room in this conception of both persons and the world for individual agency – for the expression in death of the personality of the deceased, for their own achievements and actions. Simultaneously, the behaviour of a drunk must be controlled by forces outside the individual body – by deities who prevent the disintegration of communal personhood into individual desires. At Chiusi, where communal personhood as a way of self-conception appears to have been so deeply entrenched, it is entirely unsurprising that a form of ceramic experience focused upon the promotion and development of a distinctly personal self should be carefully and cautiously adopted, hedged with references to values enshrined in indigenous pottery traditions. While eventually, even here, both burial rites (i.e. the development of later personalised burial urns of the 5th and 4th centuries BCE) and ceramic experience would come to reflect the adoption of individual selfhood and abandonment of communal personhood by Etruscan society. This interpretation fits well with Chiusine practices. Yet it still has not answered the question as to why the inhabitants of Tarquinia and Vulci were prepared to abandon communal personhood more quickly and more definitively than their contemporaries to the north. I would argue that in these southern coastal cities, with their myriad opportunities for trade and self-aggrandisement, the promotion of the individual person over the communal person had already begun. In a context of economic growth and increasing urbanism, intensified through contacts made through individual journeys and individual agency, the deeds of the singular person stand out from their familial and community background. A person could transform their prospects, make new trading contacts, establish new networks of exchange – all outside the traditional boundaries of Etruscan society, all defying the ideology of personhood as community. In Tarquinia and Vulci, where cremation burial had long been abandoned, imported ceramic experiences which emphasised and trumpeted the prowess of the individual fell on fallow soil. The coastal communities had already to a large extent discarded communal personhood in favour of the personality – a form of pottery which encouraged and played off that transformation in the conception of the self would be self-evidently successful. Through linking experience to definitions of personhood, a new value is ascribed to imported vessels – a value based on economies of agency, enjoyment and self-definition. The description of experience has led to an explanation of change which is centred on choice.

9.4 Back to the Future

This concluding chapter has, so far, been focused on interpretative conclusions. I have pulled together the conclusions of each of the four previous chapters of analysis, and woven them together into a narrative which describes in detail each aspect of the ceramic experiences associated with indigenous and imported pottery in Etruria during the Archaic period. From this characterisation, I have gone on to develop and draw out two different models of alcohol consumption allied to these forms of ceramic experience. Through ethnographic analogies and social theory, I have demonstrated that these models have continued to structure interactions between humans and intoxication, in contexts far from the Italian Iron Age. I have also put forward ideas about models of social change, produced from a combination of the analysis of ceramic experience and the definition of these two ontologies of alcohol, each allied to a particular way of being-in-the-world and drinking-in-the-world. By focusing on the experience of an Etruscan person as a point at which to determine the value of an object, as opposed to externally dictated economic or aesthetic principles, I have been able to develop a new answer to old and frustrating questions about the nature of change in Etruria. This idea of the changing conception of personhood is a reach from a pottery-grounded analysis, yet it is very much the product of an experiential philosophy and phenomenological analysis.

These extended conclusions, related to Etruscan ceramics and their relationship with society, to some extent prefigure the more general conclusions of the final points I wish to make. They could not have been arrived at without some degree of theoretical and methodological success – both facets of this study working together to produce a longer narrative linked outwards to wider questions than the ceramic experience of the original research question. Yet there are three future directions which complete this assessment of the success of the study. Each is centred upon a particular aspect of my analysis, and considers the potential of theory and method for expansion both in Etruscan archaeology and more widely in the archaeological analysis of ceramics. In evaluating these potential expansions, the strengths of my approach are made clear. In moving from conclusions about the deep Etruscan past to the future of the sub-discipline, this section finishes this book by pointing firmly forwards.

The first of these relates to the development of an experiential methodology for ceramic analysis. This methodology has been one of the most successful aspects of this study, and it would be exciting to test it on different assemblages of vessels from different contexts. I have demonstrated that phenomenology can be applied to objects successfully, providing an estimation of experience in the past which is not purely subjective. A particularly interesting extension of the methodology would be to apply it to a wider range of ceramic material from the European Iron Age – examining the patterns of pottery experience across a wider area. Smaller case studies could also prove enlightening – perhaps a comparison of ceramic experience across a single site, or even between individual tomb assemblages. The opportunity to access individual experiences through small collections of ceramics is particularly exciting – variations in practice and preference could be used to reconstruct personal agency and choice in the past. An experiential methodology for pottery analysis could be applied in any examination involving ceramics – a supplement to more traditional petrological and typological categorisation.

The second area for future exploration lies within the more specific world of Etruscan studies. The use of this methodology at four sites could be extended to cover a wider corpus of ceramic material from Etruria. This extension could test the conclusions from this study, expanding them through an analysis of unpublished material and incorporating physical examination of ceramics from museums to ensure entirely accurate results, moving beyond the limited scope of a single research project. This process could also be entirely digitised, contributing to an online corpus of Etruscan ceramics for future research – providing a consistent array of information about each individual vessel, and a link to the institution which held them. This research could also form part of a project exploring whether local traditions of pottery experience formed specific groups across Etruria, and whether the hints of regional preferences in imported pottery hold across other Etruscan settlements. Alternatively, the tentative conclusions about gendered representation in pottery could be tested over a wider area, and, as suggested above, contrasted with ceramic assemblages from Greece, examining the variety in experience for more specific pottery users of both genders.

The implications of such a wider analysis would be deeply relevant to a series of significant arguments which continually occupy and concern Etruscan scholars. By investigating changes in the experience of pottery over key moments of transition, the relationship between ceramic design and usage and Etruscan social activity could potentially be charted. For example, during the increasing urbanisation of the seventh century BCE, mapping the complexity and variation in ceramic form could reflect increasing concerns with the maintenance of elite identities in a newly urban world. In a town setting, behaviour is intensely public – negative responses to alcohol are no longer hidden – the wider community becomes aware of dangerous and inappropriate behaviour almost instantly in an enclosed area. At the same time, a newly urban lifestyle is filled with opportunities to impress – through the acquisition of imposing objects, and the mastery of their potentially embarassing shapes. An extension of this analysis into metal containers of bronze and silver from Etruria would contribute significantly to such arguments – applying the same methodologies developed for ceramics to other vessels, and allowing for comparison between the two. The changing role of ceramics in funerary assemblages could also be a further extension – examining the different experiences gathered together in individual tombs, taking the brief analysis of Chapter 4 a stage further to question why pots were placed in Etruscan tombs at all. Such an approach could problematise traditional assumptions of pottery as conduits for a feast in the afterlife, pushing for a more nuanced appreciation of the connections between pots, their contents and the identity of their owners.

The third area in which this research could be extended is also bounded in Etruscan studies. The use of archaeological theory in the development of this experiential methodology has been central to the production of new conclusions about Etruscan ceramic use. The continued opportunities that theoretical engagement provides for increasing the breadth and intricacy of archaeological engagement has been recognised in other areas of Italian prehistory, but not embraced in Etruscology. Integrating historiography into archaeological research, resulting in an appreciation and respect for the underlying reasons behind the apprehension with which theory has been treated by Etruscan specialists is the first step to moving forward. The successful and practical application of theoretical ideas to specifically Etruscan problems, while simultaneously valuing traditional approaches, as demonstrated in these conclusions, is the best way to demonstrate the relevance of theory to Etruscology. I would hope that the presentation of a series of concrete results produced by a methodology which owes equal inspiration to tradition and innovation, used to answer questions which have plagued Etruscan studies for years, might be an example of this type of work. The most exciting steps to be made from the completion of this project may be those incorporating other applications of theory in Etruscan archaeology: whether focused on pottery or landscapes, burials or houses. Pragmatic phenomenology has provided a series of striking insights into the relationship between persons and pots in Etruria. The potential for future use of theory in Etruscan studies provides a tantalising promise of more ideas about the Etruscans as people, and the social objects they left behind.

Appendix 1

Pottery Corpus

This appendix details the ceramics included within this book, providing details of their original provenance, current location and relevant bibliographic information. It firstly presents the imported vessels, and secondly the indigenously produced vessels. In the case of singular publications such as volumes and journal articles, the bibliographic reference follows the Harvard style of referencing used throughout the book, with an individual page reference for each vessel. In addition to these more traditional publishing formats, a significant proportion of the corpus utilised information provided by online catalogues – those of Boston Museum of Fine Arts, the British Museum, the Fitzwilliam Museum in Cambridge, the Metropolitan Museum New York, and the Poggio Civitate Archive. In these cases, the online catalogue is referred to, and the vessel may be found by use of the museum reference number as a search term on these portals. Direct links to individual pages have not been used, to avoid the likely impact of changes to online data storage systems in the future breaking the links. The full references for each publication used to bring together the corpus are listed in full in the second part of this appendix, as a separate bibliography. The appendix ends with the online sources used; collected together as a series of URLs, alongside the date each was last consulted.

Bibliographic Reference	Museum Reference	Site	Museum
Beazley (1927: 1)	CUP516	Vulci	Oxford Ashmolean Museum
Beazley (1927: 1)	CUP515	Vulci	Oxford Ashmolean Museum
Beazley (1927: 20)	1922.8	Vulci	Oxford Ashmolean Museum
Beazley (1927: 3)	CUP303	Chiusi	Oxford, Ashmolean Museum
Beazley (1927: 38)	288	Chiusi	Oxford, Ashmolean Museum
Beazley (1927: 5)	CUP300	Chiusi	Oxford, Ashmolean Museum
Beazley (1927: 5)	1914.729	Vulci	Oxford Ashmolean Museum
Beazley (1927: 7)	521	Vulci	Oxford Ashmolean Museum
Beazley (1964: 826.29)	96.9.32	Tarquinia	Metropolitan Museum, New York
Beazley (1971: 305)	F166	Vulci	Louvre
Beazley (1971: 355)	97.368	Vulci	Boston Museum of Fine Arts
Beazley (1971: 422)	F2299	Vulci	Berlin Antiquarium
Bermond (1957: 77)	PU285	Vulci	Bologna Museo Civico
Bielefield (1959: 28-29)	222	Vulci	Altenburg Staatliches Lindenau
Bielefield (1959: 31)	218	Vulci	Altenburg Staatliches Lindenau
Bielefield (1959: 31-32)	217	Vulci	Altenburg Staatliches Lindenau
Bielefield (1959: 32-33)	202	Vulci	Altenburg Staatliches Lindenau
Bielefield (1959: 33-34)	203	Vulci	Altenburg Staatliches Lindenau
Bielefield (1959: 34-35)	204	Vulci	Altenburg Staatliches Lindenau
Bielefield (1960: 19)	234	Vulci	Altenburg Staatliches Lindenau
Bielefield (1960: 20-22)	211	Vulci	Altenburg Staatliches Lindenau
Bielefield (1960: 21)	229	Vulci	Altenburg Staatliches Lindenau
Blinkenberg and Friis Johansen (1928: 105)	INV.CHR.VIII. 320	Vulci	Copenhagen National Museum
Blinkenberg and Friis Johansen (1928: 106)	INV.CHR.VIII 340	Vulci	Copenhagen National Museum
Blinkenberg and Friis Johansen (1928: 108)	INV.CHR.VIII. 458	Vulci	Copenhagen National Museum
Blinkenberg and Friis Johansen (1928: 109)	INV.CHR.VIII.326	Vulci	Copenhagen National Museum
Blinkenberg and Friis Johansen (1928: 80)	INV.CHR.VIII323	Vulci	Copenhagen National Museum
Blinkenberg and Friis Johansen (1928: 81)	INV.CHR.VIII 375	Vulci	Copenhagen National Museum
Blinkenberg and Friis Johansen (1928: 82)	INV.7783	Tarquinia	Copenhagen National Museum
Blinkenberg and Friis Johansen (1928: 84)	INV.CHR.VIII797	Vulci	Copenhagen National Museum
Blinkenberg and Friis Johansen (1928: 86)	INV.CHR.VII 321	Vulci	Copenhagen National Museum
Blinkenberg and Friis Johansen (1929: 115-116)	INV.CHR. VIII794	Vulci	Copenhagen National Museum

APPENDIX

Bibliographic Reference	Museum Reference	Site	Museum
Boston Museum of Fine Arts Online Catalogue	0.338	Tarquinia	Boston Museum of Fine Arts
Boston Museum of Fine Arts Online Catalogue	0.345	Tarquinia	Boston Museum of Fine Arts
Boston Museum of Fine Arts Online Catalogue	0.344	Tarquinia	Boston Museum of Fine Arts
Boston Museum of Fine Arts Online Catalogue	0.334	Tarquinia	Boston Museum of Fine Arts
Boston Museum of Fine Arts Online Catalogue	0.335	Tarquinia	Boston Museum of Fine Arts
Boston Museum of Fine Arts Online Catalogue	24.453	Vulci	Boston Museum of Fine Arts
Boston Museum of Fine Arts Online Catalogue	13.67	Vulci	Boston Museum of Fine Arts
Boston Museum of Fine Arts Online Catalogue	95.61	Vulci	Boston Museum of Fine Arts
Boston Museum of Fine Arts Online Catalogue	95.28	Vulci	Boston Museum of Fine Arts
Boston Museum of Fine Arts Online Catalogue	1.8057	Vulci	Boston Museum of Fine Arts
Boston Museum of Fine Arts Online Catalogue	89.272	Vulci	Boston Museum of Fine Arts
Boston Museum of Fine Arts Online Catalogue	0.352	Vulci	Boston Museum of Fine Arts
British Museum Online Catalogue	Vase B211	Chiusi	British Museum
British Museum Online Catalogue	1907,1020.1	Chiusi	British Museum
British Museum Online Catalogue	1893,1115.6	Chiusi	British Museum
British Museum Online Catalogue	Vase E80	Chiusi	British Museum
British Museum Online Catalogue	Vase E1	Chiusi	British Museum
British Museum Online Catalogue	Vase E182	Chiusi	British Museum
British Museum Online Catalogue	Vase E447	Chiusi	British Museum
British Museum Online Catalogue	1926,0410.34	Tarquinia	British Museum
British Museum Online Catalogue	Vase E15	Tarquinia	British Museum
British Museum Online Catalogue	Vase E180	Tarquinia	British Museum
British Museum Online Catalogue	Vase B289	Vulci	British Museum
British Museum Online Catalogue	1896,1022.1	Vulci	British Museum
British Museum Online Catalogue	1899,0721.3	Vulci	British Museum
British Museum Online Catalogue	Vase B180	Vulci	British Museum
British Museum Online Catalogue	Vase B271	Vulci	British Museum
British Museum Online Catalogue	Vase B280	Vulci	British Museum
British Museum Online Catalogue	Vase B222	Vulci	British Museum
British Museum Online Catalogue	Vase B231	Vulci	British Museum
British Museum Online Catalogue	Vase B200	Vulci	British Museum
British Museum Online Catalogue	Vase B181	Vulci	British Museum
British Museum Online Catalogue	Vase B187	Vulci	British Museum
British Museum Online Catalogue	Vase B169	Vulci	British Museum
British Museum Online Catalogue	Vase B202	Vulci	British Museum
British Museum Online Catalogue	Vase B178	Vulci	British Museum
British Museum Online Catalogue	Vase B168	Vulci	British Museum
British Museum Online Catalogue	Vase B184	Vulci	British Museum
British Museum Online Catalogue	Vase B179	Vulci	British Museum
British Museum Online Catalogue	Vase B185	Vulci	British Museum
British Museum Online Catalogue	Vase B177	Vulci	British Museum
British Museum Online Catalogue	Vase B198	Vulci	British Museum
British Museum Online Catalogue	Vase B614	Vulci	British Museum
British Museum Online Catalogue	Vase B144	Vulci	British Museum
British Museum Online Catalogue	Vase E282	Vulci	British Museum
British Museum Online Catalogue	Vase B163	Vulci	British Museum
British Museum Online Catalogue	Vase E267	Vulci	British Museum
British Museum Online Catalogue	Vase B195	Vulci	British Museum
British Museum Online Catalogue	Vase E258	Vulci	British Museum
British Museum Online Catalogue	Vase B168	Vulci	British Museum
British Museum Online Catalogue	Vase B134	Vulci	British Museum

Bibliographic Reference	Museum Reference	Site	Museum
British Museum Online Catalogue	Vase B171	Vulci	British Museum
British Museum Online Catalogue	Vase B201	Vulci	British Museum
British Museum Online Catalogue	Vase E271	Vulci	British Museum
British Museum Online Catalogue	Vase E265	Vulci	British Museum
British Museum Online Catalogue	Vase B162	Vulci	British Museum
British Museum Online Catalogue	Vase B147	Vulci	British Museum
British Museum Online Catalogue	Vase B166	Vulci	British Museum
British Museum Online Catalogue	Vase B153	Vulci	British Museum
British Museum Online Catalogue	Museum Secretum W39	Vulci	British Museum
British Museum Online Catalogue	Vase B194	Vulci	British Museum
British Museum Online Catalogue	Vase B164	Vulci	British Museum
British Museum Online Catalogue	Vase B213	Vulci	British Museum
British Museum Online Catalogue	Vase B271	Vulci	British Museum
British Museum Online Catalogue	Vase B210	Vulci	British Museum
British Museum Online Catalogue	Vase E262	Vulci	British Museum
British Museum Online Catalogue	Vase B205	Vulci	British Museum
British Museum Online Catalogue	Vase B133	Vulci	British Museum
British Museum Online Catalogue	Vase B196	Vulci	British Museum
British Museum Online Catalogue	Vase B241	Vulci	British Museum
British Museum Online Catalogue	Vase B234	Vulci	British Museum
British Museum Online Catalogue	Vase B246	Vulci	British Museum
British Museum Online Catalogue	Vase B679	Vulci	British Museum
British Museum Online Catalogue	Vase B207	Vulci	British Museum
British Museum Online Catalogue	Vase B206	Vulci	British Museum
British Museum Online Catalogue	Vase B239	Vulci	British Museum
British Museum Online Catalogue	Vase B161	Vulci	British Museum
British Museum Online Catalogue	Vase B199	Vulci	British Museum
British Museum Online Catalogue	Vase B215	Vulci	British Museum
British Museum Online Catalogue	Vase E263	Vulci	British Museum
British Museum Online Catalogue	Vase B146	Vulci	British Museum
British Museum Online Catalogue	Vase E261	Vulci	British Museum
British Museum Online Catalogue	Vase B158	Vulci	British Museum
British Museum Online Catalogue	Vase E256	Vulci	British Museum
British Museum Online Catalogue	Vase B208	Vulci	British Museum
British Museum Online Catalogue	Vase E255	Vulci	British Museum
British Museum Online Catalogue	Vase B228	Vulci	British Museum
British Museum Online Catalogue	Vase B220	Vulci	British Museum
British Museum Online Catalogue	Vase E257	Vulci	British Museum
British Museum Online Catalogue	Vase B167	Vulci	British Museum
British Museum Online Catalogue	Vase B204	Vulci	British Museum
British Museum Online Catalogue	Vase B398	Vulci	British Museum
British Museum Online Catalogue	Vase B367	Vulci	British Museum
British Museum Online Catalogue	1896,0621.2	Vulci	British Museum
British Museum Online Catalogue	Vase B428	Vulci	British Museum
British Museum Online Catalogue	Vase E817	Vulci	British Museum
British Museum Online Catalogue	Vase E818	Vulci	British Museum
British Museum Online Catalogue	Vase E54	Vulci	British Museum
British Museum Online Catalogue	Vase E53	Vulci	British Museum
British Museum Online Catalogue	Vase E154	Vulci	British Museum
British Museum Online Catalogue	Old Catalogue 1020	Vulci	British Museum
British Museum Online Catalogue	Vase E58	Vulci	British Museum

Appendix

Bibliographic Reference	Museum Reference	Site	Museum
British Museum Online Catalogue	Vase E6	Vulci	British Museum
British Museum Online Catalogue	Vase B331	Vulci	British Museum
British Museum Online Catalogue	Vase E9	Vulci	British Museum
British Museum Online Catalogue	Vase E8	Vulci	British Museum
British Museum Online Catalogue	Vase E33	Vulci	British Museum
British Museum Online Catalogue	Vase E17	Vulci	British Museum
British Museum Online Catalogue	Vase E18	Vulci	British Museum
British Museum Online Catalogue	Vase E13	Vulci	British Museum
British Museum Online Catalogue	Vase E36	Vulci	British Museum
British Museum Online Catalogue	CVA British Museum 9 49	Vulci	British Museum
British Museum Online Catalogue	Vase E61	Vulci	British Museum
British Museum Online Catalogue	Vase E16	Vulci	British Museum
British Museum Online Catalogue	Vase E38	Vulci	British Museum
British Museum Online Catalogue	Vase E102	Vulci	British Museum
British Museum Online Catalogue	Vase E57	Vulci	British Museum
British Museum Online Catalogue	Vase E82	Vulci	British Museum
British Museum Online Catalogue	Vase E53	Vulci	British Museum
British Museum Online Catalogue	Vase E83	Vulci	British Museum
British Museum Online Catalogue	Vase E81	Vulci	British Museum
British Museum Online Catalogue	Vase E100	Vulci	British Museum
British Museum Online Catalogue	Vase E84	Vulci	British Museum
British Museum Online Catalogue	Vase E104	Vulci	British Museum
British Museum Online Catalogue	Vase E77	Vulci	British Museum
British Museum Online Catalogue	Vase E55	Vulci	British Museum
British Museum Online Catalogue	Vase E60	Vulci	British Museum
British Museum Online Catalogue	Vase B409	Vulci	British Museum
British Museum Online Catalogue	Vase B423	Vulci	British Museum
British Museum Online Catalogue	Vase B387	Vulci	British Museum
British Museum Online Catalogue	Vase B410	Vulci	British Museum
British Museum Online Catalogue	Vase E39	Vulci	British Museum
British Museum Online Catalogue	Vase B424	Vulci	British Museum
British Museum Online Catalogue	Vase B399	Vulci	British Museum
British Museum Online Catalogue	Vase E49	Vulci	British Museum
British Museum Online Catalogue	Vase E52	Vulci	British Museum
British Museum Online Catalogue	Vase E48	Vulci	British Museum
British Museum Online Catalogue	Vase B425	Vulci	British Museum
British Museum Online Catalogue	Vase E67	Vulci	British Museum
British Museum Online Catalogue	Vase E78	Vulci	British Museum
British Museum Online Catalogue	Vase E68	Vulci	British Museum
British Museum Online Catalogue	Vase E75	Vulci	British Museum
British Museum Online Catalogue	Vase E44	Vulci	British Museum
British Museum Online Catalogue	Vase E69	Vulci	British Museum
British Museum Online Catalogue	Vase E62	Vulci	British Museum
British Museum Online Catalogue	Vase B419	Vulci	British Museum
British Museum Online Catalogue	Vase E20	Vulci	British Museum
British Museum Online Catalogue	Vase E21	Vulci	British Museum
British Museum Online Catalogue	Vase B402	Vulci	British Museum
British Museum Online Catalogue	1896,0621.1	Vulci	British Museum
British Museum Online Catalogue	Vase E70	Vulci	British Museum
British Museum Online Catalogue	Vase E35	Vulci	British Museum
British Museum Online Catalogue	Vase E7	Vulci	British Museum

Bibliographic Reference	Museum Reference	Site	Museum
British Museum Online Catalogue	Vase E816	Vulci	British Museum
British Museum Online Catalogue	Vase E40	Vulci	British Museum
British Museum Online Catalogue	Vase B173	Vulci	British Museum
British Museum Online Catalogue	Vase B203	Vulci	British Museum
British Museum Online Catalogue	Vase B427	Vulci	British Museum
British Museum Online Catalogue	Vase B418	Vulci	British Museum
British Museum Online Catalogue	Vase E10	Vulci	British Museum
British Museum Online Catalogue	Vase E41	Vulci	British Museum
British Museum Online Catalogue	Vase E45	Vulci	British Museum
British Museum Online Catalogue	Vase E12	Vulci	British Museum
British Museum Online Catalogue	Vase E76	Vulci	British Museum
British Museum Online Catalogue	Vase E64	Vulci	British Museum
British Museum Online Catalogue	1952,1202.10.a	Vulci	British Museum
British Museum Online Catalogue	1952,1202.10.b	Vulci	British Museum
British Museum Online Catalogue	Vase B62	Vulci	British Museum
British Museum Online Catalogue	1899,0721.4	Vulci	British Museum
British Museum Online Catalogue	Vase B308	Vulci	British Museum
British Museum Online Catalogue	Vase B342	Vulci	British Museum
British Museum Online Catalogue	Vase B332	Vulci	British Museum
British Museum Online Catalogue	Vase B340	Vulci	British Museum
British Museum Online Catalogue	Vase B344	Vulci	British Museum
British Museum Online Catalogue	Vase B318	Vulci	British Museum
British Museum Online Catalogue	Vase B345	Vulci	British Museum
British Museum Online Catalogue	Vase B343	Vulci	British Museum
British Museum Online Catalogue	Vase B317	Vulci	British Museum
British Museum Online Catalogue	Vase B335	Vulci	British Museum
British Museum Online Catalogue	Vase E177	Vulci	British Museum
British Museum Online Catalogue	Vase E211	Vulci	British Museum
British Museum Online Catalogue	Vase E162	Vulci	British Museum
British Museum Online Catalogue	Vase E176	Vulci	British Museum
British Museum Online Catalogue	Vase B319	Vulci	British Museum
British Museum Online Catalogue	Vase B306	Vulci	British Museum
British Museum Online Catalogue	Vase B337	Vulci	British Museum
British Museum Online Catalogue	Vase B321	Vulci	British Museum
British Museum Online Catalogue	Vase B336	Vulci	British Museum
British Museum Online Catalogue	Vase E19	Vulci	British Museum
British Museum Online Catalogue	Vase E160	Vulci	British Museum
British Museum Online Catalogue	Vase B301	Vulci	British Museum
British Museum Online Catalogue	Vase B312	Vulci	British Museum
British Museum Online Catalogue	Vase B339	Vulci	British Museum
British Museum Online Catalogue	Vase B302	Vulci	British Museum
British Museum Online Catalogue	Vase B327	Vulci	British Museum
British Museum Online Catalogue	Vase B330	Vulci	British Museum
British Museum Online Catalogue	Vase E169	Vulci	British Museum
British Museum Online Catalogue	Vase E163	Vulci	British Museum
British Museum Online Catalogue	Vase B303	Vulci	British Museum
British Museum Online Catalogue	Vase E168	Vulci	British Museum
British Museum Online Catalogue	Vase B334	Vulci	British Museum
British Museum Online Catalogue	Vase B322	Vulci	British Museum
British Museum Online Catalogue	Vase B328	Vulci	British Museum
British Museum Online Catalogue	Vase B323	Vulci	British Museum

Appendix

Bibliographic Reference	Museum Reference	Site	Museum
British Museum Online Catalogue	Vase E815	Vulci	British Museum
British Museum Online Catalogue	Vase B304	Vulci	British Museum
British Museum Online Catalogue	Vase B316	Vulci	British Museum
British Museum Online Catalogue	Vase E161	Vulci	British Museum
British Museum Online Catalogue	Vase E165	Vulci	British Museum
British Museum Online Catalogue	Vase B305	Vulci	British Museum
British Museum Online Catalogue	Vase B329	Vulci	British Museum
British Museum Online Catalogue	Vase B338	Vulci	British Museum
British Museum Online Catalogue	1977,1201.33	Vulci	British Museum
British Museum Online Catalogue	Vase E461	Vulci	British Museum
British Museum Online Catalogue	Old Catalogue 1020	Vulci	British Museum
British Museum Online Catalogue	Vase E496	Vulci	British Museum
British Museum Online Catalogue	Vase B470	Vulci	British Museum
British Museum Online Catalogue	Vase B463	Vulci	British Museum
British Museum Online Catalogue	Vase B462	Vulci	British Museum
British Museum Online Catalogue	Vase B465	Vulci	British Museum
British Museum Online Catalogue	Vase B466	Vulci	British Museum
British Museum Online Catalogue	Vase E808	Vulci	British Museum
British Museum Online Catalogue	Old Catalogue 715	Vulci	British Museum
British Museum Online Catalogue	Vase B429	Vulci	British Museum
British Museum Online Catalogue	Vase E4	Vulci	British Museum
British Museum Online Catalogue	Vase B430	Vulci	British Museum
British Museum Online Catalogue	Vase B433	Vulci	British Museum
British Museum Online Catalogue	Vase B680	Vulci	British Museum
British Museum Online Catalogue	Vase B434	Vulci	British Museum
British Museum Online Catalogue	Vase E11	Vulci	British Museum
British Museum Online Catalogue	Vase B436	Vulci	British Museum
British Museum Online Catalogue	Vase E2	Vulci	British Museum
British Museum Online Catalogue	Vase E23	Vulci	British Museum
British Museum Online Catalogue	Vase E14	Vulci	British Museum
British Museum Online Catalogue	Vase E37	Vulci	British Museum
British Museum Online Catalogue	Vase E5	Vulci	British Museum
British Museum Online Catalogue	1896,0621.3	Vulci	British Museum
British Museum Online Catalogue	1836,0224.53	Vulci	British Museum
British Museum Online Catalogue	Vase B53	Vulci	British Museum
British Museum Online Catalogue	Vase B643	Vulci	British Museum
British Museum Online Catalogue	Vase B687	Vulci	British Museum
British Museum Online Catalogue	1836,0224.53	Vulci	British Museum
British Museum Online Catalogue	Vase B660	Vulci	British Museum
British Museum Online Catalogue	Vase B404	Vulci	British Museum
British Museum Online Catalogue	Vase B395	Vulci	British Museum
British Museum Online Catalogue	Vase B412	Vulci	British Museum
British Museum Online Catalogue	Vase B421	Vulci	British Museum
British Museum Online Catalogue	Vase B403	Vulci	British Museum
British Museum Online Catalogue	Vase B401	Vulci	British Museum
British Museum Online Catalogue	Vase B375	Vulci	British Museum
British Museum Online Catalogue	Terracotta 1617	Vulci	British Museum
British Museum Online Catalogue	Terracotta 1619	Vulci	British Museum
British Museum Online Catalogue	Terracotta 1609	Vulci	British Museum
British Museum Online Catalogue	Vase B223	Vulci	British Museum
British Museum Online Catalogue	Vase B615	Vulci	British Museum

Bibliographic Reference	Museum Reference	Site	Museum
British Museum Online Catalogue	Vase B272	Vulci	British Museum
British Museum Online Catalogue	1980,1029.1	Vulci	British Museum
British Museum Online Catalogue	Vase B256	Vulci	British Museum
British Museum Online Catalogue	Vase B286	Vulci	British Museum
British Museum Online Catalogue	Vase B288	Vulci	British Museum
British Museum Online Catalogue	Vase B283	Vulci	British Museum
British Museum Online Catalogue	Vase B277	Vulci	British Museum
British Museum Online Catalogue	Vase B24	Vulci	British Museum
British Museum Online Catalogue	Vase B273	Vulci	British Museum
British Museum Online Catalogue	Vase B259	Vulci	British Museum
British Museum Online Catalogue	Vase B176	Vulci	British Museum
British Museum Online Catalogue	Vase E283	Vulci	British Museum
British Museum Online Catalogue	Vase B236	Vulci	British Museum
British Museum Online Catalogue	Vase B252	Vulci	British Museum
British Museum Online Catalogue	Vase B274	Vulci	British Museum
British Museum Online Catalogue	Vase B279	Vulci	British Museum
British Museum Online Catalogue	Vase B232	Vulci	British Museum
British Museum Online Catalogue	Vase B245	Vulci	British Museum
British Museum Online Catalogue	Vase B191	Vulci	British Museum
British Museum Online Catalogue	Vase B260	Vulci	British Museum
British Museum Online Catalogue	Vase B254	Vulci	British Museum
British Museum Online Catalogue	Vase B248	Vulci	British Museum
British Museum Online Catalogue	Vase B238	Vulci	British Museum
British Museum Online Catalogue	Vase B267	Vulci	British Museum
British Museum Online Catalogue	Vase B227	Vulci	British Museum
British Museum Online Catalogue	Vase B251	Vulci	British Museum
British Museum Online Catalogue	Vase B257	Vulci	British Museum
British Museum Online Catalogue	Vase B243	Vulci	British Museum
British Museum Online Catalogue	Vase B249	Vulci	British Museum
British Museum Online Catalogue	Vase E304	Vulci	British Museum
British Museum Online Catalogue	Vase E275	Vulci	British Museum
British Museum Online Catalogue	Vase E266	Vulci	British Museum
British Museum Online Catalogue	Vase B242	Vulci	British Museum
British Museum Online Catalogue	Vase B218	Vulci	British Museum
British Museum Online Catalogue	Vase B224	Vulci	British Museum
British Museum Online Catalogue	Vase B267	Vulci	British Museum
British Museum Online Catalogue	Vase B245	Vulci	British Museum
British Museum Online Catalogue	Vase B232	Vulci	British Museum
British Museum Online Catalogue	Vase E274	Vulci	British Museum
British Museum Online Catalogue	Vase B230	Vulci	British Museum
British Museum Online Catalogue	Vase B264	Vulci	British Museum
British Museum Online Catalogue	Vase B214	Vulci	British Museum
British Museum Online Catalogue	Vase E278	Vulci	British Museum
British Museum Online Catalogue	Vase B47	Vulci	British Museum
British Museum Online Catalogue	Vase B275	Vulci	British Museum
British Museum Online Catalogue	Vase B217	Vulci	British Museum
British Museum Online Catalogue	Vase B244	Vulci	British Museum
British Museum Online Catalogue	Old Catalogue 635	Vulci	British Museum
British Museum Online Catalogue	Vase B478	Vulci	British Museum
British Museum Online Catalogue	Vase B515	Vulci	British Museum
British Museum Online Catalogue	Vase B494	Vulci	British Museum

APPENDIX

Bibliographic Reference	Museum Reference	Site	Museum
British Museum Online Catalogue	Vase B497	Vulci	British Museum
British Museum Online Catalogue	Vase B519	Vulci	British Museum
British Museum Online Catalogue	Vase B493	Vulci	British Museum
British Museum Online Catalogue	Vase B475	Vulci	British Museum
British Museum Online Catalogue	Vase B477	Vulci	British Museum
British Museum Online Catalogue	Vase B518	Vulci	British Museum
British Museum Online Catalogue	Vase B632	Vulci	British Museum
British Museum Online Catalogue	Vase B501	Vulci	British Museum
British Museum Online Catalogue	Vase B512	Vulci	British Museum
British Museum Online Catalogue	Vase B489	Vulci	British Museum
British Museum Online Catalogue	Vase B484	Vulci	British Museum
British Museum Online Catalogue	Vase B508	Vulci	British Museum
British Museum Online Catalogue	Vase B513	Vulci	British Museum
British Museum Online Catalogue	Vase B499	Vulci	British Museum
British Museum Online Catalogue	Vase B476	Vulci	British Museum
British Museum Online Catalogue	Vase B496	Vulci	British Museum
British Museum Online Catalogue	Vase B522	Vulci	British Museum
British Museum Online Catalogue	Vase B523	Vulci	British Museum
British Museum Online Catalogue	Vase E523	Vulci	British Museum
British Museum Online Catalogue	Vase B524	Vulci	British Museum
British Museum Online Catalogue	Vase B620	Vulci	British Museum
British Museum Online Catalogue	Vase B617	Vulci	British Museum
British Museum Online Catalogue	Vase B483	Vulci	British Museum
British Museum Online Catalogue	Vase E510	Vulci	British Museum
British Museum Online Catalogue	Vase E511	Vulci	British Museum
British Museum Online Catalogue	Vase E514	Vulci	British Museum
British Museum Online Catalogue	Vase D14	Vulci	British Museum
British Museum Online Catalogue	Vase B621	Vulci	British Museum
British Museum Online Catalogue	Vase B507	Vulci	British Museum
British Museum Online Catalogue	Vase B492	Vulci	British Museum
British Museum Online Catalogue	Vase B474	Vulci	British Museum
British Museum Online Catalogue	Vase B131	Vulci	British Museum
British Museum Online Catalogue	Vase B132	Vulci	British Museum
British Museum Online Catalogue	Vase E380	Vulci	British Museum
British Museum Online Catalogue	Vase E383	Vulci	British Museum
British Museum Online Catalogue	Vase E375	Vulci	British Museum
British Museum Online Catalogue	Vase E410	Vulci	British Museum
British Museum Online Catalogue	Vase E382	Vulci	British Museum
British Museum Online Catalogue	Vase B368	Vulci	British Museum
British Museum Online Catalogue	Vase B589	Vulci	British Museum
British Museum Online Catalogue	Vase B591	Vulci	British Museum
British Museum Online Catalogue	Vase E136	Vulci	British Museum
British Museum Online Catalogue	Vase E137	Vulci	British Museum
British Museum Online Catalogue	Vase E135	Vulci	British Museum
British Museum Online Catalogue	Vase B299	Vulci	British Museum
British Museum Online Catalogue	Vase B366	Vulci	British Museum
British Museum Online Catalogue	Vase E450	Vulci	British Museum
British Museum Online Catalogue	Vase E448	Vulci	British Museum
British Museum Online Catalogue	Vase E453	Vulci	British Museum
British Museum Online Catalogue	Vase E444	Vulci	British Museum
British Museum Online Catalogue	Vase E440	Vulci	British Museum

Bibliographic Reference	Museum Reference	Site	Museum
British Museum Online Catalogue	Vase E439	Vulci	British Museum
British Museum Online Catalogue	Vase E452	Vulci	British Museum
British Museum Online Catalogue	Vase E454	Vulci	British Museum
British Museum Online Catalogue	Vase E441	Vulci	British Museum
British Museum Online Catalogue	Vase E443	Vulci	British Museum
British Museum Online Catalogue	Vase E451	Vulci	British Museum
British Museum Online Catalogue	Vase E445	Vulci	British Museum
British Museum Online Catalogue	Vase E51	Vulci	British Museum
British Museum Online Catalogue	Vase E512	Vulci	British Museum
British Museum Online Catalogue	Vase E442	Vulci	British Museum
British Museum Online Catalogue	Vase E264	Vulci	British Museum
British Museum Online Catalogue	Vase B174	Vulci	British Museum
British Museum Online Catalogue	Vase B294	Vulci	British Musuem
British Museum Online Catalogue	Vase E410	Vulci	British Museum
British Museum Online Catalogue	Vase E382	Vulci	British Museum
British Museum Online Catalogue	Vase B368	Vulci	British Museum
British Museum Online Catalogue	Vase B589	Vulci	British Museum
British Museum Online Catalogue	Vase B591	Vulci	British Museum
British Museum Online Catalogue	Vase E136	Vulci	British Museum
British Museum Online Catalogue	Vase E448	Vulci	British Museum
British Museum Online Catalogue	Vase E453	Vulci	British Museum
British Museum Online Catalogue	Vase E444	Vulci	British Museum
British Museum Online Catalogue	Vase E440	Vulci	British Museum
British Museum Online Catalogue	Vase E439	Vulci	British Museum
British Museum Online Catalogue	Vase E452	Vulci	British Museum
British Museum Online Catalogue	Vase E454	Vulci	British Museum
British Museum Online Catalogue	Vase E441	Vulci	British Museum
British Museum Online Catalogue	Vase E443	Vulci	British Museum
British Museum Online Catalogue	Vase E451	Vulci	British Museum
British Museum Online Catalogue	Vase E445	Vulci	British Museum
British Museum Online Catalogue	Vase E51	Vulci	British Museum
British Museum Online Catalogue	Vase E512	Vulci	British Museum
British Museum Online Catalogue	Vase E442	Vulci	British Museum
British Museum Online Catalogue	Vase E264	Vulci	British Museum
British Museum Online Catalogue	Vase B174	Vulci	British Museum
British Museum Online Catalogue	Vase B294	Vulci	British Musuem
Smith (1936: 19)	01/08/81	Chiusi	Berkeley
Campus (1981: 1)	INV603	Tarquinia	Tarquinia Museo Nazionale
Campus (1981: 100)	RC5187	Tarquinia	Tarquinia Museo Nazionale
Campus (1981: 101)	INV6848	Tarquinia	Tarquinia Museo Nazionale
Campus (1981: 103)	RC6217	Tarquinia	Tarquinia Museo Nazionale
Campus (1981: 104)	RC6218	Tarquinia	Tarquinia Museo Nazionale
Campus (1981: 104)	RC6216	Tarquinia	Tarquinia Museo Nazionale
Campus (1981: 105)	RC6219	Tarquinia	Tarquinia Museo Nazionale
Campus (1981: 11)	INV596	Tarquinia	Tarquinia Museo Nazionale
Campus (1981: 12)	INV?CAT7	Tarquinia	Tarquinia Museo Nazionale
Campus (1981: 14)	INV1749	Tarquinia	Tarquinia Museo Nazionale
Campus (1981: 17)	RC5658	Tarquinia	Tarquinia Museo Nazionale
Campus (1981: 18)	RC5992	Tarquinia	Tarquinia Museo Nazionale
Campus (1981: 20)	INV592	Tarquinia	Tarquinia Museo Nazionale
Campus (1981: 22)	INV1629	Tarquinia	Tarquinia Museo Nazionale

Appendix

Bibliographic Reference	Museum Reference	Site	Museum
Campus (1981: 24)	RC2431	Tarquinia	Tarquinia Museo Nazionale
Campus (1981: 25)	INV595	Tarquinia	Tarquinia Museo Nazionale
Campus (1981: 27)	RC5659	Tarquinia	Tarquinia Museo Nazionale
Campus (1981: 28)	RC2461	Tarquinia	Tarquinia Museo Nazionale
Campus (1981: 31)	RC5657	Tarquinia	Tarquinia Museo Nazionale
Campus (1981: 33)	INV?CAT19	Tarquinia	Tarquinia Museo Nazionale
Campus (1981: 35)	RC1059	Tarquinia	Tarquinia Museo Nazionale
Campus (1981: 35)	INV590	Tarquinia	Tarquinia Museo Nazionale
Campus (1981: 38)	RC3245	Tarquinia	Tarquinia Museo Nazionale
Campus (1981: 39)	INV?CAT22	Tarquinia	Tarquinia Museo Nazionale
Campus (1981: 41)	RC1046	Tarquinia	Tarquinia Museo Nazionale
Campus (1981: 42)	INV710	Tarquinia	Tarquinia Museo Nazionale
Campus (1981: 43)	INV605	Tarquinia	Tarquinia Museo Nazionale
Campus (1981: 44)	INV602	Tarquinia	Tarquinia Museo Nazionale
Campus (1981: 47)	RC5174	Tarquinia	Tarquinia Museo Nazionale
Campus (1981: 48)	RC5198	Tarquinia	Tarquinia Museo Nazionale
Campus (1981: 5)	RC1044	Tarquinia	Tarquinia Museo Nazionale
Campus (1981: 50)	INV? CAT28	Tarquinia	Tarquinia Museo Nazionale
Campus (1981: 6)	INV601	Tarquinia	Tarquinia Museo Nazionale
Campus (1981: 62)	RC3033	Tarquinia	Tarquinia Museo Nazionale
Campus (1981: 63)	INV612	Tarquinia	Tarquinia Museo Nazionale
Campus (1981: 64)	INV613	Tarquinia	Tarquinia Museo Nazionale
Campus (1981: 65)	INV610	Tarquinia	Tarquinia Museo Nazionale
Campus (1981: 66)	INV609	Tarquinia	Tarquinia Museo Nazionale
Campus (1981: 67)	RC5169	Tarquinia	Tarquinia Museo Nazionale
Campus (1981: 68)	RC5289	Tarquinia	Tarquinia Museo Nazionale
Campus (1981: 7)	RC1045	Tarquinia	Tarquinia Museo Nazionale
Campus (1981: 71)	RC5175	Tarquinia	Tarquinia Museo Nazionale
Campus (1981: 72)	INV559	Tarquinia	Tarquinia Museo Nazionale
Campus (1981: 73)	INV2935	Tarquinia	Tarquinia Museo Nazionale
Campus (1981: 74)	RC1632	Tarquinia	Tarquinia Museo Nazionale
Campus (1981: 75)	INV611	Tarquinia	Tarquinia Museo Nazionale
Campus (1981: 76)	RC3034	Tarquinia	Tarquinia Museo Nazionale
Campus (1981: 77)	INV615	Tarquinia	Tarquinia Museo Nazionale
Campus (1981: 78)	RC3035	Tarquinia	Tarquinia Museo Nazionale
Campus (1981: 79)	RC5287	Tarquinia	Tarquinia Museo Nazionale
Campus (1981: 8)	INV? CAT5 (Campus)	Tarquinia	Tarquinia Museo Nazionale
Campus (1981: 80)	INV?CAT56	Tarquinia	Tarquinia Museo Nazionale
Campus (1981: 81)	RC3036	Tarquinia	Tarquinia Museo Nazionale
Campus (1981: 86)	INV?CAT60	Tarquinia	Tarquinia Museo Nazionale
Campus (1981: 88)	INV593	Tarquinia	Tarquinia Museo Nazionale
Campus (1981: 91)	INV597	Tarquinia	Tarquinia Museo Nazionale
Campus (1981: 94)	RC3308	Tarquinia	Tarquinia Museo Nazionale
Campus (1981: 96)	INV?CAT66	Tarquinia	Tarquinia Museo Nazionale
Campus (1981: 97)	INV?CAT67	Tarquinia	Tarquinia Museo Nazionale
Campus (1981: 98)	INV?CAT68	Tarquinia	Tarquinia Museo Nazionale
Campus (1981:30)	INV591	Tarquinia	Tarquinia Museo Nazionale
Descoeudres (1981: 107-108)	KA 421	Vulci	Basle Antikenmuseum
Descoeudres (1981: 186-187)	BS 1921.328	Vulci	Basle Antikenmuseum
Elarth (1933: 30)	2595	Chiusi	Ann Arbor
Elarth (1933: 31)	2594	Chiusi	Ann Arbor

Bibliographic Reference	Museum Reference	Site	Museum
Ferrari (1988: 101)	RC7455	Tarquinia	Tarquinia Museo Nazionale
Ferrari (1988: 103)	RC973	Tarquinai	Tarquinia Museo Nazionale
Ferrari (1988: 105)	INV683	Tarquinia	Tarquinia Museo Nazionale
Ferrari (1988: 108)	INV704	Tarquinia	Tarquinia Museo Nazionale
Ferrari (1988: 111)	INV701	Tarquinia	Tarquinia Museo Nazionale
Ferrari (1988: 113)	INV696	Tarquinia	Tarquinia Museo Nazionale
Ferrari (1988: 115)	RC1912	Tarquinia	Tarquinia Museo Nazionale
Ferrari (1988: 116)	RC1914	Tarquinia	Tarquinia Museo Nazionale
Ferrari (1988: 121)	RC1916	Tarquinia	Tarquinia Museo Nazionale
Ferrari (1988: 123)	RC1918	Tarquinia	Tarquinia Museo Nazionale
Ferrari (1988: 125)	RC2982	Tarquinia	Tarquinia Museo Nazionale
Ferrari (1988: 126)	RC2983	Tarquinia	Tarquinia Museo Nazionale
Ferrari (1988: 129)	RC6846	Tarquinia	Tarquinia Museo Nazionale
Ferrari (1988: 134)	RC5590	Tarquinia	Tarquinia Museo Nazionale
Ferrari (1988: 135)	RC5589	Tarquinia	Tarquinia Museo Nazionale
Ferrari (1988: 139)	RC5281	Tarquinia	Tarquinia Museo Nazionale
Ferrari (1988: 146)	INV703	Tarquinia	Tarquinia Museo Nazionale
Ferrari (1988: 149)	RC2984	Tarquinia	Tarquinia Museo Nazionale
Ferrari (1988: 151)	RC2067	Tarquinia	Tarquinia Museo Nazionale
Ferrari (1988: 153)	INV698	Tarquinia	Tarquinia Museo Nazionale
Ferrari (1988: 154)	RC5771	Tarquinia	Tarquinia Museo Nazionale
Ferrari (1988: 157)	RC1116	Tarquinia	Tarquinia Museo Nazionale
Ferrari (1988: 159)	INV692	Tarquinia	Tarquinia Museo Nazionale
Ferrari (1988: 161)	INV689	Tarquinia	Tarquinia Museo Nazionale
Ferrari (1988: 17)	RC6843	Tarquinia	Tarquinia Museo Nazionale
Ferrari (1988: 23)	RC6848	Tarquinia	Tarquinia Museo Nazionale
Ferrari (1988: 29)	RC1091	Tarquinia	Tarquinia Museo Nazionale
Ferrari (1988: 31)	RC1911	Tarquinia	Tarquinia Museo Nazionale
Ferrari (1988: 34)	RC5292	Tarquinia	Tarquinia Museo Nazionale
Ferrari (1988: 39)	INV699	Tarquinia	Tarquinia Museo Nazionale
Ferrari (1988: 43)	RC1123	Tarquinia	Tarquinia Museo Nazionale
Ferrari (1988: 46)	87778	Tarquinia	Tarquinia Museo Nazionale
Ferrari (1988: 49)	RC2066	Tarquinia	Tarquinia Museo Nazionale
Ferrari (1988: 55)	RC2074	Tarquinia	Tarquinia Museo Nazionale
Ferrari (1988: 57)	RC1129	Tarquinia	Tarquinia Museo Nazionale
Ferrari (1988: 59)	RC5293	Tarquinia	Tarquinia Museo Nazionale
Ferrari (1988: 63)	RC1130	Tarquinia	Tarquinia Museo Nazionale
Ferrari (1988: 66)	87783	Tarquinia	Tarquinia Museo Nazionale
Ferrari (1988: 71)	RC2660	Tarquinia	Tarquinia Museo Nazionale
Ferrari (1988: 73)	RC4196	Tarquinia	Tarquinia Museo Nazionale
Ferrari (1988: 76)	INV711	Tarquinia	Tarquinia Museo Nazionale
Ferrari (1988: 80)	RC7456	Tarquinia	Tarquinia Museo Nazionale
Ferrari (1988: 83)	RC2989	Tarquinia	Tarquinia Museo Nazionale
Ferrari (1988: 87)	RC2398	Tarquinia	Tarquinia Museo Nazionale
Ferrari (1988: 89)	87781	Tarquinia	Tarquinia Museo Nazionale
Ferrari (1988: 90)	RC992	Tarquinia	Tarquinia Museo Nazionale
Ferrari (1988: 96)	RC8261	Tarquinia	Tarquinia Museo Nazionale
Ferrari (1988:144)	87779	Tarquinia	Tarquinia Museo Nazionale
Ferrari (1988:94)	RC2460	Tarquinia	Tarquinia Museo Nazionale
Fitzwilliam Museum Online Catalogue	GR.27.1864	Vulci	Fitzwilliam
Fitzwilliam Museum Online Catalogue	GR.28.1864	Vulci	Fitzwilliam

APPENDIX

Bibliographic Reference	Museum Reference	Site	Museum
Fitzwilliam Museum Online Catalogue	GR.29.1864	Vulci	Fitzwilliam
Fitzwilliam Museum Online Catalogue	GR.30.1864	Vulci	Fitzwilliam
Fitzwilliam Museum Online Catalogue	GR.31.1864	Vulci	Fitzwilliam
Fitzwilliam Museum Online Catalogue	GR.32.1864	Vulci	Fitzwilliam
Fitzwilliam Museum Online Catalogue	GR.23.1864	Vulci	Fitzwilliam
Fitzwilliam Museum Online Catalogue	GR.24.1864	Vulci	Fitzwilliam
Fitzwilliam Museum Online Catalogue	GR.26.1864	Vulci	Fitzwilliam
Fitzwilliam Museum Online Catalogue	GR.39.1864	Vulci	Fitzwilliam
Fitzwilliam Museum Online Catalogue	GR.40.1864	Vulci	Fitzwilliam
Fitzwilliam Museum Online Catalogue	GR.41.1864	Vulci	Fitzwilliam
Fitzwilliam Museum Online Catalogue	GR.44.1864	Vulci	Fitzwilliam
Fitzwilliam Museum Online Catalogue	GR.45.1864	Vulci	Fitzwilliam
Fitzwilliam Museum Online Catalogue	GR.46.1864	Vulci	Fitzwilliam
Fitzwilliam Museum Online Catalogue	GR.49.1864	Vulci	Fitzwilliam
Fitzwilliam Museum Online Catalogue	GR.50.1864	Vulci	Fitzwilliam
Fitzwilliam Museum Online Catalogue	GR.48.1864	Vulci	Fitzwilliam
Fitzwilliam Museum Online Catalogue	GR.51.1864	Vulci	Fitzwilliam
Fitzwilliam Museum Online Catalogue	GR.15.1937	Vulci	Fitzwilliam
Fitzwilliam Museum Online Catalogue	GR.16.1937	Vulci	Fitzwilliam
Fitzwilliam Museum Online Catalogue	GR.17.1937	Vulci	Fitzwilliam
Fitzwilliam Museum Online Catalogue	GR.25.1864	Vulci	Fitzwilliam
Fitzwilliam Museum Online Catalogue	GR.33.1864	Vulci	Fitzwilliam
Fitzwilliam Museum Online Catalogue	GR.34.1864	Vulci	Fitzwilliam
Fitzwilliam Museum Online Catalogue	GR.35.1864	Vulci	Fitzwilliam
Fitzwilliam Museum Online Catalogue	GR.36.1864	Vulci	Fitzwilliam
Fitzwilliam Museum Online Catalogue	GR.126.1864	Vulci	Fitzwilliam
Fitzwilliam Museum Online Catalogue	GR.147.1864	Vulci	Fitzwilliam
Flot (1924: 10-11)	no 1068	Vulci	Musee de Compiegne
Flot (1924: 11)	no. 1022	Vulci	Musee de Compiegne
Flot (1924: 12)	no. 1045	Vulci	Musee de Compiegne
Flot (1924: 4)	no. 1094	Vulci	Musee de Compiegne
Flot (1924: 4)	no. 1044	Vulci	Musee de Compiegne
Flot (1924: 5)	no. 1091	Vulci	Musee de Compiegne
Flot (1924: 6)	no. 1075	Vulci	Musee de Compiegne
Flot (1924: 6)	no. 1073	Vulci	Musee de Compiegne
Flot (1924: 7)	no. 1097	Vulci	Musee de Compiegne
Flot (1924: 8)	no. 1085	Vulci	Musee de Compiegne
Flot (1924: 8)	no. 1020	Vulci	Musee de Compiegne
Flot (1924: 8)	no. 1008	Vulci	Musee de Compiegne
Flot (1924: 9)	no. 1032	Vulci	Musee de Compiegne
Flot (1924: 9)	no. 1009	Vulci	Musee de Compiegne
Flot (1924: 9)	no. 1040	Vulci	Musee de Compiegne
Flot (1924: 9)	no. 993	Vulci	Musee de Compiegne
Flot (1927: 3.2)	no. 982	Vulci	Musee de Compiegne
Flot (1927: 3.3-4)	no. 979	Vulci	Musee de Compiegne
Flot (1927: 3.7-8)	no. 1050	Vulci	Musee de Compiegne
Flot (1927: 4.1-2)	no. 981	Vulci	Musee de Compiegne
Flot (1927: 4.5-8)	no. 987	Vulci	Musee de Compiegne
Flot (1929: 4.9)	no. 986	Vulci	Musee de Compiegne
Flot (1929: 5.1-8)	no. 976	Vulci	Musee de Compiegne
Giglioli (1925: 3)	24998	Tarquinia	Rome, Museo Nazionale di Villa Giulia

Bibliographic Reference	Museum Reference	Site	Museum
Griefenhagen (1962a: 16-18)	F2279	Vulci	Berlin Antiquarium
Griefenhagen (1962a: 22)	F2303	Vulci	Berlin Antiquarium
Griefenhagen (1962a: 22-23)	F2293	Vulci	Berlin Antiquarium
Griefenhagen (1962a: 25-26)	F2294	Vulci	Berlin Antiquarium
Griefenhagen (1962a: 31)	F2289	Vulci	Berlin Antiquarium
Griefenhagen (1962a: 32)	F2288	Vulci	Berlin Antiquarium
Griefenhagen (1962a: 33-34)	F2291	Vulci	Berlin Antiquarium
Griefenhagen (1962a: 34-35)	F2290	Vulci	Berlin Antiquarium
Griefenhagen (1962a: 35)	F2292	Vulci	Berlin Antiquarium
Griefenhagen (1962a: 39-40)	F2522	Tarquinia	Berlin Antiquarium
Griefenhagen (1962a: 41)	F2534	Vulci	Berlin Antiquarium
Griefenhagen (1962a: 7-9)	F2278	Vulci	Berlin Antiquarium
Griefenhagen (1962a:. 28-29)	F2284	Vulci	Berlin Antiquarium
Griefenhagen (1962b: 13)	F2532	Vulci	Berlin Antiquarium
Griefenhagen (1962b: 13-14)	F2537	Tarquinia	Berlin Antiquarium
Griefenhagen (1962b: 13-14)	F2538	Vulci	Berlin Antiquarium
Griefenhagen (1962b: 18)	F2531	Vulci	Berlin Antiquarium
Griefenhagen (1962b: 19)	F2263	Vulci	Berlin Antiquarium
Griefenhagen (1962b: 19)	F2262	Vulci	Berlin Antiquarium
Griefenhagen (1962b: 19-20)	3251	Vulci	Berlin Antiquarium
Griefenhagen (1962b: 24)	F2318	Vulci	Berlin Antiquarium
Griefenhagen (1962b: 26)	F2319	Tarquinia	Berlin Antiquarium
Griefenhagen (1962b: 28-29)	F2416	Tarquinia	Berlin Antiquarium
Griefenhagen (1962b: 7)	F2530	Vulci	Berlin Antiquarium
Griefenhagen (1962b: 8-9)	F2282	Vulci	Berlin Antiquarium
Hayes (1981: 10-11)	919.5.141	Tarquinia	Royal Ontario Museum Toronto
Hayes (1981: 1-2)	919.5.176	Tarquinia	Royal Ontario Museum Toronto
Hayes (1981: 13-14)	925.97	Vulci	Royal Ontario Museum Toronto
Hayes (1981: 17-18)	919.5.136	Tarquinia	Royal Ontario Museum Toronto
Hayes (1981: 20)	919.5.145	Tarquinia	Royal Ontario Museum Toronto
Hayes (1981: 7-8)	06/08/80	Tarquinia	Royal Ontario Museum Toronto
Hemelrijk (1988: 12)	2228	Vulci	Allard Pierson Museum Amsterdam
Hemelrijk (1988: 1-3)	997	Vulci	Allard Pierson Museum Amsterdam
Hemelrijk (1988: 23-25)	3361	Vulci	Allard Pierson Museum Amsterdam
Hemelrijk (1988: 4-5)	888	Vulci	Allard Pierson Museum Amsterdam
Hemelrijk (1988: 46-47)	2246	Vulci	Allard Pierson Museum Amsterdam
Hoffman (1973: 11-12)	98.916	Vulci	Boston Museum of Fine Arts
Hoffman (1973: 16-17	99.517	Vulci	Boston Museum of Fine Arts
Hoffman (1973: 31-32	89.257	Tarquinia	Boston Museum of Fine Arts
Hoffman (1973: 36-37	89.258	Tarquinia	Boston Museum of Fine Arts
Hoffman (1973: 40)	99.52	Vulci	Boston Museum of Fine Arts
Iacopi (1956: 37.3)	RC997	Tarquinia	Tarquinia Museo Nazionale
Kahill and Dunant (1982: 32-33	MF240	Tarquinia	Geneva Musee de l'Art et l'Histoire
Lambrino (1928: 19)	no. 191	Vulci	Paris Bibliotheque Nationale
Lambrino (1928: 22)	no. 178	Vulci	Paris Bibliotheque Nationale
Lambrino (1928: 26-26)	no. 227	Vulci	Paris Bibliotheque Nationale
Lambrino (1928: 27-28)	no.207	Vulci	Paris Bibliotheque Nationale
Lambrino (1928: 35)	no. 258	Vulci	Paris Bibliotheque Nationale
Lambrino (1928: 8)	no. 85	Vulci	Paris Bibliotheque Nationale
Lambrino (1928: 9-10)	no. 81	Vulci	Paris Bibliotheque Nationale
Lambrino (1930: 38-39)	no. 321	Vulci	Paris Bibliotheque Nationale

APPENDIX

Bibliographic Reference	Museum Reference	Site	Museum
Lambrino (1930: 43-45)	no. 255	Vulci	Paris Bibliotheque Nationale
Lambrino (1930: 45-46)	no. 256	Vulci	Paris Bibliotheque Nationale
Lambrino (1930: 47)	no. 275	Vulci	Paris Bibliotheque Nationale
Lambrino (1930: 48)	no 269	Vulci	Paris Bibliotheque Nationale
Lambrino (1930: 52-54)	no. 355	Vulci	Paris Bibliotheque Nationale
Lambrino (1930: 59-60)	no.284	Vulci	Paris Bibliotheque Nationale
Lambrino (1930: 65-66)	no. 298	Vulci	Paris Bibliotheque Nationale
Lambrino (1930: 73)	no. 335	Vulci	Paris Bibliotheque Nationale
Lambrino (1930: 88.1-6)	no. 244	Vulci	Paris Bibliotheque Nationale
Laurenzi (1931: 301-302)	1437	Vulci	Bologna Museo Civico
Laurenzi (1997: 111-113)	PU270	Chiusi	Bologna Museo Civico
Laurenzi (1997: 18-19)	PU271	Vulci	Bologna Museo Civico
Magi (1984: 13)	PD265	Chiusi	Florence Museo Archeologico
Magi (1984: 13)	PD273	Chiusi	Florence Museo Archeologico
Magi (1984: 14)	PD269	Chiusi	Florence Museo Archeologico
Magi (1984: 15)	76103	Chiusi	Florence Museo Archeologico
Magi (1984: 16)	PD276	Chiusi	Florence Museo Archeologico
Magi (1984: 17)	PD271	Chiusi	Florence Museo Archeologico
Magi (1984: 18)	PD371	Chiusi	Florence Museo Archeologico
Magi (1984: 18)	PD564	Chiusi	Florence Museo Archeologico
Magi (1984: 18)	PD372	Chiusi	Florence Museo Archeologico
Magi (1984: 19)	PD272	Chiusi	Florence Museo Archeologico
Magi (1984: 20)	PD267	Chiusi	Florence Museo Archeologico
Magi (1984: 33)	4020	Chiusi	Florence Museo Archeologico
Magi (1984: 35)	76895	Chiusi	Florence Museo Archeologico
Magi (1984: 36)	n. 4013	Chiusi	Florence Museo Archeologico
Magi (1984: 44)	81268	Chiusi	Florence Museo Archeologico
Magi (1984: 50)	n. 4227	Chiusi	Florence Museo Archeologico
Magi (1984: 6)	72724	Chiusi	Florence Museo Archeologico
Magi (1984: 9)	PD356	Chiusi	Florence Museo Archeologico
Magi (1984: 9)	INV 3922	Chiusi	Florence Museo Archeologico
Magi (1984: 98)	70800	Tarquinia	Florence Museo Archeologico
Magi (1984: 99)	76363	Tarquinia	Florence Museo Archeologico
Marconi-Bovio (1938: 10.1-2)	V659	Chiusi	Palermo, Museo Nazionale
Marconi-Bovio (1938: 11. 4)	V661A	Chiusi	Palermo, Museo Nazionale
Marconi-Bovio (1938: 11.1)	V660	Chiusi	Palermo, Museo Nazionale
Marconi-Bovio (1938: 11.2-3)	V661	Chiusi	Palermo, Museo Nazionale
Marconi-Bovio (1938: 13.1-2)	V662	Chiusi	Palermo, Museo Nazionale
Marconi-Bovio (1938: 17.1-2)	V664	Chiusi	Palermo, Museo Nazionale
Marconi-Bovio (1938: 18.1-3)	V665	Chiusi	Palermo, Museo Nazionale
Marconi-Bovio (1938: 29.1-4)	V762	Chiusi	Palermo, Museo Nazionale
Marconi-Bovio (1938: 3.1.3)	V651	Chiusi	Palermo, Museo Nazionale
Marconi-Bovio (1938: 31.1-5)	V763	Chiusi	Palermo, Museo Nazionale
Marconi-Bovio (1938: 32.1-5)	V766	Chiusi	Palermo, Museo Nazionale
Marconi-Bovio (1938: 41.2-3)	V788	Chiusi	Palermo, Museo Nazionale
Marconi-Bovio (1938: 5.1-3)	V653	Chiusi	Palermo, Museo Nazionale
Marconi-Bovio (1938:.1-2)	V663	Chiusi	Palermo, Museo Nazionale
Metropolitan Museum Online Catalogue	09/09/96	Tarquinia	Metropolitan Museum, New York
Metropolitan Museum Online Catalogue	06.1021.17	Tarquinia	Metropolitan Museum, New York
Metropolitan Museum Online Catalogue	1972.118.142	Tarquinia	Metropolitan Museum, New York
Metropolitan Museum Online Catalogue	06.1021.203	Vulci	Metropolitan Museum, New York

Bibliographic Reference	Museum Reference	Site	Museum
Metropolitan Museum Online Catalogue	20.246	Vulci	Metropolitan Museum, New York
Metropolitan Museum Online Catalogue	12.231.1	Vulci	Metropolitan Museum, New York
Metropolitan Museum Online Catalogue	12.198.2	Vulci	Metropolitan Museum, New York
Metropolitan Museum Online Catalogue	21/11/78	Vulci	Metropolitan Museum, New York
Metropolitan Museum Online Catalogue	41.162.133	Vulci	Metropolitan Museum, New York
Metropolitan Museum Online Catalogue	41.162.129	Vulci	Metropolitan Museum, New York
Metropolitan Museum Online Catalogue	41.162.128	Vulci	Metropolitan Museum, New York
Metropolitan Museum Online Catalogue	41.162.1	Vulci	Metropolitan Museum, New York
Metropolitan Museum Online Catalogue	23.160.1	Vulci	Metropolitan Museum, New York
Metropolitan Museum Online Catalogue	06.1021.47	Vulci	Metropolitan Museum, New York
Metropolitan Museum Online Catalogue	22.139.32	Vulci	Metropolitan Museum, New York
Metropolitan Museum Online Catalogue	10/11/81	Vulci	Metropolitan Museum, New York
Metropolitan Museum Online Catalogue	05/11/93	Vulci	Metropolitan Museum, New York
Metropolitan Museum Online Catalogue	06.1021.162	Vulci	Metropolitan Museum, New York
Moignard (1989: 14-16)	1872.23.12	Vulci	Edinburgh National Museum
Mommsen (1980: 54)	F1874	Tarquinia	Berlin Antikenmuseum
Mommsen (1980: 28-29)	F1702	Vulci	Berlin Antikenmuseum
Mommsen (1980: 30-31)	F1717	Vulci	Berlin Antikenmuseum
Mommsen (1980: 32-33)	F1870	Vulci	Berlin Antikenmuseum
Mommsen (1980: 38-39)	F1852	Vulci	Berlin Antikenmuseum
Mommsen (1980: 42-43)	F1846	Vulci	Berlin Antikenmuseum
Mommsen (1980: 43-45)	F1856	Vulci	Berlin Antikenmuseum
Mommsen (1980: 47-49)	F1845	Vulci	Berlin Antikenmuseum
Mommsen (1980: 50-52)	F1830	Vulci	Berlin Antikenmuseum
Mommsen (1980: 55-56)	F1873	Vulci	Berlin Antikenmuseum
Mommsen (1980: 58-60)	F1879	Vulci	Berlin Antikenmuseum
Mommsen (1980: 59-59)	F1833	Vulci	Berlin Antikenmuseum
Mommsen (1980: 68-69)	F1880	Vulci	Berlin Antikenmuseum
Mommsen (1985: 14-15)	F1722	Chiusi	Berlin Antikenmuseum
Pierro (1984: 119)	RC8562	Tarquinia	Tarquinia Museo Nazionale
Pierro (1984: 119)	RC2395	Tarquinia	Tarquinia Museo Nazionale
Pierro (1984: 121)	INV2007	Tarquinia	Tarquinia Museo Nazionale
Pierro (1984: 122)	RC4194	Tarquinia	Tarquinia Museo Nazionale
Pierro (1984: 124)	INV616	Tarquinia	Tarquinia Museo Nazionale
Pierro (1984: 125)	INV614	Tarquinia	Tarquinia Museo Nazionale
Pierro (1984: 129)	RC7951	Tarquinia	Tarquinia Museo Nazionale
Pierro (1984: 129)	RC7951	Tarquinia	Tarquinia Museo Nazionale
Pierro (1984: 133)	RC7949	Tarquinia	Tarquinia Museo Nazionale
Pierro (1984: 137)	RC7948	Tarquinia	Tarquinia Museo Nazionale
Pierro (1984: 157)	RC8306	Tarquinia	Tarquinia Museo Nazionale
Pierro (1984: 158)	RC1919	Tarquinia	Tarquinia Museo Nazionale
Pierro (1984: 159)	INV583	Tarquinia	Tarquinia Museo Nazionale
Pierro (1984: 163)	RC4200	Tarquinia	Tarquinia Museo Nazionale
Pierro (1984: 167)	INV569	Tarquinia	Tarquinia Museo Nazionale
Pierro (1984: 168)	RC967	Tarquinia	Tarquinia Museo Nazionale
Pierro (1984: 169)	INV584	Tarquinia	Tarquinia Museo Nazionale
Pierro (1984: 170)	INV571	Tarquinia	Tarquinia Museo Nazionale
Pierro (1984: 173)	RC4201	Tarquinia	Tarquinia Museo Nazionale
Pierro (1984: 174)	RC994	Tarquinia	Tarquinia Museo Nazionale
Pierro (1984: 175)	RC4203	Tarquinia	Tarquinia Museo Nazionale
Pierro (1984: 175)	RC2412	Tarquinia	Tarquinia Museo Nazionale

Appendix

Bibliographic Reference	Museum Reference	Site	Museum
Pierro (1984: 177)	INV578	Tarquinia	Tarquinia Museo Nazionale
Pierro (1984: 178)	RC4202	Tarquinia	Tarquinia Museo Nazionale
Pierro (1984: 179)	RC3866	Tarquinia	Tarquinia Museo Nazionale
Pierro (1984: 181)	RC1092	Tarquinia	Tarquinia Museo Nazionale
Pierro (1984: 182)	RC2070	Tarquinia	Tarquinia Museo Nazionale
Pierro (1984: 185)	INV570	Tarquinia	Tarquinia Museo Nazionale
Pierro (1984: 186)	RC990	Tarquinia	Tarquinia Museo Nazionale
Pierro (1984: 189)	RC2385	Tarquinia	Tarquinia Museo Nazionale
Pierro (1984: 190)	INV572	Tarquinia	Tarquinia Museo Nazionale
Pierro (1984: 190)	INV581	Tarquinia	Tarquinia Museo Nazionale
Pierro (1984: 191)	RC1913	Tarquinia	Tarquinia Museo Nazionale
Pierro (1984:158)	RC8307	Tarquinia	Tarquinia Museo Nazionale
Plaoutine (1941: 13)	314	Vulci	Palais des Beaux Arts P'tit Palais
Plaoutine (1941: 14)	310	Vulci	Palais des Beaux Arts P'tit Palais
Plaoutine (1941: 21)	330	Tarquinia	Palais des Beaux Arts P'tit Palais
Plaoutine (1941: 22)	325	Tarquinia	Palais des Beaux Arts P'tit Palais
Plaoutine (1941: 29)	371	Vulci	Palais des Beaux Arts P'tit Palais
Plaoutine (1941: 8-10)	304	Vulci	Palais des Beaux Arts P'tit Palais
Plaoutine (1941: 9-10)	311	Vulci	Palais des Beaux Arts P'tit Palais
Plaoutine, Pottier and Merlin (1938: 19-20)	G81	Vulci	Louvre
Plaoutine, Pottier and Merlin (1938: 80.1-7)	F72	Vulci	Louvre
Plaoutine, Pottier and Merlin (1938: 81.3-10)	F75	Vulci	Louvre
Plaoutine, Pottier and Merlin (1938: 82.2-5)	F78	Vulci	Louvre
Plaoutine, Pottier and Merlin (1938: 84.6-11)	F86	Vulci	Louvre
Plaoutine, Pottier and Merlin (1938: 86.1-5)	F90	Vulci	Louvre
Plaoutine, Pottier and Merlin (1938: 86.6-8)	F91	Vulci	Louvre
Plaoutine, Pottier and Merlin (1938: 87.1-4)	F92	Vulci	Louvre
Pottier (1928: 365)	G30	Vulci	Louvre
Pottier (1928: 366)	G42	Vulci	Louvre
Pottier (1929: 410)	F297	Vulci	Louvre
Pottier (1929: 411)	F298	Vulci	Louvre
Pottier (1929: 411)	F301	Vulci	Louvre
Pottier (1929: 431)	G50	Vulci	Louvre
Rastrelli (1981: 10)	n. 543	Chiusi	Chiusi Museo Nazionale
Rastrelli (1981: 10)	n. 297	Chiusi	Chiusi Museo Nazionale
Rastrelli (1981: 11)	n. 1083	Chiusi	Chiusi Museo Nazionale
Rastrelli (1981: 13)	n. 1806	Chiusi	Chiusi Museo Nazionale
Rastrelli (1981: 14)	n. 1794	Chiusi	Chiusi Museo Nazionale
Rastrelli (1981: 15)	n. 1812	Chiusi	Chiusi Museo Nazionale
Rastrelli (1981: 20)	n. 492	Chiusi	Chiusi Museo Nazionale
Rastrelli (1981: 24)	n. 296	Chiusi	Chiusi Museo Nazionale
Rastrelli (1981: 8)	n. 1802	Chiusi	Chiusi Museo Nazionale
Rastrelli (1981: 9)	n. 1804	Chiusi	Chiusi Museo Nazionale
Rastrelli (1982: 10)	n. 1849	Chiusi	Chiusi Museo Nazionale
Rastrelli (1982: 10)	Coll n. 1841	Chiusi	Chiusi Museo Nazionale
Rastrelli (1982: 10)	-	Chiusi	Chiusi Museo Nazionale
Rastrelli (1982: 12)	n. 1838	Chiusi	Chiusi Museo Nazionale
Rastrelli (1982: 12)	n. 266	Chiusi	Chiusi Museo Nazionale
Rastrelli (1982: 13)	n. 1836	Chiusi	Chiusi Museo Nazionale
Rastrelli (1982: 13)	n. 1839	Chiusi	Chiusi Museo Nazionale
Rastrelli (1982: 13)	n. 1840	Chiusi	Chiusi Museo Nazionale

Bibliographic Reference	Museum Reference	Site	Museum
Rastrelli (1982: 14)	n. 1835	Chiusi	Chiusi Museo Nazionale
Rastrelli (1982: 14)	n. 1843	Chiusi	Chiusi Museo Nazionale
Rastrelli (1982: 16)	n. 1830	Chiusi	Chiusi Museo Nazionale
Rastrelli (1982: 16)	n. 269	Chiusi	Chiusi Museo Nazionale
Rastrelli (1982: 16)	n. 814	Chiusi	Chiusi Museo Nazionale
Rastrelli (1982: 17)	n. 1831	Chiusi	Chiusi Museo Nazionale
Rastrelli (1982: 17)	n. 515	Chiusi	Chiusi Museo Nazionale
Rastrelli (1982: 17)	n. 489	Chiusi	Chiusi Museo Nazionale
Rastrelli (1982: 18)	n. 481	Chiusi	Chiusi Museo Nazionale
Rastrelli (1982: 18)	n. 1826	Chiusi	Chiusi Museo Nazionale
Rastrelli (1982: 18)	n. 1797	Chiusi	Chiusi Museo Nazionale
Rastrelli (1982: 18)	n. 218	Chiusi	Chiusi Museo Nazionale
Rastrelli (1982: 18)	n. 300	Chiusi	Chiusi Museo Nazionale
Rastrelli (1982: 18)	n. 833	Chiusi	Chiusi Museo Nazionale
Rastrelli (1982: 19)	n. 1829	Chiusi	Chiusi Museo Nazionale
Rastrelli (1982: 19)	n. 327	Chiusi	Chiusi Museo Nazionale
Rastrelli (1982: 19)	n. 603	Chiusi	Chiusi Museo Nazionale
Rastrelli (1982: 20)	n. 1801	Chiusi	Chiusi Museo Nazionale
Rastrelli (1982: 20)	n. 447	Chiusi	Chiusi Museo Nazionale
Rastrelli (1982: 23)	n. 537	Chiusi	Chiusi Museo Nazionale
Rastrelli (1982: 24)	n. 596	Chiusi	Chiusi Museo Nazionale
Rastrelli (1982: 24)	n. 295	Chiusi	Chiusi Museo Nazionale
Rastrelli (1982: 5)	Coll. n. 1849	Chiusi	Chiusi Museo Nazionale
Rastrelli (1982: 5)	n. 1850	Chiusi	Chiusi Museo Nazionale
Rastrelli (1982: 6)	Coll. n. 1850	Chiusi	Chiusi Museo Nazionale
Rastrelli (1982: 6)	Coll. n. 1822	Chiusi	Chiusi Museo Nazionale
Rastrelli (1982: 6)	n. 1822	Chiusi	Chiusi Museo Nazionale
Rastrelli (1982: 6)	n. 596	Chiusi	Chiusi Museo Nazionale
Rastrelli (1982: 7)	Coll. Paolozzi n. 596	Chiusi	Chiusi Museo Nazionale
Rastrelli (1982: 7)	n. 1827	Chiusi	Chiusi Museo Nazionale
Rastrelli (1982: 7)	n. 1805	Chiusi	Chiusi Museo Nazionale
Rastrelli (1982: 8)	Coll. n. 1827	Chiusi	Chiusi Museo Nazionale
Rastrelli (1982: 8)	Coll. n. 1823	Chiusi	Chiusi Museo Nazionale
Rastrelli (1982: 8)	n. 1823	Chiusi	Chiusi Museo Nazionale
Rastrelli (1982: 8)	Coll. n. 1847	Chiusi	Chiusi Museo Nazionale
Rastrelli (1982: 8)	n. 270	Chiusi	Chiusi Museo Nazionale
Rastrelli (1982: 9)	Coll. n. 1842	Chiusi	Chiusi Museo Nazionale
Rastrelli (1982: 9)	Coll. Paolozzi n. 605	Chiusi	Chiusi Museo Nazionale
Rastrelli (1982: 9)	no. 241	Chiusi	Chiusi Museo Nazionale
Richter (1946: 15)	96.9.36	Tarquinia	Metropolitan Museum, New York
Richter (1946: 16)	09.221.39	Tarquinia	Metropolitan Museum, New York
Robinson (1934: 8)	-	Chiusi	Robinson Collection Baltimore
Robinson (1936: 11)	-	Chiusi	Robinson Collection Baltimore
Robinson (1936: 11)	-	Chiusi	Robinson Collection Baltimore
Robinson (1936: 12)	-	Chiusi	Robinson Collection Baltimore
Robinson (1936: 13)	-	Chiusi	Robinson Collection Baltimore
Robinson (1936: 14)	-	Chiusi	Robinson Collection Baltimore
Robinson (1936: 15)	-	Chiusi	Robinson Collection Baltimore
Robinson (1936: 16)	-	Chiusi	Robinson Collection Baltimore
Rohde (1990: 11-15)	F2264	Vulci	Berlin Antikensammlung
Rohde (1990: 15-16)	VI3217	Vulci	Berlin Antikensammlung

Appendix

Bibliographic Reference	Museum Reference	Site	Museum
Rohde (1990: 16-17)	F2274	Chiusi	Berlin Antikensammlung
Rohde (1990: 22-23)	F2172	Vulci	Berlin Antikensammlung
Rohde (1990: 24-26)	F2178	Vulci	Berlin Antikensammlung
Rohde (1990: 26-27)	F2300	Chiusi	Berlin Antikensammlung
Rohde (1990: 26-29)	F2179	Vulci	Berlin Antikensammlung
Rohde (1990: 29-30)	F2377	Vulci	Berlin Antikensammlung
Rohde (1990: 36-39)	F2388	Vulci	Berlin Antikensammlung
Rohde (1990: 59-64)	F2634	Vulci	Berlin Antikensammlung
Smith (1936: 19)	01/08/81	Chiusi	Berkeley
Tronchetti (1983: 103)	RC5165	Tarquinia	Tarquinia Museo Nazionale
Tronchetti (1983: 106)	RC6847	Tarquinia	Tarquinia Museo Nazionale
Tronchetti (1983: 107)	RC8217	Tarquinia	Tarquinia Museo Nazionale
Tronchetti (1983: 109)	RC7687	Tarquinia	Tarquinia Museo Nazionale
Tronchetti (1983: 111)	INV588	Tarquinia	Tarquinia Museo Nazionale
Tronchetti (1983: 113)	RC1063	Tarquinia	Tarquinia Museo Nazionale
Tronchetti (1983: 115)	RC7207	Tarquinia	Tarquinia Museo Nazionale
Tronchetti (1983: 116)	RC985	Tarquinia	Tarquinia Museo Nazionale
Tronchetti (1983: 118)	RC1077	Tarquinia	Tarquinia Museo Nazionale
Tronchetti (1983: 119)	RC2438	Tarquinia	Tarquinia Museo Nazionale
Tronchetti (1983: 121)	INV589	Tarquinia	Tarquinia Museo Nazionale
Tronchetti (1983: 122)	INV620	Tarquinia	Tarquinia Museo Nazionale
Tronchetti (1983: 124)	-	Tarquinia	Tarquinia Museo Nazionale
Tronchetti (1983: 125)	INV1937	Tarquinia	Tarquinia Museo Nazionale
Tronchetti (1983: 126)	INV2223	Tarquinia	Tarquinia Museo Nazionale
Tronchetti (1983: 129)	RC2439	Tarquinia	Tarquinia Museo Nazionale
Tronchetti (1983: 131)	RC2837	Tarquinia	Tarquinia Museo Nazionale
Tronchetti (1983: 19)	INV628	Tarquinia	Tarquinia Museo Nazionale
Tronchetti (1983: 24)	INV508	Tarquinia	Tarquinia Museo Nazionale
Tronchetti (1983: 29)	RC2802	Tarquinia	Tarquinia Museo Nazionale
Tronchetti (1983: 29)	INV633	Tarquinia	Tarquinia Museo Nazionale
Tronchetti (1983: 31)	INV619	Tarquinia	Tarquinia Museo Nazionale
Tronchetti (1983: 36)	INV618	Tarquinia	Tarquinia Museo Nazionale
Tronchetti (1983: 37)	RC7370	Tarquinia	Tarquinia Museo Nazionale
Tronchetti (1983: 38)	INV631	Tarquinia	Tarquinia Museo Nazionale
Tronchetti (1983: 40)	-	Tarquinia	Tarquinia Museo Nazionale
Tronchetti (1983: 41)	INV625	Tarquinia	Tarquinia Museo Nazionale
Tronchetti (1983: 46)	INV621	Tarquinia	Tarquinia Museo Nazionale
Tronchetti (1983: 48)	RC7170	Tarquinia	Tarquinia Museo Nazionale
Tronchetti (1983: 49)	INV617	Tarquinia	Tarquinia Museo Nazionale
Tronchetti (1983: 51)	INV626	Tarquinia	Tarquinia Museo Nazionale
Tronchetti (1983: 52)	RC3030	Tarquinia	Tarquinia Museo Nazionale
Tronchetti (1983: 54)	-	Tarquinia	Tarquinia Museo Nazionale
Tronchetti (1983: 55)	RC3008	Tarquinia	Tarquinia Museo Nazionale
Tronchetti (1983: 57)	-	Tarquinia	Tarquinia Museo Nazionale
Tronchetti (1983: 59)	RC2449	Tarquinia	Tarquinia Museo Nazionale
Tronchetti (1983: 63)	RC4796	Tarquinia	Tarquinia Museo Nazionale
Tronchetti (1983: 65)	RC4798	Tarquinia	Tarquinia Museo Nazionale
Tronchetti (1983: 67)	INV 624	Tarquinia	Tarquinia Museo Nazionale
Tronchetti (1983: 70)	INV651	Tarquinia	Tarquinia Museo Nazionale
Tronchetti (1983: 73)	RC3984	Tarquinia	Tarquinia Museo Nazionale
Tronchetti (1983: 75)	RC5654	Tarquinia	Tarquinia Museo Nazionale

Bibliographic Reference	Museum Reference	Site	Museum
Tronchetti (1983: 77)	RC7205	Tarquinia	Tarquinia Museo Nazionale
Tronchetti (1983: 79)	RC2421	Tarquinia	Tarquinia Museo Nazionale
Tronchetti (1983: 80)	RC3003	Tarquinia	Tarquinia Museo Nazionale
Tronchetti (1983: 82)	RC968	Tarquinia	Tarquinia Museo Nazionale
Tronchetti (1983: 85)	RC8262	Tarquinia	Tarquinia Museo Nazionale
Tronchetti (1983: 87)	RC1880	Tarquinia	Tarquinia Museo Nazionale
Tronchetti (1983: 89)	RC5166	Tarquinia	Tarquinia Museo Nazionale
Tronchetti (1983: 90)	RC1058	Tarquinia	Tarquinia Museo Nazionale
Tronchetti (1983: 92)	-	Tarquinia	Tarquinia Museo Nazionale
Tronchetti (1983: 93)	RC1816	Tarquinia	Tarquinia Museo Nazionale
Tronchetti (1983: 94)	INV649	Tarquinia	Tarquinia Museo Nazionale
Tronchetti (1983: 96)	INV664	Tarquinia	Tarquinia Museo Nazionale
Tronchetti (1983: 99)	RC984	Tarquinia	Tarquinia Museo Nazionale
True (1978: 18-19)	99.522	Vulci	Boston Museum of Fine Arts
True (1978: 22-23)	1.8058	Vulci	Boston Museum of Fine Arts
True (1978: 26-27)	62.1185	Vulci	Boston Museum of Fine Arts
Villard and Merlin (1951: 10.2-9)	G6	Vulci	Louvre
Villard and Merlin (1951: 106.4-7)	F121	Vulci	Louvre
Villard and Merlin (1951: 107.1-2)	F132	Vulci	Louvre
Villard and Merlin (1951: 7.2-6)	F125	Vulci	Louvre
Villard and Merlin (1951: 9.2-3)	G5	Vulci	Louvre
Villard and Merlin (1951: 98.7-9)	F122	Vulci	Louvre
von Bothmer (1963: 12)	20.244	Vulci	Metropolitan Museum, New York
von Bothmer (1963: 14-15)	12.198.4	Vulci	Metropolitan Museum, New York
von Bothmer (1963: 36-37)	41.162.193	Vulci	Metropolitan Museum, New York
von Bothmer (1963: 40-41)	20/11/40	Vulci	Metropolitan Museum, New York
Bonamici (1974: 36)	-	Tarquinia	Tarquinia Museo Nazionale
Bonamici (1974: 41)	Bonamici n. 49	Vulci	Museo Gregoriano Etrusco (Vatican)
Bonamici (1974: 41)	MVG64578	Vulci	Museo Nazionale Villa Giulia
Boston Museum of Fine Arts Online Catalogue	61.942	Vulci	Boston Museum of Fine Arts
Boston Museum of Fine Arts Online Catalogue	80.596	Vulci	Boston Museum of Fine Arts
Boston Museum of Fine Arts Online Catalogue	80.595	Vulci	Boston Museum of Fine Arts
British Museum Online Catalogue	Etruscan Bucchero no. 212	Chiusi	British Museum
British Museum Online Catalogue	Etruscan Bucchero no. 213	Chiusi	British Museum
British Museum Online Catalogue	Etruscan Bucchero no. 56	Chiusi	British Museum
British Museum Online Catalogue	Etruscan Bucchero no. 70	Chiusi	British Museum
British Museum Online Catalogue	Etruscan Bucchero no. 255	Chiusi	British Museum
British Museum Online Catalogue	Etruscan Bucchero no. 129	Chiusi	British Museum
British Museum Online Catalogue	Etruscan Bucchero no. 89	Chiusi	British Museum
British Museum Online Catalogue	Etruscan Bucchero no. 16	Chiusi	British Museum
British Museum Online Catalogue	Vase H191	Chiusi	British Museum
British Museum Online Catalogue	Vase H190	Chiusi	British Museum
British Museum Online Catalogue	Vase H194	Chiusi	British Museum
British Museum Online Catalogue	Etruscan Bucchero no. 93	Chiusi	British Museum
British Museum Online Catalogue	Vase H207	Chiusi	British Museum
British Museum Online Catalogue	Vase H226	Chiusi	British Museum
British Museum Online Catalogue	Vase H188	Chiusi	British Museum
British Museum Online Catalogue	Etruscan Bucchero no. 127	Chiusi	British Museum
British Museum Online Catalogue	Etruscan Bucchero no. 128	Chiusi	British Museum
British Museum Online Catalogue	Vase H189	Chiusi	British Museum
British Museum Online Catalogue	Vase H187	Chiusi	British Museum

Appendix

Bibliographic Reference	Museum Reference	Site	Museum
British Museum Online Catalogue	Vase H208	Chiusi	British Museum
British Museum Online Catalogue	British Museum	Vulci	British Museum
British Museum Online Catalogue	British Museum	Vulci	British Museum
British Museum Online Catalogue	British Museum	Vulci	British Museum
British Museum Online Catalogue	British Museum	Vulci	British Museum
British Museum Online Catalogue	British Museum	Vulci	British Museum
British Museum Online Catalogue	British Museum	Vulci	British Museum
British Museum Online Catalogue	British Museum	Vulci	British Museum
British Museum Online Catalogue	1928,0614.1	Vulci	British Museum
British Museum Online Catalogue	Vase F480	Vulci	British Museum
British Museum Online Catalogue	Vase B63	Vulci	British Museum
British Museum Online Catalogue	Vase B64	Vulci	British Museum
British Museum Online Catalogue	Vase B61	Vulci	British Museum
British Museum Online Catalogue	Terracotta 1683	Vulci	British Museum
British Museum Online Catalogue	Amphore C643	Chiusi	Louvre
British Museum Online Catalogue	Amphore C619	Chiusi	Louvre
British Museum Online Catalogue	C641	Chiusi	Louvre
Fitzwilliam Museum Online Catalogue	GR.23.1952	Vulci	Fitzwilliam Museum, Cambridge
Fitzwilliam Museum Online Catalogue	GR.24.1952	Vulci	Fitzwilliam Museum, Cambridge
Ginge (1987: 18)	RC1051	Tarquinia	Tarquinia Museo Nazionale
Ginge (1987: 20)	INV529	Tarquinia	Tarquinia Museo Nazionale
Ginge (1987: 22)	RC1979	Tarquinia	Tarquinia Museo Nazionale
Ginge (1987: 23)	RC7946	Tarquinia	Tarquinia Museo Nazionale
Ginge (1987: 27)	INV632	Tarquinia	Tarquinia Museo Nazionale
Ginge (1987: 28)	RC7176	Tarquinia	Tarquinia Museo Nazionale
Ginge (1987: 29)	INV867	Tarquinia	Tarquinia Museo Nazionale
Ginge (1987: 34)	INVSN (CAT N10)	Tarquinia	Tarquinia Museo Nazionale
Ginge (1987: 35)	RC7945	Tarquinia	Tarquinia Museo Nazionale
Ginge (1987: 35)	RC5285	Tarquinia	Tarquinia Museo Nazionale
Ginge (1987: 36)	RC7451	Tarquinia	Tarquinia Museo Nazionale
Ginge (1987: 37)	INVSN (CAT N14)	Tarquinia	Tarquinia Museo Nazionale
Ginge (1987: 38)	INVSN (CATN14)	Tarquinia	Tarquinia Museo Nazionale
Ginge (1987: 39)	INV1049	Tarquinia	Tarquinia Museo Nazionale
Ginge (1987: 39)	RC5709	Tarquinia	Tarquinia Museo Nazionale
Ginge (1987: 45)	RC947	Tarquinia	Tarquinia Museo Nazionale
Ginge (1987: 47)	RC7289	Tarquinia	Tarquinia Museo Nazionale
Ginge (1987: 47)	RC6884	Tarquinia	Tarquinia Museo Nazionale
Ginge (1987: 49)	RC960	Tarquinia	Tarquinia Museo Nazionale
Ginge (1987: 50)	SN CATN22	Tarquinia	Tarquinia Museo Nazionale
Ginge (1987: 51)	RC1042	Tarquinia	Tarquinia Museo Nazionale
Ginge (1987: 54)	INV858	Tarquinia	Tarquinia Museo Nazionale
Ginge (1987: 55)	INV856	Tarquinia	Tarquinia Museo Nazionale
Ginge (1987: 58)	INV965	Tarquinia	Tarquinia Museo Nazionale
Ginge (1987: 59)	INV1940	Tarquinia	Tarquinia Museo Nazionale
Ginge (1987: 60)	RC5284	Tarquinia	Tarquinia Museo Nazionale
Ginge (1987: 61)	RC1881	Tarquinia	Tarquinia Museo Nazionale
Ginge (1987: 63)	INV857	Tarquinia	Tarquinia Museo Nazionale
Ginge (1987: 64)	RC2803	Tarquinia	Tarquinia Museo Nazionale
Ginge (1987: 65)	RC3303	Tarquinia	Tarquinia Museo Nazionale
Ginge (1987: 69)	INV859	Tarquinia	Tarquinia Museo Nazionale
Ginge (1987: 71)	INV3223	Tarquinia	Tarquinia Museo Nazionale

Bibliographic Reference	Museum Reference	Site	Museum
Ginge (1987: 72)	RC2779	Tarquinia	Tarquinia Museo Nazionale
Ginge (1987: 73)	RC2780	Tarquinia	Tarquinia Museo Nazionale
Ginge (1987: 74)	RC3216	Tarquinia	Tarquinia Museo Nazionale
Ginge (1987: 76)	INV2432	Tarquinia	Tarquinia Museo Nazionale
Ginge (1987: 77)	RC5310	Tarquinia	Tarquinia Museo Nazionale
Ginge (1987: 78)	RC5311	Tarquinia	Tarquinia Museo Nazionale
Ginge (1987: 80)	INV1939	Tarquinia	Tarquinia Museo Nazionale
Ginge (1987: 81)	RC2663	Tarquinia	Tarquinia Museo Nazionale
Ginge (1987: 82)	RC1760	Tarquinia	Tarquinia Museo Nazionale
Ginge (1987: 83)	RC3869	Tarquinia	Tarquinia Museo Nazionale
Ginge (1987: 84)	INV860	Tarquinia	Tarquinia Museo Nazionale
Ginge (1987: 85)	RC2836	Tarquinia	Tarquinia Museo Nazionale
Ginge (1987: 86)	RC1628	Tarquinia	Tarquinia Museo Nazionale
Iacopi (1956: 2.1)	138861	Tarquinia	Tarquinia Museo Nazionale
Iacopi (1956: 2.2)	139084	Tarquinia	Tarquinia Museo Nazionale
Iacopi (1956: 2.3)	139082	Tarquinia	Tarquinia Museo Nazionale
Metropolitan Museum Online Catalogue	24.97.7	Vulci	Metropolitan Museum, New York
Metropolitan Museum Online Catalogue	96.9.78	Vulci	Metropolitan Museum, New York
Pottier (1929:39)	C645	Tarquinia	Paris, Louvre
Pottier (1929: 39)	C639	Tarquinia	Paris, Louvre
Poggio Civitate Project Online Archive	PC19720321	Poggio Civitate	Museo Etrusco di Murlo
Poggio Civitate Project Online Archive	PC19700343	Poggio Civitate	Museo Etrusco di Murlo
Poggio Civitate Project Online Archive	PC19660111	Poggio Civitate	Museo Etrusco di Murlo
Poggio Civitate Project Online Archive	PC19660151	Poggio Civitate	Museo Etrusco di Murlo
Poggio Civitate Project Online Archive	PC19670067	Poggio Civitate	Museo Etrusco di Murlo
Poggio Civitate Project Online Archive	PC19670069	Poggio Civitate	Museo Etrusco di Murlo
Poggio Civitate Project Online Archive	PC19670071	Poggio Civitate	Museo Etrusco di Murlo
Poggio Civitate Project Online Archive	PC19680431	Poggio Civitate	Museo Etrusco di Murlo
Poggio Civitate Project Online Archive	PC19690095	Poggio Civitate	Museo Etrusco di Murlo
Poggio Civitate Project Online Archive	PC19700071	Poggio Civitate	Museo Etrusco di Murlo
Poggio Civitate Project Online Archive	PC19700117	Poggio Civitate	Museo Etrusco di Murlo
Poggio Civitate Project Online Archive	PC19700122	Poggio Civitate	Museo Etrusco di Murlo
Poggio Civitate Project Online Archive	PC19700199	Poggio Civitate	Museo Etrusco di Murlo
Poggio Civitate Project Online Archive	PC19710051	Poggio Civitate	Museo Etrusco di Murlo
Poggio Civitate Project Online Archive	PC19710083	Poggio Civitate	Museo Etrusco di Murlo
Poggio Civitate Project Online Archive	PC19710327	Poggio Civitate	Museo Etrusco di Murlo
Poggio Civitate Project Online Archive	PC19710392	Poggio Civitate	Museo Etrusco di Murlo
Poggio Civitate Project Online Archive	PC19710490	Poggio Civitate	Museo Etrusco di Murlo
Poggio Civitate Project Online Archive	PC19710491	Poggio Civitate	Museo Etrusco di Murlo
Poggio Civitate Project Online Archive	PC19710553	Poggio Civitate	Museo Etrusco di Murlo
Poggio Civitate Project Online Archive	PC19710558	Poggio Civitate	Museo Etrusco di Murlo
Poggio Civitate Project Online Archive	PC19710564	Poggio Civitate	Museo Etrusco di Murlo
Poggio Civitate Project Online Archive	PC19710550	Poggio Civitate	Museo Etrusco di Murlo
Poggio Civitate Project Online Archive	PC19710569	Poggio Civitate	Museo Etrusco di Murlo
Poggio Civitate Project Online Archive	PC19710616	Poggio Civitate	Museo Etrusco di Murlo
Poggio Civitate Project Online Archive	PC19710825	Poggio Civitate	Museo Etrusco di Murlo
Poggio Civitate Project Online Archive	PC19720319	Poggio Civitate	Museo Etrusco di Murlo
Poggio Civitate Project Online Archive	PC19720320	Poggio Civitate	Museo Etrusco di Murlo
Poggio Civitate Project Online Archive	PC19720321	Poggio Civitate	Museo Etrusco di Murlo
Poggio Civitate Project Online Archive	PC19720322	Poggio Civitate	Museo Etrusco di Murlo
Poggio Civitate Project Online Archive	PC19720323	Poggio Civitate	Museo Etrusco di Murlo

APPENDIX

Bibliographic Reference	Museum Reference	Site	Museum
Poggio Civitate Project Online Archive	PC19730274	Poggio Civitate	Museo Etrusco di Murlo
Poggio Civitate Project Online Archive	PC19730275	Poggio Civitate	Museo Etrusco di Murlo
Poggio Civitate Project Online Archive	PC19730276	Poggio Civitate	Museo Etrusco di Murlo
Poggio Civitate Project Online Archive	PC19730278	Poggio Civitate	Museo Etrusco di Murlo
Poggio Civitate Project Online Archive	PC19730280	Poggio Civitate	Museo Etrusco di Murlo
Poggio Civitate Project Online Archive	PC19730313	Poggio Civitate	Museo Etrusco di Murlo
Poggio Civitate Project Online Archive	PC19730315	Poggio Civitate	Museo Etrusco di Murlo
Poggio Civitate Project Online Archive	PC19730319	Poggio Civitate	Museo Etrusco di Murlo
Poggio Civitate Project Online Archive	PC19770031	Poggio Civitate	Museo Etrusco di Murlo
Poggio Civitate Project Online Archive	PC19780010	Poggio Civitate	Museo Etrusco di Murlo
Poggio Civitate Project Online Archive	PC19780030	Poggio Civitate	Museo Etrusco di Murlo
Poggio Civitate Project Online Archive	PC19800204	Poggio Civitate	Museo Etrusco di Murlo
Poggio Civitate Project Online Archive	PC19840034	Poggio Civitate	Museo Etrusco di Murlo
Poggio Civitate Project Online Archive	PC19870052	Poggio Civitate	Museo Etrusco di Murlo
Poggio Civitate Project Online Archive	PC19870088	Poggio Civitate	Museo Etrusco di Murlo
Poggio Civitate Project Online Archive	PC20040129	Poggio Civitate	Museo Etrusco di Murlo
Poggio Civitate Project Online Archive	PC20050063	Poggio Civitate	Museo Etrusco di Murlo
Poggio Civitate Project Online Archive	PC20070101	Poggio Civitate	Museo Etrusco di Murlo
Poggio Civitate Project Online Archive	PC19710561	Poggio Civitate	Museo Etrusco di Murlo
Poggio Civitate Project Online Archive	PC19710562	Poggio Civitate	Museo Etrusco di Murlo
Poggio Civitate Project Online Archive	PC19720563	Poggio Civitate	Museo Etrusco di Murlo
Poggio Civitate Project Online Archive	PC19730235	Poggio Civitate	Museo Etrusco di Murlo
Poggio Civitate Project Online Archive	PC19730239	Poggio Civitate	Museo Etrusco di Murlo
Poggio Civitate Project Online Archive	PC19730268	Poggio Civitate	Museo Etrusco di Murlo
Poggio Civitate Project Online Archive	PC19730269	Poggio Civitate	Museo Etrusco di Murlo
Poggio Civitate Project Online Archive	PC19730270	Poggio Civitate	Museo Etrusco di Murlo
Poggio Civitate Project Online Archive	PC19730272	Poggio Civitate	Museo Etrusco di Murlo
Poggio Civitate Project Online Archive	PC19730318	Poggio Civitate	Museo Etrusco di Murlo
Poggio Civitate Project Online Archive	PC19870084	Poggio Civitate	Museo Etrusco di Murlo
Poggio Civitate Project Online Archive	PC19780112	Poggio Civitate	Museo Etrusco di Murlo
Poggio Civitate Project Online Archive	PC19730239	Poggio Civitate	Museo Etrusco di Murlo
Poggio Civitate Project Online Archive	PC19730260	Poggio Civitate	Museo Etrusco di Murlo
Poggio Civitate Project Online Archive	PC19730261	Poggio Civitate	Museo Etrusco di Murlo
Poggio Civitate Project Online Archive	PC19720279	Poggio Civitate	Museo Etrusco di Murlo
Poggio Civitate Project Online Archive	PC19720115	Poggio Civitate	Museo Etrusco di Murlo
Poggio Civitate Project Online Archive	PC19870082	Poggio Civitate	Museo Etrusco di Murlo
Poggio Civitate Project Online Archive	PC19730258	Poggio Civitate	Museo Etrusco di Murlo
Scalia (1968: 362)	INV106	Chiusi	Altenburg Staatliches Lindenau
Scalia (1968: 362)	INV427	Chiusi	Berlin Antiquarium
Scalia (1968: 362)	INV80535	Chiusi	Boston Museum of Fine Arts
Scalia (1968: 362)	INV2323	Chiusi	Chiusi Museo Nazionale
Scalia (1968: 362)	S/N	Chiusi	Chiusi Museo Nazionale
Scalia (1968: 364)	INV18	Chiusi	Bologna, Museo Civico
Scalia (1968: 364)	INV80553	Chiusi	Boston Museum of Fine Arts
Scalia (1968: 364)	s/n	Chiusi	Chiusi Museo Nazionale
Scalia (1968: 367)	INV 4	Chiusi	Bologna, Museo Civico
Scalia (1968: 367)	sn	Chiusi	Chiusi Museo Nazionale
Scalia (1968: 368)	INV 411	Chiusi	Berlin Antiquarium
Scalia (1968: 370)	INV 1431	Chiusi	Chiusi Museo Nazionale
Scalia (1968: 370)	INV 322	Chiusi	Chiusi Museo Nazionale
Scalia (1968: 371)	INV 7231	Chiusi	Sevres Musee Nationale

Bibliographic Reference	Museum Reference	Site	Museum
Scalia (1968: 374)	INV 399	Chiusi	Chiusi Museo Nazionale
Scalia (1968: 374)	INV 591	Chiusi	Chiusi Museo Nazionale
Scalia (1968: 374)	SN	Chiusi	Chiusi Museo Nazionale
Scalia (1968: 375)	INV 198	Chiusi	Chiusi Museo Nazionale
Scalia (1968: 375)	INV 302	Chiusi	Chiusi Museo Nazionale
Scalia (1968: 375)	SN	Chiusi	Chiusi Museo Nazionale
Scalia (1968: 375)	SN	Chiusi	Chiusi Museo Nazionale
Scalia (1968: 376)	INV469	Chiusi	Chiusi Museo Nazionale
Scalia (1968: 376)	INV723	Chiusi	Chiusi Museo Nazionale
Scalia (1968: 376)	INV 905	Chiusi	Chiusi Museo Nazionale
Scalia (1968: 376)	INV2935	Chiusi	Florence Museo Archeologico
Scalia (1968: 378)	INV 1371	Chiusi	Chiusi Museo Nazionale
Scalia (1968: 378)	INV 1372	Chiusi	Chiusi Museo Nazionale
Scalia (1968: 378)	INV 1374	Chiusi	Chiusi Museo Nazionale
Scalia (1968: 378)	SN	Chiusi	Chiusi Museo Nazionale
Scalia (1968: 379)	INV 76210	Chiusi	Boston Museum of Fine Arts
Scalia (1968: 379)	INV 77433	Chiusi	Florence Museo Archeologico
Scalia (1968: 380)	INV 416	Chiusi	Berlin Antiquarium
Scalia (1968: 384)	INV R137	Chiusi	Brussels Royal Museum
Scalia (1968: 385)	SN	Chiusi	Chiusi Museo Nazionale
Scalia (1968: 389)	INV 407	Chiusi	Berlin Antiquarium
Scalia (1968: 389)	INV 1386	Chiusi	Chiusi Museo Nazionale
Scalia (1968: 389)	INV 1430	Chiusi	Chiusi Museo Nazionale
Scalia (1968: 389)	SN	Chiusi	Chiusi Museo Nazionale
Scalia (1968: 389)	INV 79266	Chiusi	Florence Museo Archeologico
Scalia (1968: 390)	INV 1996	Chiusi	Berlin Antiquarium
Scalia (1968: 390)	SN	Chiusi	Chiusi Museo Nazionale
Scalia (1968: 390)	SN	Chiusi	Chiusi Museo Nazionale
Scalia (1968: 390)	INV 4211	Chiusi	Copenhagen National Museum
Scalia (1968: 392)	INV 3	Chiusi	Bologna, Museo Civico
Scalia (1968: 392)	INV 14	Chiusi	Bologna, Museo Civico
Scalia (1968: 393)	INV 1437	Chiusi	Chiusi Museo Nazionale
Scalia (1968: 393)	INV 178	Chiusi	Chiusi Museo Nazionale
Scalia (1968: 396)	INV186	Chiusi	Chiusi Museo Nazionale
Scalia (1968: 396)	INV 187	Chiusi	Chiusi Museo Nazionale
Scalia (1968: 396)	INV 247	Chiusi	Chiusi Museo Nazionale
Scalia (1968: 396)	INV 188	Chiusi	Chiusi Museo Nazionale
Scalia (1968: 398)	INV 1237	Chiusi	Sevres Musee Nationale
Scalia (1968: 399)	INV P334	Chiusi	Chiusi Museo Nazionale
Scalia (1968: 400)	INV 415	Chiusi	Berlin Antiquarium
Scalia (1968: 400)		Chiusi	Bologna, Museo Civico
Scalia (1968:366)	INV 5	Chiusi	Bologna, Museo Civico
Scalia (1968:366)	INV1337	Chiusi	Chiusi Museo Nazionale
Scalia (1968:366)	INV1389	Chiusi	Chiusi Museo Nazionale
Scalia (1968:366)	sn	Chiusi	Chiusi Museo Nazionale
Scalia (1968:366)	INV 258	Chiusi	Chiusi Museo Nazionale
Scalia (1968:366)	INV 431	Chiusi	Chiusi Museo Nazionale
Scalia (1968:366)	INV 77436	Chiusi	Florence Museo Archeologico
Scalia (1968:366)	INV 77435	Chiusi	Florence Museo Archeologico
Scalia (1968:366)	INV 77434	Chiusi	Florence Museo Archeologico
Spivey (1987: 10)	843	Vulci	Munich Antikenmuseum

APPENDIX

Bibliographic Reference	Museum Reference	Site	Museum
Spivey (1987: 12)	842	Vulci	Munich Antikenmuseum
Spivey (1987: 12)	844	Vulci	Munich Antikenmuseum
Spivey (1987: 13)	846	Vulci	Munich Antikenmuseum
Spivey (1987: 13)	2757	Vulci	Naples
Spivey (1987: 14)	2717	Vulci	Naples Museo Nazionale
Spivey (1987: 16)	43544	Vulci	Museo Nazionale Villa Giulia
Spivey (1987: 17)	E776	Vulci	Louvre
Spivey (1987: 19)	INV4812	Vulci	Copenhagen National Museum
Spivey (1987: 20)	91	Vucli	Vatican
Spivey (1987: 20)	862	Vulci	Munich Antikenmuseum
Spivey (1987: 20)	861	Vulci	Munich Antikenmuseum
Spivey (1987: 21)	4139	Vulci	Florence Museo Archeologico
Spivey (1987: 21)	239	Vulci	Museo Gregoriano Etrusco (Vatican)
Spivey (1987: 22)	895	Vulci	Munich Antikenmuseum
Spivey (1987: 22)	898	Vulci	Munich Antikenmuseum
Spivey (1987: 22)	236	Vulci	Museo Gregoriano Etrusco (Vatican)
Spivey (1987: 23)	928	Vulci	Munich Antikenmuseum
Spivey (1987: 26)	2152	Tarquinia	Berlin Antiquarium
Spivey (1987: 26)	853	Vulci	Munich Antikenmuseum
Spivey (1987: 26)	854	Vulci	Munich Antikenmuseum
Spivey (1987: 27)	896	Vulci	Munich Antikenmuseum
Spivey (1987: 32)	863	Vulci	Munich Antikenmuseum
Spivey (1987: 38)	865	Vulci	Munich Antikenmuseum
Spivey (1987: 42)	871	Vulci	Munich Antikenmuseum
Spivey (1987: 44)	rac gug 92	Vulci	Museo Gregoriano Etrusco (Vatican)
Spivey (1987: 8)	894	Vulci	Munich Antikenmuseum
Spivey (1987: 8)	908	Vulci	Munich Antikenmuseum
Spivey (1987: 9)	925	Vulci	Munich Antikenmuseum
Spivey (1987: pl 54)	1498	Chiusi	Palermo Museo Nazionale
Spivey (1987:13)	845	Vulci	Munich Antikenmuseum
Spivey (1987:38)	866	Vulci	Munich Antikenmuseum
Spivey (1987:pl 55)	1499	Chiusi	Palermo Museo Nazionale
Valentini (1969: 420)	INV 1545	Chiusi	Chiusi Museo Nazionale
Valentini (1969: 420)	SN	Chiusi	Chiusi Museo Nazionale
Valentini (1969: 420)	INV 402	Chiusi	Chiusi Museo Nazionale
Valentini (1969: 421)	sn	Chiusi	Chiusi Museo Nazionale
Valentini (1969: 421)	INV 1394	Chiusi	Chiusi Museo Nazionale
Valentini (1969: 421)	INV 1398	Chiusi	Chiusi Museo Nazionale
Valentini (1969: 421)	INV 77587	Chiusi	Florence Museo Archeologico
Valentini (1969: 421)	INV 259	Vulci	Istituto Heman Ferre Puerto Rico
Valentini (1969: 423)	INV 76195	Chiusi	Boston Museum of Fine Arts
Valentini (1969: 423)	INV 390	Chiusi	Chiusi Museo Nazionale
Valentini (1969: 423)	SN	Chiusi	Chiusi Museo Nazionale
Valentini (1969: 423)	INV 1378	Chiusi	Chiusi Museo Nazionale
Valentini (1969: 423)	SN	Chiusi	Chiusi Museo Nazionale
Valentini (1969: 423)	INV 77587	Chiusi	Florence Museo Archeologico
Valentini (1969: 423)	INV 76164	Vulci	Florence Museo Archeologico
Valentini (1969: 423)	INV 71045	Vulci	Florence Museo Archeologico
Valentini (1969: 424)	INV 922	Chiusi	Musee du Compiegne
Valentini (1969: 426)	INV 58	Chiusi	Bologna, Museo Civico
Valentini (1969: 426)	INV 925	Chiusi	Musee du Compiegne

Bibliographic Reference	Museum Reference	Site	Museum
Valentini (1969: 427)	INV 305	Vulci	Berlin Antiquarium
Valentini (1969: 427)	INV 35	Chiusi	Bologna, Museo Civico
Valentini (1969: 427)	INV 491	Chiusi	Chiusi Museo Nazionale
Valentini (1969: 427)	SN	Chiusi	Chiusi Museo Nazionale
Valentini (1969: 427)	INV 121	Chiusi	Musee du Compiegne
Valentini (1969: 429)	INV 488	Chiusi	Chiusi Museo Nazionale
Valentini (1969: 430)	INV V. 201	Chiusi	Florence Museo Archeologico
Valentini (1969: 430)	SN	Vulci	Roma, Coll. Hercle
Valentini (1969: 432)	INV V. 216	Chiusi	Florence Museo Archeologico
Valentini (1969: 433)	SN	Vulci	Proprieta Bongiovi
Valentini (1969: 433)	SN	Vulci	Proprieta dellEnte Maremma
Valentini (1969: 435)	INV 507	Chiusi	Copenhagen National Museum
Valentini (1969: 435)	INV V. 215	Chiusi	Florence Museo Archeologico
Valentini (1969: 436)	not given n. 59	Chiusi	Museo Gregoriano Etrusco (Vatican)

Bibliography

Corpus Bibliography

Beazley, J. 1927. *Corpus Vasorum Antiquorum: Oxford Ashmolean* vol.1. Oxford: Clarendon Press.

Bermond, G. 1957. *Corpus Vasorum Antiquorum: Bologna Museo Civico* vol. 4. Rome: Libreria dello Stato.

Bielefield, E. 1959. *Corpus Vasorum Antiquorum: Altenburg Staatliches Lindenau Museum* vol. 1. Berlin: Akademie Verlag.

Bielefield, E. 1960. *Corpus Vasorum Antiquorum: Altenburg Staatliches Lindenau Museum* vol. 2. Berlin: Akademie Verlag.

Blinkenberg, C. and Friis Johansen, K. 1928. *Corpus Vasorum Antiquorum: Copenhagen National Museum* vol.3. Paris: E. Champion.

Blinkenberg, C. and Friis Johansen, K. 1929. *Corpus Vasorum Antiquorum: Copenhagen National Museum* vol. 4. Paris: E. Champion.

Bonamici, M. 1974. *I buccheri con figurazioni graffite*. Florence: Biblioteca di Studi Etruschi 8.

Campus, L. 1981. *Ceramica attica a figure nere: piccoli vasi e vasi plastici. Museo Archeologico Nazionale di Tarquinia*. Roma: L'Erma di Breitschneider.

Descoeudres, J.P. 1981. *Corpus Vasorum Antiquorum: Basel Antikemuseum* vol.1. Bern: P. Lang.

Elarth, W. 1933. *Corpus Vasorum Antiquorum: Michigan, Ann Arbor* vol.1. Cambridge, MA: Harvard University Press.

Ferrari, G. 1988. *I vasi attici a figure rosse del periodo arcaico. Tarquinia Museo Nazionale*. Rome: G. Breitschneider.

Flot, M. 1924. *Corpus Vasorum Antiquorum: Compiègne Musée National* vol.1. Paris: E. Champion.

Flot, M. 1927. *Corpus Vasorum Antiquorum: Compiègne Musée National* vol.3. Paris: E. Champion.

Flot, M. 1929. *Corpus Vasorum Antiquorum: Compiègne Musée National* vol. 4. Paris: E Champion.

Giglioli, G.Q. 1925. *Corpus vasorum antiquorum: Italia. Museo Nazionale di Villa Giulia in Roma* vol. 1. Roma: Istituto poligrafico dello Stato.

Ginge, B. 1987. *Ceramiche etrusche a figure nere. Tarquinia Museo Nazionale*. Roma: Giorgio Breitschneider.

Greifenhagen, A. 1962a. *Corpus Vasorum Antiquorum: Berlin Antiquarium* vol. 2. Munchen: Beck.

Greifenhagen, A. 1962b. *Corpus Vasorum Antiquorum: Berlin Antiquarium* vol.3. Munchen: Beck.

Hayes, J.W. 1981. *Corpus Vasorum Antiquorum: Toronto Royal Ontario Museum* vol. 1. Oxford: Oxford University Press.

Hemelrijk, J.M. 1988. *Corpus Vasorum Antiquorum: Allard Pierson Museum Amsterdam* vol. 1. Amsterdam: The Museum Press.

Hoffman, H. 1973. *Corpus Vasorum Antiquorum: Boston Museum of Fine Arts* vol.1. Boston: Museum of Fine Arts.

Iacopi, G. 1956. *Corpus Vasorum Antiquorum: Tarquinia* vol.2. Rome: Libreria dello Stato.

Kahill, L. and Dunant, C. 1982. *Corpus Vasorum Antiquorum: Geneva Musée de l'Art et de l'Histoire* vol. 2. Berne: H. Lang.

Lambrino, M. 1928. *Corpus Vasorum Antiquorum: Paris Bibliotheque National* vol.1. Paris: E. Champion.

Lambrino, M. 1930. *Corpus Vasorum Antiquorum: Paris Bilbiotheque National* vol.2. Paris: E. Champion.

Laurenzi, L. 1931. *Corpus Vasorum Antiquorum: Bologna Museo Civico* vol. 2. Milan: Tumminelli.

Laurenzi, L. 1997. *Corpus Vasorum Antiquorum: Bologna Museo Civico* vol. 5. Rome: L'Erma di Breitschneider.

Moignard, E.1989. *Corpus Vasorum Antiquorum: Edinburgh National Museum* vol.1. Oxford: Oxford University Press.

Magi, A. 1981. *Corpus Vasorum Antiquorum: Florence Museo Archeologico* vol.3. Milan: Tumminelli.

Magi, A. 1984. *Corpus Vasorum Antiquorum: Florence Museo Archeologico* vol.4. Milan: Tumminelli.

Marconi Bovio, J. 1938. *Corpus Vasorum Antiquorum: Palermo Museo Nazionale* vol.1. Rome: Libreria dello Stato.

Mommsen, H. 1980. *Corpus Vasorum Antiquorum: Berlin Antikenmuseum* vol. 5. Munchen: Beck.

Mommsen, H. 1985. *Corpus Vasorum Antiquorum: Berlin Antikenmuseum* vol. 7. Munchen: Beck.

Pierro, E. 1984. *Ceramiche ioniche non figurate e coppe attiche a figure nere. Museo Archeologico Nazionale di Tarquinia*. Roma: L'Erma di Breitschneider.

Plaoutine, N. 1941. *Corpus Vasorum Antiquorum: Paris Musée du Petit Palais* vol.1. Paris: E. Champion.

Plaoutine, N., Pottier, E., and Merlin, A. 1938. *Corpus Vasorum Antiquorum: Musée du Louvre* vol. 9. Paris: E. Champion.

Pottier, E. 1928. *Corpus Vasorum Antiquorum: Musée du Louvre* vol. 5. Paris: E. Champion.

Pottier, E. 1929. *Corpus Vasorum Antiquorum: Musée du Louvre* vol. 6. Paris: E. Champion.

Rastrelli, A. 1981. *Corpus Vasorum Antiquorum: Chiusi Museo Nazionale* vol.1. Rome: Multigrafica Editrice.

Rastrelli, A. 1982. *Corpus Vasorum Antiquorum: Chiusi Museo Nazionale* vol.2. Rome: Multigrafica Editrice.

Richter, G. 1946. *Corpus Vasorum Antiquorum: New York Metropolitan Museum* vol. 2. Cambridge, MA: Harvard University Press.

Robinson, D. 1934. *Corpus Vasorum Antiquorum: Robinson Collection Baltimore* vol.1. Cambridge, MA: Harvard University Press.

Robinson, D. 1936. *Corpus Vasorum Antiquorum: Robinson Collection Baltimore* vol. 2. Cambridge, MA: Harvard University Press.

Rohde, E. 1990. *Corpus Vasorum Antiquorum: Berlin Staatliches Museum Antikensammlung* vol.1. Berlin: Akademie Verlag.

Scalia, F. 1968. I cilindretti di tipo chiusino con figure umane (contributo allo studio dei buccheri neri a cilindretto *Studi Etruschi* 36: 357-402.

Smith, H. 1936. *Corpus Vasorum Antiquorum: California, University of California Berkeley* vol.1. Cambridge, MA: Harvard University Press.

Spivey, N. 1987. *The Micali Painter and his followers.* Oxford, Clarendon Press.

Tronchetti, C. 1983. *Ceramica attica a figure nere: grande vasi, anfore, pelikai, cratere. Tarquinia Museo Nazionale.* Roma: L'Erma di Breitschneider.

True, M. 1978. *Corpus Vasorum Antiquorum: Boston Museum of Fine Arts* vol. 2. Boston: Museum of Fine Arts.

Valentini, G. 1969. Il motivo della potnia theron sui vasi di bucchero. *Studi Etruschi* 37: 413-432.

Villard, F. and Merlin, A. 1951. *Corpus Vasorum Antiquorum: Musée du Louvre* vol.10. Paris: E. Champion.

von Bothmer, D. 1963. *Corpus Vasorum Antiquorum: New York Metropolitan Museum* vol. 3. Cambridge, MA: Harvard University Press.

Digital Bibliography

Boston Museum of Fine Arts Online Catalogue (last accessed October 2013)
https://www.mfa.org/collections

British Museum Online Catalogue (last accessed October 2013)
http://www.britishmuseum.org/research/collection_online/search.aspx

Fitzwilliam Museum Online Catalogue (last accessed October 2013)
http://www.fitzmuseum.cam.ac.uk/explorer/

Metropolitan Museum, New York Online Catalogue (last accessed October 2013)
http://www.metmuseum.org/collections

Poggio Civitate Online Archive (last accessed October 2013)
http://poggiocivitate.classics.umass.edu/index.asp

Historical and Literary Sources

Alighieri, D. 2005. *Convivio*. Rome: Garzanti Libri.

Alighieri, D.1987. *The Divine Comedy*. Trans. Kirkpatrick. Cambridge: Cambridge University Press.

Boccaccio 1985. *L'Ameto*. Trans. J. Serafini-Sauli New York: Garland. Bruni, L. Historiarum Florentini populi libri XII. In L. A. Muratori (ed.), *Rerum Italicarum Scriptores* [1723-1751], vol. XIX, 3, Città di Castello 1914-26: 3-288.

D'Arezzo, R. 1872 [1282]. *La composizione del mondo di Ristoro d'Arezzo : testo italiano del 1282*. Roma: Enrico Narducci and Francesco Fontani. Dempster, T. 1723. *De Etruria Regali*. Ed. T. Coke, with further explanations by F. Buonarotti. Firenze.

Dionysius of Halicarnassus. *Roman Antiquities*. Trans. Cary, 1968. London: Heinemann.

Eubulus. Dionysus and Semele. In Athenaeus, *Deipnosophistae*. Trans. Burton Gulick, 1927. London: LCL.

Herodotus. *Histories*. Trans. Waterfield, 2008. Oxford: Oxford World Classics.

Hesiod. *Theogony and Works and Days*. Trans. West, 1999. Oxford: Oxford University Press.

Homer. *The Iliad*. Trans. Fagles, 1991. London: Penguin Classics.

Livy. *History of Rome*. Trans. Ogilvie and de Selincourt, 2002. London: Penguin Classics.

Plato. *Laws*. Trans. Pangle, 1980. Chicago: University of Chicago Press.

Shakespeare, W. 1992 [1613]. *Macbeth*. London: Wordsworth Classics.

Theopompus of Chios. Histories. In Athenaeus, *Deipnosophistae*. Trans. Burton Gulick, 1927. London: LCL.

Thucydides. *Histories vol I and vol II*. Trans. Stuart-Jones, 1963. Oxford, Clarendon Press.

Wickstead, P. (ed.) and Selfe, R. (trans). 1872. *Selections from the Croniche Fiorentine of Villani*. London: Archibald Constable.

Bibliography

Achilli, A., Olivieri, A., Pala, M., Matspalu, E., Fornarino, S., Battaglia, V. and Torroni, A. 2007. Mitochondrial DNA variation of modern Tuscans supports the Near Eastern origin of Etruscans. *The American Journal of Human Genetics* 80, 759–68.

Adamson, W. L. 1989. Fascism and culture: avant-gardes and secular religion in the Italian case. *Journal of Contemporary History* 24: 411-435.

Agnihotri, A.K., Agnihotri, S., Jeebun, N. and Googoolye, K. 2008. Prediction of stature using hand dimensions. *Journal of Forensic and Legal Medicine* 15: 479-482.

Alasuutari, P. 1982. *Desire and Craving: A Cultural Theory of Alcohol.* Albany, NY: State University of New York Press.

Alberti, B. Jones, A. and Pollard, J. (eds.) 2013. *Archaeology after Interpretation. Materials, Relations, Becomings.* Walnut Creek, CA: Left Coast Press.

Ambrosini, L. 2013. Candelabra, Thymiateria and Kottaboi at Banquets: Greece and Etruria in Comparison. *Etruscan Studies* 16: 1-38.

Amorelli, M.T.F. 1983. *Vulci: scavi Bendinelli.* Roma: Paleani. Amorelli, M. T. F. 1987. *Vulci: scavi Mendinelli.* Roma: Borgia.

Andersen, H. D. The origins of Potnia Theron in Central Italy. *Hamburger Beiträge zur Archäologie* 19: 20.

Arafat, K. and Morgan, C. 1989. Pots and potters in Athens and Corinth: a review. *Oxford Journal of Archaeology* 8: 311-346.

Arafat, K. and Morgan, C. 1994. Athens, Etruria and the Heuneburg: mutual misconceptions in the study of Greek-Barbarian relations. In I. Morris (ed.) *Classical Greece: Ancient histories and modern archaeologies.* Cambridge: Cambridge University Press: 108-134.

Arbib, M. A. Liebal, K. and Pika, S. 2008. Primate vocalization, gesture, and the evolution of human language. *Current Anthropology* 49: 1053-1076.

Armstrong, P.F. 1988. L'Ordine Nuovo: The legacy of Antonio Gramsci and the education of adults. *International Journal of Lifelong Education* 7: 249-259.

Arnold, D.E. 1988. *Ceramic theory and cultural process.* Cambridge: Cambridge University Press.

Avramidou, A. 2006. Attic vases in Etruria: Another view on the divine banquet cup by the Codrus Painter. *American Journal of Archaeology* 110: 565-579.

Bamford, D. and Finlay, N. 2008. Introduction: Archaeological approaches to lithic production, skill and craft learning. *Journal of Archaeological Method and Theory* 15: 1-27.

Bandinelli, R. B. 1925. Clusium: Ricerche archeologiche e topografiche su Chiusi e il suo territorio in età etrusca. *Monumenti Antichi dall'Accademia dei Lincei* 30: 209-552.

Bandinelli, R.B. 1927. *Edizione archeologia della carta d'Italia al 100.000: saggio per la zona di Chiusi.* Firenze: Istituto Geografico Militare.

Bandinelli, R.B. 1928. *Sovana: topografia ed arte: contributo alla conoscenza dell'architettura etrusca.* Firenze: Rinascimento del libro.

Bandinelli, R.B. 1950 [1943]. *Storicità dell'arte classica.* Firenze: Electa.

Bandinelli, R.B, 1961. *L'origine del ritratto in Grecia e in Roma.* Roma: Edizioni Ricerche.

Bandinelli, R. B. 1972. Qualche osservazione sulle statue acroteriali di Poggio Civitate (Murlo). *Dialoghi di Archeologia* 6: 236-45.

Bandinelli, R.B. 1979. *Archeologia e cultura.* Roma: Editori Riuniti. Bandinelli, R.B. 1995. *Hitler e Mussolini, 1938. Il viaggio del Führer in Italia.* Roma: Edizione e/o.

Barbanero, M. 2000. *Ranuccio Bianchi Bandinelli e il suo mondo.* Bari: Edipuglia.

Barbanero, M. 2003. *Ranuccio Bianchi Bandinelli: biografia ed epistolario di un grande archeologo.* Milano: Skira.

Barbanero, M. (ed.) 2009. *L'occhio dell'archeologo: Ranuccio Bianchi Bandinelli nella Siena del primo '900.* Cinisello Balsamo: Silvana.

Barbagli, D. and Iozzo, M. 2007. *Etruschi: Chiusi, Siena, Palermo: la collezione Bonci Casuccini.* Siena: Protagon.

Barker, G. 1985. Landscape archaeology in Italy. In C. Malone and S. Stoddart (eds.) *Papers in Italian Archaeology IV: The Cambridge Conference. Part I: the Human Landscape.* Oxford: Archaeopress: 1-19.

Barker, G. 1988. Archaeology and the Etruscan countryside. *Antiquity* 62: 772-785.

Barker, G. and Rasmussen, T. 1999. *The Etruscans.* Oxford: Blackwell.

Barlett, P. 1980. Reciprocity and the San Juan fiesta. *Journal of Anthropological Research* 36: 116-130.

Barrett, J. and Ko, I. 2009. A phenomenology of landscape: a crisis in British landscape archaeology? *Journal of Social Archaeology* 9: 275-294.

Barth, F. (ed.) 1969. *Ethnic groups and boundaries: the social organization of culture difference.* Bergen: University of Bergen.

Bartlett, K.R. 1980. The Strangeness of Strangers: English Impressions of Italy in the Sixteenth Century. *Quaderni d'Italianistica* 1: 46-63.

Bartoloni, G. and Bocci Pacini, P. 2003. The importance of Etruscan antiquity in the Tuscan Renaissance. *Acta Hyperborea: Danish Studies in Classical Archaeology* 10: 449-472.

Beazley, J. 1947. *Etruscan Vase-Painting.* Oxford, Clarendon Press. Beazley, J. 1963. *Attic red figure vase painters.* Oxford, Oxford University Press.

Beazley, J. 1971. *Paralipomena: additions to Attic black figure vase painters and to Attic red figure vase painters.* Oxford, Oxford University Press.

Beazley, J. 1978. *Attic black figure vase painters.* Oxford, Oxford University Press.

Beazley, J. 1986. *The development of Attic black figure.* Oxford, Oxford University Press.

Becker, H. 2009. The economic agency of the Etruscan temple: Elites, Dedications and Display. In M. Gleba and H. Becker (eds.) *Votives, Places and Rituals in Etruscan Religion: Studies in Honour of Jean MacIntosh Turfa.* Leiden: Brill, 87-99.

Becker, H. 2010. The written word and proprietary inscriptions in Etruria. *Etruscan Studies* 13: 131-148.

Becker, H. and Wallace, R. 2010. Introduction: historical approaches to Etruscan epigraphy. *Etruscan Studies* 13: 107-108.

Belknap, P. and Leonard, W. 1991. A conceptual replication and extension of Erving Goffman's study of gender advertisements. *Sex Roles* 25: 103-118.

Bérard, C. 1983. Imagiers et artistes. *Etudes des Lettres* 4: 2-37.

Bérard, C. 1989. *A city of images: iconography and society in Ancient Greece.* Princeton, NJ: Princeton University Press.

Bergson, H. 1991. *Matter and Memory.* New York: Zone Books.

Berkin, J. 2004. *The Orientalizing Bucchero from the Lower Building at Poggio Civitate (Murlo).* Philadelphia: Pennsylvania Museum of Archaeology Press.

Betts, E. 2003. The sacred landscape of Picenum (900-100 BC): towards a phenomenology of cult places. *Accordia Research Papers* 5: 101-120.

Bittarello, M.B. 2009. The construction of Eturscan 'Otherness' in Latin Literature. *Greece and Rome* 56: 211-233.

Black, J. 1992. *The British Abroad: The Grand Tour in the Eighteenth Century.* London: St. Martin's Press.

Boardman, J. 1974. *Athenian black figure vases: a handbook.* Oxford, Oxford University Press.

Boardman, J. 1979. *Athenian red figure vases: the Archaic period: A handbook.* Oxford, Oxford University Press.

Boardman, J. 1986. *The Greeks Overseas.* London, Penguin.

Bocci Pacini, P. 1992. Il Museo dell'accademia nel 700. In P. Bocci Pacini, A.M. Maetzke, and A. Paolucci (eds.) *Il Museo dell'Accademia etrusca di Cortona.* Firenze: Cassa di risparmio di Firenze: 31-39.

Boitani, P. (ed.) 1985. *Chaucer and the Italian Trecento.* Cambridge: Cambridge University Press.

Bonfante, G. 1998. The Origin of Cannibalism in Dante. *Etruscan Studies* 5: 3-6.

Bonfante, L. 1973. Etruscan Women. A Question of Interpretation. *Archaeology* 26: 242-249.

Bonfante, L. 1975. *Etruscan Dress.* Baltimore: Johns Hopkins University Press.

Bonfante, L. 1980. An Etruscan mirror with 'spiky garland' in the Getty Museum. *The J.Paul Getty Museum Journal* 8: 147-154.

Bonfante, L. 1981. Etruscan couples and their aristocratic society. *Women's Studies:* 8: 157-187.

Bonfante, L. 1989. Nudity as a costume in classical art. *American Journal of Archaeology* 93: 543-570.

Bonfante, L. 1993. *Fufluns Pacha: the Etruscan Dionysus.* Ithaca and London: Cornell University Press.

Bonfante, L. and Bonfante, G. 2002. *The Etruscan language: an introduction.* Manchester: Manchester University Press.

Bonfante, L. 2011. The Etruscans: Mediators between northern barbarians and Classical Civilizations. In L. Bonfante (ed.) *The Barbarians of Ancient Europe: Realities and Interactions.* Cambridge: Cambridge University Press: 233-282.

Bonfante, L. (ed.) 1986. *Etruscan Life and Afterlife: a handbook of Etruscan Studies.* Detroit, MI: Wayne State University Press.

Bonghi Jovino, M. 1986a. Gli scavi nell'abitato di Tarquinia e la scoperta dei 'bronzi' in un preliminare inquadramento. In M. Bonghi Jovino and C. Chiaramonte Trere (eds.) *Tarquinia – ricerche, scavi e prospettive: Atti del convegno internazionale di studi La Lombardia per gli Etruschi.* Milano: Edizioni ET: 59-77.

Bonghi Jovino, M. 1986b. *Gli Etruschi di Tarquinia.* Modena: Panini.

Bonghi Jovino, M. 1989. Scavi recenti nell'abitatio di Tarquinia. In G. Maetzke (ed.) *Atti del secondo congresso internazionale Etrusco. Firenze, 26 maggio – 2 giugno 1985.* Vol. 1. Rome: 315-19.

Bonghi Jovino, M. 1991. Osservazioni sui sistemi di costruzione a Tarquinia: tecniche locale ed uso del 'muro a pilastri' fenico. *Archeologia Classica* 43: 171-192.

Bonghi Jovino, M. 2001. *Tarquinia: scavi sistematici nell'abitato, campagne 1982-1988: i materiali.* Roma, L'Erma di Breitschneider.

Bonghi Jovino, M. 2010. The Tarquinia Project: a summary of 25 years of excavation. *American Journal of Archaeology* 114: 161-180.

Bourdieu, P. 1990. *The Logic of Practice.* Stanford, CA: Stanford University Press.

Bradley, R. 1990. *The passage of arms: an archaeological analysis of prehistoric hoards and votive deposits.* Cambridge: Cambridge University Press.

Bradley, R. 1991. Ritual, time and history. *World Archaeology* 23: 209-219.

Bradley, R. 1997. *Rock art and the prehistory of Atlantic Europe: signing the land.* London: Psychology Press.

Bradley, R. 1998. Ruined buildings, ruined stones: Enclosures, tombs and natural places in the Neolithic of south-west England. *World Archaeology* 30: 13-22.

Bradley, R. 2000. *An archaeology of natural places.* London: Routledge.

Bradley, R. 2002. *The significance of monuments: on the shaping of human experience in Neolithic and Bronze Age Europe.* London: Routledge.

Bradley, R. 2003. Seeing Things: Perception, Experience and the Constraints of Excavation. *Journal of Social Archaeology* 3: 151-168.

Bradley, R. 2005. *Ritual and domestic life in prehistoric Europe.* London: Psychology Press.

Brand, C.P. 2011. *Italy and the English Romantics: the Italianate fashion in early nineteenth-century England.* Cambridge: Cambridge University Press.

Brendel, O.J. 1978. *Etruscan Art.* London: Harmondsworth.

Briquel, D. 1991. *L'origine lydienne des Étrusques: histoire de la doctrine dans l'antiquité.* Rome: École Française de Rome.

Briquel, D. 2001. Le origini degli Etruschi: una questione di battuta fin dall'antichita. In M. Torelli (ed.) *Gli Etruschi.* London: Thames and Hudson: 43-51.

Brück, J. 1998. In the footsteps of the ancestors: A review of Christopher Tilley's A Phenomenology of Landscape: Places, paths and monuments. *Archaeological Review from Cambridge* 15: 23-36.

Brück, J. 2005. Experiencing the past? The development of a phenomenological archaeology in British prehistory. *Archaeological Dialogues* 12: 45-72.

Burgwyn, J.H. 1993. *The legend of the mutilated victory: Italy, the Great War, and the Paris Peace Conference, 1915-1919.* Westport, CT: Greenwood Press.

Butler, J. 1988. Performative Acts and Gender Constitution: An Essay in Phenomenology and Feminist Theory. *Theatre Journal* 40: 519-531.

Butler, J. 1993. *Bodies that Matter. On the Discursive Limits of Sex.* London: Routledge.

Butler, J. 1997. *Excitable Speech: A Politics of the Performative.* London: Routledge.

Butler, J. 1999 [1989]. *Gender Trouble: Feminism and the Subversion of Identity.* London: Routledge.

Caferro, W. 2006. *John Hawkwood: an English mercenary in Fourteenth-Century Italy.* Baltimore, MR: Johns Hopkins University Press.

Camerini, G. 1985. *Il bucchero etrusco.* Roma: L'Erma di Breitscheider.

Camporeale, G. 1994. Un gruppo di vasi bronzei chiusini di facies orientalizzante. *Studi Etruschi* 54: 29-37.

Camporeale, G. 1997. On Etruscan origins, again. *Etruscan Studies* 4: 45–51.

Camporeale, G. 2004. Etruscan Civilisation. In G. Camporeale and P. Bernardini (eds.) *The Etruscans outside Etruria.* New York, Getty: 12-77.

Campus, L. 1981. *Ceramica attica a figure nere: piccoli vasi e vasi plastici. Museo Archeologico Nazionale di Tarquinia.* Roma: L'Erma di Breitschneider.

Cappellini, E., Chiarelli, B., Sineo, L., Casoli, A., Di Gioia, A., Vernesi, C., and Caramelli, D. 2004. Biomolecular study of the human remains from tomb 5859 in the Etruscan necropolis of Monterozzi, Tarquinia (Viterbo, Italy). *Journal of Archaeological Science* 31: 603-612.

Carandini, A. 1979a. *Archeologia e cultura materiale: dai 'lavori senza gloria' nell'antichità a una politica dei beni culturali.* Bari: De Donato.

Carandini, A. 1979b. *Schiavi e padrone nell'Etruria romana: la villa di Settefinestre dallo scavo allo mostra.* Bari: De Donato.

Carandini, A. 1979c. *L'anatomia della scimmia: la formazione economiche della società prima del Capitale.* Torino: Einaudi.

Carandini, A. 1997. *La nascita di Roma: dèi, lari, eroi e uomini all'alba di una civiltà.* Torino: Einaudi.

Carandini, A. 2000. *Giornale di uno scavo: pensieri sparsi di un archeologo.* Torino: Einaudi.

Carandini,, A. 2006. *Remo e Romolo: dai rioni dei Quiriti alla città dei Romani (775/750-700/675 a C circa).* Torino: Einaudi.

Carandini, A. 2007. *Roma: il primo giorno.* Roma: Laterza.

Carsten, F.L. 1982. *The rise of Fascism.* Berkeley, CA: University of California Press.

Cavagnaro-Vanoni, L. 1972. Sei tombe a camera nella necropoli dei Monterozzi, localita Calvario. *Notizie degli Scavi di Antichità* 26: 148-194.

Cavagnaro-Vanoni, L. 1977. Sei tombe intatte nella necropoli dei Monterozzi in localita Calvario. *Notizie degli Scavi di Antichità* 31: 157-210.

Cavaliero, R. 2007. *Italia Romantica: English Romantics and Italian Freedom.* London: IB Tauris.

Chadwick, A. 2012. Routine magic, mundane ritual: towards a unified notion of depositional practice. *Oxford Journal of Archaeology* 31: 283-315.

Chai, A. 2011. Consumer specialization and the Romantic transformation of the British Grand Tour of Europe. *Journal of Bioeconomics* 13: 181-203.

Chami, F. 1999a. Roman beads from the Rufiji Delta: first incontrovertible link with the periplus. *Current Anthropology* 40: 237-242.

Chami, F. 1999b. Greco-Roman trade link and the Bantu migration theory. *Anthropos* 94: 205-215.

Chami, F. and Msemwa, P. 1997. A new look at culture and trade on the Azanian coast. *Current Anthropology* 38: 673-677.

Chaney, E. 2000. *The evolution of the grand tour: Anglo-Italian cultural relations since the Renaissance.* London: Frank Cass.

Christenson, A.L. 1989. Introduction. In A.L. Christenson (ed.) *Tracing archaeology's past: the historiography of archaeology.* Carbondale, Illinois: SIU Press: 1-5.

Champion, T.C. (ed.) 1995. *Centre and Periphery: Comparative Studies in Archaeology.* London: Routledge.

Chamption, T.C. and Diaz-Andreu, M. 1996. Introduction. In Champion,T.C. and Diaz-Andreu, M. (eds.) *Nationalism and archaeology in Europe.* London: UCL Press: 1-7.

Cipriani, G. 1980. *Il mito etrusco nel rinascimento fiorentino.* Florence: Leo S. Olschki Editore.

Clairmont, C. 1953. Studies in Greek Mythology and Vase-Painting. *American Journal of Archaeology* 57: 85-94.

Clark, L. 1983. Notes on Small Textile Frames Pictured on Greek Vases. *American Journal of Archaeology* 87: 91-96.

Clarke, M. 2004. On the semantics of ancient Greek smiles. In D.L Cairns (ed.) *Body language in the Greek and Roman World*. Swansea: Classical Press of Wales, 37 – 46.

Cohen, R. 1978. Ethnicity: Problem and focus in anthropology. *Annual Review of Anthropology* 7: 379-403.

Colonna, G. 1970. *Bronzi votivi umbro-sabellici a figura umana. Periodo Arcaico*. Firenze: Sansoni.

Colonna, G. (ed.) 1996. *L'altorilievo a Pyrgi: dei ed eroi greci in Etruria*. Roma: L'Erma di Breitschneider.

Colonna, G. 2000. *Piceni popolo d'Europa*. Roma: De Luca.

Colonna, G. 2005. *Italia ante Romanum Impericum: scritti di antichità etrusche, italiche e romane*. Pisa: Istituti editoriali e poligrafici internazionali.

Comaroff, J.L. 1987. Of totemism and ethnicity: consciousness, practice and the signs of inequality. *Ethnos* 52: 301-323.

Cornell, T. 1991. The tyranny of the evidence: a discussion of the possible uses of literacy in Etruria and Latium in the archaic age. In *Literacy in the Roman World*. Journal of Roman Archaeology Supplementary Series 3. Ann Arbor, MI: University of Michigan Press.

Costin, C.L. and Hagstrum, M. 1995. Standardisation, labour investment, skill and the organisation of ceramic production in late prehispanic highland Peru. *American Antiquity* 60: 619-639.

Cristofani, M. 1965. *La tomba delle iscrizioni a Cerveteri*. Firenze: Sansoni.

Cristofani, M. 1970. *La tomba del Tifone: cultura e società di Tarquinia in età tardo etrusca*. Roma: Accademia Nazionale dei Lincei.

Cristofani, M. 1975a. *Statue cinerario chiusine di età classica*. Roma: G. Breitschneider.

Cristofani, M. 1975b. Considerazioni su Poggio Civitate. *Prospettiva* 1: 9-17.

Cristofani, M. 1975c. Il 'dono' nell'Etruria arcaica. *La parola del passato* 30: 132-152.

Cristofani, M. 1978. *L'arte degli Etruschi: produzione e consumo*. Torino: Einaudi.

Cristofani, M. 1979. *The Etruscans: a new investigation*. London: Orbis Publishing.

Cristofani, M. 1983. *La scoperta degli Etruschi: archeologia e antiquaria nel '700*. Rome: Consiglio Nazionale di Ricerca.

Cristofani, M. 1987. Il banchetto in Etruria. In Ministero per i beni culturali e ambientali (ed.) *L'alimentazione nel mondo antico*. Roma: Istituto Poligrafico dello Stato.

Daniel, G. 1975. *A hundred and fifty years of archaeology*. London: Duckworth.

Davidson, A. 1977. *Antonio Gramsci. Towards an intellectual biography*. London: Merlin Press.

Davies, M. 1971. The suicide of Ajax: a bronze Etruscan statuette from the Kapelli Collection. *Antike Kunst* 14: 148-157.

Davis, W. 1990. Style and history in art history. In M.W. Conkey and C. Holtorf (eds.) *The uses of style in archaeology*. Cambridge: Cambridge University Press: 18-31.

D'Agostino, B. 1977. *Tombe 'principesche' dell'orientalizzante antico da Pontecagnano*. Roma: Accademia Nazionale dei Lincie.

D'Agostino, B. 1983. L'immagine, la pittura e la toba nell'Etruria arcaica. *Prospettiva* 32: 2-12.

D'Agostino, B. 1985. Società dei vivi, comunità dei morti: un rapporto difficile in Archeologia e antropologia. *Dialoghi di Archeologia Roma* 3: 47-58.

D'Agostino, B. 1991. The Italian perspective on theoretical archaeology. In I. Hodder (ed.) *Archaeological Theory in Europe: The Last Three Decades*. London: Routledge: 54-62.

D'Agostino, B. and Cerchai, L. 1999. *Il mare, la morte, l'amore: gli Etruschi, i Greci e l'immagine*. Roma: Donzelli Editore.

DeBeauvoir, S. 2012 [1952]. *The Second Sex*. London: Vintage.

DeGrummond, N. T. 1986. Rediscovery. In L. Bonfante (ed.) *Etruscan Life and Afterlife: a handbook of Etruscan studies*. Detroit, MI: Wayne State University Press: 18-46.

Del Chiaro, M. 1970. Two Unusual Vases of the Etruscan Torcop Group: One with Head of Eita (Hades). *American Journal of Archaeology* 74: 292-294.

Dennis, G. 1848. *The cities and cemeteries of Etruria*. London: John Murray.

Dietler, M. 1990. Driven by drink: the role of drinking in the political economy and the case of Early Iron Age France. *Journal of Anthropological Archaeology* 9: 352-406.

Dietler, M. 2001. Theorizing the feast: Rituals of consumption, commensal politics, and power in African contexts. In M. Dietler and B. Hayden (eds.) *Feasts: Archaeological and ethnographic perspectives on food, politics, and power*. Tuscaloosa, AL: University of Alabama Press: 65-114.

Dietler, M. 2003. Clearing the Table. In T. Bray (ed.) *The archaeology and politics of food and feasting in early states and empires*. New York: Kluwer Press: 271-282.

Dietler, M. 2006. Alcohol: anthropological/archaeological perspectives. *Annual Reviews of Anthropology* 35: 229-249.

Dobres, M.A. and Robb, J. 2005.'Doing' agency: Introductory remarks on methodology. *Journal of Archaeological Method and Theory* 12: 159-166.

Dooley, B.M. 1987. *Science, politics, and society in eighteenth-century Italy: the Giornale de' letterati d'Italia and its world*. New York: Garland.

Dover, K.J. 1989. *Greek Homosexuality*. Boston, MA: Harvard University Press.

Dragendorff, H. 1895. Terra sigillata. Ein Beitrag zur Geschichte der griechischen und römischen Keramik. *Bonner Jahrbücher* 96:18-155.

Drews, R. 1992. Herodotus 1.94, the Drought ca. 1200 B.C., and the Origin of the Etruscans. *Historia: Zeitschrift für Alte Geschichte* 41: 14-39.

Duggan, C. 2008. *The Force of Destiny: a history of Italy since 1796*. London: Houghton Mifflin Harcourt.

Ericsson, K. and Lehmann, C. 1996. Expert and exceptional performance: Evidence of maximal adaptation to task constraints. *Annual Review of Psychology* 47: 273-305.

Edlund Gantz, I. 1972. The Seated Statue Akroteria from Poggio Civitate (Murlo). *Dialoghi di Archeologia* 6: 167-235.

Edlund-Berry, I. 1994. *Ritual Destruction of Cities and Sanctuaries: the 'unfounding' of the archaic monumental building at Poggio Civitate (Murlo)*. In R. dePuma and J. P. Small (eds.) Murlo and the Etruscans. Madison, WI: University of Wisconsin Press: 16-28.

Fabrizi, F. 2001. *Il labirinto di Chiusi: storia, scavi, esplorazioni*. Cortona: Caloschi.

Faraone, C. 1996. Taking the 'Nestor's Cup' Inscription Seriously: Erotic Magic and Conditional Curses in the Earliest Inscribed Hexameters. *Classical Antiquity* 15: 77-112.

Farnsworth, M. 1971. Corinthian pottery: technical studies. *American Journal of Archaeology* 74: 9-20.

Ferrari, G. 2003. Myth and Genre on Athenian Vases. *Classical Antiquity* 22: 37-54.

Ferrone, V. 1995. *The intellectual roots of the Italian Enlightenment: Newtonian science, religion, and politics in the early eighteenth century*. Atlantic Highlands, NJ: Humanities Press.

Filippelli, R.L. 1989. *American Labor and Postwar Italy: 1943-1953: A Study of Cold War Politics*. Stanford, CA: Stanford University Press.

Fleming, A. 2006. Post-processual landscape archaeology: a critique.*Cambridge Archaeological Journal* 16: 267-280.

Fortin, D.R. and Dholakia, R. 2005. Interactivity and vividness effects on social presence and involvement with a weB –based advertisement. *Journal of Business Research* 58: 387-396.

Fowler, D. 1997. On the shoulders of giants: intertextuality and classical studies. *Materiali e discussioni per l'analisi dei testi classici* 39: 13-34.

Franzosi, R. 1995. *The Puzzle of Strikes: Class and State Strategies in Postwar Italy*. Cambridge: Cambridge University Press.

Gàldy, A.M., 2009. *Cosimo I de' Medici as Collector: Antiquities and Archaeology in Sixteenth-Century Florence*. Cambridge: Cambridge Scholars Publishing.

Gatens, M. 1996. *Imaginary Bodies: Ethics, Power and Corporeality*. London: Routledge.

Geertz, C. 1973. Thick description: towards an interpretative theory of culture. In C. Geertz (ed.) The *Interpretation of Culture: Selected Essays*. New York: Basic Books, 3-30.

Geissler, S. 2012. The social significance of communal dining in Etruscan Italy from the 7th to the 4th centuries BC: an iconographical approach. University of Edinburgh MPhil thesis, published online.

Gelder, B. de. 2006. Towards the neurobiology of emotional body language. *Nature Reviews Neuroscience* 7: 242-249.

Gell, A. 1992. The technology of enchantment and the enchantment of technology. In J. Coote and A. Shelton (eds.) *Anthropology, art and aesthetics*. Oxford: Oxford University Press: 40-63.

Gell, A. 1993. *Wrapping in images: tattooing in Polynesia*. Oxford: Clarendon Press.

Gell, A. 1998. *Art and agency*. Oxford: Clarendon Press.

Gentile, E. 1986. Fascism in Italian historiography: in search of an individual historical identity. *Journal of Contemporary History* 21: 179-208.

Giglioli, G.Q. 1925. *Corpus vasorum antiquorum: Italia. Museo Nazionale di Villa Giulia in Roma*. Roma: Istituto poligrafico dello Stato.

Giglioli, G.Q. 1926. *Corpus vasorum antiquorum: Italia. Musei Capitolini di Roma*. Roma: Istituto poligrafico dello Stato.

Giglioli, G.Q. 1935. *L'arte etrusca*. Milano: Treves.

Gill, D. 1991. Pots and Trade: Spacefillers or Objets d'art? *Journal of Hellenic Studies* 111: 29-47.

Gill, D. 1994. Positivism, pots and long-distance trade. In I. Morris (ed.) *Classical Greece: Ancient histories and modern archaeologies*. Cambridge: Cambridge University Press: 99-107.

Gillet, M. 2013. *Inventing Identities: Graeco-Roman Constructions of the Etruscans*. Unpublished PhD thesis, Macquarie University.

Ginge, B. 1987. *Ceramiche etrusche a figure nere*. Museo Archeologico Nazionale di Tarquinia. Roma: L'Erma di Breitschneider.

Giudici, F. and Giudici, I. 2009. Seeing the Image: Constructing a Data-Base of the Imagery on Attic Pottery from 635-300 BC. In R. Oakley and O. Pallagia (eds.) *Athenian Potters and Painters II*. Oxford: Oxbow.

Given, M. 1999. *The Archaeology of the Colonised*. Oxford: Oxbow

Goffman, E. 1979. *Gender Advertisements*. Boston, MA: Harvard University Press.

Gosden, C. and Marshall, Y.M. 1999. The cultural biography of objects.*World Archaeology* 31, 169-178.

Gramsci, A. 2010. *Prison notebooks*. New York: Columbia University Press.

Grosz, E. 1993. *Volatile Bodies: Towards a Corporeal Feminism*. New York: Allen and Unwin.

Gsell, S. 1898. *Fouilles dans la nécropole de Vulci*. Paris: E. Thorin.

Guidi, A. 1985. An application of the rank-size rule to protohistoric settlements in the middle Tyrhennian area. In C.A. Malone and S.K. Stoddart (eds.)

Papers in Italian Archaeology vol.IV: The Cambridge Conference, part 3, Patterns in Protohistory. Oxford: Archaeopress: 217-42.

Guidi, A.1996. Nationalism without a nation: the Italian case. In T.C. Champion and M. Diaz-Andreu (eds.) *Nationalism and archaeology in Europe.* London: UCL Press:108-118.

Guidi, A., 2010. The Historical Development of Italian Prehistoric Archaeology: A Brief Outline. *Bulletin of the History of Archaeology* 20: 13-21.

Habinek, T.N. 2001. *The politics of Latin literature: writing, identity, and empire in ancient Rome.* Princeton, NY: Princeton University Press.

Hadfield, A. 1998. *Literature, travel, and colonial writing in the English Renaissance, 1545-1625.* Oxford: Oxford University Press.

Hall, J. 1985. Livy's Tanaquil and the image of assertive Etruscan women in Latin historical literature of the early empire. *Augustan Age* 4: 31-38.

Hall, T. and Chase-Dunn, C. 1993. The world-systems perspective and archaeology: Forward into the past. *Journal of Archaeological Research* 1: 121-143.

Hamilakis, Y. 1996. Wine, oil and the dialectics of power in Bronze Age Crete: a review of the evidence. *Oxford Journal of Archaeology* 15: 1-32.

Hamilakis, Y. 1999. Food technologies/technologies of the body: the social context of wine and oil production and consumption in Bronze Age Crete. *World Archaeology* 31: 38-54.

Hamilakis, Y. 2002. Experience and Corporeality. Introduction. In Y. Hamilakis, M. Pluciennik, and S. Tarlow (eds.) *Thinking Through the Body: Archaeologies of Corporeality.* London: Kluwer Academic/Plenum: 99-103.

Hamilakis, Y. 2008. Time, performance, and the production of a mnemonic record: from feasting to an archaeology of eating and drinking. In L. Hitchcock, L. R. Laffineur. and J. Crowley, (eds.) *DAIS: The Aegean Feast.* Liege, Belguim, Austin, US. University of Liege and University of Texas at Austin. Austin, University of Texas Press 3-20.

Hamilton, S. and Whitehouse, R. 2006. Three Senses of Dwelling: beginning to socialise the Neolithic ditched villages of the Tavoliere, southeast Italy. *Journal of Iberian Archaeology* 8: 159-84.

Hamilton, S. 2002. Between ritual and routine: interpreting British prehistoric pottery production and distribution. In A. Woodward and J.D. Hill (eds.) *Prehistoric Britain: the ceramic basis.* Oxford: Oxbow, 38-53.

Hamilton, S., Whitehouse, R., Brown, K., Combes, P., Herring, E., and Thomas, M.S. 2006. Phenomenology in Practice: Towards a Methodology for a 'Subjective' Approach. *European Journal of Archaeology* 9: 31-71.

Hansen, P. A. Pithecusan humour. The interpretation of 'Nestor's cup' reconsidered. *Glotta* 54: 25-44.

Hardwick, L. 1990. Ancient Amazons-Heroes, Outsiders or Women? *Greece & Rome* 37: 14-36.

Harrison, K. Taylor, L. and Marske, L. 2006. Women's and men's eating behaviour following exposure to ideal body images and text. *Communication Research* 33: 507-529.

Hawkes, C. 1959. The problem of the origins of the archaic cultures in Etruria and its main difficulties. *Studi Etruschi* 27: 363-382.

Haynes, S. 1965. *Etruscan bronze utensils.* London: British Museum Press.

Haynes, S. 1971. *Etruscan sculpture.* London: British Museum Press. Haynes, S. 1985. *Etruscan bronzes.* Cambridge: Cambridge University Press.

Haynes, S. 2005. *Etruscan civilization: a cultural history.* Los Angeles, CA: J. Paul Getty Museum.

Heath, M. 2002. *Interpreting classical texts.* London: Duckbacks.

Hegel, G. F. 1979 [1807]. *The Phenomenology of Spirit.* Trans. A.V. Miller. Oxford, Oxford University Press.

Heidegger, M. 1962 [1927] *Being and Time.* New York: Harper.

Hercle. 1968. *Vulci: zona dell'Osteria, scavi della Hercle.* Roma: Hercle.

Hewes, G.W. 1973. Primate communication and the gestural origin of language. *Current Anthropology* 14: 5-24.

Hill, J.D. 1995. *Ritual and rubbish in the Iron Age of Wessex: a study on the formation of a particular archaeological record.* Oxford: British Archaeological Reports.

Hingley, R. 2001. An Imperial Legacy: the contribution of Classical Rome to the Character of the English. In Hingley, R. (ed.) *Images of Rome: perceptions of Ancient Rome in Europe and the United States in the modern age.* Portsmouth, R.I.: Journal of Roman Archaeology, Supplementary Series: 145-66.

Hingley, R. 2002. *Roman officers and English gentlemen: the imperial origins of Roman archaeology.* London, Routledge.

Hodder, I. 1982. *Symbols in action: ethnoarchaeological studies of material culture.* Cambridge: Cambridge University Press.

Hodder, I. 1987. *The Archaeology of Contextual Meanings.* Cambridge, Cambridge University Press.

Hodder, I. 1988. *The meanings of things: material culture and symbolic expression.* London: Unwin Hyman.

Hodder, I. 1989. This is not an article about material culture as text. *Journal of Anthropological Archaeology* 8: 250-269.

Hodder, I. 1991. Interpretive archaeology and its role. *American Antiquity* 56: 7-18.

Hodder, I. 2003. The interpretation of documents and material culture. In N.K. Denzin and Y.S. Lincoln (eds.) *Collecting and interpreting qualitative materials.* New York: Sage 155-175.

Hodos, T. 2009. Colonial engagements in the global Mediterranean Iron Age. *Cambridge Archaeological Journal* 19: 221-41.

Holt, P. 1989. The End of the Trachiniai and the Fate of Herakles. *Journal of Hellenic Studies* 109: 69-80.

Höttemann, B. 2011. *Shakespeare and Italy*. Münster: LIT Verlag.

Horowitz, D.L. (ed.) 1985. *Ethnic Groups in Conflict*. Berkeley, CA: University of California Press.

Hus, A. 1971. Vulci *étrusque et étrusco-romain*. Paris: Klinckseick.

Husserl, E. 1990 [1913]. *Ideas pertaining to a pure phenomenology and to a phenomenological philosophy*. London: Kluwer Academic Publishing.

Iaia, C. 1999. *Simbolismo funerario e ideologia alle origini di una civiltà urbana: forme rituali nelle sepolture villanoviane a Tarquinia e Vulcie nel loro entroterra*. Firenze: All'insegna del giglio.

Iaia, C. 2005. *Produzioni toreutiche della prima età del ferro in Italia centro-settentrionale: stili decorativi, circolazioni, significato*. Pisa: Istituti editoriali poligrafici internazionali.

Iaia, C. 2006. Prima del' simposio': vasi in bronzo e contesto sociale nell'Etruria meridionale protostorica. *Revista d'arqueologia de Ponent* 16: 261-270.

Ianziti, G. 2007. Challenging Chronicles: Leonardo Bruni's History of the Florentine People. In S. Dale, A. Williams Lewin, and D. Osheim (eds.) *Chronicling history: chroniclers and historians in Medieval and Renaissance Italy* University Park, PA: Pennsylvania University Press: 249-273.

Iozzo, M. 2007. *Materiali dimenticate recuperate: restauri e acquisizioni nel Museo Archeologico Nazionale. Chiusi*. Chiusi: Edizioni Lui.

Irigaray, L. 1993. *An Ethics of Sexual Difference*. London: Continuum.

Izzet, V. 2001. Form and meaning in Etruscan ritual space. *Cambridge Archaeological Journal* 11: 185-200.

Izzet, V. 2003. Cerveteri. *Archaeological Reports* 49: 100-101.

Izzet, V. 2004a. Winckelmann and Etruscan art. *Etruscan Studies* 10: 223-238.

Izzet, V. 2004b. Purloined letters: the Aristonothos Inscription and Krater. In B. Shefton and K. Lomas (eds.) *Greek Identity in the Western Mediterranean: Papers in Honour of Brian Shefton*. London: Brill, 191-210.

Izzet, V. 2005. The Mirror of Theopompus: Etruscan Identity and Greek Myth. *Papers of the British School of Rome* 73: 1-22.

Izzet, V. 2007a. *The Archaeology of Etruscan Society*. Cambridge, Cambridge University Press.

Izzet, V. 2007b. Changing Perspectives: Greek Myth in Etruria. In P. Attema, A. Nijboer, and A. Zifferero. *Papers in Italian Archaeology: Communities and Settlements from the Neolithic to the Early Medieval Period.6th Conference of Italian Archaeology*. Oxford, UK. Oxford: Archaeopress, 822-827. (BAR International, 2 VI).

Izzet, V. 2007c. Greeks Make It; Etruscans Fecit: the Stigma of Plagiarism in the Reception of Etruscan Art. *Etruscan Studies* 10: 18.

Jannot, J.R. 2000.The Etruscans and the Afterworld. *Etruscan Studies* 7: 81-102.

Jones, A. 1998. Where Eagles Dare: Landscape, Animals and the Neolithic of Orkney. *Journal of Material Culture* 3: 301-324.

Joy, J. 2009. Reinvigorating object biography: reproducing the drama of object lives. *World Archaeology* 41: 540-556.

Joyce, R.A. 1993. Women's Work: Images of Production and Reproduction in Pre-Hispanic Southern Central America. *Current Anthropology* 34: 255-274.

Joyce, R.A. 1998. Performing the body in Pre-hispanic Central America. *RES: Anthropology and Aesthetics* 33: 147-65.

Joyce, R.A. 2000a. Girling the girl and boying the boy: the production of adulthood in ancient Mesoamerica. *World Archaeology* 31: 473-483.

Joyce, R.A. 2000b. *Gender and power in Pre-hispanic Mesoamerica*. Austin: University of Texas Press.

Joyce, R.A. 2001. Burying the dead at Tlatilco: Social memory and social identities. *Archeological Papers of the American Anthropological Association* 10: 12-26.

Joyce, R.A. 2003. Making something of herself: embodiment in life and death at Playa de los Muertos, Honduras. *Cambridge Archaeological Journal* 13: 248-261.

Joyce, R.A. 2004. Embodied Subjectivity: Gender, Femininity, Masculinity, Sexuality. In L. Meskell and R.W. Preucel (eds.) *A Companion to Social Archaeology*. Oxford: Blackwell.

Kipp, R.S and Schortman, E.M. 1989. The Political Impact of Trade in Chiefdoms. *American Anthropologist* 91: 370-385.

Kopytoff, I. 1986. The cultural biography of things. In I. Kopytoff and A. Appadurai (eds.) *The Social Life of Things: commodities in cultural perspective*. Cambridge: Cambridge University Press, 64-91

Lavine, H. Sweeney, D. and Wagner, S. 1999. Depicting women as sex objects in television advertising: effects on body dissatisfaction. *Personality and Social Psychology Bulletin* 25: 1049-1058.

Lawrence, D.H. 2007 [1932]. *Sketches of Etruscan Places*. London: Penguin. Layton, E. 1974. Technology as knowledge. *Technology and Culture* 15: 31-41.

Leighton, R. 2004. *Tarquinia: an Etruscan city*. Oxford: Duckbacks.

Leoni, M. and Trabucchi, C. 1962. Alcuni dati tecnici sulla colorazione nera dei buccheri etruschi. *Studi Etruschi* 80: 257-267.

Levi, J. L. 1992. Commoditizing the Vessels of Identity: Transnational Trade and the Reconstruction of Rarámuri Ethnicity. *Museum Anthropology* 16: 7-24.

Lewis, S. 2003. Representation and reception: Athenian pottery in its Italian context. In J.B. Wilkins and E. Herring (eds.) *Inhabiting Symbols: symbol and image in the ancient Mediterranean*. London: Accordia Research Institute, 175-92.

Lewis, S. 2006. Iconography and the Study of Gender In S. Schroer (ed.) *Images and Gender: Contributions to the Hermeneutics of Reading Ancient Art*. Fribourg: Academic Press, 23-39.

Lewis, S. 2009. Athletics on Attic Pottery: Export and Imagery. In V. Norskov, L. Hannestad, C. Isler-Kerenyi and S. Lewis (eds.) *The World of Greek Vases*. Edizioni Quasar 41:133-148.

Ligota, C.R. 1987. Annius of Viterbo and historical method. *Journal of the Warburg and Courtauld Institutes* 50: 44-56.

Lissarague, F. 1987. Voyages d'images: iconographie et aires culturelles. *Revue des Etudes Anciennes* 89:261-270.

Lowenstam, S. 1993. The arming of Achilleus on early Greek vases. *Classical Antiquity* 12: 199-218.

Lowenstam, S. 1997. Talking vases: the relationship between the Homeric poems and archaic representations of epic myth. *Transactions of the American Philological Association* 127: 21-76.

Lynch, K. 2011. *The symposium in context: pottery from a Late Archaic house near the Athenian Agora*. Athens: American School of Classical Studies at Athens.

Lyttleton, A. 2003. The origins of a national monarchy: Tradition and innovation in the cult of the House of Savoy during the risorgimento. *Proceedings of the British Academy* 17: 2001 Lectures 117: 325 – 353.

Malkin, I. 2002. A colonial middle ground: Greek, Etruscan, and local élites in the Bay of Naples. In C. Lyons and J. Papadopoulos (eds.) *The Archaeology of Colonialism*. New York: Getty: 151-181.

Malkin, I. 2004. Post-colonial concepts and Ancient Greek Colonisation. *Modern Language Quarterly* 65: 341-364.

Mandolesi, A. 1999. *La 'prima' Tarquinia: l'insediamento protostorico sulla Civita e nel territorio circostante*. Firenze: All'insegna del giglio.

Mansuelli, G. 1966. *Etruria and early Rome*. London: Methuen.

Marrapodi, M. (ed.) 1997. *Shakespeare's Italy: functions of Italian locations in Renaissance drama*. Manchester: Manchester University Press.

Marinis, S. de. 1961. *La tipologia del banchetto nell'arte etrusca arcaica*. Roma: L'Erma di Breitschneider.

Merleau-Ponty, M. 1962. *The Phenomenology of Perception*. Trans. C. Smith. London, Routledge.

Merleau-Ponty, M. 1963. *The Structure of Behaviour*. Trans. A.L. Fisher. Boston: Beacon Press.

Milani, L.A. 1884 Tombe etrusche sulla linea ferroviaria Orte. *Notizie degli Scavi di antichità* 13: 185-227.

Miles, G. 1997. *Livy: reconstructing early Rome*. Ithaca, NY: Cornell University Press.

Millett, M. 1979. The dating of Farnham (Alice Holt) pottery. *Britannia* 10: 121-77.

Mitchell, T. 2004. *Intoxicated Identities: Alcohol's Power in Mexican History and Culture*. London: Routledge.

Montemurro, B. and McClure, B. 2005. Changing gender norms for alcohol consumption: Social drinking and lowered inhibitions at bachelorette parties. *Sex Roles* 52: 279-288.

Moore, A. 1985. *Norfolk and the Grand Tour: eighteenth-century travellers abroad and their souvenirs*. Norwich: Norfolk Museums Service.

Moore, A. 2008. Thomas Coke's Grand Tour. *Papers of the British School of Rome* 76: 313-314.

Moretti, M. 1962. *Tarquinia: la tomba della nave*. Milano: Lerici. Moretti, M. 1966. *Tomba Martin Marescotti*. Milano: Lerici.

Moretti, M. 1970. *New monuments of Etruscan painting*. University Park, PA: Pennsylvania University Press.

Moretti, M. 1975. *Nuove scoperte e acquisizioni nell'Etruria meridionale*. Roma: Artistica.

Moretti, M. 1977. *Cerveteri*. Novara: Istituto Geografico DeAgostini.

Morris, I. 1992. *Death ritual and social structure in classical antiquity*. Cambridge: Cambridge University Press.

Moser, S. 1992. The visual language of archaeology: a case study of the Neanderthals. *Antiquity* 66: 831-844.

Moser, S. 1997. *Ancestral Images: the Iconography of Human Origins*. Ithaca, NY: Cornell University Press.

Munzi, M. 2004. Italian Archaeology in Libya From Colonial Romanità to Decolonization of the Past. In Galaty, M. and Watkinson, C. (eds.) *Archaeology under dictatorship*. New York: Springer US, 73-107.

Murray, O. 1990. Sympotic history. In O. Murray (ed.) *Sympotica: a symposium on the symposion*. Oxford: Oxford University Press, 3-11.

Murray, O. 1994. 'Nestor's cup' and the origin of the Greek symposion. *Annali di archeologia e storia antica* 1: 47-54.

Naddeo, B.A. 2005. Cultural capitals and cosmopolitanism in eighteenth-century Italy: the historiography and Italy on the Grand Tour. *Journal of Modern Italian Studies* 10: 183-199.

Neff, H. 1993. Theory, sampling, and analytical techniques in the archaeological study of prehistoric ceramics. *American Antiquity* 58: 23-44.

Nelis, J. 2007. Constructing fascist identity: Benito Mussolini and the myth of romanità. *Classical World* 100: 391-415.

Nielson, M. 1998. Etruscan women: a cross-cultural perspective. In L. L. Loven and A. Strömberg (eds.) *Aspects of women in antiquity*. Jonsered: P. Astroms, 69-84.

O'Donoghue, E. 2013. The Mute Statues Speak: The Archaic Period Acroteria from Poggio Civitate (Murlo). *European Journal of Archaeology* 16: 268-288.

O'Hara, P. 1993. 'The Willow Pattern that we knew' the Victorian literature of Blue Willow. *Victorian Studies* 36: 421-442.

Oleson, J.P. 1975. Greek myth and Etruscan imagery in the Tomb of the Bulls at Tarquinia. *American Journal of Archaeology* 79: 189-200.

Osborne, R. 1997. Men without clothes: heroic nakedness in Greek art. *Gender and History* 9: 504-488.

Osborne, R. 2001. Why did Athenian pots appeal to the Etruscans? World Archaeology 33.2 277–95.

Osborne, R. 2004. The anatomy of a mobile culture: the Greeks, their pots and their myths in Etruria. In R.

Schleisser and U. Zellman (eds.) *Mobility and Travel in the Mediterranean from Antiquity to the Middle Ages*. Münster: Lit Verlag.

Osborne, R. 2007. What travelled with Greek Pottery? *Mediterranean Historical Review* 22: 85-95.

Paleothodoros, D. 2002. Pourquoi les Etrusques achetaient-ils des vases attiques? *Les études classiques* 70: 139-160.

Paleothodoros, D. 2004. Dionysiac imagery in Archaic Etruria. *Etruscan Studies* 10: 187-202.

Paleothodoros, D. 2008. Archaeological contexts and iconographic analysis: case studies from Greece and Etruria. In V. Nørskov, L. Hannestad, C. Isler-Kerényi and S. Lewis (eds.) *The World of Greek Vases*. Roma:Edizioni Quasar: 45-62.

Paleothodoros, D. 2010. Etruscan Black figure in context. *Bollettino di Archeologia Online I* 2010 Volume Speciale C/C4: 1-11.

Paleothodoros, D. 2011. A complex approach to Etruscan Black-figure vase painting. *Mediterranea* 8: 33-82.

Pallottino, M. 1939. Sulle facies culturali arcaiche dell'Etruria. *Studi Etruschi* 13: 85-128.

Pallottino, M. 1947. *L'origine degli etruschi*. Roma: Tumminelli. Pallottino, M. 1984a (1942). *Etruscologia*. Roma: Hoepli Editore.

Pallottino, M. 1984b. *The Etruscans*. London: Routledge.

Pallottino, M. 1991. *A History of Earliest Italy*. London, Routledge.

Paolucci, G. 2005. *Documente e memorie sulle antichità e il Museo di Chiusi*. Pisa: Istituti editoriali e poligrafici internazionali.

Paolucci, G. 2007a. *Immagini etrusche. Tombe con ceramiche a figure nere dalla necropoli di Tolle a Chianciano Terme*. Milano: Silvana.

Paolucci, G. 2007b. *Chianchiano Terme*. Firenze: Bonsignori.

Parker Pearson, M. 2001. *The archaeology of death and burial*. Oxford: Berg.

Pearce, M. 1998. Reconstructing prehistoric metallurgical knowledge:the northern Italian Copper and Bronze Ages. *European Journal of Archaeology* 1: 51-70.

Pearce, M. 2008. Structured deposition in early neolithic Northern Italy. *Journal of Mediterranean Archaeology*. 21: 19-33.

Pellecchia, M., Negrini, R., Colli, L. et al. 2007. The mystery of Etruscan origins: novel clues from Bos taurus mitochondrial DNA. *Proceedings of the Royal Society* B 274:1175–79.

Perez, R. L. 2000. Fiesta as tradition, fiesta as change: Ritual, alcohol and violence in a Mexican community. *Addiction* 95: 365-373.

Perkins, P. 2007. *Etruscan bucchero in the British Museum*. London: British Museum Press.

Perkins, P. 2009. DNA and Etruscan Identity. In J. Swaddling and P. Perkins (eds.) *Etruscan by definition: the cultural, regional and personal identity of the Etruscans*. London, British Museum Press: 95-111.

Phillips, K.M. 1967. Bryn Mawr College Excavations in Tuscany 1966. *American Journal of Archaeology* 71: 133-139.

Phillips, K.M. 1968. Bryn Mawr College Excavations in Tuscany 1967. *American Journal of Archaeology* 72: 121-124.

Phillips, K.M. 1969. Bryn Mawr College Excavations in Tuscany 1968. *American Journal of Archaeology* 73: 333-339.

Phillips, K.M. 1970. Bryn Mawr College Excavations in Tuscany 1969. *American Journal of Archaeology* 74: 241-245.

Phillips, K.M. 1970. Speculations on Poggio Civitate. In K.M. Phillips & A. Talocchini (eds.) *Poggio Civitate. The Archaic Etruscan Sanctuary*. Florence: Olschki: 79-80.

Phillips, K.M. 1971. Bryn Mawr College Excavations in Tuscany. *American Journal of Archaeology* 75: 257-261.

Phillips, K.M. 1972. Bryn Mawr College Excavations in Tuscany 1971. *American Journal of Archaeology* 76: 249-255.

Phillips, K.M. 1973. Bryn Mawr College Excavations in Tuscany 1972. *American Journal of Archaeology* 77: 319-326.

Phillips, K.M. 1993. *In the hills of Tuscany. Recent excavations at the Etruscan site of Poggio Civitate (Murlo, Siena)*. Philadelphia (PA): University Museum of Pennsylvania.

Phillips, K.M. and Nielsen, E. 1974. Bryn Mawr College Excavations in Tuscany 1973. *American Journal of Archaeology* 78: 265-277.

Phillips, K.M. and Nielsen, E. 1975. Bryn Mawr College Excavations in Tuscany 1974. *American Journal of Archaeology* 79:357-366.

Phillips, K.M. and Nielsen, E. 1977. Bryn Mawr College Excavations in Tuscany 1975. *American Journal of Archaeology* 81: 85-100.

Pianù, G. 1980. *Ceramiche etrusche a figure rosse. Museo Archeologico Nazionale di Tarquinia*. Roma: L'Erma di Breitschneider.

Pieraccini, L. 2000. Families, Feasting, and Funerals: Funerary Ritual at Ancient Caere. *Etruscan Studies* 7: 35-50.

Pieraccini, L. 2009. The English, Etruscans and 'Etouria:' the Grand Tour. *Etruscan Studies* 12: 3-20.

Pieraccini, L. 2011. The wonders of wine in Etruria. In N.T. DeGrummond and I. Edlund-Berry (eds.) *The Archaeology of Sanctuaries and Ritual in Etruria*. Portsmouth, RI: Journal of Roman Archaeology Supplement 81: 127-137.

Pierro, E. 1984. *Ceramiche ioniche non figurate e coppe attiche a figure nere*. Museo Archeologico Nazionale di Tarquinia. Roma: L'Erma di Breitschneider.

Poliakoff, M.B. 1987. *Combat sports in the Ancient World*. New Haven and London: Yale University Press.

Preucel, R. and Mrozowski, S. (eds.) 2011. *Contemporary archaeology in theory: the new pragmatism*. New York: Wiley-Blackwell.

Ra'ad, B. L. 2001. Primal Scenes of Globalization: Legacies of Canaan and Etruria. PMLA 116: 89-110.

Ramage, N. 2011. The English Etruria: Wedgwood and the Etruscans. *Etruscan Studies* 14: 187-202.

Randers Pehrson, J.D. 1983. *Barbarians and Romans: the birth struggle for Europe AD 400-700*. Oklahoma: University of Oklahoma Press.

Rasmussen, T. 2004. [1979] *Bucchero Pottery from Southern Etruria*. Cambridge: Cambridge University Press.

Rathje, A. 1994. Banquet and Ideology: Some new considerations about banqueting at Poggio Civitate. In R. dePuma and J. P. Small (eds.) *Murlo and the Etruscans: Art and Society in Ancient Etruria*. Madison: University of Wisconsin Press: 95-100.

Rathje, A. 2007. Murlo, Images and Archaeology. *Etruscan Studies* 10: 175-184.

Rausser, C. 2002. *Vasen für Etruria. Verbreitung und Funktionen attischer Keramik im Etrurien des 6. und 5. Jahrhunderts vor Christus*. Zurich.

Riccioni, G. 2003. *Vasi greci da Vulci: necropoli dell'Osteria svavi Ferraguti-Mengarelli 1929-1931*. Milan: Comune di Milano.

Richards, C. 1993. Monuments as landscape: creating the centre of the world in late Neolithic Orkney. *World Archaeology* 28: 190-208.

Richards, C. 1996. Henges And Water: Towards an Elemental Understanding of Monumentality and Landscape in Late Neolithic Britain. *Journal of Material Culture* 1: 313-336.

Richter, G. and Milne, M. 1935. *Shapes and names of Greek Vases*. New York: Metropolitan Museum of New York.

Ridgway, D. 1973. Archaeology in Central Italy and Etruria, 1968-73. *Archaeological Reports* 20: 42-59.

Ridgway, D. 1984. *L'alba di Magna Graecia*. Milano: Longanesi.

Ridgway, D. 1992. *The first Western Greeks*. Cambridge: Cambridge University Press.

Ridgway, D. 1997. Nestor's Cup and the Etruscans. Oxford Journal of Archaeology 16: 325: 344.

Ridgway, D. 2002. *The world of the early Etruscans*. Stockholm: Paul Aströms.

Ridgway, D. and Ridgway, F.S. (eds.) 1979. *Italy before the Romans: the Iron Age, Orientalizing and Etruscan periods*. London: Academic Press.

Ridgway, D. and Ridgway, F.S. 1994. Demaratus and the Archaeologists. In R. dePuma and J. P. Small (eds.) *Murlo and the Etruscans: Art and Society in Ancient Etruria*. Madison: University of Wisconsin Press: 6 – 15.

Riva, C. 2005. The culture of urbanization in the Mediterranean c. 800-600. In B. Cunliffe and R. Osborne (eds.) *Mediterranean Urbanisation 800–600 BC*. London: Proceedings of the British Academy: 203-32.

Riva, C. 2006. The Orientalizing period in Etruria: sophisticated communities. In C. Riva & N. Vella (eds.) *Debating Orientalization: Multidisciplinary Approaches to Change in the Ancient Mediterranean. Monographs in Mediterranean Archaeology* 10. London: Equinox Press: 110-134.

Riva, C. 2010a. *The urbanisation of Etruria: funerary practices and social change, 700–600 BC*. Cambridge: Cambridge University Press.

Riva, C. 2010b. Trading Settlements and the Materiality of Wine Consumption in the North Tyrrhenian Sea Region. In B. Knapp and P. van Dommelen (eds.) *Material Connections: Mobility, Materiality and Mediterranean Identities*. London and New York: Routledge

Riva, C. 2010c. Tecnologie del se': il banchetto rituale collettivo in Etruria. In C. Mata, G. Pérez Jorda and Jaime Vives-Ferrándiz (eds.) *De la cuina a la taula IV reunio d'Economia en el I milleni a.C. (Caudete de las Fuentes, Octubre 2009) Saguntum*. Valencia: Papeles del Laboratorio de Arqueología: 69-80.

Robb, J. 1994a. Gender contradictions, moral coalitions and inequality in prehistoric Italy. *Journal of European Archaeology* 2: 20–49.

Robb, J. 1994b. Burial and social reproduction in the peninsular Italian neolithic. *Journal of Mediterranean Archaeology* 7: 27–71.

Robb, J. 1997. New directions in Italian burial studies: A disorganized renaissance? *American Journal of Archaeology* 100: 773–776.

Robb, J. 1999. Great persons and big men in the Italian Neolithic. In R. Tykot, J. Morter, and J. Robb (eds.) *Social dynamics of the prehistoric central Mediterranean*. London: Accordia Research Centre: 111-122.

Robb, J. 2001. Island identities: Ritual, travel, and the creation of difference in Neolithic Malta. *European Journal of Archaeology* 4: 175–202.

Robb, J. 2002. Time and biography. In Y. Hamilakis, M. Pluciennik, and S. Tarlow (eds.) *Thinking through the body: Archaeologies of corporeality*. London: Kluwer/Academic: 145-163.

Robb, J. 2008. Tradition and agency: human body representations in later prehistoric Europe. *World Archaeology* 40:332–353.

Robb, J. 2009a. The Body as Material Culture. *Current Anthropology* 50: 169–170.

Robb, J. 2009b. People of stone: Stelae, personhood, and society in prehistoric Europe. *Journal of Archaeological Method and Theory* 16: 162–183.

Robb, J. 2010. Beyond agency. *World Archaeology* 42: 493–520.

Romanelli, P. 1948. Tarquinia: scavi e ricerche nell'area della citta. *Notizie degli Scavi di Antichità* 2: 193-270.

Romualdi, A. 2009. The Late Orientalizing Bronze Works at Chiusi. In J. Swaddling and P. Perkins (eds.) *Etruscan by definition: the cultural, regional and personal identity of the Etruscans*. London: British Museum Press: 57-59.

Rowland, I. 1986. Render Unto Caesar the Things Which are Caesar's: Humanism and the Arts in the Patronage of Agostino Chigi. *Renaissance Quarterly* 39: 673-730.

Rowland, I. 1989. Etruscan Inscriptions from a 1637 Autograph of Fabio Chigi. *American Journal of Archaeology* 93: 423-428.

Rowland, I. 2004. *The Scarith of Scornello: a tale of Renaissance forgery*. Chicago: University of Chicago Press.

Russell, B.F. 2003. Wine, women and the Polis: Gender and the Formation of the City-State in Archaic Rome. *Greece and Rome* 50: 77-84.

Safran, L. 2000. Hercle in Washington: A Faliscan Vase at The Catholic University of America. *Etruscan Studies* 7: 51-80.

Said, E. 1979. *Orientalism*. London: Vintage.

Sassatelli, G. 1999. The diet of the Etruscans. In J-L Flandrin and M. Montanari (eds.) *Food: a culinary history from antiquity to the present*. New York: Columbia University Press, 106-112.

Sassatelli, G. 2011. Archeologia e Risorgimento. La scoperta degli Etruschi a Bologna. *Storicamente* 7: art. 33.

Schoonhoven, E. 2010. The Etruscan Myth in Early Renaissance Florence. Renaissance Studies 24: 459-71.

Scott, J. 2003. *The pleasures of antiquity: British collectors of Greece and Rome*. New Haven, CT: Yale University Press.

Seyfarth, R.M. 1987. Vocal communication and its relation to language. In B. Smuts, D. Cheney, R. Seyfarth, R. Wrangham and T. Struhsaker (eds.) *Primate Societies*. Chicago: University of Chicago Press, 440-451.

Sgubini-Moretti, A.M. 1993. *Vulci e il suo territorio*. Roma: Quasar.

Sgubini-Moretti, A.M. 1998. *Le antichità dei Falisci al Museo di Villa Giulia*. Roma, L'Erma di Breitschneider.

Sgubini-Moretti, A.M. (ed.) 2001a. *Tarquinia etrusca : una nuova storia: Tarquinia, Museo archeologico nazionale, Palazzo Vitelleschi, Salone delle Armi, 4 ottobre – 30 dicembre 2001*. Roma, L'Erma di Breitschneider.

Sgubini-Moretti, A.M. (ed.) 2001b. *Veio, Cerveteri, Vulci : città d'Etruria a confronto : Roma, Museo Nazionale Etrusco di Villa Giulia, Villa Poniatowski, 1° ottobre – 30 dicembre 2001*. Roma, L'Erma di Breitschneider.

Sgubini-Moretti, A.M. (ed.) 2002. *Vulci : scoperte e riscoperte : nuovi dati dal territorio e dai depositi del museo, Montalto di Castro, Palazzo del Comune, 10 maggio-30 agosto 2002*. Firenze: Edizioni Cooperativi Archeologia.

Sgubini-Moretti, A.M. (ed.) 2004a. *Eroi etruschi e miti greci: gli affreschi della Tomba François tornano a Vulci*. Roma: Ministerio per i Beni e le attività culturali.

Sgubini-Moretti, A.M. (ed.) 2004b. *Scavo nello scavo : gli Etruschi non visti : ricerche e 'riscoperte' nei depositi dei musei archeologici dell'Etruria meridionale : 5 marzo 2004-30 giugno 2004, Viterbo, Fortezza Giulioli*. Roma: Ministerio per i Beni e le attività culturali.

Shanks, M. 2004. *Art and the early Greek state*. Cambridge: Cambridge University Press.

Shapiro, H. 1984. Herakles and Kyknos. *American Journal of Archaeology* 88: 523-529.

Shipley, L. 2013a. Guelphs, Ghibellines and Etruscans: archaeological discoveries and civic identity in late Medieval and early Renaissance Tuscany. *Bulletin of the History of Archaeology* 23.

Shipley, L. 2013b. Moving through memories: site distribution, performance and practice in Etruria. In A. Chadwick and C. Gibson (eds.) *Memories Can't Wait: Memory, Myth, Materiality and Long-Term Landscape Inhabitation*. Oxford: Oxbow.

Shipley, L. (In press 2015) Potting personhood: biconical urns and the development of individual funerary identity. In Perego, E. and Scarpacosa, R. (eds.) *Burial and Social Change in pre-Roman Italy*. Oxford: Oxbow.

Skeates, R. 1994. Ritual, context, and gender in Neolithic south-eastern Italy. *Journal of European Archaeology* 2: 199-214.

Skeates, R. 1995. Animate objects: a biography of prehistoric 'axe-amulets' in the central Mediterranean region. *Proceedings of the Prehistoric Society* 61: 279-301.

Skeates, R. 2001. The social dynamics of enclosure in the Neolithic of the Tavoliere, south-east Italy. *Journal of Mediterranean Archaeology* 13: 155-188.

Skeates, R. 2007. Neolithic Stamps: Cultural Patterns, Processes and Potencies. *Cambridge Archaeological Journal* 17: 183.

Small, J.P. 1981. *Studies related to the Theban cycle on late Etruscan urns*. Rome: G. Breitscheider.

Small, J.P. 1994a. Eat, Drink, and Be Merry: Etruscan Banquets. In R. dePuma and J. P. Small (eds.) *Murlo and the Etruscans*. Madison, WI: University of Wisconsin Press: 85-94.

Small, J.P. 1994b. Scholars, Etruscans, and Attic painted vases. *Journal of Roman Archaeology* 7: 34-58.

Snodgrass, A. 1998. *Homer and the artists: text and picture in early Greek art*. Cambridge: Cambridge University Press.

Sparkes, B. 1991. *Greek Pottery: an introduction*. Oxford, Wiley Blackwell. Sparkes, B. 1996. *The red and the black: studies in Greek pottery*. London: Routledge.

Spivak, G. 1990. Can the subaltern speak? In C. Nelson and L. Grossberg (eds.) *Marxism and the Interpretation of Culture*. Urbana, IL: University of Illinois Press: 271-313.

Spivak, G. 1996. *The Spivak Reader*. London: Routledge.

Spivak, G. 2005. Scattered speculations on the subaltern and the popular. *Postcolonial Studies* 8: 475-486.

Spivey, N. J. 1987. *The Micali Painter and his followers*. Oxford: Oxford Monographs on Classical Archaeology.

Spivey, N. J. 1988. Il pittore Micali. In M.A. Rizzo (ed.) *Un artista etrusco e il suo mondo: Il pittore di Micali*. Roma: De Luca:11-21.

Spivey, N.J and Stoddart, S. 1990. *Etruscan Italy*. London: Batsford.

Spivey, N.J. 1991a. Greek vases in Etruria. In N.J. Spivey and T. Rasmussen (eds.) *Looking at Greek Vases*. Cambridge: Cambridge University Press: 131 – 150.

Spivey, N.J. 1991b. The Power of Women in Etruscan Society. *Accordia Research Papers* 2: 55-67.

Spivey, N.J. 2006. Greek vases in Etruria. *American Journal of Archaeology* 110: 659-71.

Steingräber, S. 1983. Città e necropoli dell'Etruria. Roma: L'Erma di Breitschneider.

Steingräber, S.1995. Funerary Architecture in Chiusi. *Etruscan Studies* 2: 53-83.

Stenhouse, W. 2004. Thomas Dempster, royal historian to James I, and classical scholarship in early Stuart England. *The Sixteenth Century Journal* 35: 295-401..

Stoddart, S. 1989. Divergent trajectories in central Italy, 1200-500 BC. In T. C. Champion (ed.) *Centre and Periphery: Comparative Studies in Archaeology*. London: Routledge: 88-101.

Stoddart, S. 1990. The political landscape of Etruria. *Accordia Research Papers* 1: 39-51.

Stoddart, S. 1992. Towards a historical ethnology of the Mediterranean. *Current Anthropology* 33: 599-60.

Stoddart, S. 1995. The domestication of the proto-Villanovan mind. *Antiquity* 69: 411-414.

Stoddart, S. 2007. The impact of landscape and surface survey on the study of the Etruscans. *Etruscan Studies* 10: 239–245.

Stoddart, S. and Whiteley, J. 1988. The social context of literacy in Archaic Greece and Etruria. *Antiquity* 62: 761-772.

Straus, E. 1966. *Phenomenological Psychology*. New York: Basic Books.

Theodore-Pena, J. 2011. State formation in southern coastal Etruria: an application of the Kipp-Schortman Model. In N. Terrenato and D. Haggis (eds.) *State formation in Italy and Greece: questioning the neo-evolutionist model*. Oxford: Oxbow: 179-198.

Thomas, J. 1990. Monuments from the inside: the case of the Irish megalithic tombs. *World Archaeology* 22: 168-178.

Thomas, J. 1991. *Rethinking the Neolithic*. Cambridge: Cambridge University Press.

Thomas, J. 1996. *Time, Culture, and Identity: an interpretative archaeology*. London: Psychology Press.

Tilley, C. 1994. *A Phenomenology of Landscape: places, paths and monuments*. Berg: Oxford.

Tilley, C. 1996. The powers of rocks: topography and monument construction on Bodmin Moor. *World Archaeology* 28: 161-176.

Tilley, C. 2004. *The materiality of stone: explorations in landscape phenomenology*. Berg: Oxford.

Tilley, C. 2008. *Body and Image: Explorations in landscape phenomenology 2*. Walnut Creek, CA: Left Coast Press.

Tilley, C. 2012. Walking the Past in the Present. In A. Amason et al (eds.) *Landscapes Beyond Land: Routes, Aesthetics, Narratives*. Berghahn: Oxford, 15-32.

Tobey, M. H., E. O. Nielsen, and M. W. Rowe. *Elemental analysis of Etruscan ceramics from Murlo, Italy*. In J. Olin and M. James Blackman (eds.) Proceedings of the 24th International Archaeometry Symposium. Washington, DC: Smithsonian Institution Press: 115-127.

Tobin, F. 2013. Music and musical instruments in Etruria. In J. MacIntosh Turfa (ed.) *The Etruscan World*. London: Routledge, 841-854.

Topper, K. 2007. Perseus, the maiden Medusa, and the imagery of abduction. *Hesperia* 76: 73-105.

Torelli, M. 1981. *Storia degli etruschi*. Roma: Laterza.

Torelli, M. 1987. *La società etrusca: l'età arcaica, l'età classica*. Roma: La Nuova Italia Scientifica.

Torelli, M. (ed.) 2001. *The Etruscans*. Milano: Bompiami.

Treherne, P. 1995. The warrior's beauty: the masculine body and self-identity in Bronze-Age Europe. *Journal of European Archaeology* 3: 105-144.

Trigger, B. 1990. *A history of archaeological thought*. Cambridge: Cambridge University Press.

Tronchetti, C. 1983. *Ceramica attica a figure nere: grande vasi, anfore, pelikai, cratere. Museo Archeologico Nazionale di Tarquinia*. Roma: L'Erma di Breitschneider.

Tuck, A. 1994. The Etruscan Seated Banquet: Villanovan Ritual and Etruscan Iconography. *American Journal of Archaeology* 98: 617–628.

Tuck, A. 1998. Orientalizing Period Wing-Handle Cups from Poggio Civitate: Ceramic Traditions and Regional Production in Inland Etruria. *Etruscan Studies* 6: 174-190.

Tuck, A. 2000. Architecture and Community at Poggio Civitate. *Etruscan Studies* 7: 109-112.

Tuck, A. 2010. Master and Mistress: the politics of iconography in pre-Roman Central Italy. In Arnold, A. and Counts, D. (eds.) *The Master of Animals in Old World Iconography*. Archaeolingua: Budapest, 211-223.

Tuck, A. 2011. *The necropolis of Poggio Civitate (Murlo): Burials from Poggio Aguzzo*. Roma: Archeologica 153.

Tuck, A., Rodriguez, A. and Glennie, A. 2012. *The Iron Age at Poggio Civitate: Evidence and Argument*. Poster session presented at the annual meeting of the Archaeological Institue of America, Philadelphia, PA.

Tuck, A., Bauer, J., Huntsman, T., Kreindler, K., Pancaldo, S., Powell, C., and Miller, S. 2007. Centre and Periphery in Inland Etruria: Poggio Civitate and the Etruscan Settlement in Vescovado di Murlo. *Etruscan Studies* 12: 215-240.

Tuck, A., Brunk, J., Huntsman, T., and Tallman, H. 2010. An Archaic Period well at Poggio Civitate: evidence for broader final destruction. *Etruscan Studies* 13: 93-106.

Valentini, G. 1969. Il motivo della potnia theron sui vasi di bucchero. *Studi Etruschi* 37: 413-432.

van der Meer, L.B. 1995. *Interpretatio Etrusca: Greek Myths on Etruscan Mirrors*. Amsterdam: J.C. Gieben.

van der Meer, L. B. 2004. Etruscan Origins. Language and Archaeology. *BaBesch* 79: 51-57.

van Dommelen, P. 1998. Colonial constructs: colonialism and archaeology in the Mediterranean. *World Archaeology* 28: 31-49.

van Dommelen, P. 2001. Beyond domination and resistance: colonial culture and local identities in Classical Sardinia. *American Journal of Archaeology* 105: 253-274.

Venturi, F. 1972. *Italy and the Enlightenment: studies in a cosmopolitan century*. New York: New York University Press.

Vickers, M. 1985. Imaginary Etruscans: changing perceptions of Etruria since the fifteenth century. *Hephaistos* 7: 153-168.

Wahnbaek, T. 2004. *Luxury and Public Happiness: Political economy in the Italian Enlightenment*. Oxford: Clarendon Press.

Wallace-Hadrill, A. 2001. *The British School at Rome: One Hundred Years*. London: British School at Rome Press.

Waley, D. and Dean, T. 2010. *The Italian city-republics*. London: Pearson.

Warden, G. P. 2009. Remains of the Ritual at the Sanctuary of Poggio Colla. In M. Gleba and H. Becker (eds.) *Votives, Places, and Rituals in Etruscan Religion: Studies in Honour Of Jean MacIntosh Turfa*. New York: Brill. 107-121.

Wells, P. 1995. Identities, material culture and change: 'Celts' and 'Germans' in late Iron-Age Europe. *Journal of European Archaeology* 3: 169-85.

Whitehouse, R. 1992. *Underground religion: cult and culture in prehistoric Italy*. London: Accordia Research Centre.

Whitehouse, R. 2001a. A Tale of Two Caves. The archaeology of religious experience in Mediterranean Europe. In P. Biehl, P. & F. Bertèmes (eds.) *The Archaeologies of Cult and Religion*. Budapest: Archaeolingua Foundation: 161-167.

Whitehouse, R. 2001b. Exploring gender in prehistoric Italy. *Papers of the British School at Rome* 69: 49-96.

Whitehouse, R. 2002. Gender in the South Italian Neolithic: a combinatory approach. In Rosen-Ayalon, M. & Nelson, S. (eds.) *In Pursuit of Gender*. Walnut Creek, CA: Altamira Press: 15-42.

Whitehouse, R. 2007a. Gender Archaeology and Archaeology of Women: Do We Need Both? In S. Hamilton, R. Whitehouse, and K. Wright (eds.) *Archaeology and Women. Ancient and Modern Issues*. Walnut Creek, CA: Left Coast Press (Institute of Archaeology series): 27–40.

Whitehouse, R. 2007b. Writing, identity and the state. In K. Lomas, R. Whitehouse, and J. Wilkins (eds.) *Literacy and the State in the ancient Mediterranean*. London: Accordia Research Institute: 95-106.

Williams, D. 1982. An Oinochoe in the British Museum and the Brygos Painter's Work on a White Ground. *Jahrbuch der Berliner Museen* 24: 17-40.

Winter, N. 1997. Poggio Civitate: a turning point. *Etruscan Studies* 4: 23-40.

Winter, N. (ed.) 2009. *Symbols of wealth and power. Architectural terracotta decoration in Etruria and central Italy 640-510 B.C.* Ann Arbor, MI: University of Michigan Press.

Wiseman, T. 1990. *A short history of the British School at Rome*. London: British School at Rome Press.

Wittig, M. 1994. *The Lesbian Body*. London: Beacon Press.

Woodford, S. 1993. *The Trojan War in ancient art*. Ithaca, NY: Cornell University Press.

Woodford, S. 2003. *Images of myths in classical antiquity*. Cambridge: Cambridge University Press

Wylie, A. 1992. The interplay of evidential constraints and political interests: recent archaeological research on gender. *American Antiquity* 57: 15-35.

Young, I. 1990. *Throwing Like a Girl and Other essays in Feminist Philosophy and Social Theory*. Indianapolis, IN: Indiana University Press.

Zamagni, V. 1993. *The Economic History of Italy 1860-1990*. Oxford: Oxford University Press.

Zariski, R. 1956. Problems and Prospects of Democratic Socialism in France and Italy. *The Journal of Politics* 18: 254-280.

Index

A

Agency 2, 3, 5, 6, 7, 23, 25, 26, 29, 30, 31, 33, 34, 35, 72, 77, 84, 87, 89, 93, 94, 100, 102, 104, 105, 107, 108, 110, 111, 112, 142, 144, 145, 150
Archaic period 4, 5, 38, 41, 43, 46, 68, 69, 105, 109, 110, 111, 142, 154
Arezzo 10, 11, 13, 18, 140
Attic pottery 2, 40

B

Beazley, John 2, 4, 20, 33, 40, 139
Bianchi Bandinelli, Ranuccio 14, 16, 17, 141
biography 1, 144, 145, 150, 151
Bucchero 13, 18, 39, 41, 76, 79, 103, 140, 149, 153
burial 2, 4, 39, 41, 46, 109, 111, 149, 150
Butler, Judith 23, 25, 26, 28, 32, 33, 34, 94, 143

C

Cerveteri 17, 41, 44, 151
Chiusi 13, 14, 37, 39, 41, 44, 56, 57, 58, 66, 67, 68, 73, 75, 76, 82, 86, 89, 93, 99, 100, 105, 110, 111, 139, 141, 149, 150, 152
Coke, Thomas 13, 18, 140
colonialism, 4, 5, 10, 13, 18, 19, 43, 153
Colonna, Giovanni 17, 46
Corpus Vasorum Antiquorum 36
Cristofani, Mauro 9, 13, 17, 38

D

Dante 11
Dempster, Thomas 13, 18, 20, 140, 152
Dennis, George 19, 20, 40
drinking 31, 33, 38, 39, 43, 44, 45, 48, 49, 50, 52, 55, 56, 57, 58, 59, 61, 62, 63, 64, 66, 67, 68, 69, 73, 74, 75, 76, 77, 78, 79, 85, 86, 93, 94, 96, 101, 102, 103, 105, 106, 107, 108, 109, 110, 111, 144, 146, 148

E

exchange 5, 6, 20, 39, 50, 111

F

Fascism 15, 16, 17, 141
Fascist 14
feminism 7, 25-26
Florence 10, 11, 12, 13, 15, 18, 139, 149

G

Gell, Alfred 7, 23, 30, 31, 32, 33, 34, 36, 77, 78
Giglioli, Giulio Quirinio 14, 15, 16, 139
Gramsci, Antonio 16, 17
Grand Tour 7, 13, 18, 19, 22, 142, 148, 149
Grosz, Elizabeth 23, 26, 27, 28, 30, 33, 34, 145

H

handles 49, 52, 53, 63, 78, 106
Haynes 20
Hegel 7, 23, 24
Hellenocentric 4, 5
Hellenocentrsm 5
historiography 9, 16, 112

I

iconography 2, 9, 11, 12, 17, 22, 43, 103, 110, 142, 152
Italy 1, 3, 4, 6, 7, 9, 10, 13, 14, 15, 16, 17, 18, 19, 21, 23, 40, 55, 78, 96, 103, 110, 141, 143, 144, 149, 150, 151, 152, 153

J

John Robb 6, 20

K

kottabos 44
kula 30, 31

L

Lawrence 19, 20

M

Medici, 10
Merleau-Ponty, Maurice 7, 23, 24, 25, 26, 27, 28, 33, 34, 36
music 44
Mussolini 9, 14, 15, 16, 22, 141

N

nationalism 9, 12, 14, 15 16, 22

O

origins 4, 13, 14, 15, 16, 19, 33, 38, 39, 47, 72, 76, 81, 90, 96, 141, 149

P

Pallottino, Massimo 4, 14, 15, 16, 17, 149
Performativity 26
phenomenology 1, 3, 6, 7, 23, 24, 25, 26, 27, 28, 29, 30, 31, 32, 33, 34, 35, 112, 113, 141, 142, 152
Pithekoussai 20
Poggio Civitate 36, 37, 38, 39, 41, 42, 49, 50, 56, 57, 58, 66, 68, 73, 75, 76, 78, 82, 85, 86, 92, 93, 99, 105, 109, 110, 111, 114, 140, 141, 142, 144, 145, 148, 149, 152, 153
post-processualism. 23
provenance 2, 35, 36, 37, 38, 45, 52, 58, 64, 71, 81, 82, 114

R

Raramuri 5, 6

republicanism 13, 16
rim diameter 48, 49, 50, 52, 53, 54, 58, 59, 61, 63, 64, 66, 68
Roman culture 5, 9, 10, 11, 12, 13, 17, 18, 21, 39, 140, 149, 151, 152
romanticism 18, 22

S

skill 32, 33, 34, 45, 54, 55, 63, 64, 65, 66, 67, 68, 77, 79, 80, 101, 109, 110, 141, 144
socialism 14, 16
symposion 44, 148

T

Tarquinia 11, 12, 13, 17, 36, 37, 39, 40, 42, 43, 45, 46, 56, 57, 58, 66, 67, 68, 75, 76, 82, 86, 87, 90, 93, 94, 97, 99, 100, 103, 105, 110, 111, 139, 140, 142, 148, 149, 150, 151, 152
Tavoliere-Gargano 7, 23, 30, 34
textual sources 11, 21, 30
theory, archaeological 4, 6, 7, 9, 20, 21, 22, 23, 24, 33, 36, 111, 112, 150
typologies 2, 16, 17, 22, 35, 38, 50, 58, 70, 72, 80 87

V

Veii 17
Villanovan 2, 4, 17, 38, 41, 152
Volterra 13, 17
volume 15, 16, 21, 46, 49, 50, 51, 52, 53, 54, 58, 61, 62, 63, 64, 68, 69, 75, 106, 108
Vulci 17, 36, 37, 39, 40, 41, 46, 47, 56, 57, 58, 66, 67, 68, 76, 82, 85, 86, 92, 93, 97, 99, 105, 110, 111, 141, 150, 151